LEGAL PLURALISM AND EMPI

Legal Pluralism and Empires, 1500–1850

Edited by Lauren Benton and Richard J. Ross

NEW YORK UNIVERSITY PRESS
New York and London

NEW YORK UNIVERSITY PRESS

New York and London
www.nyupress.org

References to Internet websites (URLs) were accurate at the time of writing. Neither the author nor New York University Press is responsible for URLs that may have expired or changed since the manuscript was prepared.

LIBRARY OF CONGRESS CATALOGING-IN-PUBLICATION DATA
Legal pluralism and empires, 1500-1850 / edited by Lauren Benton and Richard J. Ross.
pages cm
Includes bibliographical references and index.
ISBN 978-0-8147-7116-7 (cloth : alk. paper)
ISBN 978-0-8147-0836-1 (paperback)
1. Colonies—Law and legislation—Congresses. 2. Legal polycentricity—Congresses. I. Benton, Lauren A., editor of compilation. II. Ross, Richard Jeffrey, editor of compilation.
K3375.A6L44 2013
342'.04130903—dc23
2013001060

New York University Press books

Manufactured in the United States of America
10 9 8 7 6 5 4 3 2 1

To our parents:

Charlotte Benton and (in memoriam) George Benton
and
Leonard Ross and Lorraine Ross

CONTENTS

ACKNOWLEDGMENTS

This volume developed out of a 2010 conference on "New Perspectives on Legal Pluralism" organized by Lauren Benton and Richard Ross through the Symposium on Comparative Early Modern Legal History. Richard Ross oversees the Symposium, which gathers each year under the auspices of the Center for Renaissance Studies at the Newberry Library in Chicago to discuss the comparative legal history of the Atlantic world in the period c. 1492 to 1815. Proliferating scholarship on the layered, jurisdictionally complex, and multicentric nature of law in overseas empires suggested the value of a conference assessing legal pluralism in colonial settings. The rich papers presented at the "New Perspectives on Legal Pluralism" symposium, together with the valuable conversation they inspired among participants, prompted the organizers to think of assembling a volume on the subject.

The editors wished to produce a volume that studied the provenance, meaning, and implications of legal pluralism across a wide range of early modern empires, in settings as far apart as Peru and New Zealand, and in every century between 1500 and the middle of the nineteenth century. To that end, we drew from contributions by participants in the symposium and also invited other scholars to write for the volume. Karen Barkey, Linda Rupert, Philip Stern, and P. G. McHugh presented papers at the symposium that subsequently became chapters in this volume. Lauren Benton, Helen Dewar, Lisa Ford, Brian Owensby, and Richard Ross contributed chapters written especially for the volume. We were lucky to recruit Jane Burbank, Frederick Cooper, and Paul Halliday to write chapters presenting concluding perspectives.

The editors wish to thank the authors for their essays. All undertook revisions with dedication, care, and good humor. Several anonymous commentators for New York University Press suggested ways to improve the framing of the volume. Deborah Gershenowitz, the history and law editor at the press, expertly guided the book through the publication process. The University of Illinois College of Law provided funding for the conference out of which this volume emerged. Funds for promoting the study of legal history at New York University contributed to covering the costs of preparing the manuscript for publication. The Center for Renaissance Studies at the Newberry Library offered an ideal site for the proceedings.

1

Empires and Legal Pluralism

Jurisdiction, Sovereignty, and Political Imagination in the Early Modern World

LAUREN BENTON AND RICHARD J. ROSS

The subject of empires is both very old and very new. An old narrative of a transition from empires to nation-states has now given way to an emphasis on the centrality and persistence of empires in world history. At the heart of this history is a recognition of the importance of legal pluralism to empires, which invariably relied on layered legal arrangements within composite polities. Empires were legally plural in their core regions as well as in their overseas or distant possessions. Many empires assembled political communities boasting divergent constitutional traditions; uneasily maintained overlapping or clashing royal, ecclesiastical, local, and seigneurial jurisdictions; and encompassed a variety of forms and sources of law. Such pluralism often grew more complex in colonies and far-flung peripheries as administrators and settlers dealt with indigenous, enslaved, and conquered peoples. The resulting legal orders encompassed multiple zones with unstable and varied relationships to one another and to imperial centers.

Colonial administrators and jurists studied legal pluralism without using the term. Officials and settlers described plural institutions and practices in order to guide rulers and, sometimes, to question the justice of empire itself. The Spanish scholastic Francisco de Vitoria, for example, in the process of criticizing the conduct of Spain in the New World, developed legal rationales for European conquest and colonization that balanced Castilian and indigenous rights and jurisdictions.[1] Juan de Solórzano Pereira and Thomas Pownall were among the more prominent imperial administrators who put the problem of plural legal orders at the forefront of efforts to canvass and reform colonial governance.[2] In defending Dutch imperial interests, Hugo Grotius addressed central problems of legal pluralism and empire, in particular in evaluating the ways that jurisdiction could extend into the sea independently of claims to dominion.[3] Such preoccupations continued into late-colonial and postcolonial contexts, encompassing debates about definitions of quasi-sovereignty and the legal status of political communities borne out of the expansion, fragmentation, dissolution, and reconfiguration of empires. Across the centuries, persisting questions about the nature and structure of plural legal orders in empires reflected and informed wider currents of religious, legal, and political thought.

This volume takes as its subject the shifting structures and processes of legal pluralism as well as historically changing ways of imagining and describing legal pluralism in empires. The chapters contribute to a new narrative of world history that places empires at its center. They present new findings and pose new questions about the complex and contingent configuration of imperial law—not as a structure of command but as a set of fluid institutional and cultural practices.

Though a relatively new subject, the study of plural legal orders in empires has already passed through several phases. Legal pluralism drew the attention of scholars in the middle decades of the twentieth century who sought to map the evident legal complexity of colonial and postcolonial societies. Their efforts featured, as one scholar has put it, "a spirit of aggressive celebration of . . . [the] romantic assumption that nonstate law was more egalitarian and less coercive than state law."[4] Studies of legal pluralism in the 1970s and 1980s also argued for analysis of law not as doctrine but as a social and cultural process, a perspective developed by anthropologists in colonial and postcolonial settings, then applied by them to the examination of legal change in societies labeled as complex and modern. Legal pluralism came to be associated in the 1990s with an emphasis on the instability of legal order and a "constructionist" understanding of multicentric legal systems as contingent products of conflict.[5]

Such efforts led logically to increased scrutiny of legal processes in empires. Sally Merry, Sally Falk Moore, Martin Chanock, and other scholars bridged anthropology and imperial history in documenting the persistence of colonial jurisdictional complexities.[6] At the same time, historians were building on what had been largely national and imperial traditions of the study of law to develop rich new currents of research on the legal history of the Chinese, Ottoman, Spanish, British, French, and Russian empires, efforts that increasingly drew attention to cross-imperial comparisons.[7] Scholars began to probe, too, the degree of imperial influence on processes formerly regarded as the keys to national legal development—from currents in constitutionalism to the legal underpinnings of sovereignty. The emergence of new regional fields, meanwhile, especially the rise of Atlantic and Indian Ocean history, stimulated questions about the legal foundations of inter-imperial and global regimes.[8]

These and other projects gave new relevance—and a different spin—to the decades-old concept of "legal pluralism." Historians began to take seriously the idea that changes in the plural legal order constituted an important piece of the narrative about the shifting international order. This perspective has led to studies of the ways in which jurisdictional conflicts spurred shifts in the structure of plural legal orders, contributing, for example, to the formation of the colonial state or to "settler sovereignty."[9] Some scholars have reframed colonial legal history as a narrative of multiple and fluid imperial constitutions.[10] Still others have sought to locate debates about "rights" in the context of jurisdictionally complex imperial law, or have followed metropolitan legal practices through new variations on the edges of empire.[11]

We can now profitably take stock of these approaches to legal pluralism and empires—and also begin to look beyond initial contributions. This volume seeks to advance the field both by identifying new research directions and by connecting historical studies to broadly defined questions about the nature of law and legal politics in empires. The volume's essays enrich understandings of imperial sovereignty; analyze the legal strategies of conquered subjects, slaves, and religious minorities; probe the relation between legal pluralism and inter-imperial law; and investigate circulating ideas about legal pluralism. Many of the chapters reflect a view of legal pluralism that emphasizes its rootedness in jurisdictional politics. Some chapters explore historical actors' uses of political and religious thought to structure, justify, or undermine plural legal regimes. Jurisdictional conflicts and the strategic manipulation of ideas and information about legal pluralism are shown to have worked together in shaping the history of empires. Imperial law represented a medium of politics at the same time that it reflected ways of representing order, authority, and rights that changed more slowly and provided participants in legal disputes with a durable, if flexible, resource.

Jurisdictional vs. Normative Legal Pluralism

The concept of legal pluralism comes with a troubled past. Social scientists and legal scholars have struggled with the term's definition, vying to capture the structural relation of multiple spheres of law while also recognizing the porousness of such spheres and the fluidity of institutional arrangements.

This section summarizes problems embedded in the dominant approaches to the subject before offering an alternative perspective that defines legal pluralism as a formation of historically occurring patterns of jurisdictional complexity and conflict. Among other benefits, the approach we outline allows researchers to connect the history of legal conflicts in empires to the study of circulating ideas about legal pluralism. It also lays the foundation for comparative histories of legal pluralism in global and regional formations.

Scholars presented the study of legal pluralism as a correction to a deeply ingrained view that state law is necessarily central to all legal orders, a perspective that one influential essay defined as "the ideology of legal centralism."[12] Those who claim that all societies are characterized by legal pluralism have not, however, agreed on the multiple entities that make up composite legal orders. Some speak of "two or more legal systems," others identify multiple "semi-autonomous social fields," and still others propose a plurality of "rule systems" or "different social normative systems."[13] Many scholars writing about legal pluralism have placed in the foreground distinctions between state law and nonstate law.[14] Some propose an understanding of legal pluralism as encompassing all sources of law or rules of conduct in a given territory or social context, ranging from the state's legal commands through customs, habits, religious precepts, and codes of etiquette. They suggest that to study this "normative" legal pluralism is to canvass potentially all the rules of various origins that people feel compelled to follow, whether or not these are imposed by institutions or backed by sanctions.[15]

From our perspective as historians of empires, these overlapping approaches present three main problems. First, emphasis on a distinction between state and nonstate law draws attention away from the complexities, confusions, and conflicts within "state law" while also potentially exaggerating the homogeneity and insularity of "non-state" or "customary" law.[16] Some critics have complained that the supposition that all ordered social behavior is law-like opens a limitless horizon for the study of legal pluralism.[17] In the study of empires, such a tendency appears less dangerous than the representation of imperial legal orders as comprising sets of neatly stacked and bounded legal spheres. Layered and composite legal arrangements in empires featured overlapping public and private jurisdictions and were characterized by continual restructuring, changes that resulted in part from the legal strategies of often litigious and legally sophisticated imperial subjects.[18]

Second, a key shortcoming of many attempts to analyze legal pluralism has been a tendency to view the phenomenon ahistorically or to incorporate an overly simplified historical narrative of rising state power. This flaw is particularly clear in attempts to formulate typologies in which state law figures in opposition to "nonstate" law. Consider the common assertion that state law descended or was imposed on "other" law in linear and consistent ways across several centuries. Moore's careful description of "semi-autonomous social fields" as law-like, for example, contrasted sharply with her rendering of state law as expanding and converting customary law into a colonial "residue."[19] Tamanaha insists on an understanding of the rise of state law as "contingent," but then characterizes its dominance as a "development which occurred initially in the West."[20] Even a scholar calling for "limited, operational, historically contingent definitions of law" as a key to arriving at a sufficiently complex understanding of state law in legal pluralism comes up with a strained example of the benefits of this move: its illumination of the way state institutions "are likely to intervene" when "a private normative order . . . directly violates state law."[21] Historians of empire note that the construction of the imperial state responded to an array of political and legal problems and pressures; even (or especially) in political thought, the boundary between state and private legal spheres was not just unstable but also unclear and often a matter of fierce debate.[22]

The need for more nuanced historical analysis of legal pluralism connects to a third problem for historians of empire: a dearth of sustained analysis of the changing and often locally specific understandings of law and legal complexity as presented and debated by historical actors, including state agents. Here an emphasis of "normative" legal pluralism on rules and norms creates methodological problems by asking historians to uncover elusive subjective beliefs about the applicability and ordering of bodies of law. In contrast, to the extent that we focus on jurisdictional conflicts, we examine arenas from which documents are more likely to survive, uncover disputes in which participants gave reasons for their actions, and analyze cases whose outcomes altered the future interplay of institutions and the expectations of historical actors. It becomes possible to combine an understanding of legal pluralism as a jurisdictional web without abandoning the study of the intellectual history of legal pluralism. Recent intellectual histories of empire show that engagement with imperial conflicts drew from and informed broader trends in thought while also sometimes prompting jurisprudential and philosophical innovations.[23] Without the presumption of a connection to normative structures, the study of intellectual approaches to legal pluralism opens up interesting questions about the relation of political and legal discourse to local and regional histories, and to shifting strategies of legal actors within empires.

Over a decade ago, Lauren Benton proposed replacing the study of normative orders with a focus on patterns of jurisdictional conflicts that propelled change in the structure of colonial legal orders.[24] She applied the term "jurisdiction" to the exercise by sometimes vaguely defined legal authorities of the power to regulate and administer sanctions over particular actions or people, including groups defined by personal status, territorial boundaries, and corporate membership.

A jurisdictional perspective helps to address the problems identified in writings on legal pluralism. The study of jurisdictional politics does not depend on a general definition of "law." Nor does it require making distinctions between "state" and "nonstate" law. The jurisdictional claims of a wide range of authorities, from a guild or merchant ship captain to a conquistador or trading company, can be analyzed without their being defined neatly as public or private. Jurisdictional divides come into focus and matter most to an understanding of legal pluralism when conflicts occur, and so a methodological advantage of the approach is to focus attention on clusters of conflicts, rather than elusive and often inconsistently applied rules or norms. This approach invites historical analysis because it becomes possible to analyze structural shifts propelled by the legal strategies of parties to jurisdictional conflicts.

Of course, historical actors making legal claims did not focus exclusively on jurisdictional divides. They often cited natural law, divine precepts, the *ius gentium*, and other bodies of law or norms without connecting them explicitly to specific jurisdictions. A loose or indirect connection to jurisdictional politics in fact often made sense when people were citing laws not for forensic advantage but as a protest ideal, a resource for negotiating social status, or a vocabulary for politics. Cases of conscience literature that proliferated in early modern Europe and its colonies, for example, sorted through potentially clashing divine, natural, and civil law to guide the individual's behavior on a wide range of issues, from usury and tithes to control of labor and political allegiance.[25] Such discourse about legal pluralism exerted influence over long periods and may not be captured by an emphasis on jurisdictional tensions.

The study of jurisdictional conflicts and the analysis of evolving and circulating ideas about legal pluralism remain powerfully connected, however. Their combination can lead to rich veins of research linking engagement in legal conflicts within and across empires to the development of legal and political thought. Jurists and imperial agents drew on multiform legal repertoires, including and especially ideas about legal pluralism, in defending a range of legal proposals and actions in empires, from occupation and conquest to humanitarian reforms.[26] Further, as Benton has recently shown in relation to imperial sovereignty, and as Richard Ross and Philip Stern argue in this volume (chapter 5), the contemplation of problems of imperial rule developed together with long and varied traditions emphasizing the legitimacy of decentralized power.[27] Jurisprudence worked together with what one historian has called "jurispractice" in shaping imperial legal systems and inter-polity legal regimes.[28]

Jurisdiction and Empire

What do we know about jurisdictional politics in empires? The conflicts served as an especially powerful engine of change in the relationship of empires to one another and to settlers, merchants, imperial administrators, and indigenous peoples. Patterns of legal pluralism across empires spawned possibilities for inter-polity contact and trade, and acted as catalysts for the emergence of global legal regimes. Jurisdictional conflicts both responded to and created claims to legal authority by old and new political communities, corporations, and emerging colonial states. This section reviews some of the accomplishments and limitations of research developed within this perspective. We consider some of the ways historians might begin to advance and refine the approach, a project taken up implicitly or explicitly by many of the essays in this volume.

Studies of patterns of legal politics across empires have complicated the image of state law as uniform and bounded. When viewed as encompassing the multilayered and multicentric law of empire-states, and exhibiting patterns of jurisdictional complexity that persist into the era of robust claims about state legal hegemony, state law becomes not a single arena opposed to nonstate law but a composite of jurisdictions with unevenly exercised authority. Philip Stern's "'Bundles of Hyphens': Corporations as Legal Communities in the Early Modern British Empire" (chapter 2) demonstrates how overseas trading and settlement companies were semi-independent associations that at times competed with the state by claiming monopolistic authority over territories and peoples under their command. Corporations were not only economic entities. They oversaw religion, justice, and education; they conducted diplomacy and fought wars; and at times they spawned a "public sphere" that provided a focus for sociability and allegiance. Emphasizing the resemblance of overseas companies to a commonwealth writ small questions the conventional hierarchical distinction between supposedly superior states and dependent corporations. In this fashion, Stern fractures the state and the category of "state law."

From another direction, so does Helen Dewar's "Litigating Empire: The Role of French Courts in Establishing Colonial Sovereignties" (chapter 3).

Leaders among seventeenth-century French colonists in St. Lawrence Valley and Acadia contended for power by appealing back for support to officials in a French state that was profoundly riven by normative and jurisdictional pluralism. No unified crown or state prevented settlers from strategically invoking the most favorable among the competing customs, privileges, and jurisdictional competences available in France. Meanwhile, metropolitan powerholders sought to extend their juridical and administrative reach into New France in order to reinforce authority at home. Jurisdictional multiplicity in both the colonies and the metropolis encouraged the creation of a series of New World "feudal enclaves" delineated not by territorial boundaries so much as the effective reach of personal authority, an authority in part defined by which elements of the plural legal order in France remained in play in a given context overseas.

The study of jurisdictional pluralism sheds light on understandings of the imperial constitution. Alternative visions for the arrangements of authority encompassing sovereign power and the quasi-sovereignty of colonial entities were taken up by different constituencies in the course of conflicts over such fundamental constitutional questions as the reach of crown prerogative, the rights of subjects, and the content and scope of imperial legislation. Historians who have placed such rubrics in the framework of shifting legal pluralism have noted a long-nineteenth-century turn away from jumbled jurisdictions to the imagination of a more hierarchical and streamlined legal administrative order.[29]

In this volume, Lauren Benton and Lisa Ford explore a dimension of this shift in "Magistrates in Empire: Convicts, Slaves, and the Remaking of the Plural Legal Order in the British Empire" (chapter 7). They note that threats to order in British colonies at the turn of the nineteenth century were a matter of perspective. Colonial elites feared unruly subordinates and the intervention of imperial officials; metropolitan observers viewed legal pluralism itself as a source of disorder because it protected private jurisdictions and the exercise of arbitrary and unauthorized power in the colonies. Benton and Ford analyze cases in which these contrasting perspectives come into clear focus, then trace their convergence with regard to one proposed solution: the redefinition of magistrates as imperial agents. The call to reform the magistracy emerged in the same decades in distant and very different parts of the British Empire, in the process focusing attention on the shared jurisdictional politics of slave and convict societies.

The search for synchronous shifts in imperial legal structures has been related, further, to the attempt to use legal pluralism as a lens through which to grasp inter-imperial configurations. The multiplicity of imperial legal orders represents another dimension of legal pluralism, one that we can understand as helping to compose regional and global legal regimes. For example, the routine practice of granting a degree of autonomy over legal affairs to merchant communities in the early modern world undergirded long-distance trading diasporas by making foreign legal systems understandable to merchants and travelers.[30] The same repeated structures also established cross-polity frameworks for new jurisdictional conflicts. The strategies of indigenous people, slaves, religious minorities, and other subordinate groups contributed to pressures to change jurisdictional ordering within empires and helped to create continuities giving rise to transimperial legal regimes. An illuminating example of this dual process is explored in this volume by Linda Rupert in "'Seeking the Water of Baptism': Fugitive Slaves and Imperial Jurisdiction in the Early Modern Caribbean" (chapter 8). Rupert shows that fugitive slaves crossing imperial borders exploited inter-imperial legal complexity while also prompting Spanish efforts to streamline jurisdictions within the empire—a process that in turn influenced Dutch legal policies. The result was a transimperial legal zone encompassing Curaçao and the Spanish mainland, a micro-region in which two dimensions of legal pluralism were partly directed by patterns of marronage.

Such complexity connected directly to efforts to define and construct sovereignty in empires. Rather than representing a fully formed phenomenon in metropolitan centers that was exported to and imposed beyond the center, sovereignty itself is best understood as a multiform and mainly elusive project. Jurisdictional conflicts involving settlers and indigenous peoples in disparate parts of the British Empire at the turn of the nineteenth century generated subtle, synchronous shifts toward understanding sovereignty as territorial.[31] P. G. McHugh's "'A Pretty Gov[ernment]!': The 'Confederation of United Tribes' and Britain's Quest for Imperial Order in the New Zealand Islands during the 1830s" (chapter 9) is an exemplary study of this transition. In line with their practice in the East Indies, the British recognized plural legal orders in New Zealand in the 1830s. Britain claimed jurisdiction over their nationals while working with and through the Maori, who exercised the primary jurisdiction over the islands. Expanding settlement, lobbying by missionaries, and Maori political turbulence provided the context for the cession of "sovereignty" from indigenous chiefs to the British in the Treaty of Waitangi (1840), a transfer that partly obscured the continuing importance for decades of plural, overlapping jurisdictions. McHugh's reconstruction of pre-1840 jurisdictional pluralism helps explain the ideological and practical meaning, and the limits, of what came after: British claims to "sovereignty."

Political and Religious Imagination

To ask why a particular form of plural legal order emerged in a given empire is to invite a wide range of explanations. Limitations of money, coercive ability, and administrative capacity might favor pluralism, as might the play of political rivalries in a metropolis, tensions among inherited legal forms and institutions, the accommodation of diverse settlers' and indigenous groups' interests in the service of securing order, and so forth. Aside from such pressures, the political and religious commitments, or imagination, of imperial elites—views about ideal governance and God's expectations—shaped the structure, limits, and justifications of pluralism. Several of the essays in this volume pursue these important connections.

Karen Barkey's "Aspects of Legal Pluralism in the Ottoman Empire" (chapter 4) emphasizes how Islamic thought both supported and curtailed the partial legal autonomy that Christian and Jewish communities enjoyed under the *millet* system in the sultan's domains. On the precedent of the mid-seventh-century Pact of Umar offered to the Christians of Syria, Muslim communities, including the Ottomans, expected the "peoples of the book" to consent to subordinate status in exchange for the right to govern personal and family affairs through their own religious tribunals. Yet as Muslim thought ratified pluralism, it also limited Christian and Jewish jurisdictions, ensuring that they were neither sealed off from nor hierarchically equal to Islamic tribunals. The Ottoman's "state Islam" in conjunction with the sultan generated rules of interaction for Jewish, Christian, and Muslim courts, while insisting on the cultural and symbolic primacy of the latter. The result was not a fixed legal order but a "relational field" in which Ottoman hegemony secured scope for legal action by minority communities and in which many of the strategies they pursued, such as frequent recourse to state courts, reinforced Ottoman legal authority.

If religious and political imagination could structure and legitimate particular forms of jurisdictional interactions within a plural legal order, it could also uphold the idea of pluralism itself. Historians of early modern political thought preoccupied with the rise of the modern state have lavished attention on "centralizing" discourses, particularly theorists such as Bodin, Hobbes, and Pufendorf, represented as champions of sovereignty. But the plural legal orders so prevalent on the ground in early modern Europe did not struggle against a predominantly hostile intellectual climate. Richard Ross and Philip Stern's "Reconstructing Early Modern Notions of Legal Pluralism" (chapter 5) explores how ideological support for plural legal orders could be found in a wide range of intellectual projects. These ranged from debates over the right of resistance and the divine right of rulers through historical work on the ancient Jewish commonwealth and theological disputes over which precepts "bound conscience" and finally to writings on political economy and the place of family. Advocates of pluralism and centralism did not simply contest each other so much as emerge, interlinked, through engagement with similar problems and adoption of related vocabularies.

Our familiarity with the challenge that centralizing discourses of sovereignty posed to pluralism obscures another way in which programs of political and religious reform undermined plural legal orders—through arguments that some human good, whether piety, civility, or productivity, required the removal of selected populations from a pluralist framework. This possibility emerges as a recurrent theme in the treatment of indigenous peoples in Spanish America. Divisions between imperial and colonial law and between secular and religious jurisdictions made New Spain and Peru highly pluralist, as did the creation of a "republic of the Indians" providing native communities with a corporate identity that burdened them with labor and tribute obligations as it sustained rights of self-government and an array of special legal privileges. In the middle of the seventeenth century, Jesuit missions to the Guaraní Indians in Paraguay, in the service of better Christianizing and "civilizing" their charges, self-consciously reduced within these missions the jurisdictional multiplicity that native peoples commonly experienced.[32]

A century later, as Brian Owensby insightfully demonstrates, schemes to increase the productivity and economic value of natives weakened legal pluralism as a central organizing concept used for thinking about indigenous peoples ("Between Justice and Economics: 'Indians' and Reformism in Eighteenth-Century Spanish Imperial Thought" [chapter 6]). Seventeenth-century Spanish American rulers concentrated on the king's responsibility to preserve the common good and dispense justice to his different communities of vassals through an array of overlapping and competing jurisdictions. Several mid-eighteenth-century proposals to improve the empire focused on making indigenous peoples more economically vibrant and "useful" to Spain, casting them as producers, consumers, and laborers rather than as members of self-governing communities in the republic of the Indians. By thinking about natives within a framework of productivity, Owensby concludes, imperial reformers reduced the salience of an inherited discourse about jurisdictional multiplicity in a plural legal order. Reformers did not advocate legal centralism directly in the fashion of Bodin and Hobbes so much as efface pluralism for selected populations by reorienting discourse from one value to another, from justice to utility.

In different ways, Owensby, Ross and Stern, and Barkey explore the intellectual ecology that surrounded and sustained—or undermined—plural legal orders. Explicit, articulated political and religious thought was important, but only one part of this larger intellectual ecology, whose various aspects invite further research. Consider in this respect not only the content of reflection about law but the means of its transmission. To what extent was there an elective affinity between plural legal orders and fragmentations and asymmetries in the circulation of legal knowledge? Among the obstacles to a state-dominated judicial administration in the New World settlements was the state's relative difficulty in disseminating its views about the content of law and about the political and normative frameworks that explained law's purposes and meanings. The French, Spanish, and English empires transmitted legal knowledge across the Atlantic not only through imperial officials but also through commercial and religious networks that often pursued their own interests. Churches, colleges, and merchants no less than imperial administrative structures provided points of entry for law created or ratified in the metropolis. Within the New World, social networks proved critical to the circulation of law, often in manuscript and oral form, at times increasing the ability of neglectful or self-interested brokers to bury or transform a metropolitan sovereign's legal messages and outlook.[33] We are only beginning to understand how local domination, fracture, and variation in the means of legal communications composed the intellectual ecology that supported and shaped pluralism.

Conclusion

A peculiar challenge in the study of legal pluralism in empires is defining historical moments or settings in which jurisdictional tensions mattered in relation to other shifts. In the long period covered by this volume, two broad patterns of legal pluralism in empires have attracted special attention from historians. The growth and reconfiguration of empires to include new groups of subjects and new territories—nonlinear processes of long duration—prompted clusters of conflicts linked to the contested legal status of conquered peoples, the articulation of legal systems of colonizers and colonized, and the shifting scope of legal authority exercised by imperial offices and agents. A second pattern involved the connection between jurisdictional politics within and across empires and the move toward a more hierarchically structured legal order defined in part by the assertion (whether realized or not) of imperial jurisdiction. Examples of the first pattern stretch across the centuries; the second pattern emerged fitfully but has been associated particularly with the reconfiguration of empires in the long nineteenth century.

This broad framework has posed as many interesting questions as it has settled. Some open questions involve change inside empires. For example, what characteristics make a colonial controversy take on the qualities of "scandal" and therefore command attention across imperial peripheries and centers?[34] To what degree did the behavior of relatively powerless legal actors—think of the fugitive slaves whose legal paths are traced in this volume by Rupert—urge imperial institutional reforms? Other research questions address the broad systemic implications of legal pluralism in empires. What was the relation of micro-polities, confederations, and business enterprises to the routines and structures associated with legal pluralism in empires, and how did such relations change over time?[35] In what ways did efforts to devise a coherent imperial legal order inform the imagination of international order and international law?[36]

The chapters in this volume mark significant contributions to such questions while also pointing to new research directions. The jurisdictional autonomy of corporations described by Stern (chapter 2) and the jurisdictional puzzles stretching from metropole to colony as detailed by Dewar (chapter 3) for the French empire reveal the need for further study of the legal underpinnings of early imperial ventures in both the Atlantic and Indian Ocean worlds. Barkey's depiction of Jewish, Christian, and Islamic courts within the Ottoman *millet* system (chapter 4) and Owensby's discussion of indigenous customary law and tribunals in the Spanish empire's "republic" of the Indians (chapter 6) suggest the potential for histories of the shifting legal status of religious and political communities inside empires to expand comparative possibilities and merge intellectual and jurisdictional analyses. In reflecting on the diverse intellectual traditions that informed Europeans' thinking and writing about legal pluralism, Ross and Stern (chapter 5) pose novel questions about the activation of arguments about the legitimacy of opposition to royal authority in a wide range of imperial conflicts. They point, too, to the importance of deepening our understanding of the way analogies developed and operated across arenas of legal discourse—for example, linking the relation of religious and secular law to debates about the autonomy of corporations and households. Benton and Ford (chapter 7), Rupert (chapter 8), and McHugh (chapter 9) examine multiple and strikingly different contexts in which conflicts shaped emergent claims of imperial jurisdiction in plural legal orders between the late-eighteenth century and the mid-nineteenth century. The variety suggests a need for further analysis of the period as one of global legal transformation as well as more research on the way jurisdictional politics interacted with the formation of inter-imperial legal regimes and intra-imperial constitutional discourse.

The volume concludes with wide-ranging chapters, one by Paul Halliday and another by Jane Burbank and Frederick Cooper, which assess the previous chapters' multiple strands of analysis and point out both the hazards and potential rewards of pushing further the study of legal pluralism in empires. Halliday urges historians not to forget the genuine violence that could accompany state legal interventions, while he also reminds us that "the state's law might emanicipate as well as repress." The term "pluralities," he notes, may reflect better than "legal pluralism," with its implications of order bestowed by observers, the variegated relations of subjecthood that channeled choices for historical actors and shaped their understandings of the sources of legal diversity. While Halliday notes that state strategists in the late-eighteenth and early-nineteenth centuries increasingly viewed "plurality" as a condition to be controlled, Burbank and Cooper caution that the very normality of legal pluralism often turned the management of multiple jurisdictions into "conventional practice." Imperial officials could regard jurisdictional complexity as acting to reinforce state power rather than unleashing transformative conflicts. The dynamics of legal pluralism, they show, extended well beyond the end point of the mid-nineteenth century chosen for this volume, and beyond any other artificial marker separating "early modern" and "modern" worlds.

Both concluding chapters identify and explain the significance of directions for further research. The message is one that we, as editors, heartily embrace. The volume's findings will, we hope, form the basis for open-ended questions about legal pluralism and empires—in earlier and later periods, and in other empires and regions. Themes and phenomena explored here that deserve further investigation include the analysis of political and ideological representations of legal diversity; the relation between legal pluralism and shifting configurations of imperial sovereignty; and cross-imperial interactions, from the movements of legal subjects to the institutional echoing effect of transformations in imperial governance. The subjects and approaches of this volume overlap with parts of many fields, including the comparative history of law, colonial and imperial history, and world history. The chapters also establish the study of legal pluralism and empires as a scholarly project with its own trajectory and future.

NOTES

1. J. A. Fernández-Santamaría, *Natural Law, Constitutionalism, Reason of State, and War: Counter-Reformation Spanish Political Thought* (New York: Peter Lang, 2005).
2. Juan de Soloìrzano Pereira, *Política Indiana*, 3 vols. (reprinted, Madrid: Fundacioìn Joseì Antonio de Castro, 1996 [1648]); Thomas Pownall, *The Administration of the Colonies . . .*

Wherein Their Rights and Constitution Are Discussed and Stated (reprinted, New York: Da Capo, 1971 [4th ed., London, 1768]).

3. Edward Keene, *Beyond the Anarchical Society: Grotius, Colonialism, and Order in World Politics* (Cambridge: Cambridge University Press, 2002); Lauren Benton, *A Search for Sovereignty: Law and Geography in European Empires, 1400-1900* (Cambridge: Cambridge University Press, 2010), 120-37; Martine van Ittersum, *Profit and Principle: Hugo Grotius, Natural Rights Theories, and the Rise of Dutch Power in the East Indies, 1595-1615* (Leiden: Brill, 2006).
4. Mitra Shirafi, "Justice in Many Rooms since Galanter: De-Romanticizing Cultural Pluralism through the Cultural Defense," *Law & Contemporary Problems* 71 (2008): 139-46, 139.
5. See Sally Engle Merry, "Legal Pluralism," *Law & Society Review* 22 (1988): 869-96; cf. Brian Tamanaha, "The Folly of the 'Social Scientific' Concept of Legal Pluralism," *Journal of Law & Society* 20, no. 2 (1993): 192-217, 193.
6. Sally Engle Merry, *Colonizing Hawai'i: The Cultural Power of Law* (Princeton, NJ: Princeton University Press, 2000); Sally Falk Moore, *Social Facts and Fabrications: "Customary" Law on Kilimanjaro, 1880-1980* (Cambridge: Cambridge University Press, 1986); Martin Chanock, *Law, Custom, and Social Order: The Colonial Experience in Malawi and Zambia* (Portsmouth, NH: Heinemann, 1998); Boaventure De Sousa Santos, "Law: A Map of Misreading; Toward a Postmodern Conception of Law," *Journal of Law & Society* 14 (1987): 297-98.
7. There was also a thin strand of comparative writings on legal pluralism in empires, in particular M. B. Hooker, *Legal Pluralism: An Introduction to Colonial and Neo-Colonial Laws* (New York: Clarendon, 1975).
8. Though at first ignored by many historians of the region, of particular importance in the study of law in the Indian Ocean world was Charles Henry Alexandrowicz, *An Introduction to the History of the Law of Nations in the East Indies: 16th, 17th, and 18th Centuries* (New York: Clarendon, 1967). A foundational work on the legal pluralism in early European expansion into the Atlantic is James Muldoon, *Popes, Lawyers, and Infidels: The Church and the Non-Christian World, 1250-1550* (Philadelphia: University of Pennsylvania Press, 1979).
9. Lauren Benton, *Law and Colonial Cultures: Legal Regimes in World History, 1400-1900* (New York: Cambridge University Press, 2002); Lisa Ford, *Settler Sovereignty: Jurisdiction and Indigenous People in America and Australia, 1788-1836* (Cambridge, MA: Harvard University Press, 2010).
10. See especially Daniel Hulsebosch, *Constituting Empire: New York and the Transformation of Constitutionalism in the Atlantic World, 1664–1830* (Chapel Hill: University of North Carolina Press, 2005); and Ken MacMillan, *The Atlantic Imperial Constitution: Center and Periphery in the English Atlantic World* (New York: Palgrave Macmillan, 2011).
11. For example, Paul Halliday, *Habeas Corpus: From England to Empire* (Cambridge, MA: Harvard University Press, 2010).
12. John Griffiths, "What Is Legal Pluralism?" *Journal of Legal Pluralism & Unofficial Law* 24 (1): 3.
13. Sally Merry, "Anthropology, Law, and Transitional Processes" *Annual Review of Anthropology* 21 (1992): 357, 358; Moore, *Social Facts and Fabrications*; Tamanaha, "The Folly of the 'Social Scientific' Concept of Legal Pluralism," 212; Gordon R. Woodman, "Legal Pluralism and the Search for Justice," *Journal of African Law* 40, no. 2 (1996): 152-67, 152.

14. Griffiths ("What Is Legal Pluralism?" 38) distinguished between the "strong legal pluralism" of state law operating alongside a plurality of nonstate legal orders from "weak legal pluralism" in which pluralism occurs "within the framework of state law." Merry offered a variant of this distinction in defining "classic legal pluralism" as produced in colonial and postcolonial societies and "new legal pluralism" as characteristic of advanced industrial countries (Merry, "Legal Pluralism," 872).
15. Brian Tamanaha, "A Non-Essentialist Concept of Legal Pluralism," *Journal of Law and Society* 27 (2000): 300-301.
16. On oversimplification of state law, see Ido Shahar, "State, Society, and the Relations between Them: Implications for the Study of Legal Pluralism," *Theoretical Inquiries in Law* 9 (2008): 417-41; on assumptions about the insularity of nonstate law, see Lauren Benton, "Beyond Legal Pluralism: Towards a New Approach to Law in the Informal Sector," *Social & Legal Studies* 3 (1994): 223-42.
17. For comment on the pitfalls of this debate within the literature on legal pluralism, see Merry, "Legal Pluralism," 879; Tamanaha, "The Folly of the 'Social Scientific' Concept of Legal Pluralism," 193; Shahar, "State, Society, and the Relations between Them," 419, 439.
18. On the "layered" and "uneven" qualities of empires, see Jane Burbank and Frederick Cooper, *Empires in World History: Power and the Politics of Difference* (Princeton, NJ: Princeton University Press, 2011); and Lauren Benton, *A Search for Sovereignty*. An excellent study of the legal sophistication of low-status imperial subjects is Jane Burbank, *Russian Peasants Go to Court: Legal Culture in the Countryside, 1905-1917* (Bloomington: Indiana University Press, 2004).
19. Moore, *Social Facts and Fabrications*, 317, 324.
20. Tamanaha, "The Folly of the 'Social Scientific' Concept of Legal Pluralism," 197.
21. Shahar, "State, Society, and the Relations between Them," 433.
22. The categories of "private" and "public," for example, had no settled meaning throughout the period covered by this volume, and the location of state legal authority was a centrally disputed question between imperial centers and peripheries. See Christine Daniels and Michael V. Kennedy, eds., *Negotiated Empires: Centers and Peripheries in the Americas, 1500-1820* (New York: Routledge, 2002). As Malick Ghachem points out, the public-private distinction in some imperial settings makes sense in characterizing jurisdictional tensions, as between the imperial state and the legal authority of slave owners on the eve of the Haitian Revolution. Malick W. Ghachem, *The Old Regime and the Haitian Revolution* (New York: Cambridge University Press, 2012), 179.
23. To take just one example, consider the reexamination of liberalism and empire: Jennifer Pitts, *A Turn to Empire: The Rise of Imperial Liberalism in Britain and France* (Princeton, NJ: Princeton University Press, 2005); Uday Singh Mehta, *Liberalism and Empire: A Study in Nineteenth-Century British Liberal Thought* (Chicago: University of Chicago Press, 1999); Karuna Mantena, *Alibis of Empire: Henry Maine and the Ends of Liberal Imperialism* (Princeton, NJ: Princeton University Press, 2010); and C. S. Bayly, *Recovering Liberties: Indian Thought in the Age of Liberalism and Empire* (Cambridge: Cambridge University Press, 2012).
24. Benton, *Law and Colonial Cultures*.
25. These books instructed readers about the demands of conscience, which operated even without the intermediation of jurisdictions and whose violation imperiled the soul. Arthur R. Jonsen and Stephen Toulmin, *The Abuse of Casuistry: A History of Moral*

Reasoning (Berkeley: University of California Press, 1988); Edmund Leites, ed., *Conscience and Casuistry in Early Modern Europe* (Cambridge: Cambridge University Press, 1988); Richard J. Ross, "Distinguishing Eternal from Transient Law: Natural Law and the Judicial Laws of Moses," *Past and Present* 217 (2012): 79-115; Thomas Wood, *English Casuistical Divinity during the Seventeenth Century* (London: S.P.C.K, 1952).

26. See, for example, Lauren Benton and Benjamin Straumann, "Acquiring Empire by Law: From Roman Doctrine to Early Modern European Practice," *Law & History Review* 28 (2010): 1-38.
27. Lauren Benton, *A Search for Sovereignty*; and see also Alison LaCroix, *The Ideological Origins of American Federalism* (Cambridge, MA: Harvard University Press, 2010).
28. Katherine A. Hermes, "The Law of Native Americans, to 1815," in Michael Grossberg and Christopher Tomlins, eds. *The Cambridge History of Law in American*, vol. 1 (Cambridge: Cambridge University Press, 2008), 32-62.
29. See Benton, *Law and Colonial Cultures*, chapters 5-6.
30. Lauren Benton, "The Legal Regime of the South Atlantic World: Jurisdictional Politics as Institutional Order," *Journal of World History* 11, no. 1 (2000): 27-56.
31. Ford, *Settler Sovereignty*.
32. The Jesuit missions to the Guaraní were not unique. Settlements in the New World committed to serious programs of godly discipline often reduced levels of legal pluralism. Richard J. Ross, "Puritan Godly Discipline in Comparative Perspective: Legal Pluralism and the Sources of 'Intensity,'" *American Historical Review* 113 (2008): 975-1002, esp. 997-99 (on the Jesuits and other examples).
33. Kenneth J. Banks, *Chasing Empire across the Sea: Communications and the State in the French Atlantic, 1713-1763* (Montreal: McGill-Queen's University Press, 2002); Richard J. Ross, "Legal Communications and Imperial Governance: British North America and Spanish America Compared," in *The Cambridge History of Law in America*, volume 1, *Early America (1580-1815)*, ed. Michael Grossberg and Christopher Tomlins (Cambridge: Cambridge University Press, 2008), 104-43.
34. On the question of what makes a colonial legal case a scandal, see James Epstein, *Scandal of Colonial Rule: Power and Subversion in the British Atlantic during the Age of Revolution* (Cambridge: Cambridge University Press, 2012).
35. The question of confederations and empire is framed by José Carlos Chiaramonte, *Nación y Estado en Iberoamérica: El lenguaje politico en tiempos de las independencies* (Buenos Aires: Sudamericana, 2004); and for a study that provokes questions about the relation of diaspora to empire, see Francesca Trivellato, *The Familiarity of Strangers: The Sephardic Diaspora, Livorno, and Cross-Cultural Trade in the Early Modern Period* (New Haven, CT: Yale University Press, 2009).
36. Jennifer Pitts, "Empire and Legal Universalisms in the Eighteenth Century," *American Historical Review* 117, no. 1 (February 2012): 92-121; Duncan Bell, ed., *Victorian Visions of Global Order: Empire and International Relations in Nineteenth-Century Political Thought* (Cambridge: Cambridge University Press, 2007).

PART I

Composite Polities across Empires

2

"Bundles of Hyphens"

Corporations as Legal Communities in the Early Modern British Empire

PHILIP J. STERN

"Corporate" life has long been at the heart of our understanding of legal pluralism, whether in the sense of religious, ethnic, or commercial "corporate" groups with claims to semi-autonomous laws and legal institutions or formal corporate bodies that served as a "middle level" or "mediating institution" between state and society.[1] Understandably, such pluralism was particularly pronounced in the context of empire, which by very definition required rule over a range of different groups, with divergent legal traditions, institutions, and cultures. Far from the confident and singular project it is often represented to be, such diversity meant that overseas expansion was a matter of constant uncertainty, opportunity, negotiation, and syncretism both for governments and subjects alike.[2]

This chapter argues that overseas corporations were far more than intermediary bodies or outsourced, privatized extensions of the state. In early modern parlance, they were themselves forms of "commonwealth," bodies politic responsible for governing over the economic, political, religious, and cultural life of those under their charge, with their own claims to property, rights, and immunities at law that generated claims to jurisdiction, allegiance, and subjects and citizens. Whether in joint-stock companies, corporate colonies, incorporated municipalities, or various other institutional forms, the corporation ensured that empire was defined by layers of competing and overlapping jurisdictional authority from its very conception. Seen in such a way, legal pluralism of empire appears not just a product of the complex encounters with indigenous legal systems, other European empires, and the motley and often violent nature of rule overseas. Rather, legal pluralism was embedded in the enterprise itself, found in the nature of Anglo-British political and juridical institutions as much as in their "entanglements" with others.[3] Yet, while pluralism provided the flexibility and diversity necessary for managing such an empire, it also produced jurisdictional tension and fissure, between corporations and the state as well as within and among corporations themselves. In this sense, the jurisdictional and institutional diversity engendered by corporations rendered the British imperial "constitution" a constantly moving target, located not in any static set of rules but in its ongoing negotiation of the ever-shifting dynamic between corporate pluralism and the centralism—one might say, *e pluribus unum* —of more singular notions of state and empire.

Corporate Sovereignty

What is a corporation? While today the term perhaps most immediately calls to mind an economic firm, a corporation as a legal and political idea was far broader and far more public in its nature. Tracing its origins back to Roman law, corporations came in various different shapes and sizes: perhaps most notably and foundationally as cities and towns but also as churches and religious organizations, schools, learned societies, hospitals, charity organizations, professional and voluntary associations, and, of course, companies for commerce, public works, and colonization. The eighteenth-century jurist William Blackstone, following on Littleton and Coke, offered a simple concentric taxonomy into which all corporations could be fit: sole and aggregate, with aggregate being divided among ecclesiastical and lay and lay being divided into civil and charitable.[4] The corporation sole was a peculiar and rare concept, most famously exemplified in the monarch's two bodies: the mortal and profane body natural and the transcendent body politic. Thus, even the absolutist and divinely ordained Crown was itself a form of corporation. Yet, as F. W. Maitland noted, the very notion seemed not to come from political theory but to have been modeled on the way the law dealt with the distinction between a vicar as an individual and the property he held on behalf of the church; that is, as Maitland ridiculed it, the monarchical corporation sole was less a "personification" of the state than its "parsonification."[5]

Far more common and pervasive, of course, were aggregate corporations. As Edward Coke observed, what bound them together legally and conceptually was simply their status as "*collegium* or *universitas*": that is, a collectivity vested with a legal personality, or a group of such bodies.[6] From this basic concept of collegiality flowed the very notion of corporate behavior, particularly in the urban corporation, whose "whole point," the twentieth-century political theorist Harold Laski observed, "lies in the organization of a group of men into something like an unity."[7] Yet while most any group could simply come together voluntarily, corporations uniquely possessed the right and responsibility to frame laws, bind their members to obedience, and obtain immunities and rights on behalf of the group as a whole.[8] Put more simply, as a 1702 digest of corporation laws insisted, "The general Intent and End of all Civil Incorporation is for better Government; either general or special."[9]

Ongoing modern controversies notwithstanding, for the vast majority of the corporation's long lifespan the dilemmas surrounding it have been much less about its identity as a rights-bearing individual than as a form of society.[10] As an artificial person, a corporation was subject to and protected by English laws, particularly with respect to property; yet, as a government, it was immune as a body from many of the very same strictures. It could sue and be sued but could not be guilty of a crime. It was immortal, and had no soul, and thus could administer but not take oaths, commit treason, be outlawed or excommunicated, perform homage, or even actually be summoned to appear.[11] Their charters called into being not people but "bodies corporate and politick," understood by contemporaries, especially in the context of urban government, as forms of "*res publica*," or "commonwealth," a typically early modern fusion of private capacities of property ownership and legal personality mixed with the responsibilities and rights to govern over a particular form of public and its well-being.[12] As Andrew Fitzmaurice has explained, "For the early modern English, ["commonwealth"] meant simply a coherent political body defined by mutual obligations. A commonwealth could be a guild, a business, a parish, a town, a city, or . . . a colony."[13]

Moreover, corporations were also forms of association, fellowship, and society.[14] Even the joint-stock company, Otto von Gierke argued, "has in every respect the legal status of a fellowship personality. . . . [T]herefore, the association does not exercise merely private rights, but general corporate rights: autonomy, a specific area of jurisdiction."[15] In England, perpetual succession and the incorporated structure of the joint-stock company also descended from medieval guilds, which too were not only economic but organizations with distinct "bond[s] of union" and social functions that went far beyond their immediate commercial purposes.[16] Corporations offered a form of citizenship, particularly via their "freedoms," which, in conferring a right to participate in governance as well as particular immunities, constituted "a form of political as much as social or economic identity."[17] Even more widely, corporations offered other forms of service and participation, from their courts and systems of adjudication to a range of offices with public functions.[18] Public ceremonies, architecture, and other performances of *stateliness* further reinforced the authority of the corporation and its corporators.[19] Among variations of chartered bodies politic, each and all possessed unique privileges, social practices, and political duties that overlapped, complemented, conflicted with, and confused other forms of civic relationships, including with the Crown itself, and in their own way generated a form of "public sphere."[20]

The early modern English "state" was in this sense a composite of agents, networks, and "grids of power" that operated within, aside, and sometimes in conflict with the sovereign Crown.[21] The corporation—whether through its franchises, its courts, or the variety of forms of offices it offered—forces us, as Mark Goldie has put it, to abandon a vision of "early modern England as a bipolar society of rulers and ruled . . . in favor of a vocabulary of agency, reciprocity, mediation, participation and negotiation."[22] Each of these jurisdictions and communities required law and government, and were often equated with and analogized to one another. For example, the early-seventeenth-century clergyman Robert Sanderson argued that "*positive Laws* and Sanctions" were necessary for "all *Government* and *Order*," including "*Churches, Kingdoms, Corporations, Families,* and all other both greater and lesser *Societies* of men."[23] "The same Reason which appoints general Laws to govern Kingdoms," one treatise in 1712 noted, "ought to allow particular Laws for governing particular Societies, it being admitted that Discipline is requisite in both."[24] As William Prynne observed, that all people had to contribute, through taxation, to their own welfare was "[t]he Fundamentall Law and originall compact of every Kingdom, Citie, Corporation, Company or Fraternitie of men in the World."[25]

Of course, some argued with Bodin and others—and far more simply assumed—that these "lesser" or "particular" societies were inferior to or extensions of the sovereign; after all, as Elisha Coles's 1677 dictionary defined it, a corporation was indeed "a body politick," but one "form'd by the King's charter."[26] Similarly, Thomas Smith understood citizens and burgesses of an urban corporation to be of "none accompt" to all but Parliament.[27] Yet, even Bodin recognized that different forms of corporation predated the state and was never quite clear on how or why the sovereign came to be superior to them.[28] Of course, this was borne out in practice. Some corporations, like

London, were so "ancient" they were said simply to exist by prescription, "time whereof the memory of many runneth not to the contrary; and therefore are looked upon in law to be well created."[29] Yet, even charters were not so clear-cut. While on the one hand they were issued by the sovereign, their very concessions and limitations on his power created certain paradoxes. Some jurists held that corporations, once formed, could not be dissolved without their own consent. Moreover, charters that provided conditions for their revocation also often promised an expectation of immortality and self-perpetuation. Even the later Stuarts' aggressive assault on the privileges of municipalities, including London, could not be done by fiat, but rather had to be prosecuted through the questionable instrument of *quo warranto*: that is, questioning at law the very foundation of the charter and whether it had been mismanaged or abused by its holders. Moreover, some corporations could create other corporations, and could be embedded within and among one another; in 1575, one even finds the two prominent corporations in Cambridge referring to themselves collectively as "the commonwealth of this University and Town."[30] With a few exceptions, the monarch rarely had any direct say, outside of express political pressure or his own shareholding, in how those corporations were governed. As Maitland noted, "the king was no more a corporator of Rhode Island than he was a corporator of the city of Norwich or of the East India Company, and . . . the Governor of Connecticut was as little a deputy of the king as was the Governor of the Bank of England."[31]

Thus it was, Maitland argued, that "there seems to be a genus of which State and Corporation are species. They seem to be permanently organised groups of men; they seem to be group-units; we seem to attribute acts and intents, rights and wrongs to these groups, to these units." Those who assumed that the state ought to be and has always been paramount and generically distinct as a political body were not reacting to historical reality, but rather were simply "slaves of a jurist's theory."[32] Even Carl Schmitt—Thomas Hobbes's heir and great critic of Laski, Maitland, and the so-called English pluralists—admitted that sovereignty was simply a matter of intensity; to recognize a corporation, association, or anything as political alongside the state was to render the very concept of the political "nonexistent," but there was no necessary reason why the political could not "derive its energy from the most varied of human endeavors" or that the "association or dissociation of human beings" could not be "religious, national (in the ethnic or cultural sense), economic or of another kind."[33] Thus, what bothered Schmitt particularly was not the pluralists' notion that associations were critical to society but their rejection of any notion of *the* political, a singular form of association above and exclusive of all others. Harold Laski obviously did not share Schmitt's confidence. "Ours is a time of deep question about the state," he observed in 1917. "Theories of corporate personality have challenged in decisive fashion its proud claim to preeminence. Its central character of uniqueness seems hardly to have survived the acid test of skeptical inquiry. The groups it has claimed to control seem, often enough, to lead a life no less full and splendid than its own."[34] The corporation and the variety of associational life, which had been historically layered throughout society, simply undermined the national state's claim to absolute and singular authority. As he put it elsewhere,

> Everywhere we find groups within the state which challenge its supremacy. . . . They are, it may be, in relations with the state, a part of it; but one with it they are not. They refuse the reduction to unity. . . . Men belong to it; but, also, they belong to other groups, and a competition for allegiance is continuously possible. . . . Whether we will or no, we are bundles of hyphens.[35]

Corporate Colonies

If corporations were so foundational to political life in Europe, it should be no surprise that they would prove critical to European expansion abroad. For Laski and others, the ubiquity of the corporation and associational life did not just challenge the singularity of domestic sovereignty; it called into question the state's exclusivity in international relations as well. After all, if corporations were societies and forms of public, states could not be persons, acting as if they spoke with one unified voice for an entire nation.[36] This was particularly true within European empires, which by their very nature could not even pretend, like many states, to govern even over coherent nations or singular juridical traditions. Across early modern Europe, Asia, and the Atlantic, imperial sovereignty was less a singularity than a composite "patchwork" of overlapping and competing governments, jurisdictions, and empires.[37] Corporations and corporate forms were deeply embedded in this overseas Eurasian enterprise. Certainly, the Spanish Atlantic was replete with varieties of corporate power, including not only municipalities, companies, and guilds but also corporate rights assigned to particular groups, clergy, the military, and even the so-called *república de los indios*.[38] Hugo Grotius's argument that the Dutch East India Company was perfectly capable of making treaties and alliances in Asia, as well as waging just and legitimate war, led him to a theory of divisible sovereignty in which individuals and groups outside the state could possess rights to a public legal personality, particularly in the extra-European world.[39]

To Maitland, it was precisely in overseas expansion that one could see a "unicellular" England converted into a "multicellular" British state and empire that could join the ranks of robust pluralism found in its continental neighbors. As he put it in the introduction to his translation of Gierke's *Political Theories of the Middle Age*,

> The adventures of an English joint-stock company which happened into a rulership of the Indies, the adventures of another English company which while its charter was still very new had become the puritan commonwealth of Massachusett's [sic] Bay should be enough to show that our popular English *Staatslehre* if, instead of analysing the contents of a speculative jurist's mind, it seriously grasped the facts of English history, would show some inclination to become a *Korporationslehre* also.[40]

While the English in many ways lagged behind their European rivals, corporations played a particular role in overseas expansion, given the degree to which that empire relied upon nonstate actors for both its economic and its infrastructural foundations. Without "domestic" municipalities, universities, and other incorporated institutions, many overseas ventures would have found it impossible in the first place to secure fiscal, political, and ideological footing for their enterprises. English monarchs did not have the resources or even really the political will to command trade and colonial life abroad. This should not have been surprising; the English state was hardly in the business of raising militia or building churches at home, let alone across the Atlantic or on the other side of the world. It was also not always clear that the Crown could do so even if it had wanted. Some English corporations—particularly but not exclusively London—participated as bodies politic in this enterprise, providing investment, directorship, and promotion of colonial and commercial enterprises, and were literally reproduced both orthographically and structurally throughout the Atlantic world: *London*derry, *Plymouth* plantation, and so on.[41] Municipal and university corporations were also deeply invested in underwriting colonial promotion and propaganda, from petitions and pamphlets to geography and cartography. They also underscored these enterprises indirectly by supporting other institutions, such as Gresham College, created by the London corporation and the Mercer's Company to emphasize education in "practical" subjects like commerce.[42]

More directly, Tudor and Stuart England witnessed an explosion of corporations for overseas trade, exploration, and empire: East India, Virginia, Guinea, Guiana, Africa, Russia, Northwest Passage, Levant, Somers Island, Providence Island, Plymouth and Massachusetts Bay, Hudson's Bay, and so on.[43] These companies, like "domestic" corporations, were not simply commercial firms but forms of political and social association; thus, the East India Company's 1600 charter identified it as a "fellowship," and Ferdinando Gorges, early promoter of New England plantation, imagined his Plymouth Company as "a Corporation-company or Brotherhood."[44] All corporations called upon a wide range of rights and privileges, but those involved in overseas settlement, to whatever degree, were of a different order. As Thomas Pownall put it in 1773, all "emigrations and settlements *in partibus caeteris*" possessed

> the like powers of incorporation . . . of acquiring, purchasing and possessing lands and hereditaments within the realm . . . of property and joint stock . . . of direction and government . . . of permission of emigration and of transporting emigrants . . . of trading, making settlements, and of establishing factories . . . to build forts and otherwise fortify their possessions; to make war and peace with the natives, not Christians . . . of establishing government, and of appointing governors and all necessary officers, civil and military, as have been given to all other colonists and emigrants.[45]

Even supposedly "commercial" companies that involved forms of plantation, like the East India Company or the Hudson's Bay Company, ultimately maintained these same rights and obligations, which in turn dovetailed with claims to exclusive jurisdiction over the people within the bounds of their authority, English, European, and indigenous alike. This in a sense meant that corporate companies, in claiming jurisdiction over people, could also claim them as subjects.[46]

As with domestic charters, these rights were quite resistant to interference. As a property right in itself, charters, once granted, were both in theory and certainly in practice extremely difficult if not impossible to withdraw without the corporation's consent. Moreover, corporations like New York City themselves possessed and dispensed of real property, which blurred the lines between their public and private functions and defined their role as a government and its relationship with both royal and provincial forms of government.[47] Until the late seventeenth century, it was fairly well established that statute law did not reach beyond the borders of England and Wales, yet there was a sense in which the absolute power of the king to grant charters also ironically limited his power abroad. "In all other places & Plantacons his Majesty's Charter gives the Law and his power is despoticall," the East India Company argued in 1689, "*if he has not bounded it by some Charter of his own to the first Planters or Adventurers,* as in the Plantations of the Matathusis or Boston in new England and that of Pistataqua or Plimouth in New England."[48] Even Charles II's own attorney general argued in 1681 that the right to make "Locall" law in foreign plantations devolved on the proprietor, as absolute and beholden to the same principles as if it were the king himself.[49] Thus, in 1687, the East India Company cited "that Maxim of the Law *Nullum tempus Occurit Regi aut Ecclesiae*"—that is, the principle that there can be no statute of limitations on the powers of the king or Church—as a justification for invalidating a planter's attempts to transfer his land and cattle into the name of another planter to avoid impending condemnation. The foundation for this, they continued, was the even more general principle that "the Company must always have the Preference in India as his Majesty justly hath here, which you must ever observe as a standing rule & law in that Island" and that Company laws and orders were to be "as good Law as Magna Charta is to England."[50] Common restrictions like the so-called repugnancy principle—clauses that required colonial laws made abroad not to contradict English law—apparently subsumed colonies into a coherent English legal system but were notoriously ambiguous, open to interpretation, and subject to both intercolonial and transatlantic legal dispute; after all, colonial laws differed from the laws of England and one another in substantive ways, from questions of probate and primogeniture to ecclesiastical and religious policy to slave and labor codes.[51] Charters for overseas activities were also further complicated by the fact that they were necessarily ambivalent documents: looking, on the one hand, to domestic law and, on the other, to international politics and the law of nations. Accordingly, as Ken Macmillan has shown, despite all of the vitriol English colonial promoters directed at the Catholic Spanish and Portuguese claims to *imperium* abroad, English charters possessed a striking resemblance—in their languages and legal foundations—with the notorious papal bulls *inter caetera* upon which those Iberian claims had rested for a century.[52]

It was possible to argue that overseas charters stood on even firmer ground still, quite literally. Even if English monarchs had the clear authority to make a corporation, what right did they have to own or possess the actual property granted in these charters? To some, that right was vested in "no other Right than what is deriv'd from the native Lords of the Soil"—that is what was *purchased* of Native Americans—and the labor and improvement put into that soil, both of which were the work of corporations and their settlers, not the

Crown.[53] Even if one did not accept this radical a position, for many corporations as well as settlers abroad, charters became a form of written constitution (in itself a fundamental difference with the English polity) that secured their rights both in the colony and vis-à-vis Crown authorities.[54] Moreover, not every corporation's charter so clearly descended from the monarch. Settlers in Massachusetts, from its earliest days, argued that the expansive and nebulous nature of their corporation prevented oversight and intervention from London.[55] English emigrants on the *Mayflower,* who, discovering that they had landed some two hundred miles outside of their authorized destination, improvised their own "compact" for self-government at Plymouth colony, forming themselves into "a civil body politic." The fact that the Massachusetts Bay Company's governor and General Court met across the Atlantic and had physically removed their charter to New England also effectively transformed their "commercial charter into an instrument of government" and a corporate company into a corporate colony; until the 1680s, English state attempts to revoke the charter were hampered by the simple fact that Massachusetts refused to repatriate the document itself.[56] The New England confederation, which lasted from 1643 until the creation of the (short-lived) Dominion of New England in 1684, was also established with little reference to authority from England, and generated authorities ranging from negotiating boundaries and defense to the propagation of the Gospel.[57] Likewise, early New Yorkers took their charter not as a dispensation but as "a license for internal autonomy."[58]

Of the three basic constitutional forms that Blackstone (and many others) identified in English colonial rule—Crown or state "provinces," proprietary rule, and "charter," or corporate rule—corporations also seemed to have the greatest claims to autonomy.[59] Colonies ruled directly by the Crown were themselves, at least initially, exceptional. More common of course were proprietorships. While vested in charters like corporations, proprietary grants were essentially fiefdoms. In the Atlantic, these charters tended to allocate lands *in capite,* that is, directly held of the monarch, as in a manor; such an arrangement, rooted in palatinates and bishoprics in England—Durham was often the model—offered a vast amount of power, particularly to administer justice and alienate land, but it also theoretically placed great burdens upon its holders. Conversely, corporations could not be considered vice-regents nor, in a technical sense, manorial lords. Their colonial holdings tended to be neither issued *in capite* nor rooted in a particular manor but rather in the peculiar language "*as of* the Manor of East Greenwich." While both proprietary and corporate grants were grants in socage (that is, requiring no feudal service, which was, in any event, abolished across the board after the 1650s), the "Greenwich" formula effectively identified the property in question as wasteland, consigning any extant claims, whether by other landholders or by other sovereign powers, to legal oblivion. As it had for certain land grants in England as well, such as drainage projects in the English fenlands, this type of grant was particularly designed to create allodial, freehold property under the exclusive jurisdiction of the patent holder, completely independent of any previous local customs or claims. That patents were not held in feudal tenure also meant they could not be summarily recalled, require service or obligation beyond the payment of rent, or behold the patent holder to the immediate supervision of the Crown. In short, the grant of free tenure actually implied a significant latitude of rights with respect to self-government, and confused rather than clarified the division of rights of government among Crown, patentee, and settler.[60] Certainly, down to the American Revolution, the "Manor of Greenwich" formula remained an argument for the limited reach of parliamentary statute in the making of the colonial constitution, and thus central imperial authority.[61]

These distinctions, of course, were also ideal legal types; many settlement efforts offered what appeared to be a fusion of both the palatine and the corporate traditions. In 1627, the Council for New England granted land to the voluntary organization calling itself the New England Company, which promptly sought incorporation as the Massachusetts Bay Company, along the lines of the earlier Virginia Company though with a number of features that resembled the more recent proprietary ventures' emphasis on governing over territory, settlers, and religion. In 1639, Gorges sought a form of palatine jurisdiction in Maine, but under the rubric of his corporate company.[62] The admission of so many new settlers to the freedom of the Massachusetts colony prompted its government to restrict their franchise from direct to representative government; the system of deputies that ensued was premised on Governor John Winthrop's insistence that the government was now "in the nature of a parliament" rather than a mayor and corporate council.[63] New York city's corporation was hybrid in its very origins as a Dutch colony, and the New York colony, as Daniel Hulsebosch has put it, represented a mélange of forms: "part proprietary, part corporation, part country, and part replica of the whole of England."[64] The charter for Rhode Island was, in a sense, "a cross between the small municipalities that dotted the English countryside and a business company."[65] Carolina and Georgia were proprietorships, but, as they were vested in consortia rather than individual proprietors, they also shared critical commonalities with corporations. In the 1660s and 1670s, the East India Company obtained royal charters for the governance of Bombay and St. Helena, which similarly called upon the "Manor of Greenwich" formula, but also referred to the company as the "Lords and Proprietors" of the land, which in turn seemed to confer on the company some expectation of manorial rights in governing the colonies, such as control over land, justice, and people.[66] Thus, one finds the governor and council at St. Helena not only claiming the right to govern the island but also alienating land under whatever sorts of tenure it saw fit and justifying administering justice and issuing fines for "all cases of trespass, misbehaviour, breach of the peace, or high misdemeanor," as similar to "his Majesty in our courts at Westminster and at all Court Leets to the respective Lords of the manner."[67]

Corporate Government

Corporate government permitted the exercise of a particular form of sovereignty and jurisdiction, which, as in colonial New York, "provided a continuum of governmental powers running from the almost purely governmental to the purely private."[68] It was also a familiar way to organize political life in the profoundly unfamiliar circumstances of overseas trade and settlement. The cross-fertilization of English corporate life and colonial governance rested, of course, on the legal, ideological, and structural continuities between the two forms: the roots of colonial enterprise in both incorporated English cities and corporate companies and ventures, the claims on rights and responsibilities that were rooted in the ubiquity of corporate law, and self-conscious reproduction of municipal and other corporate forms in colonial contexts. The English did not invent their colonial system *ex nihilo,* but rather rooted it in established legal tradition; this was perhaps unsurprising, given that so many corporate proprietors and governors necessarily had great amounts of previous experience in urban commerce and municipal government. As a result, Daniel Hulsebosch has observed, the New York colony at least "resembled a county or municipal corporation" and its government employed "specific practices over centuries in English counties and cities."[69] American colonies were thus already embedded in a pluralistic legal system, which some, like Jeremiah Dummer, argued served as a necessary check on the arbitrary rule of Crown governors and officials.[70] Less polemically, the consultative structure of their governance and the hybrid nature of their legal and political foundations made corporations ever more likely to tend ideologically toward a sort of normative pluralism, in an amalgam of legal traditions, theories, and precedent: republican, feudal, common, civil, natural, martial, and despotic forms of law, including the extremely common but often vague notion of "equity," not to mention the ability to absorb and accommodate indigenous law and custom as well as the accumulated customs of a colony itself.[71]

Unsurprisingly, then, the regulation of trade and governing of the market, which were primarily and initially matters for local corporate institutions and particularly guilds, were also of great concern to corporate government abroad.[72] The initial charter for Virginia specifically provided for the rights to plant, fortify, and govern, but also to exploit natural resources—"lands, woods, soil, grounds havens, ports, rivers, mines, minerals, marshes, waters, fishings, commodities, and heriditaments"—some of which would normally have fallen under royal prerogative.[73] Similarly, the charter for Massachusetts Bay made clear the rights for "planting, ruling, ordering and governing of Newe England in America," which included "mynes and Myneralls," as well as "all Jurisdiccons, Rights, Royalties, Liberties, Freedomes, Immunities, Priviledges, Franchises, Preheminences, and Comodities whatsoever."[74] Though hardly exclusive among colonial ventures in doing so, corporations also micromanaged both agriculture and commerce. At places like Bombay and Madras, the East India Company similarly encouraged the organization of inhabitants' trade, even including encouraging settlers, English and otherwise, to create joint-stock corporations of their own.[75] As Karen Kupperman has put it, early settlers at Providence Island, as at Barbados, "were hit with a veritable barrage of advice and instructions about the products they should grow."[76] Like municipal corporations at home, corporations abroad were thus responsible for governing and regulating a range of aspects of social and economic life, from promoting "virtue" and piety to adjudicating creditor-debtor relationships, inspecting and setting prices of goods, licensing and regulating particular activities such as tavern-keeping, providing for the poor and others in times of crisis and dearth. They thus also had the right and responsibility to tax their subjects to provide for those conditions. The Fundamental Constitutions of Carolina (1669) made it clear that all freehold grants would be subject to taxation in silver from the proprietors. It also authorized duties on certain economic resources should they be discovered, such as mines, whale fishing, ambergris, and gems and other minerals—again, a privilege that in England might have been reserved solely for the Crown.[77] Conversely, the Providence Island Company's *failure* to properly balance taxation (as well as property rights in land) with the rights and interests of settlers contributed, Kupperman has argued, to the corporation's ultimate failure.[78]

Government over people and property, of course, required not just provision for social welfare but also venues for enforcing law and adjudicating conflicts, whether in the form of political intervention from governors and councils or legal intervention from a variety of forms of courts. Corporations' courts, of course, did far more than this, as they enforced both civil disputes and criminal law, adjudicated wills and probate, and even engaged affairs of state. As Thomas Lechford noted in 1642, Massachusetts courts had the "power of Parliament, King's Bench, Common Pleas, Chancery, High Commission and Star-Chamber, and all other Courts of England."[79] The degree to which the decisions of these courts could be appealed also varied across the English colonial world; chartered incorporation, particularly as a form of franchise, often complicated appeals outside the body politic, limitations that were dynamic, changing over time and fundamentally structuring the nature of the relationship among franchises, corporations, and the state.[80]

Corporate courts and governments also determined the nature of both individual and corporate relationship with property. The settlers in Plymouth, for example, initially organized their property in common, but in 1627 divided it up into parcels for private ownership; the Massachusetts Bay General Court gave land to towns as "corporate entitites," which tended then to distribute it as freehold tenure, reserving some lands as common as well.[81] Rhode Island's land banks essentially issued paper currency without direct royal assent or Privy Council review, but rather on the foundation of its corporate charter.[82] This, of course, raised another crucial function and responsibility of both corporate and proprietary government: namely, to create these courts, banks, offices, and even other corporations and colonies, with varying degrees of relation to royal control.[83] Sometimes with royal consent and sometimes not, colonies and companies themselves created corporations; after all, as Maitland reminded, "a body politic may be a member of another body politic."[84] Like many others, the 1663 charter for Carolina empowered proprietors specifically to charter municipalities, corporations, and markets and fairs; its amendment in 1665 extended that power to creating "counties, barronies, and colonies." The Fundamental Constitutions of Carolina (1669) further specified that every town should be governed with a mayor, aldermen, and common council, yet named almost forty different categories of office, as well as sub-proprietorships, territorial nobility, and county jurisdictions; within these jurisdictions were to meet courts leet and baron, with sheriffs and justices on the county level, a steward and justices on the precinct level, and mayors, aldermen, and councilors at the municipal level. There were also eight supreme courts, with their attendant juridical officers, attendants, and assistants. Pennsylvania's charter similarly included the right to constitute incorporated towns, boroughs, and fairs; Penn's charter of incorporation to the Free Society of Traders, for example, offered it a manorial holding of twenty thousand acres, the right to convene manorial courts, and the right to adjudicate disputes, particularly with the goal of peopling the territory with farmers and tradesmen.[85] Indeed, such was the enthusiasm for this incorporating function of the corporation that John Smith felt compelled to caution New England colonists in the 1630s that "privileges for Cities, Charters for Corporations, Universities, Free-schooles, and Glebeland" often quixotically preceded any people there to actually populate, fund, or support them.[86]

Corporations within colonies were intended to facilitate defense, public expenditure, local government, and justice; they constituted another layer of jurisdiction, legal authority, and site of colonial life.[87] Both manorial and corporate urban government was also a particular prophylaxis to the natural evolution of rural life, which colonial proprietors like Shaftesbury saw as exposing settlers to "inconvenience and Barbarisme."[88] Moreover, the financial, judicial, and administrative responsibilities of such corporations did not originate in the vague clauses of the royal charters but were determined in the acts and chartering of colonial corporations, governments, legislatures, statutes; no municipality in colonial North America was ever chartered directly from the Crown, and no colonial government ever initiated processes of *quo warranto* against them.[89] Even after the assumption of Crown rule in Virginia, courts sat monthly at Charles City and Elizabeth City, two of the four original incorporated cities in the colony, allowing appeals only to the governor and council; Massachusetts similarly relied on a court structure that rested at the town or city level.[90] King's College (later Columbia University) in New York received its charter from the colony's governor on behalf of the king, but many colonists insisted they had the right to charter such an institution themselves and certainly commanded the governance of the institution once established.[91]

Like the colonies, proprietors, and companies that created them, such corporations were sites of pluralistic legal orders in potential conflict with their progenitors. Corporation officials, like mayors and aldermen, registrars, militia captains, and tax collectors, could easily fall into jurisdictional tension with other county, colonial, and royal officials alike. The express desires of the London committees of the East India Company, for example, that Madras—which it had incorporated in 1687—be broadly representative of the inhabitants of the town were quickly upset not only by the domination of English residents in the mayorality and among the aldermen but also by the constant impositions of authority from the company's governor and council over its affairs, such as appeals from its Mayor's Court.[92] William Penn's vision of manorial settlement was often in tension with the corporate rights of the city of Philadelphia, not to mention the evolution of townships, farmsteads, and noncontiguous family landholdings throughout Pennsylvania, under the local jurisdictional authority of county courts and officials.[93] The Ohio Company, though chartered by the Crown, arose in mid-eighteenth-century Virginia as a means to further plantation inland along the Ohio river valley, to solidify Virginia's land claims against Native American, French, *and* Pennsylvanian claims alike.[94] In New England, where corporate government had been particularly pronounced from its foundations, the corporate town and city—of which there were hundreds—became, in Christopher Tomlins's words, a primary "unit of collective proprietorship, settlement, land distribution, and local governance." The creation and settlement of corporate townships also structured New England's northward expansion into New Hampshire, Maine, and Nova Scotia during and in the wake of the Seven Years War, a means toward more effectively securing both private interest and collective rights.[95]

If corporate status at every level provided alternative forms of legal jurisdiction and venue, it also offered opportunities for rights claims by individuals and groups. Claims on the ancient rights and privileges of "freeman" status, for example, could complicate lines of allegiance and obedience; corporate freedoms were in this sense as much a franchise and office as they were an economic right, if not more so. They also drew lines within colonies and cities, between insiders and outsiders, those who belonged and those who were strangers. This also meant that colonial subjecthood would articulate itself in different ways in different places and times.[96] The late-seventeenth-century merchant elite in New York rested on its status as one "body Politick and Corporate" to push for elected aldermen, constables, and assessors in city wards, and to protect the city's control over flour packing, bread making, and the shipping of other merchandise in and out of the colony.[97] In the face of external pressure, the corporation reasserted itself in a variety of ways: reformulating its oath in 1707 in imitation of the centuries-old oath taken by freemen of the corporation of London; registering hundreds of new freemen, issuing licenses, and collecting taxes; allowing officers, lawyers, and inspectors to persist in claiming their rights vis-à-vis traders and workers in the city; calling upon laborers for civic service; and engaging the construction of buildings, institutions, and public works that had traditionally been its purview. In turn, a variety of New York's inhabitants continued to appeal as "citizens" of the "ancient" corporation to the Common Council for redress of grievances, welfare, and favor.[98] Corporate freedoms, whether municipal or commercial, thus served both to tie people to government and to allow for them to participate in and manipulate its legal and political regimes. For locals in New York as much as patent holders of the East India Company, the corporation was, in its beginning as much as its end, a "contractual bond" with government.[99]

Pluralism, Centralism, and the Corporation

That the corporation insisted upon a pluralistic legal order in the early modern empire did not, of course, mean that everyone was particularly comfortable with such an arrangement. Certainly, the seventeenth-century English state was hardly divested of interest in colonial government, and there were manifold examples of its attempts to intervene abroad.[100] As early as the 1620s, the initial enthusiasm for corporate charters waned in favor of palatine proprietorship.[101] Often Crown attempts to intervene or assume government directly were accompanied by arguments that corporations were, indeed, inferior forms of government: "[A] company or corporation to whom it may be proper to trust matters of trade and commerce," Crown officials argued in their dissolution of the Virginia Company in 1624, "cannot be fit or safe to communicate the ordering of State affairs, be they never of so mean consequence."[102] Whether in Cromwell's Western Design or Charles II's short-lived enterprise in Tangier, there were certainly attempts to rule abroad directly, and instruments like Navigation Acts and the extension of Vice-Admiralty courts also revealed a constant attempt by the Crown to both enforce corporate monopoly but also rein it in for its purposes. Massachusetts, Rhode Island, and Connecticut all had at various points to defend their charters against Crown intervention, ultimately unsuccessfully. By the late century, some saw such assaults as continuous with the *quo warranto* attacks at home; "in this general Ruin of Charters at Home," Jeremiah Dummer wrote, "it could not be expected that those in *America* should escape." Those fears were not entirely ungrounded; as early as 1679, the Council of Trade had considered a *quo warranto* assault of its own on the Bermuda company, and others in New England followed.[103] James II's short-lived Dominion of New England also clearly took aim at corporate autonomy, appointing sheriffs, JPs, clerks, and other officials who were intended to upend the previously localized selection of jurors and undermine the legitimacy of their courts in the process.[104] On the other hand, the later Stuarts paradoxically also endorsed new urban corporations in the empire, which had varying degrees of independence from their rule, from Charles's Tangier to James's New York to the East India Company's Madras.[105]

As in England, the English state could assault the legal pluralism of empire indirectly, by erecting itself as an arbitrator in juridical and jurisdictional disputes among corporations and other forms of colonial enterprise. Through the late seventeenth century, the East India Company's battles with the Levant Company, South Sea Company, Hudson's Bay Company, as well as, of course, private traders over jurisdiction in Persia, the East Indies, and the Pacific were waged in Crown courts and even Parliament. Conflicts within corporations could create rival new corporations, whether in the "new" East India Company created in the 1690s or in Massachusetts' spawning, more famously, of Connecticut and Rhode Island. Boundary and jurisdictional disputes, say between Massachusetts and Rhode Island or Pennsylvania and Maryland, played out in appeals to English authorities. The Rhode Island charter of 1663 was the first specifically to authorize appeals from the colony to the Crown, for matters pertaining to disputes with other colonies.[106] Such instances provided royal courts and agency a prime opportunity to redefine the terms of corporate autonomy; for example, adjudicating the boundary dispute between Rhode Island and Massachusetts in 1741, the Lord Chief Justice "intimated that the Patent was only from Council of Plymo. and not from the Crown, and that one Corporation cou'd not grant Jurisdiction to an other Corporation &ca."[107] In defense of the colony, Rhode Island's agent in London cited the "great precedent" to be found in the Court of King's Bench refusal to overturn the *quo warranto* dissolution of the corporation of Maidstone in Kent, since it "makes greatly for us as being a good precedent, from whence we may conclude that they will not permit any Review or rehearing" in the case of its successful resolution of its border dispute with Massachusetts.[108]

Thus, corporate autonomy could be tenuous, as it was assaulted from without, by authorities in England, and from within, as different forms of corporation competed with one another for jurisdiction and authority. Its degrees, of course, also differed quite radically from one situation to another, and over time. Though pronounced under the late Stuarts, such assaults continued after the Glorious Revolution, as bodies like the Privy Council, Board of Trade, Admiralty courts, and other institutions with clearer ties to the "center" took aim at the pluralism of the Atlantic and Asian empire.[109] The greater place for Parliament in the empire only furthered this assault. Charters were recalled, Navigation Acts renewed, and corporations and companies investigated and brought under greater scrutiny. Smuggling, piracy, and customs evasion served as grounds for more Crown agents, courts, and supervision in the American colonies, and in many instances, for scrutinizing the behavior of corporate authorities. For example, in 1698, Edward Randolph, the Crown's surveyor in the American colonies, in the same breath indicted the governor, deputy governor, recorder, and House of Deputies of Rhode Island to the Board of Trade in London for supporting pirates and collecting taxes from those "Inhabitants as are not freemen of the Corporation which they have no power by their Charter to do."[110] Through the 1690s, the English state entertained the annexation of Connecticut to New York and Rhode Island to New England, again under the general ambition of curbing corruption, smuggling, and piracy.[111] Bodies like the Board of Trade also signaled this greater involvement and regulation of imperial venture by the national state, and as a result the viability of monopolies, such as the Royal African Company, was increasingly tenuous.[112]

The corporation continued into the eighteenth century to be a flashpoint of conflict over colonial authority, which was in many cases apparently paradoxical and self-contradictory. While the British state continued to expand its claims on authority across the Atlantic, some corporate rights expanded; the 1730 charter for New York City, designed to confirm the city's right to governance, formally pledged that the Crown would never to take out an action of *quo warranto* against it.[113] Still, by the 1760s and 1770s, a number of arguments in favor of more uniform legal authority abroad in fact cited the corporate status of *both* the American plantations and the East India Company alike, using one to highlight the propriety of assaults on the other. Thomas Whately, for example, dismissed the claim that colonial assemblies implied the right to representation in matters of taxation by noting that neither London, which had a common council, nor the East India Company could claim such a right.[114] Crown institutions claimed greater rights to oversight of corporate activities across the Atlantic, especially on questions of the "repugnancy clause"; Mary Sarah Bilder has argued that in this history one can also find the foundation for the concept of judicial review.[115] The East India Company came under similar scrutiny, as did its own corporations. In 1726, Calcutta and Bombay were first given corporate status under Crown rather than company charter; along with Madras, which was rechartered under the same authority, their Mayor's Courts became for the first time subject to Privy Council appeals and their laws much more dependent upon metropolitan legal ideas and practices.[116] It should also thus be little surprise that advocates for the company, in battling against parliamentary regulations of the 1770s, should fall upon some of the same "rhetoric of resistance" to parliamentary oversight as American revolutionaries.[117] While those American revolutionaries were ironically participating in the assault on the East India Company, its tea, and its corporate privileges,[118] their status as "corporations" also became a foundation for regulation and intervention, not independence. Thus, John Wesley could now justify transatlantic parliamentary taxation because "[a]n English colony is . . . a corporation. . . . As a corporation they make laws for themselves, but as a corporation subsisting by a grant from higher authority, to the control of that authority, they still continue subject."[119] Likewise, under some pressure, Thomas Hutchinson hedged his position on American legislative independence, suggesting that though their distance required "a more extensive Legislative Power to be necessary for a Colony than for a Corporation in England," both remained under the "supreme" power of Parliament.[120] For Thomas Pownall, the fact that the East India Company possessed the same rights "*in partibus caeteris*" as an American colony was not an advocacy for its independence, but rather an argument for the obvious ability of the state to regulate, tax, and control both.[121]

If corporations made for a pluralistic form of empire, assaulting their independence and subsuming them more firmly under the parliamentary state became crucial to both the making of a more coherent British empire and the establishment of the new American republic. As Maitland put it, "When a Statute declared that the *Herrschaft* [rule] which the East India Company had acquired in India was held 'in trust' for the Crown of Great Britain, that was no idle proposition but the settlement of a great dispute."[122] It was, as Maitland noted elsewhere, at the core of a "modern absolutism," and "the pulverising, macadamising tendency in all its glory, working from century to century, reducing to impotence, and then to nullity, all that intervenes between Man and State."[123] The modern insistence on the separation of public and private, of state and economy, has done a great deal to dismantle the notion that corporations, as societies and self-governing bodies politic, carried with them particular rights and responsibilities not just as *persons* but as *governments*. Of course, the endurance of these dichotomies might very well be called into question, as the problem of the "sovereign corporation" and its genealogy in this earlier corporate and colonial history has taken on a new urgency, in the wake of globalization, neoliberalism, and the failure of (particularly postcolonial) states and quasi-states across the globe.[124] As we remained preoccupied with notions of whether corporations can be people—with rights, for example, to free speech—the relationship between the "nation" and both the domestic and global multinational corporation itself continues to be unclear and in a process of negotiation, as we once again, it seems, become "bundles of hyphens."

NOTES

1. Lauren Benton, *Law and Colonial Cultures: Legal Regimes in World History, 1400-1900* (New York: Cambridge University Press, 2001), 55; Erwin K. Scheuch, "Societies, Corporations, and the Nation State," in E. K. Scheuch and D. Sciulli, eds., *The Annals of the International Institute of Sociology,* New Series, vol. 7: *Societies, Corporations, and the Nation State* (Leiden: Brill, 2000), 3; David Konig, "Jurisprudence and Social Policy in the New American Republic," in Konig, ed., *Devising Liberty: Preserving and Creating Freedom in the New American Republic* (Stanford, CA: Stanford University Press, 1995), 207.

2. Brian Z. Tamanaha, "Understanding Legal Pluralism: Past to Present, Local to Global," *Sydney Law Review* 30 (2008): 375. See also J. P. Greene, *Negotiated Authorities: Essays in Colonial Political and Constitutional History* (Charlottesville: University of Virginia Press, 1994); Elizabeth Mancke, "Negotiating an Empire: Britain and Its Overseas Peripheries, c. 1550-1780," in Christine Daniels and Michael Kennedy, eds., *Negotiated Empire: Centers and Peripheries in the Americas, 1500-1820* (New York: Routledge, 2002).
3. Benton, *Law and Colonial Cultures;* Lauren Benton, *A Search for Sovereignty: Law and Geography in European Empires, 1400-1900* (New York: Cambridge University Press, 2009); Eliga Gould, "Zones of Law, Zones of Violence: The Legal Geography of the British Atlantic, circa 1772," *William and Mary Quarterly* 60, no. 3 (2003); "AHR Forum: Entangled Empires in the Atlantic World," *American Historical Review* 112, no. 3 (June 2007); Lisa Ford, *Settler Sovereignty: Jurisdiction and Indigenous People in America and Australia* (Cambridge, MA: Harvard University Press, 2010); Richard White, *The Middle Ground: Indians, Empires, and Republics in the Great Lakes Region, 1650-1815* (Cambridge: Cambridge University Press, 1991); Richard White, "Legal Pluralism and Native Sovereignty," *William and Mary Quarterly* 68, no. 4 (2011): 720-24.
4. Sir William Blackstone, *Commentaries on the Laws of England*, vol. 1 (Oxford: Clarendon, 1765), 457-59.
5. F. W. Maitland, "The Crown as Corporation," *Law Quarterly Review* 17 (1901): 133; F. W. Maitland, "The Corporation Sole," *Law Quarterly Review* 16 (1900); Ernst Kantorowicz, *The King's Two Bodies: A Study in Medieval Political Theology* (Princeton, NJ: Princeton University Press, 1957).
6. Edward Coke, *The First Part of the Institutes of the Laws of England; or, A Commentary Upon Littleton, Not the Name of the Author Only, but of the Law Itself* (Philadelphia: Robert H. Small, 1853), II: 250a (l.3, c.6, sec. 413).
7. Harold Laski, "The Early History of the Corporation in England," *Harvard Law Review* 30, no. 6 (1917): 581.
8. Blackstone, *Commentaries,* I: 455-56.
9. *The Law of Corporations: Containing the Laws and Customs of All the Corporations and Inferior Courts of Record in England* (London, 1702), 2.
10. See also Daniel J. H. Greenwood, "The Semi-Sovereign Corporation" (March 20, 2005), Utah Legal Studies Paper No. 05-04. Available at SSRN: http://ssrn.com/abstract=757315.
11. *Law of Corporations,* 2, 6-7; Paul D. Halliday, *Dismembering the Body Politic: Partisan Politics in England's Towns, 1650-1730* (Cambridge: Cambridge University Press, 1998), 32-33.
12. Phil Withington, *The Politics of Commonwealth: Citizens and Freemen in Early Modern England* (Cambridge: Cambridge University Press, 2005).
13. Andrew Fitzmaurice, *Humanism and America: An Intellectual History of English Colonisation, 1500-1625* (Cambridge: Cambridge University Press, 2003), 6.
14. See, most recently, Phil Withington, *Society in Early Modern England: The Vernacular Origins of Some Powerful Ideas* (Cambridge, MA: Polity, 2010).
15. Otto von Gierke, *Community in Historical Perspective,* trans. Mary Fischer, ed. Antony Black (Cambridge: Cambridge University Press, 1990), 201. See also Eric Wilson, "The VOC, Corporate Sovereignty, and the Republican Sub-Text of *De iure praedae,*" in *Property, Piracy, and Punishment: Hugo Grotius on War and Booty in De Iure Praedae—Concepts and Contexts* (Leiden: Brill, 2009), 337.
16. William Robert Scott, *The Constitution and Finance of English, Scottish, and Irish Joint-Stock Companies to 1720*, 3 vols. (reprinted, Gloucester, MA: Peter Smith, 1968 [London:

1912]), I: 3, 152; K. G. Davies, *The Royal African Company* (London: Longmans, Green, 1957), 24-25.

17. Phil Withington, "Citizens, Community, and Political Culture in Restoration England," in Alexandra Shepard and Phil Withington, eds., *Communities in Early Modern England* (Manchester, UK: Manchester University Press, 2000), 138.
18. Mark Goldie, "The Unacknowledged Republic: Officeholding in Early Modern England," in Tim Harris, ed., *The Politics of the Excluded, c. 1500-1850* (Houndmills, UK: Palgrave, 2001).
19. Robert Tittler, "Political Culture and the Built Environment of the English Country Town, c. 1540-1620," in Dale Hoak, ed., *Tudor Political Culture* (Cambridge: Cambridge University Press, 2002), 133-56.
20. Phil Withington, "Public Discourse, Corporate Citizenship, and State Formation in Early Modern England," *American Historical Review* 112, no. 4 (October 2007): esp. 1017-20. See also Halliday, *Dismembering the Body Politic,* esp. 29-55; Jacqueline Hill, "Corporatist Ideology and Practice in Ireland, 1660-1800," in S. J. Connolly, ed., *Political Ideas in Eighteenth-Century Ireland* (Dublin: Four Courts Press, 2000), 65-82; Timothy L. Alborn, *Conceiving Companies: Joint-Stock Politics in Victorian England* (London: Routledge, 1998), 3-4; Catherine Patterson, *Urban Patronage in Early Modern England: Corporate Boroughs, the Landed Elite, and the Crown, 1580-1640* (Stanford, CA: Stanford University Press, 1999).
21. E.g., Michael Braddick and John Walter, "Introduction: Grids of Power; Order, Hierarchy, and Subordination in Early Modern Society," in Michael Braddick and John Walter, eds., *Negotiating Power in Early Modern Society: Order, Hierarchy, and Subordination in Britain and Ireland* (New York: Cambridge University Press, 2001), 38-39.
22. Goldie, "Unacknowledged Republic," 154-55.
23. Robert Sanderson, *XXXVI Sermons, viz. XVI ad aulam, VI ad clerum, VI ad magistratum, VIII ad populum, with a Large Preface* (London, 1686), 81-82.
24. *Laws concerning Trade and Tradesmen* ([London], 1712), 2.
25. William Prynne, *The Fourth Part of the Soveraigne Power of Parliaments and Kingdoms* (London, 1643), 22.
26. Elisha Coles, *An English Dictionary Explaining the Difficult Terms That Are Used in Divinity, Husbandry, Physick, Phylosophy, Law, Navigation, Mathematicks, and Other Arts and Sciences* (London, 1677), s.v., "corporation."
27. Thomas Smith, *De Republica Anglorum: The Maner of Government or Policie of the Realme of England* (London, 1583), 29.
28. Preston King, *The Ideology of Order: A Comparative Analysis of Jean Bodin and Thomas Hobbes* (London: Allen & Unwin, 1974), 96-105.
29. Blackstone, *Commentaries,* I: 460-61.
30. Quoted by Alexandra Shepard, "Contesting Communities? 'Town' and 'Gown' in Cambridge, c. 1560-1640," in Shepard and Withington, eds., *Communities in Early Modern England,* 222.
31. Maitland, "Crown as Corporation," 140.
32. F. W. Maitland, "Extract from Maitland's Introduction to *Political Theories of the Middle Age* by Otto von Gierke," in Maitland, *State, Trust, and Corporation*, ed. David Runciman and Magnus Ryan (Cambridge: Cambridge University Press, 2003), 1; for a slightly different version of this argument see David Runciman, "The Concept of the State: The Sovereignty of a Fiction," in Quentin Skinner and Bo Stråth, eds., *States and Citizens: History, Theory, Prospects* (Cambridge: Cambridge University Press, 2003), 29. See also David

Runciman, *Pluralism and the Personality of the State* (Cambridge: Cambridge University Press, 1997); Quentin Skinner, "The State," in Terence Ball, James Farr, and Russell Hanson, eds., *Political Innovation and Conceptual Change* (Cambridge: Cambridge University Press, 1989).

33. Carl Schmitt, *The Concept of the Political*, trans. and intro. George Schwab (Chicago: University of Chicago Press, 1996, repr. 2007), 37-39; see also, Carl Schmitt, "Ethic of State and Pluralistic State," in Chantal Mouffe, ed., *The Challenge of Carl Schmitt* (London: Verso, 1999), 195-208; Richard Boyd, "Thomas Hobbes and the Perils of Pluralism," *Journal of Politics* 63 (2001): 392-413.
34. Laski, "Early History of the Corporation," 561.
35. Harold Laski, "The Personality of Associations," *Harvard Law Review* 29, no. 4 (1916): 425.
36. Jeanne Morefield, "States Are Not People: Harold Laski on Unsettling Sovereignty, Rediscovering Democracy," *Political Research Quarterly* 58, no. 4 (2005).
37. J. H. Elliott, *Empires of the Atlantic World: Britain and Spain in America, 1492-1830* (New Haven, CT: Yale University Press, 2006), 118; Sanjay Subrahmanyam, "Holding the World in Balance: The Connected Histories of the Iberian Overseas Empires, 1500-1640," *American Historical Review* 112, no. 5 (December 2007): 1359.
38. Elliott, *Empires of the Atlantic World*, 170, 300.
39. Edward Keene, *Beyond the Anarchical Society: Grotius, Colonialism, and Order in World Politics* (Cambridge: Cambridge University Press, 2002), 93; Martine van Ittersum, *Profit and Principle: Hugo Grotius, Natural Rights Theories, and the Rise of Dutch Power in the East Indies, 1595-1615* (Leiden: Brill, 2006); Wilson, "The VOC," 310-40. On Dutch Company practices of sovereignty, see, among others, J. van Goor, "Seapower, Trade, and State Formation: Pontianak and the Dutch," in J. van Goor, ed., *Trading Companies in Asia, 1600-1830* (Utrecht: HES Uitgevers, 1986), 85; George Winius and Markus Vink, *The Merchant-Warrior Pacified: The VOC (The Dutch East India Company) and Its Changing Political Economy in India* (Delhi: Oxford University Press, 1991), esp. 4-5; Tonio Andrade, "Political Spectacle and Colonial Rule: The *Landdag* on Dutch Taiwan, 1629-1648," *Itinerario* 21 (1997).
40. Maitland, "Extract from Maitland's Introduction," 2.
41. *E.g.*, David Harris Sacks, *The Widening Gate: Bristol and the Atlantic Economy, 1450-1700* (Berkeley and Los Angeles: University of California Press, 1991); Kenneth Morgan, *Bristol and the Atlantic Trade in the Eighteenth Century* (Cambridge: Cambridge University Press, 1993); Theodore Rabb, *Enterprise and Empire* (Cambridge, MA: Harvard University Press, 1967), 22-26.
42. Kenneth R. Andrews, *Trade, Plunder, and Settlement: Maritime Enterprise and the Genesis of the British Empire, 1480-1630* (Cambridge: Cambridge University Press, 1984), 30.
43. On these, see Scott, *Constitution and Finance*, esp. vol. 2.
44. Sir Ferdinando Gorges, *America Painted to the Life. A True History of the Originall Undertakings of the Advancement of Plantations into Those Parts with a Perfect Relation of Our English Discoveries Shewing Their Beginning, Progress, and Continuence from the Year 1628 to 1658* (London, 1658), 13.
45. Thomas Pownall, *The Right, Interest, and Duty of Government, as Concerned in the Affairs of the East Indies* (London: Printed for J. Almon, 1773), 7.
46. Philip J. Stern, *The Company-State: Corporate Sovereignty and the Early Modern Foundations of the British Empire in India* (New York: Oxford University Press, 2011); Edward Cavanagh, "A Company with Sovereignty and Subjects of Its Own? The Case of the

Hudson's Bay Company, 1670-1763," *Canadian Journal of Law and Society* 26, no. 1 (2011): 25-50.

47. Hendrik Hartog, *Public Property and Private Power: The Corporation of the City of New York in American Law, 1730-1870* (Chapel Hill: University of North Carolina, 1983).
48. London to St. Helena, 5 April 1689, India Office Records [hereafter IOR], E/3/92 f. 17 (emphasis added); Stern, *Company-State,* 26.
49. Report of the Attorney General Concerning Interlopers, 16 Nov. 1681, the National Archives [hereafter TNA], CO 77/49 f. 247.
50. London to St. Helena, 3 Aug. 1687, IOR E/3/91 f. 180-81; Stern, *Company-State*, 26.
51. Mary Sarah Bilder, *The Transatlantic Constitution: Colonial Legal Culture and the Empire* (Cambridge, MA: Harvard University Press, 2004).
52. Quoted by Ken Macmillan, *Sovereignty and Possession in the New World: The Legal Foundations of Empire 1576-1640* (Cambridge: Cambridge University Press, 2006), 107; Ken MacMillan, "Common and Civil Law? Taking Possession of the English Empire in America, 1575-1630," *Canadian Journal of History* 38 (2003): 415-18. James Muldoon, "The Contribution of the Medieval Canon Lawyers to the Formation of International Law," *Traditio* 28 (1972): 497; Anthony Pagden, *Lords of All the World: Ideologies of Empire in Spain, Britain, and France c.1500-c.1800* (New Haven, CT: Yale University Press, 1995), 64.
53. Jeremiah Dummer, *A Defence of the New-England Charters* (London, 1721), 14-15.
54. Craig Yirush, *Settlers, Liberty, and Empire: The Roots of Early American Political Theory, 1675-1775* (Cambridge: Cambridge University Press, 2011), 53.
55. Edward M. Cook Jr., "Enjoying and Defending Charter Privileges: Corporate Status and Political Culture in Eighteenth-Century Rhode Island," in Robert Olwell and Alan Tully, eds., *Cultures and Identities in Colonial British America* (Baltimore, MD: Johns Hopkins University Press, 2006), 250.
56. Virginia DeJohn Anderson, "New England in the Seventeenth Century," in Nicholas Canny, ed., *Oxford History of the British Empire,* vol. 1, *Origins of Empire* (Oxford: Oxford University Press, 1998), 196, 198; Elizabeth Mancke, "Empire and State," in David Armitage and Michael Braddick, eds., *The British Atlantic World, 1500-1800* (Basingstoke, UK: Palgrave, 2002), 189-90.
57. Alison LaCroix, *The Ideological Origins of American Federalism* (Cambridge, MA: Harvard University Press, 2010), 21, 24.
58. Daniel Hulsebosch, *Constituting Empire: New York and the Transformation of Constitutionalism in the Atlantic World, 1664-1830* (Chapel Hill: University of North Carolina Press, 2005), 88.
59. However, Herbert Osgood argued in a series of articles in 1896 and 1897 that Blackstone's taxonomy was flawed, and proposed instead only two forms: provincial and corporate. See Herbert L. Osgood, "The Corporation as a Form of Colonial Government, I," *Political Science Quarterly* 11, no. 2 (1896): 259-77, as well as parts II (issue 3, pp. 502-33) and III (issue 4, pp. 694-715).
60. Christopher Tomlins, *Freedom Bound: Law, Labor, and Civic Identity in Colonizing English America, 1550-1865* (Cambridge: Cambridge University Press, 2010), 161 n. 87, 166-68, 170-71; Yirush, *Settlers, Liberty, and Empire,* 52 n. 5; On the proprietary colonies and the palatinate model, see Vicki Hsueh, *Hybrid Constitutions: Challenging Legacies, of Law, Privilege, and Culture in Colonial America* (Durham, NC: Duke University Press, 2010). See also B. H. McPherson, "Revisiting the Manor of East Greenwich," *American Journal of Legal History* 42 (1998); Michael Craton, "Property and Propriety: Land Tenure and Slave

Property in the Creation of a British West Indian Plantocracy, 1612-1740," in Susan Staves and John Brewer, eds., *Early Modern Conceptions of Property* (London: Routledge, 1996), 499; Edward Keene, *Beyond the Anarchical Society: Grotius, Colonialism, and Order in World Politics* (Cambridge: Cambridge University Press, 2002), 62-68.

61. See Benjamin Franklin, "On the Tenure of the Manor of East Greenwich," *Gazetteer and New Daily Advertiser*, 11 January 1766; James Muldoon, "Discovery, Grant, Charter, Conquest, or Purchase: John Adams on the Legal Basis for English Possession of North America," in Bruce H. Mann and Christopher L. Tomlins, eds., *The Many Legalities of Early America* (Chapel Hill: University of North Carolina Press, 2001); Richard Tuck, *The Rights of War and Peace: Political Thought and the International Order from Grotius to Kant* (Oxford: Oxford University Press, 1999), 121-22; Daniel J. Hulsebosch, "*Imperia in Imperio*: The Multiple Constitutions of Empire in New York, 1750-1777," *Law & History Review* 16, no. 2 (1998): 319-79.
62. Tomlins, *Freedom Bound*, 173-75.
63. Osgood, "The Corporation as a Form of Colonial Government," 515.
64. Hulsebosch, *Constituting Empire*, 43, 52-55, 87-90.
65. Cook Jr., "Enjoying and Defending Charter Privileges," 247, 258.
66. Stern, *Company-State*, 24-25.
67. London to Bombay, 25 Aug. 1686, British Library, IOR, E/3/91 f. 84.
68. Hartog, *Public Property and Private Power*, 19.
69. Hulsebosch, *Constituting Empire*, 51.
70. Dummer, *A Defence of the New-England Charters*, 35, 38-39.
71. Hsueh, *Hybrid Constititutions*, 64-65; Tomlins, *Freedom Bound*, 188.
72. Thomas Nachbar, "Monopoly, Mercantilism, and the Politics of Regulation," *Virginia Law Review* 91, no. 6 (2005): 1320.
73. *First Charter of Virginia* (1606).
74. *Charter of Massachusetts Bay* (1629).
75. George Forrest, ed., *Selections from the Letters, Despatches, and Other State Papers Preserved in the Bombay Secretariat*, 2 vols. (Bombay: Government Central Press, 1887), I: 52.
76. Karen Kupperman, *Providence Island, 1630-1641: The Other Puritan Colony* (Cambridge: Cambridge University Press, 1993), 83.
77. *Fundamental Constitutions of Carolina* (March 1, 1669), secs. 113-14, avalon.law.yale.edu/17th_century/nc05.asp, last accessed November 27, 2012.
78. Kupperman, *Providence Island*, 208.
79. Quoted by Mary Sarah Bilder, "Salamanders and Sons of God: The Culture of Appeal in Early New England," in Christopher L. Tomlins and Bruce H. Mann, eds., *The Many Legalities of Early America* (Chapel Hill: University of North Carolina Press, 2001), 68.
80. Mary Sarah Bilder, "The Corporate Origins of Judicial Review," *Yale Law Journal* 116, no. 502 (2006): 503-66; Bilder, "Salamanders and Sons of God," 58-59, 63-64; Stern, *Company-State*, 26, 28-29, 55.
81. Anderson, "New England," 197, 199.
82. Cook Jr., "Enjoying and Defending Charter Privileges," 256-57.
83. Maitland, "Crown as Corporation," 141.
84. Maitland, "Crown as Corporation," 144.
85. Hsueh, *Hybrid Constitutions*, 68-69; Tomlins, *Freedom Bound*, 178-83, 287.
86. John Smith, *Advertisements for the Unexperienced Planters of New-England, or Any Where; or, The Path-Way to Experience to Erect a Plantation*, quoted by Tomlins, *Freedom Bound*, 3, 13.

87. Alan Taylor, *American Colonies: The Settling of North America* (New York: Penguin, 2002), 170.
88. Quoted by Robert Home, *Of Planting and Planning: The Making of British Colonial Cities* (London: E&FN Spon, 1997), 9.
89. Howard Lee McBain, "The Legal Status of the American Colonial City," *Political Science Quarterly* 2, no. 40 (1925): 186, 191, 198-200.
90. Bilder, "Salamanders and Sons of God," 64-65.
91. Hulsebosch, *Constituting Empire,* 89.
92. Stern, *Company-State,* 94.
93. Tomlins, *Freedom Bound,* 284; William M. Offut Jr., *Of "Good Laws" and "Good Men": Law and Society in the Delaware Valley, 1680-1710* (Urbana: University of Illinois Press, 1995), 9.
94. Herbert T. Leyland, "The Ohio Company: A Colonial Corporation," *Quarterly Publication of the Historical and Philosophical Society of Ohio* 16 (1921): 1-20.
95. Tomlins, *Freedom Bound,* 221-22; Osgood, "The Corporation as a Form of Colonial Government," 511; Elizabeth Mancke, "Corporate Structure and Private Interest: The Mid-Eighteenth-Century Expansion of New England," in Margaret Conrad, ed., *They Planted Well: New England Planters in Maritime Canada* (Fredericton, Canada: Acadiensis, 1988), 161-77.
96. See Simon Middleton, *From Privileges to Rights: Work and Politics in Colonial New York City* (Philadelphia: University of Pennsylvania Press, 2006), 154; Beverly McAnear, "The Place of the Freeman in Old New York," *New York History* 21 (1940): 418-30.
97. Middleton, *From Privileges to Rights,* 76.
98. Middleton, *From Privileges to Rights,* 153-54.
99. Graham Russell Hodges, "Legal Bonds of Attachment: The Freemanship Law of New York City, 1648-1801," *Slavery, Freedom, and Culture among Early American Workers* (New York: Sharpe, 1998), 3.
100. Ken Macmillan, *The Atlantic Imperial Constitution: Center and Periphery in the English Atlantic World* (New York: Palgrave Macmillan, 2011).
101. Hsueh, *Hybrid Constititutions.*
102. Quoted by Macmillan, *Sovereignty and Possession,* 104.
103. Dummer, *Defence of the New-England Charters*, 3; Yirush, *Settlers, Liberty, and Empire,* 66, 91, 187-88; Halliday, *Dismembering the Body Politic,* 200.
104. Offut Jr., *Of "Good Laws" and "Good Men,"* 14.
105. Hartog, *Public Property and Private Power,* 29.
106. Bilder, "Salamanders and Sons of God," 67.
107. Richard Partridge to Joseph Whipple, 15 Dec. 1744, in Gertrude Selwyn Kimball, ed., *The Correspondence of the Colonial Governors of Rhode Island, 1723-1775* (Boston: Houghton, Mifflin, 1902), 292.
108. Richard Partridge to William Sharpe, 22 May 1745, in Kimball, ed., *Correspondence,* 359.
109. Yirush, *Settlers, Liberty, and Empire,* 79-80.
110. Randolph to Board of Trade, 30 May 1698, TNA CO 324/6 f. 182.
111. Report of the Commissioners of the Customs upon Mr. Randolph's Memoriall Relating to the Acts of Trade &c in America, 17 Jan. 1695/6, TNA 324/5 f. 369.
112. Mancke, "Empire and State," 190-91.
113. Hartog, *Public Property and Private Power,* 30.
114. Yirush, *Settlers, Liberty, and Empire,* 226-27.
115. Bilder, "The Corporate Origins of Judicial Review," 503-66.

116. See A. M. Fraas, "'They Have Travailed into a Wrong Latitude': The Laws of England, Indian Settlements, and the British Imperial Constitution, 1726-1773" (Ph.D. dissertation, Duke University, 2011).
117. Mancke, "Negotiating an Empire," 247.
118. James Fichter, *So Great a Proffit: How the East Indies Trade Transformed Anglo-American Capitalism* (Cambridge, MA: Harvard University Press, 2010).
119. John Wesley, *A Calm Address to Our American Colonies* (London, 1775).
120. Quoted by LaCroix, *Ideological Origins,* 99-100.
121. Pownall, *Right, Interest, and Duty.*
122. F. W. Maitland, "Trust and Corporation," in Maitland, *State, Trust, and Corporation*, 127.
123. F. W. Maitland, "Moral Personality and Legal Personality," in Maitland, *State, Trust, and Corporation*, 66.
124. Paul Schiff Berman, "The New Legal Pluralism," *Annual Review of Law and Social Science* 5 (2009): 225-42; Joshua Barkan, "A Genealogy of the Corporation: Articulating Sovereign Power and Capitalism" (Ph.D, dissertation, University of Minnesota, 2006); Alfred D. Chandler Jr. and Bruce Mazlish, eds., *Leviathans: Multinational Corporations and the New Global History* (Cambridge: Cambridge University Press, 2005); Tamanaha, "Understanding Legal Pluralism"; David Vogel, "The Corporation as Government: Challenges and Dilemmas," *Polity* 8, no. 1 (1975): 5–37; for popular treatment, see, e.g., William Greider, "Sovereign Corporations," *The Nation* (April 30, 2011), http://www.thenation.com/article/sovereign-corporations.

3

Litigating Empire

The Role of French Courts in Establishing Colonial Sovereignties

HELEN DEWAR

In seventeenth-century northeastern North America, rival titleholders gradually constructed sovereignty through the assertion of and contest over competing claims. While the struggle among European powers, especially the French and English, to effectively occupy coastal and riverine regions has traditionally received the most attention, rivalries among Frenchmen in the Saint Lawrence Valley and Acadia played at least as important a role in the evolution of French territorial claims. Contending parties fought for ascendancy on the ground through the use of instruments of metropolitan legal authority and personal power, at the court of kings Henri IV and Louis XIII, and also in the kingdom's courts of justice. The plural legal order in France, rooted as it was in the patchwork of customary laws and privileges of each province and Roman law in part of the kingdom, affected the ability of titleholders to govern and enjoy their trading rights overseas. To a certain extent, all (imperial) politics was local. Competing titleholders projected local legal regimes onto imperial contexts. Litigation among these claimants and between them and outside traders over the first three decades of the century highlights the exercise of power through the distribution of privileges and the incompatibility of exclusive trading privileges in this context. Royal reliance on provincial and local officials to implement overseas commissions underscores the reality of the French empire as a deeply divided, indeed multiple, entity. Legal pluralism connected to the contested and interdependent processes of state formation at home and sovereignty assertion abroad.

The role of legal pluralism in France in the construction of sovereignty in New France underscores the transatlantic dimensions of the latter process. The subject of legal pluralism in an imperial context brings most readily to mind two parallel systems of justice for colonizer and colonized.[1] To be sure, the beginnings of French colonization in North America saw the coexistence of a European justice system, first under the lieutenant to the viceroy and then under the colony's governor, and indigenous understandings of justice. Parties on both sides committed transgressions of varying degrees of seriousness, which brought the two conceptions of justice into conflict. In the context of close and frequent contact among the two peoples through trade, military alliance, evangelization, and settlement, Samuel de Champlain, the French commander for much of the first three decades of the seventeenth century, preferred intercultural negotiation to trials under the French system.[2] There is, however, another dimension to legal pluralism that helped to shape governance in the French empire. As much as in New France, legal pluralism existed in the ununified imperial center. While historians of early modern Europe have acknowledged the multiple legal and political authorities that made up early modern polities, little attention has been given to how this situation affected the ways in which parties advocated and defended their claims overseas.[3] This essay addresses that question. Apart from the legal authority vested in the colony's lieutenant—who remained the source of European justice in New France until midcentury when the governor established a court system—privileges, customs, and an intimate knowledge of metropolitan judicial procedures rushed in with members of privileged trading companies, outside traders, and the viceroy's representatives.[4] This situation forces us to reconsider the assumption that overseas spaces were without entrenched interests; a new geographic space, New France became a new judicial battleground where old legal conflicts over long-held privileges and customs in France could be fought—albeit with new stakes and conditions.

The plural legal order rested on a particular understanding of the relationship between subjects and the French king. The person of the monarch united all provinces together, but his relationship to each, politically and juridically, was particular. Upon annexation to the Crown, a province like Brittany on the kingdom's northwest periphery entered what it saw as a contractual agreement with the king by which justice would be rendered "in the customary form and manner" in exchange for the province's allegiance.[5] All justice emanated from the king throughout France in theory, but there were multiple sources of law: provincial custom and local usage, Roman law (especially equity), and royal statutes, in descending order of influence. If law is considered one "official form of ordering," then privileges in France were another.[6] Privileges created layers of jurisdiction, status, and law, ranging from a town's exemption from the legal jurisdiction of its seigneur to a port's designation as a "port franc" or free port, in which import and export duties were waived, and from a province's enjoyment of administrative autonomy to a guild's regulation of its trade. King and province mutually benefited from such arrangements: the king delegated parts of his authority that were better managed locally and increased his revenue; the province and its towns rose in political and economic standing.[7] The king was, at the same time, constrained by such privileges in his ability, for example, to implement royal statutes across France. In the context of overseas expansion, we see that privileges permeated even areas of royal law such as navigation and commerce.

This essay examines, then, the interplay between a legally and politically plural order in France and the solidification of French claims in North America. What becomes clear is that the instability of trading and colonizing ventures in New France—often portrayed as failures in the historiography—was connected in part to the patchwork of customs, privileges, rights, and laws in France. The essay, based on court documents, petitions, travel accounts, and notarial records, takes in turn six specific legal conflicts among parties active in the colony. The first two occurred primarily on the ground in New France and involved the selective use of law, personal authority, and force. The following four consider the role of New France in interjurisdictional rivalries in France, particularly over the consolidation of maritime authority. Through the lens of metropolitan jurisdictional complexity, we see that the exercise of power overseas was not a matter that concerned only the Crown and private enterprise but also other levels of authority in France for whom the stakes were very high. For some, participation in the privileged enterprise and in the governance of the colony provided an opportunity to enhance authority at home; for others, the Crown's involvement overseas threatened their own political agency in France. Sovereignty overseas was inextricably tied to questions of royal reach in France itself.

A number of scholars of Anglo-America and Britain have begun to explore the connections between state formation and sovereignty overseas, arguing that these were not parallel but interdependent processes.[8] Historians of the French Atlantic have been slower to engage with this subject.[9] I follow scholars of the state who have moved beyond a narrow institutional framework to include the entire "network of agents exercising political power," from the lowest officeholder to the king himself.[10] This conception, which encompasses both locality and center, avoids the tendency to reify the state and see it as an autonomous being that exercises power over a more or less passive society.[11] There is a strong tendency to equate state formation with the creation of bureaucratic forms of government; however, in the early modern period, "elite cooption" through clientele networks, privileges, trade monopolies, tax farms, and offices was a crucial feature of the growing reach of the state.[12] This understanding of state formation foregrounds its chief characteristic: it came about as a result of the actions of many parties rather than a "central will."[13] Accordingly, its evolution was not linear but subject to challenges, setbacks, contingencies, and accommodations.

The intersections of state formation and sovereignty in the colonial realm varied across European empires. In the British case, this connection is perhaps most visible in the fact that international quarrels arising from colonial activities required the Crown to intervene, which put colonies under the category of foreign policy and were thus part of the Crown's prerogative. In the French case, the king's traditional practice of granting a broad range of privileges to individuals and corporate groups to command loyalty throughout the realm meant that the dynamics among titleholders overseas not infrequently related to the distribution and exercise of power and privileges in France itself.[14] The construction of colonial sovereignty, like the process of state formation, was not a simple matter of planting absolute authority overseas; rather, subjects, foreign rivals, and native peoples alike kept empire constantly in a "state of becoming" through sets of claims and counterclaims. Just as the activities of subjects in Europe led to a greater state presence in society, so their activities overseas prompted states to become more involved in colonial expansion.[15]

The historiography of New France has generally tended to treat the numerous lawsuits that arose over colonial claims in the early seventeenth century as but another reason for French "failure" overseas. To some, they were petty quarrels among merchants whose greed stymied the nobler intentions of adventurers like Samuel de Champlain; for others, they disrupted the supposedly linear process of colonization, contributing to the instability and sluggishness of the enterprise; for others still, they are simply invisible.[16] While some lawsuits over New France had more to do with internal wrangling common to many organizations than with sovereignty in the colonial realm, many others reveal that participants viewed their overseas and metropolitan activities as two sides of the same coin, both shaped variously by personal, local, provincial, and royal interests. Claimants brought royal and other courts—not disinterested parties themselves—into overseas spaces to play the role of arbiters of competing claims to "wealth, power, and status."[17] In this context, the construction of sovereignty comes to look less linear, as a variety of factors on both sides of the Atlantic determined who exercised authority and enjoyed trading privileges in the colony, to what extent, and for how long.

Conflicts and lawsuits were, of course, not singular to New France or French overseas expansion. Indeed, the most well-known seventeenth-century colonial crises are found in Anglo-America, from the power struggles in the early 1620s within the Virginia Company, which led eventually to its replacement by a royally appointed government, to the steadfast defiance of the heads of the Massachusetts Bay Colony in the face of Crown directives in the 1660s, 1670s, and 1680s.[18] While comparatively unknown, this series of French crises of authority, in which law was invoked in New France and justice sought in France, constituted the crucible within which various state, social, and commercial actors struggled to shape French imperial expansion in the service of their own interests. The involvement of a variety of jurisdictions tied the assertion of claims overseas to metropolitan struggles. Law then becomes something that was not simply transferred in all its diverse forms to and modified in America, but a window into the interactions between state formation in Europe and empire building overseas.

I. French Beginnings in North America

Although the French made attempts at colonization in North America during the sixteenth century, it was not until the end of the Wars of Religion in 1598 that they directed concerted energy toward solidifying their claims to much of the continent through settlement. Like its rivals, the French Crown, unable or unwilling to absorb directly the considerable risks and expense of such ventures, engaged private enterprise to this end. Where joint-stock plantation companies established many of the first English colonies in America, proprietors undertook initial French forays. After several unsuccessful attempts at settlement by various Frenchmen, Pierre du Gua, sieur de Monts received two commissions in 1603: one from Henri IV appointing him lieutenant-general of New France, the other from Admiral of France Charles de Montmorency naming him vice-admiral of the colony. Like most proprietors, de Monts was given the power to distribute land, establish forts and other buildings, and engage in trade relations with the native inhabitants of Acadia; to offset the costs of colonization, he received exclusive trading privileges for ten years. De Monts formed a commercial association with merchants from Rouen, La Rochelle, and Saint-Malo to execute his commission. The Compagnie de Monts established two settlements in Acadia before founding Quebec in 1608 under the command of de Monts's lieutenant,

Samuel de Champlain. Despite de Monts's intense lobbying at court, he lost his privileges prematurely on account of fierce domestic opposition. His situation further deteriorated with the assassination and resignation, respectively, of his two main patrons, Henri IV in 1610 and Charles de Montmorency in 1612; shortly thereafter, he lost the titles of lieutenant-general and vice-admiral of New France.[19]

The man chosen as the next proprietor in late 1612 reflected a change in tack by those involved in the New France enterprise. Henri de Bourbon, prince de Condé, a prince of the blood and governor and lieutenant general of Guyenne, had no particular connection to New France; rather, what was important was his potential as an advocate and protector at court, given his close relationship to the young king, Louis XIII. He thus played a primarily symbolic role, reflecting the Crown's commitment to the occupation of New France. Condé delegated his administrative authority to Champlain as his lieutenant and his trading privileges to the Company of Rouen and Saint-Malo (CRSM), an association of merchants from the two ports.[20] The prince's tenure established the broad pattern of governance that prevailed for the next fifteen years: two delegated authorities with separate but somewhat overlapping jurisdictions. It also saw the division of Quebec and Acadia into separate enterprises, with the viceroy's representatives henceforth concentrating on the former.[21] At each change in lieutenant general—or viceroy, as they were subsequently called—Champlain obtained a new commission. In 1620, under the duc de Montmorency, the CRSM lost its privileges to a new company led by Guillaume de Caen, a captain in the king's navy. In 1627, Cardinal Richelieu, chief minister to Louis XIII and grand master of navigation and commerce, became personally involved, with the creation of the Company of New France (CNF) or Cent Associés, granted administrative, judicial, commercial, and seigneurial authority throughout the Saint Lawrence Valley and Acadia.[22] Although the period prior to 1627 typically receives much less attention in the historiography than the subsequent one under the CNF, the early years were formative ones that saw the greatest number of competing claims in the history of New France.[23]

II. Struggles for Power in New France

As de Monts and his successors in New France discovered, the considerable power and privileges granted in commissions and contracts could prove to be rather chimerical in practice. Accorded jurisdiction over often vast territories with unspecified limits, titleholders faced the challenge of effectively enforcing their authority and policing their privileged trading area. This task was rendered more difficult by the thriving coastal fishery, which continued to be open to all Frenchmen, and by the presence of other titleholders in the region also intent on exercising their rights. As might be expected, the majority of disputes began on the ground, with the struggle for power over New France itself at their core.[24] Each party, from the Basque and Breton fishermen long accustomed to trading for furs with the native inhabitants to newly formed companies with exclusive trading privileges, used various strategies to advance their claims and legitimate their actions. As several legal scholars have recently argued, European subjects overseas brought knowledge of metropolitan law and a range of legal practices with them, which they then applied creatively depending on the particular circumstances.[25] According to Lauren Benton, through such "legal posturing," subjects sought to reinforce their relationship to their sovereign, position themselves for continued patronage and rewards, and defend any contested actions before metropolitan courts.[26] In this context, law was an instrument that both extended the monarch's sovereignty and provided subjects with a framework within which to affirm and defend their own privileges and challenge other claims.

The 1621 season in the Saint Lawrence saw jockeying for position among rival French traders and by the viceroy's representatives, characterized at once by frequent recourse to royal decrees and other legal instruments and a willingness to abandon such strategies when others proved more effective in the establishment of claims. The May arrival of a ship carrying the new viceroy Montmorency's commissioners delivered the news to Champlain and the habitation's residents that he had replaced the Company of Rouen and Saint-Malo with Guillaume de Caen and his associates. There followed letters from the viceroy's intendant of New France with instructions to Champlain to seize the goods of the former company, and from de Caen, who signaled his imminent arrival with two armed ships and "some good declarations in his favour." Without a decree from the king authorizing a seizure and outnumbered by the employees of the CRSM, Champlain opted to allow the latter to continue trading until the arrival of de Caen, "who had all proper authority, bearing with him a decree in his favour."[27] A suit between the new and old companies before the royal council in France had not yet fully settled the matter in either's favor.[28]

At the beginning of June, the approach of a CRSM vessel carrying company agent François Gravé, sieur du Pont, and three clerks prompted Champlain to arm a group of men in the half-completed fort at Quebec: "in this way we could hold our own in negotiation, and meantime continue to work at the fort to strengthen its defences."[29] Pont-Gravé's ship had left France before the council had made its decision and in spite of the admiralty's refusal to grant it a license. With none of the customary papers, the CRSM's associates and agents "had determined to fall back on simple obedience to the King." While Champlain rebuked them for their actions, the clerks in turn questioned his authority to put a man in charge of the fort "without instructions from the King." This maneuvering continued until the arrival of de Caen with a decree from the royal council, which allowed both companies to trade for the 1621 season.[30] Despite the decree's warning against "causing the other any hindrance or violence on pain of death," de Caen announced his intention to seize Pont-Gravé's vessel, which he planned to use to pursue interlopers in the river.[31] Champlain then

> [took] the Sieur du Pont's vessel under my protection, wishing to preserve it in order to uphold the King's authority and the honour of my said Lord, before all his crew: afterwards he [de Caen] could do as he liked, as he had force on his side; but in order to preserve the form of legality, I had to take up that position.

Upon the lieutenant's departure, de Caen seized the vessel, refusing to recognize "any jurisdiction in that locality."[32] In the event, de Caen returned the ship to Pont-Gravé, declaring it insufficiently armed. One suspects that the show was far more important than the outcome.

This series of events exposes the fluidity, instability, and contention associated with the use of both law and force. Each party pledged to recognize the legitimacy of royal decrees, but could, at the same time, produce decrees that contradicted or conflicted with those of others. De Caen used his commission from Montmorency, which accorded him exclusive rights to trade in the colony, as the basis for seizing Pont-Gravé's ship and thus countering the royal decree allowing both companies to trade that season.[33] This practice highlights the multiple and competing authorities in France. Courts anxious to defend their jurisdiction from encroachment by rivals and to assert their institutional power were more than willing to accede to a request, perhaps especially if it challenged another court's sentence. The result was a series of sentences that did not follow the hierarchy of first instance and appeal but the logic of home jurisdictions and institutional rivalries. The structure of the legal system encouraged parties to seek out and act on favorable decrees, regardless of subsequent ones to the contrary.

Almost as frequent as calls for the presentation of decrees to substantiate claims were invocations of royal sovereignty, reflecting a political culture defined by service to king and patron.[34] The CRSM agents, for one, could come up with no other legitimate justification for their presence in New France. In manning the fort and protecting Pont-Gravé's ship, Champlain reminded witnesses of the king's imperium in New France and of his own position as the legitimate legal authority in his name. Indeed, he claimed sole authority for the upholding of law in the colony, employing the languages of law, sovereignty, and fidelity to Montmorency and juxtaposing them with de Caen's use of force.[35] The climactic showdown between de Caen and Champlain also underscores the personal and feudal foundations of power. De Caen was far from unusual in using aggression to assert his prerogatives; faced with competing claimants themselves, seigneurs and governors in France frequently turned to such tactics.[36] The Crown, lacking the infrastructure to exercise its power directly throughout the realm, conferred commissions and privileges on individuals, corporations, and local institutions. Their multiplicity produced struggles similar to those in New France, resulting in a pattern of feudal enclaves. Claimants in the colony not only brought legal instruments with them but also knowledge of the structural conditions that rationalized their use.

The plural political and legal order in France encouraged the use of personal authority by de Caen and others to establish and extend their privileges in New France. This was particularly the case during periods of metropolitan political instability. The beginning of the 1610s saw a child king ascend the throne, the young Louis XIII, ushering in seven years of government under the queen regent, Marie de Medici. Regencies were notoriously unstable periods, as members of the nobility and overlapping authorities typically took advantage of a weak Crown to improve their own positions. Changes at the very top of the social and political hierarchy reverberated outward, precipitating reversals in the political fortunes of those at court and in provincial circles. Such shuffling extended to New France as well. While de Monts lost his dual commission of vice-admiral and lieutenant general of New France, the Biencourts, father and son, received support from the queen regent for their colonizing and trading activities at Port Royal in Acadia. From 1611, the son, Charles de Biencourt, was vice-admiral of New France. Like others with his title, he was to exercise authority in the admiral's absence, from the inspection of vessels to the issuing of licenses. Like de Caen, Biencourt pursued his personal privileges aggressively in a bid to receive what he considered his due. From 1611 to 1616, he, his agent, David Lomeron, and his father, Jean de Poutrincourt, crossed the Bay of Fundy from Port-Royal to the "pays des Etchemins" (in present-day New

Brunswick), where Frenchmen, especially Bretons and Normans, frequently traded, to demand the presentation of their charterparties and licenses and to collect one-fifth of their profits.[37]

Although this assertion of jurisdiction at times went unchallenged, at others, seizures or violence prompted one or other party to seek redress before the courts.[38] One such suit involved the Company of Rouen and Saint-Malo. In the spring of 1614, a ship in the name of Biencourt seized two of the CRSM's ships that had been trading in the fur-rich area along the Saint John River, an area of supposedly open trade. The "clerk judge of the Admiralty of New France" called for the "confiscation to the profit of the said sieur de Poitrincourt [sic] of the ships, arms, munitions, merchandise and victuals" belonging to the company.[39] That fall, back in France, the company associates obtained an order for Biencourt, Poutrincourt, and two fur merchants from La Rochelle to appear before the royal council "to see themselves condemned to return to them all that they had plundered, their men, ships and merchandise, interests, damages and expenses."[40] The main rulings on the seizure to 1632 were in the CRSM's favor, first ordering the return of the seized furs and later allowing the company to seize the defendant's property to the value of the lost merchandise.[41] By a decree in late August 1632, however, the admiralty dismissed the charges against Biencourt and Poutrincourt; the Rouennais and Malouin associates were permitted only to pursue an earlier action against Lomeron and the ship's captain. An appeal the following year before the Parlement de Rouen upheld this decision.[42]

Incidents like the above have traditionally been used as evidence that Biencourt grossly abused his powers in Acadia. Marcel Trudel has observed that it is not clear in what capacity Biencourt was acting when he went to the "pays des Etchemins" to claim one-fifth of a ship's merchandise. This is certainly true. After all, the Admiral of France had the right to a duty of only one-tenth.[43] While one-fifth could, instead, have been a seigneurial right, it seems unlikely that the seigneury of Port Royal could have legitimately extended across the Bay of Fundy to the area around the Sainte-Croix and Saint John Rivers. Trudel concludes from these ambiguities that Biencourt "readily gave himself permission to commit abuses based on his vice-admiral's commission."[44] The vice-admiral did, it appears, overextend his reach, but to condemn it as an abuse of power is to misunderstand the exercise of authority in the seventeenth-century French Atlantic. In France, the Crown had long relied on the personal as much as the administrative power of the admiral to strengthen royal naval authority in the face of competing interests. With overlapping and imprecise jurisdictions common, the exercise of personal authority, through the collection of duties, for example, greatly affected how much space, either on land or at sea, one controlled in practice. French naval historian Alan James has recently argued that the often heavy-handed nature of policing, long a subject of complaint among merchants, was essential to the establishment of the authority of both the king and the admiral.[45] There was, then, a similar constellation of competing claims in New France. In this context, claims were only as good as one's ability to enforce them, whether through personal authority, legal forms, or force.

Biencourt's and de Caen's use of personal authority highlights the tension that existed between the Crown's reliance on the method to extend and maintain its own control and the challenge such authority could pose to state building. Both men used their commissions, as vice-admiral and head of the privileged trading company, respectively, as justification to go beyond their instructions. De Caen asserted his new position with a show of force designed to deter others from challenging his authority. His refusal to recognize any authority in the colony beyond himself sparked considerable unrest within the Quebec habitation.[46] Biencourt, for his part, tested the limits of his own authority by requesting duties from ships fishing and trading in areas open to all. The Crown relied on both to capture interlopers (French and foreign) and to defend and extend its North American dominions in the face of European and native competition, but it lacked the power to curb the personal interests of each on its own, particularly during periods of regency rule. In the absence of any other methods in early modern France, the personal authority of multiple titleholders kept others in check. The exercise of authority and the continuation of patronage, then, depended not on following the letter of the law but on legitimating one's actions in the eyes of those in France and New France alike.

If personal authority was a double-edged sword on both sides of the Atlantic, it nevertheless produced quite different results for the Crown in each case. In France, during periods of strength, the Crown could play individual titleholders and institutions off against one another to ensure that its own interests would be served; in times of weakness, personal authority left the Crown vulnerable to plays for power by nobles, *parlementaires*, and others, who could assemble armies of loyal supporters or block royal directives. In New France, while metropolitan political instability certainly emboldened titleholders at various times, the vast territories and powers granted contrasted sharply with the relatively small area over which each titleholder managed to establish effective control. Indeed, what is remarkable about the litigation brought before French courts concerning New France is that so little involved rival titleholders. With the highest number of claimants in the history of New France, this period saw three commissions—vice-admiral, viceroy, and seigneur of land from the Saint Lawrence south to Florida—overlap, potentially creating conflict over prerogatives. The interest lies not in the fact that they overlapped, a common phenomenon in Europe and colonies alike, but in the relatively small effect this appeared to have on the exercise of authority and what this in turn suggests about early empire formation.[47] Only those who had to work together, such as Champlain and the Company of Rouen and Saint-Malo, came into conflict over their respective jurisdictions. Those with more sweeping powers did not. The absence of *more* legal conflict highlights an important point about the way in which sovereignty was established: titleholders created a pattern of small French enclaves in a territory otherwise under the sovereign control of native peoples. In New France, then, different sorts of delegated authority, theoretically overlapping, ended up being the basis for territorially circumscribed de facto zones of authority.[48]

III. The Admiral of France Extends His Authority to New France

Some lawsuits ostensibly over privileges in New France were at their heart efforts to enhance legal and political authority in France. In 1620, the appointment of a new viceroy incorporated the colony into an existing metropolitan institution. After purchasing the position from the prince de Condé in November 1619, Henri de Montmorency, Admiral of France, received letters patent from the king.[49] The motives behind the acquisition, the manner in which Montmorency asserted his vice-regal authority, and the ensuing lawsuit with the CRSM over trading privileges together show that at bottom this was about strengthening the admiral's authority and, by extension, the Crown's.

The authority of the admiral had long been extensive in theory and restricted in practice due to the competing claims of seigneurs, governors, and other admirals. Since 1582, the Admiral of France had claimed control over ports, fortifications, ships, munitions, and maritime justice in Picardy, Normandy, Poitou, Saintonge, Guyenne, and Brittany. In practice, his authority was only secured in the first two provinces; elsewhere, resistance was high and other titleholders shared or exercised the admiral's jurisdiction.[50] From the start of his tenure as admiral in 1612, Henri de Montmorency, with the king's encouragement, concentrated his energies on centralizing his jurisdiction through a mixture of personal and administrative authority. He purchased the office of admiral of Guyenne from the comte de Coligny, attempted to strengthen the local admiralty courts and regional *tables de marbre*, which heard appeals from the local courts, and sent personal agents to ports to collect the duties owed him from these proceedings.[51]

It is in this context that Montmorency's purchase of the viceroyalty of New France should be seen. As viceroy, Condé had the power to issue licenses in France to traders going to the Saint Lawrence, a prerogative that competed with, if not undermined, the admiral's control of all those entering and leaving French ports.[52] Like the acquisition of the admiralty of Guyenne, becoming viceroy of New France eliminated a rival, expanded Montmorency's jurisdiction, and consolidated his power. For the first time, control over maritime traffic in France was linked to control over territory overseas.

To establish his new jurisdiction, Montmorency brought the full weight of the admiralty to bear and, in so doing, asserted the legal power of the admiralty courts in the face of other jurisdictions. In the fall of 1620, upon the return of the CRSM's ships to France, the viceroy ordered his intendant of the admiralty of Normandy and the king's *procureur* to seize the company's merchandise at Honfleur.[53] While this type of action was, as we have seen, not unusual in France or New France, the decision to make such a show of force rather than simply give notice of the change in personnel to the company is nevertheless indicative of Montmorency's approach to his new position. The viceroyalty of New France being part of the consolidation of his authority as admiral, he planned to use the legal and administrative apparatus of the admiralty in its favor. As with many aggressive displays of personal authority, the seizure proved to be just the beginning of a vigorous contest over rights. After the associates protested the action, the parties reached a compromise out of court by which the intendant of New France agreed to release the goods on condition that the CRSM reimburse the admiralty of Normandy for the costs of the seizure and storage of the merchandise. Although the company associates initially agreed to "desist . . . from all pretentions . . . to continue in the future the said voyages and trade to the said country of New France, under the guise of power by treaties made formerly . . . with the preceding governors of the said countries for the king, without license, confirmation and consent from the said seigneur de Montmorency viceroy," they later withdrew their consent.[54] Before the courts once more, the ensuing dispute came to involve several third parties and did not end until 1622.[55]

Montmorency's prosecution of the admiralty showed that he wished to extend his jurisdiction as far as Frenchmen ventured by sea. He was already the official patron of the French East India Company (EIC).[56] As early as November 1620, he entered a contract with Guillaume de Caen and his uncle Ezechiel, a Rouennais merchant, for the establishment of the Company of Montmorency. If the manner in which Montmorency divested the CRSM of its privileges signaled his intention to exercise fully his prerogatives in New France, the establishment of a new trading company offered a very practical means of doing so. He could assume direct control over its composition, organization, and terms. Indeed, while the de Caens may not have been actual clients of Montmorency, it is notable that they were both already in his service in other capacities. Ezechiel, in particular, was one of the administrators of the EIC. Montmorency also intended to have the proceedings of the Company of Montmorency closely supervised by his agents, specifically the intendant of either the admiralty or New France.[57] This provision effectively removed the association's headquarters from the ports where ships would be outfitted to Montmorency's base in Paris. More than a dispute over the prerogatives of the viceroy and those of the CRSM, the lawsuit reflected Montmorency's bid to incorporate the company with trading privileges to the colony into the existing structure of authority of the Admiral of France.

IV. The Transatlantic Contest for Maritime Control

While the king encouraged the extension of the admiral's jurisdiction as a means to increase the Crown's own authority, the admiral's growing personal strength could also run counter to royal interests. By 1626, various factors persuaded the Crown to take a more active interest in maritime affairs. Continued confrontations with French Huguenots, particularly on the Atlantic coast, had exposed France's dependence on foreign navies to defend its own territory.[58] The accumulation of gold and silver through overseas ventures by the Spanish, English, and Dutch provided both a target—colonies—to undermine Spanish supremacy in Europe and a method—commercial companies—to acquire similar wealth. In addition, the decade of the 1620s saw countries throughout Europe strengthening their naval resources to prepare for a potential renewal of maritime conflict and to protect commerce at sea: England embarked on a program in 1618 to build a fleet of warships within five years; Spain introduced the "Almirantazgo" or Seville Admiralty for the regulation and protection of shipping and the Flanders Armada, a traditional naval force.[59] To this growing naval threat was added a commercial one. In France, there was a widely held view that the country lagged commercially, being too generous to and dependent on foreign shippers and traders while their own were harshly treated in foreign ports.[60]

The complexity of jurisdictions in France influenced the way in which the Crown proceeded to assert its control over the sea. In 1626, Cardinal Richelieu began to gather maritime commercial and naval authority about his person. As one who believed strongly that real maritime security could only be achieved under the Crown, the cardinal considered the admiralty a central obstacle. Richelieu attempted to reduce the latter's power through the creation of universal companies, which aimed to reestablish commerce and the navy. He entered contracts with two sets of associates for the establishment of the Compagnie de Morbihan, with jurisdiction over all French commerce on land and sea, and the Compagnie de la Nacelle Saint-Pierre fleurdelisée, which would control the fisheries and manufactures.[61] Unlike other maritime enterprises, neither was subject to the authority of the admiral, Montmorency; both fell, instead, under the jurisdiction of the "superintendant general of commerce," the cardinal himself. Richelieu's target might have been Montmorency, but his actions also challenged the maritime jurisdiction of the province of Brittany, the proposed site of the Compagnie de Morbihan. Reacting to both the attempt to undercut the provincial governor, under whose authority the admiralty customarily fell, and the exclusive commercial privileges awarded to the company, the province's sovereign court refused to register the edict. While the provincial estates did verify it, they did so with conditions so severe as to completely undermine its intent. The universal companies appeared to be a subtle route to undermine one jurisdiction, the admiralty, but came up against two provincial jurisdictions' privileges, resulting in the enterprises' eventual abandonment.[62] Fragmented maritime authority thus helped to shape the parameters of commercial and colonizing ventures overseas and efforts to strengthen French maritime standing.

Richelieu's personal and institutional rivalry with Montmorency and Brittany's protection of its jurisdiction and privileges shed light on the complex dynamics of the plural legal order and its encouragement of personal authority. Abandoning the company route, Richelieu obtained his original objective by other means. By letters patent of October 1626, the king appointed him "Grand Master, Chief and superintendant general of navigation and commerce of France," displacing the admiral in the jurisdiction of maritime affairs.[63] Despite the new title of the office, Richelieu's prosecution of it closely resembled the admiral's. Relying largely on personal authority, he bought up governorships and other positions that competed with his own, installed receivers in ports to collect his duties, and placed relatives and clients in administrative positions. Richelieu's acquisition of the governorship of Brittany prompted a gift of one hundred thousand livres from the province. A conventional courtesy, it nevertheless demonstrates that personal authority was an essential tool in a plural order.[64] By becoming governor, Richelieu legitimated his control over the admiralty; Breton officials, through their gift, recognized their dependence on him as their patron and guarantor of their privileges. As much as personal authority could prove risky to the Crown, as we saw in the cases of Montmorency, Biencourt, and de Caen, it was indispensable to governance across a patchwork of jurisdictions and authorities.

Richelieu's consolidation of maritime authority and simultaneous strengthening of his personal empire at the expense of Montmorency extended to New France in 1627-1628. In January of 1628, the royal council ordered the Company of New France to begin its voyages to the colony that spring and forbade the Company of Montmorency to engage in the trade. De Caen and his associates protested, requesting permission to "continue the voyages and trade to the said country of New France for the time that remains of their treaty." Rejecting this plea, the council nevertheless ordered the directors of the CNF "to proceed with the liquidation of compensation" to the former company.[65] Thus began a case that did not end until 1636. On the one side, de Caen and his associates wanted to trade for the remaining eight years of their contract or receive compensation for their losses; on the other, the CNF argued that its already heavy colonizing obligations more than offset its privileges and its contract had not stipulated that it would have to compensate its predecessor. Decrees from the two royal councils in the years following alternated between the two parties in granting requests for the execution or suspension of earlier sentences.[66] With the court's proposed compensation terms satisfying neither de Caen nor the company, the two reached an agreement out of court in 1636. In the end, the full amount agreed upon does not appear to have ever been paid.[67]

While the two companies were trying to preserve their own corporate interests, Richelieu was attempting to enhance royal and personal authority at home and overseas. From his perspective, it was crucial that the control of trade in New France rest in his hands. With strong ties to the admiralty and Montmorency, de Caen was connected to the institution and person capable of challenging the cardinal's maritime plans.[68] The government was not interested in having the Company of Montmorency join the new enterprise, as the CRSM had done in 1621. Compensation, despite the financial setback it represented for the CNF, was the preferred option. Several characteristics of the company point to Richelieu's desire to exercise personal control over the company. He invited several of his clients to submit a proposal for the CNF's establishment. The company's subscription lists, originally comprised of one hundred associates, show that, apart from the cardinal himself, a considerable number of his clients as well as highly placed officials in the naval and financial administrations were persuaded or pressured into joining.[69] The extension of maritime authority to New France under the Crown involved replacing one feudal-like authority with another.

Despite the impression at first glance that the CNF represented a significant transformation in the governance structure of the colony, as has traditionally been argued, there remained considerable continuity in organization with the previous period. Recalling Montmorency's tenure, the cardinal reestablished the position of intendant and had people report to him regularly in both official and unofficial capacities on the state of the company and colony.[70] He shared, in many respects, Montmorency's approach to consolidating maritime affairs: they both saw companies on the Dutch and English models as essential to increasing naval and commercial strength, were directly involved in more than one enterprise as shareholders, and incorporated New France into their maritime revitalization programs.[71] The story of litigation between the two companies can in some senses be seen as a microcosm of a larger struggle over personal and institutional control, a struggle that underscores the Crown's attempts to profit from the advantages of personal authority all the while not letting titleholders get out of hand. Once encouraged to consolidate his maritime jurisdiction, Montmorency's authority came to extend further geographically and deeper into clientele networks than either the Crown's security interests or Richelieu's personal ambitions could allow. Employing Montmorency's own strategies to bind institutions and notables to the center, one powerful, well-placed individual replaced another, now deemed too threatening. In the context of a plural legal order, personal authority was at once essential to the governance of the French empire and a potential danger if allowed to grow too strong.

V. Provincial Autonomy and Royal Reach

The Crown's initiatives to extend its oversight of maritime affairs overseas raised questions about sovereignty at home. By the early seventeenth century, voyages combining rich fishing off the coasts of Acadia and Newfoundland with fur trading were well established among Basques, Bretons, and Normans. As was the practice, the king granted commercial privileges to a variety of ports, allowing them to trade to certain regions or be exempt from import duties.[72] The southern whaling port of Saint Jean de Luz, for example, had received permission from François I in 1539 to travel and trade to the area that became New France, a privilege confirmed by subsequent monarchs.[73] Traders thus came to regard such privileges as customary rights. Moreover, the Crown had not traditionally concerned itself with overseas fishing and trading ventures, according traders considerable independence. When the king began to grant exclusive trading privileges in New France to proprietors, who in turn delegated them to one company only, vocal opposition erupted in several provinces. While these activities were economically important to many ports, the more potent issue was the perceived Crown encroachment on provincial jurisdiction they represented.

For provinces such as Brittany, exclusive trading privileges to New France were considered in the same light as attempts by the Crown and Admiral of France to wrest naval power from the province's governor, both a direct threat to provincial autonomy. The various strategies of delay and obstruction pursued by Brittany and Normandy, the two jurisdictions with the most traders to North America, at once reflect this concern and demonstrate the limits to royal power. By law, letters patent from the king had to be registered in the kingdom's sovereign courts to take full effect. Provincial parlements, notoriously protective of their jurisdiction, took this prerogative very seriously, often submitting remonstrances to the king. When de Monts received his commission in November 1603, he encountered significant delays before these bodies. Indeed, faced with refusals from the courts of Paris, Bordeaux, and Brittany to register it, Henri IV ordered the Parlement of Paris to "read, register, keep and observe" the commission in 1605.[74] Shortly thereafter, the parlement obeyed, following on the heels of the Parlement of Bordeaux. It was, however, the Parlement of Brittany that proved the most recalcitrant. Although it finally ratified the commission in June, a caveat rendered this action all but meaningless: the court rejected the provision granting trading privileges to de Monts.[75] The long delay in recognizing the letters patent—and their partial registration—severely weakened their force. Neither de Monts nor his associates could expect redress in the event of infraction in any of these jurisdictions in 1604. Although the king issued commissions and edicts intended to apply throughout the kingdom, in practice their application varied. By refusing to register royal letters patent, provincial courts wielded their power and protected the interests of their ports.[76]

Even after a commission was registered, its execution depended on the cooperation of local and regional officials, many of whom, like the *parlementaires*, tended to see such matters as royal infringements on provincial affairs. In 1609, when de Monts lost his trading privileges largely as a result of petitions from the community of inhabitants of Saint-Malo for a return to liberty of trade, it was on condition that "this community [of inhabitants of Saint-Malo] will pay to monsieur Dumont part of the costs that he incurred to Canada, the sum of six or ten thousand livres."[77] In Saint-Malo, the community of inhabitants was a strong and influential body, which exercised powers comparable to those of an admiralty, from supervising ship traffic to maintaining port facilities. In response to the decree, Saint-Malo categorically declared that "this community will not submit itself to pay the said six or ten thousand livres, to the said sieur Du Mont, but if any individuals from here who traffic to Canada want to submit themselves to paying . . . if they see fit, will do so without the general body of this community entering into the said obligation."[78] Lacking the power to force the community to comply, the royal council instead ordered "the inhabitants of Saint-Malo, Bayonne, towns and parishes aforementioned and other subjects of His said Majesty trafficking to the said places" to pay six thousand livres to de Monts. The sum was to be divided among them by the admiralties of Saint-Malo and Bayonne according to each ship's tonnage.[79] There was no mention of how these traders would be identified. Indeed, given the date of the decree, many if not all ships would have already returned to port. The implementation of the council's decision thus depended heavily on the vigilance and initiative of local officials. Given the vehemence with which Malouin traders had protested against de Monts's privileges since 1603, it is hardly surprising that he never collected his compensation. The combination of a province's determination to protect its autonomy and the king's reliance on local and regional authorities to execute royal commissions, decrees, and trading bans often meant that decrees were simply not observed or openly flouted.

Traders' mobilization of the community of Saint-Malo and the Estates of Brittany illuminates the ways in which the power and prerogatives of various bodies limited the king's own authority during regency rule and traders brought such regional influence into overseas spaces.[80] In 1616, after the return to exclusive trading privileges under Viceroy Condé, the Estates of Brittany accepted a remonstrance from Saint-Malo, which they then brought before the royal council. The grievance asked the king to "revoke the said commissions granted . . . as prejudicial to the common good of the country, and in consequence to declare the said traffic of Canada open and free to all your subjects without discrimination."[81] The king acceded to the request, suspending the Company of Rouen and Saint-Malo's trading privileges without having heard from the association first. In response, representatives of the CRSM requested the restoration of their privileges and the ban of all other traders.[82] Although the council eventually reaffirmed the company's exclusive trading privileges, the Estates of Brittany took advantage of the political confusion at court to assert their prerogatives and customary rights against what they regarded as the unjust extension of the Crown's reach overseas.[83] Due to their institutional power, the estates were in a strong position to push for the restoration of liberty of trade in the face of an even moderately weak Crown. As a *pays d'état*, Brittany had the power to negotiate with the king over the taxes it would pay each year in exchange for its status. The king's dependence on these and other exceptional sums and the province's frontier position meant that both he and his council paid attention to lobbying by the body. The ability of traders to exploit the upswing in influence of the multiple local and provincial jurisdictions during regency rule underscores the contingency of authority and privileges on both sides of the Atlantic.

If exclusive trading privileges to New France represented an attack on provincial autonomy by the Crown, litigation on the subject prompted no less fierce a rivalry among provincial jurisdictions. In a lawsuit between the CRSM and powerful Rochelais traders accused of contravening the company's privileges, both parties perceived that they would obtain the best results in their respective home provinces. The Rochelais merchants made frequent appeals to the Admiralty of La Rochelle, where they expected—and usually received—a favorable hearing, as well as to the royal councils. The Rouennais and Malouins appeared most often before the Admiralty of Rouen. A request by one party in one jurisdiction was frequently met with a counter-request in another, resulting in contradictory sentences.[84] Revealing the strength of regional jealousies and suspicion, the Rochelais requested in 1618 that the suit between the two parties be heard before the Admiralty of La Rochelle or another judge appointed by the king "outside the province of Normandy" or before the royal council.[85] With such strong rivalries among Rochelais and Norman traders, each court was biased. Rival and overlapping jurisdictions encouraged such strategies as seeking sentences in one's home province, "shopping around" for a sympathetic jurisdiction, or prolonging a case in the hopes of a favorable sentence. Courts were happy to pronounce upon a case if it privileged their power over another's and employed their own tactics, from taking their time to send particular documents to another court to ruling on a case expressly reserved to the royal council.[86] Legal authority in France, then, was as much at stake in these lawsuits as was power in New France.

VI. Conclusion

The ununified political and legal order in the imperial center shaped the establishment of claims to governance and trade in New France. Company representatives, agents to the viceroy, and outside traders came armed with knowledge of customary privileges, legal instruments, and the labyrinthine justice system in France. The concept of exclusive trading privileges to New France was highly problematic in an empire in which the exercise of authority was based on a patchwork of rights and privileges belonging to various corporate groups, provincial bodies, municipalities, and individuals. In this context, the ability to govern in New France—to capture interlopers, to execute royal orders, and to enter trade and military alliances with native peoples—depended on the extent to which the plural legal order was in play at a given moment. Thus de Monts lost his privileges in 1609 due to provincial, local, and guild opposition, parties all with avenues to court at the time. By contrast, Admiral Montmorency's tenure as viceroy saw little protest from other jurisdictions, most notably the very voluble Saint-Malo and the powerful Estates of Brittany. Montmorency brought the colony under the protection of the legal and administrative apparatus of the admiralty. Governance in New France required participants to build similar networks across jurisdictions as those cultivated by Saint-Malo. Colonial state building in the early modern period is usually seen in terms of an actively engaged Crown or the delegation of power and privileges to private enterprise, either a company or an individual proprietor. This view, however, discounts the existence of multiple legal and political authorities in France and other European countries all acting under the Crown but with their own interests and jurisdictions to protect. The role of "government," then, in overseas enterprise was not uncomplicated. The king relied on the personal authority of titleholders on both sides of the Atlantic to keep rival jurisdictions at bay and extend his reach. Both Montmorency and Richelieu consolidated maritime control in this fashion, incorporating New France into their jurisdictions. At the same time, personal authority could be a means to challenge royal directives and jurisdiction, as in the case of de Caen's seizure of Pont-Gravé's vessel. Legal pluralism in France to a certain degree encouraged such actions as it increased the chances of finding a sympathetic jurisdiction. Considering the construction of sovereignty overseas in the context of legal pluralism in the imperial center highlights its connections to state formation at home and the contingent nature of struggles over authority and privileges in the seventeenth-century French Atlantic.

NOTES

The author would like to thank the volume's editors, Richard Ross and Lauren Benton, as well as Allan Greer and Paul Cohen, for their comments on previous versions of this essay.

1. My understanding of legal pluralism is drawn primarily from Lauren Benton, *Law and Colonial Cultures* (Cambridge: Cambridge University Press, 2002), 9-15; Sally Engle Merry, "Legal Pluralism," *Law and Society Review* 22, no. 5 (1988): 869-96. The plural legal order that is the subject of this essay hews more closely to the jurisdictional complexity and conflict outlined in Benton than the two parallel systems of justice—within one culture or of different cultures—privileged by Merry.
2. For one notable example involving the murder of two Frenchmen by natives, see H. P. Biggar, ed., *The Works of Samuel de Champlain* (Toronto: University of Toronto Press, 1971 [1922-35]), 3: 181-213; David Hackett Fischer, *Champlain's Dream: The European Founding of North America* (New York: Simon and Schuster, 2008), 357-59.
3. The landmark article on this subject is J. H. Elliott, "A Europe of Composite Monarchies," *Past & Present* 137 (November 1992): 48-71. For recent challenges to this view, see, among others, John J. Hurt, *Louis XIV and the Parlements: The Assertion of Royal*

Authority (Manchester, UK: Manchester University Press, 2004); Robert Descimon and Fanny Cosandey, *L'Absolutisme en France: histoire et historiographie* (Paris: Seuil, 2002). On overlapping and rival jurisdictions in the Spanish and English justice systems, see Richard L. Kagan, *Lawsuits and Litigants in Castile, 1500-1700* (Chapel Hill: University of North Carolina Press, 1981), 32, 35, 45, 82; Warren M. Billings, "The Transfer of English Law to Virginia, 1606-50," in K. R. Andrews, N. P. Canny, P. E. H. Hair, eds., *The Westward Enterprise* (Liverpool, UK: Liverpool University Press, 1978), 233-34. Two notable exceptions to the historiography's silence on the effects of multiple jurisdictions in the metropole on overseas territories are Tamar Herzog, *Defining Nations: Immigrants and Citizens in Early Modern Spain and Spanish America* (New Haven, CT: Yale University Press, 2003), esp. chaps. 3 and 5; Phillip J. Stern, *The Company-State: Corporate Sovereignty and the Early Modern Foundations of the British Empire in India* (New York: Oxford University Press, 2011). See also Phillip J. Stern, "Bundles of Hyphens': Corporations as Legal Communities in the Early Modern British Empire" in this volume.

4. For the argument that overseas spaces were "full of law," see Lauren Benton, *A Search for Sovereignty: Law and Geography in European Empires, 1400-1900* (Cambridge: Cambridge University Press, 2010), 33.
5. The king's perception of this arrangement was different: not a contractual obligation, his recognition of the province's customs and privileges was due to his "pure and simple liberality." See Joël Cornette, *Histoire de la Bretagne et des Bretons* (Paris: Seuil, 2005), 1: 547 (my translation), also 426-28; Jean-Jacques Monnier and Jean-Christophe Cassard, eds., *Toute l'histoire de Bretagne: des origines à la fin du XXe siècle*, 2nd ed. (Morlaix: Skol Vreizh, 1997), 326.
6. Merry, "Legal Pluralism," 872-73. On the degree to which royal legislative sovereignty existed in seventeenth-century France, see David Parker, "Sovereignty, Absolutism, and the Function of Law in Seventeenth-Century France," *Past & Present* 122 (1989): 36-74; Descimon and Cosandey, *L'Absolutisme en France: histoire et historiographie.*
7. Zoë A. Schneider, *The King's Bench: Bailiwick Magistrates and Local Governance in Normandy, 1670-1740* (Rochester, UK: University of Rochester Press, 2008), chaps. 1 and 4; Séverine Debordes-Lessillour, *Les sénéchaussées royales de Bretagne: la monarchie d'ancien régime et ses juridictions ordinaires, 1532-1790* (Rennes: Presses universitaires de Rennes, 2006), 239-40, 317-18, 416-17; François Olivier-Martin, *Histoire du droit français des origines à la Révolution*, 2nd ed. (Paris: CNRS Editions, 1995 [1948]), 158, 164, 351.
8. Michael J. Braddick, *State Formation in Early Modern England: c. 1550-1700* (Cambridge: Cambridge University Press, 2000), chap. 9; Elizabeth Mancke, "Empire and State," in David Armitage and Michael J. Braddick, eds., *The British Atlantic World, 1500-1800*, 2nd ed. (New York: Palgrave Macmillan, 2009), 193-213; Elizabeth Mancke and John G. Reid, "Elites, States, and the Imperial Contest for Acadia," in John G. Reid, ed., *The "Conquest" of Acadia, 1710: Imperial, Colonial, and Aboriginal Constructions* (Toronto: University of Toronto Press, 2004), 25-47; James Muldoon, *Empire and Order: The Concept of Empire, 800-1800* (New York: St. Martin's, 1999), esp. 8, 145-46.
9. Catherine Desbarats, "La question de l'Etat en Nouvelle-France," in Philippe Joutard and Thomas Wien, eds., *Mémoires de la Nouvelle-France. De France en Nouvelle-France* (Rennes: Presses universitaires de Rennes, 2005), 187-98.

10. Braddick, *State Formation in Early Modern England*, 6; John Brewer and Eckhart Hellmuth, "Introduction: Rethinking Leviathan," in John Brewer and Eckhart Hellmuth, eds., *Rethinking Leviathan: The Eighteenth-Century State in Britain and Germany* (Oxford: Oxford University Press, 1999), 20.
11. Michael J. Braddick, "State Formation and Social Change in Early Modern England: A Problem Stated and Approaches Suggested," *Social History* 16, no.1 (January 1991): 6. On the autonomy of the state as both reality and illusion, see Timothy Mitchell, "The Limits of the State: Beyond Statist Approaches and Their Critics," *American Political Science Review* 85, no. 1 (1991): 81-89, 91-95.
12. Mancke and Reid, "Elites, States, and the Imperial Contest for Acadia," 28-31, quotation 29; Braddick, *State Formation in Early Modern England*, 24-39; William Beik, *Absolutism and Society in Seventeenth-Century France: State Power and Provincial Aristocracy in Languedoc* (Cambridge: Cambridge University Press, 1989), 31-32, 219, 281; Thomas Ertman, *Birth of the Leviathan: Building States and Regimes in Medieval and Early Modern Europe* (Cambridge: Cambridge University Press, 1997), 28; John Brewer, *The Sinews of Power: War, Money, and the English State, 1688-1783* (Boston: Unwin Hyman, 1989), 12-17. On the persistence of personal connections over "impersonal rules of procedure" in a judicial context, see Parker, "Sovereignty, Absolutism, and the Function of Law," 65-69.
13. Braddick, *State Formation in Early Modern England*, 47.
14. Mancke and Reid, "Elites, the State, and the Imperial Contest for Acadia," 29; Mancke, "Empire and State," 207.
15. Ann Laura Stoler, "On Degrees of Imperial Sovereignty," *Public Culture* 18, no. 1 (2006): 125-46, quotation 135-36; Desbarats, "La question de l'Etat en Nouvelle-France," 189. On the role of claims and counterclaims in keeping polities unstable, see Benton, *A Search for Sovereignty*, esp. chap. 1; James J. Sheehan, "The Problem of Sovereignty in European History," *American Historical Review* 111, no. 1 (February 2006): 1-15. On subjects' bringing states into overseas spaces, see Elizabeth Mancke, "Chartered Enterprise and the Evolution of the British Atlantic World," in Elizabeth Mancke and Carole Shammas, eds., *The Creation of the British Atlantic World* (Baltimore, MD: Johns Hopkins University Press, 2005), 239, 262.
16. On the greed of merchants, see H. P. Biggar, *Early Trading Companies of New France, 1534-1632* (St. Clair Shores, MI: Scholarly Press, 1972 [1901]). On the false starts of the New France enterprise, see Marcel Trudel, *Histoire de la Nouvelle-France*, vol. 2, *Le Comptoir* (Montreal: Fides, 1966). On the omission of lawsuits altogether, see Fischer, *Champlain's Dream*, chap. 17, esp. 377-78. Fischer discusses the crisis of authority of 1621 in New France without reference to the acrimonious lawsuit among the two companies trading to New France and Viceroy Montmorency. This dispute is discussed below.
17. The phrase is Parker's. See "Sovereignty, Absolutism, and the Function of Law," 69-70.
18. See, among others, Kenneth R. Andrews, *Trade, Plunder, and Settlement: Maritime Enterprise and the Genesis of the British Empire, 1480-1630* (Cambridge: Cambridge University Press, 1984), 325-26; Percival Griffiths, *A Licence to Trade: The History of English Chartered Companies* (London: E. Benn, 1974), 154-55, 196-99.
19. There appears to have been some overlap between de Monts's commission as vice-admiral and that of Charles de Biencourt, Sieur de Saint-Just, who became vice-admiral sometime in 1611. See Gabriel Marcel, ed., *Factum du procès entre Jean de Biencourt, Sieur de Poutrincourt et les pères Biard et Massé, Jésuites* (Paris: Maisonneuve et Charles Leclerc, 1887).

20. For Champlain's commission, see *Works*, 2: 244, n. 1. For the CRSM's contract of 15 November 1613, see *Nouveaux documents sur Champlain et son époque* (hereafter *Nouv. docs.*), ed. Robert Le Blant and René Baudry, vol. 1 (1560-1622), 310-21.
21. In 1604, de Monts ceded the seigneury of Port Royal to Jean de Biencourt, sieur de Poutrincourt; he passed the rest of the lands in his commission—"all the lands, ports and harbors of new France from the great river [the Saint Lawrence] to Florida, excluding only Port Royal"—to Madame de Guercheville, a prominent financial supporter of Jesuit missions overseas. After one unsuccessful venture, Guercheville left her commission largely unfulfilled. Poutrincourt and his son, Charles de Biencourt, dominated the area until its capture by the English under Samuel Argall in 1613.
22. "Acte pour l'établissement de la Compagnie des cent Associés pour le commerce du Canada . . . le 29 Avril, 1627," in *Édits, ordonnances royaux, déclarations et arrêts du Conseil d'État du Roi, concernant le Canada* (Québec: P.E. Desbarats, 1803-1806), 1-17.
23. This fact is generally overlooked because of the tendency to separate the study of Acadia and the Saint Lawrence River habitations in this period. See, for example, Trudel, *Histoire de la Nouvelle-France*, vol. 2.
24. An example of a similar conflict over authority elsewhere among Europeans occurred in New Netherland, where the West India Company, the proprietor, and patroons, who had received land and rights, vied for control over government and emoluments in the colony. See Jaap Jacobs, "Dutch Proprietary Manors in America: The Patroonships in New Netherland," in L. H. Roper and B. van Ruymbeke, eds., *Constructing Early Modern Empires: Proprietary Ventures in the Atlantic World, 1500-1750* (Leiden: Brill, 2007), 301-26.
25. Lauren Benton, *A Search for Sovereignty*, 23-33; Ken MacMillan, *Sovereignty and Possession in the English New World: The Legal Foundations of Empire, 1576-1640* (Cambridge: Cambridge University Press, 2006) 13, 41-42, 79, 115, 206; Christopher Tomlins, "Law's Empire: Chartering English Colonies on the American Mainland in the Seventeenth Century," in Diane Kirkby and Catharine Coleborne, eds., *Law, History, Colonialism: The Reach of Empire* (Manchester, UK: Manchester University Press, 2001), 27-28. On the existence of a global and pluralistic legal regime in the early modern period, see Lauren Benton, *Law and Colonial Cultures*, esp. chaps. 1 and 2. These authors, who focus on various forms of law brought by individual settlers, take a different approach to the use and influence of law and legal instruments in the process of colonization than the traditional literature, which examines the development of law and legal systems in colonial America itself, usually from an institutional perspective. See, for example, Billings, "The Transfer of English Law to Virginia," 215-44; George L. Haskins, "Law and Colonial Society," in David H. Flaherty, ed., *Essays in the History of Early American Law* (Chapel Hill: University of North Carolina Press, 1969) 41-51; Peter Charles Hoffer, *Law and People in Colonial America* (Baltimore, MD: Johns Hopkins University Press, 1992), esp. 23.
26. Benton, *A Search for Sovereignty*, 23-26, 30-31, quotation 24.
27. *Works*, 5: quotations (in order of appearance) 16, 17.
28. *Works*, 5: 18, 22-23. In 1620, the CRSM launched a suit against Montmorency over the revocation of their trading privileges. De Caen and his associates intervened sometime after assigning a *procureur* to the case in April 1621. See Library and Archives Canada (hereafter LAC) (Ottawa), Minutier Central (hereafter MC), vol. I, étude XVI, no. 48, "Procuration en blanc par Guillaume de Caen pour intervenir au procès pendant entre le duc de Montmorency et le Sieur Legendre et ses associés," 1 April 1621 and below p. 61.

29. *Works*, 5: 25-28, quotation 26.
30. *Works*, quotations (in order of appearance) 5: 28, 30-31, also 35.
31. *Nouv. docs.*, 435. All documents cited in this collection are my translation. On the protests that ensued, see Trudel, *Histoire de la Nouvelle-France*, 2: 279-80.
32. *Works*, 5: 46-47.
33. On the practice of using one decree against another, see Isabelle Carrier, "Virtuosité procédurière: Pratiques judiciaires à Montpellier au Grand Siècle" (Ph.D. diss., McGill University, 2003), 79. On the use of a variety of legal instruments in distant places, see Benton, *A Search for Sovereignty*, 56.
34. On individuals' construction of cases and use of rhetoric, see Benton, *A Search for Sovereignty*, 26, 77, 97, 101.
35. On forts as symbols of imperium, Macmillan, *Sovereignty and Possession in the English New World*, chap. 4, esp. 122, 144-45; Benton, *A Search for Sovereignty*, 8-9. On the concentration of law in one pair of hands overseas, see David Thomas Konig, "Regionalism in Early American Law," in Michael Grossberg and Christopher Tomlins, eds., *The Cambridge History of Law in America* (New York: Cambridge University Press, 2008), 1: 159.
36. On the assertion of power by these titleholders, see Alan James, *The Navy and Government in Early Modern France, 1572-1661* (Rochester, NY: Royal Historical Society and Boydell Press, 2004), 35-38, 67.
37. *The Jesuit Relations and Allied Documents*, ed. Reuben Gold Thwaites (New York: Pageant, 1959), 2: 178, 3: 186. On the importance of personal authority in the exercise of the admiral's jurisdiction, see James, *The Navy and Government in Early Modern France*, 36-38.
38. For an attempted seizure that went awry when a barrel of gunpowder exploded, see Marcel, ed., *Factum du procès entre Jean de Biencourt, Sieur de Poutrincourt et les pères Biard et Massé, Jésuites*, 30; Trudel, *Histoire de la Nouvelle France*, 2: 119-20. Poutrincourt attempted to assert his own authority along the Saint John River as judge in 1610 in a dispute between Robert Gravé, the son of François Pont-Gravé, and native peoples of the area. Gravé, however, refused to recognize his prerogative, as Poutrincourt was neither vice-admiral nor possessing any position other than seigneur of Port-Royal, a good distance away. See *Factum du procès*, 19; Trudel, *Histoire de la Nouvelle France*, 2: 90, esp. n. 44.
39. *Nouv. docs.*, 368. This is the only reference to an admiralty court in New France that I have come across.
40. *Nouv. docs.*, 379.
41. LAC (Ottawa), Extraits des diverses séries, Parlement de Rouen, 12 July 1633.
42. For both the sentence of 27 August 1632 and the appeal decision, see LAC (Ottawa), Extraits des diverses séries, Parlement de Rouen, 12 July 1633. This case lasted so long because two of the parties, the CRSM and the Rochelais merchants, were simultaneously involved in two other acrimonious lawsuits. Both parties exploited one dispute in the hopes of gaining an upper hand in another. For one of the other lawsuits, which concerned the violation of the CRSM's privileges in the Saint Lawrence by the Rochelais, see p. 68 in this chapter.
43. Roland Mousnier, *Les institutions de la France sous la monarchie absolue, 1598-1789*, vol. 2, *Les organes de l'Etat et la Société* (Paris: Presses universitaires de France, 1980), 294.
44. Trudel, *Histoire de la Nouvelle France*, 2: 98, n. 70; my translation.
45. James, *The Navy and Government in Early Modern France*, 36-38, 67, 75.
46. The absence of one universally accepted authority was hardly unique to French colonies. On disorder that arose in Maine under similar circumstances, see John G. Reid,

Acadia, Maine, and New Scotland: Marginal Colonies in the Seventeenth Century (Toronto: Published in association with Huronia Historical Parks, Ontario Ministry of Culture and Recreation by University of Toronto Press, 1981), 106-7, 108.

47. During the 1610s, Biencourt held the position of vice-admiral of New France; the prince de Condé was lieutenant-general and viceroy of New France; the Company of Rouen and Saint-Malo enjoyed trading privileges from Matane to Quebec and beyond; Poutrincourt was seigneur of Port Royal; and Madame de Guercheville held the remainder of de Monts's commission. On the frequency of overlapping jurisdictions overseas, see Tomlins, "Law's Empire," 30.

48. Condé's viceroyalty was in practice coextensive with his trading privileges, Biencourt and his father effectively controlled Port-Royal and the surrounding area, and Guercheville's claims remained largely theoretical after the short-lived settlement of Saint-Sauveur, established in 1613.

    It should also be noted that the small number of settlers and the limited resources at their disposal, as well as native sovereign control over much of the territory, were contributing factors in the creation and persistence of a series of enclaves and corridors of French control. I would like to thank John Reid for bringing this point to my attention. E-mail communication, 9 May 2011.

    On the jurisdictional rather than territorial basis of sovereignty and the resultant "zones of authority" rather than linear boundaries in early modern France and Europe, more generally, see the introduction to Peter Sahlins, *The Making of France and Spain in the Pyrénées* (Berkeley: University of California Press, 1989); idem, "The Nation in the Village: State-Building and Communal Struggles in the Catalan Borderland during the Eighteenth and Nineteenth Centuries," *Journal of Modern History* 60, no. 2 (June 1988): 234-63.

49. Although a commission from the king, the viceroyalty became venal with Montmorency's purchase from Condé in return for thirty thousand livres. See Mousnier, *Les institutions de la France*, 2: 457.

50. For example, in Brittany the governor claimed admiralty rights; the Basque inhabitants of St. Jean de Luz ran their own admiralty; and the Huguenot stronghold of La Rochelle created its own admiralty whenever it was in conflict with the Crown, a frequent occurrence in the 1610s and 1620s. See James, *The Navy and Government in Early Modern France*, 34-36; David Parker, *La Rochelle and the French Monarchy: Conflict and Order in Seventeenth-Century France* (London: Royal Historical Society, 1980), 74-76.

51. James, *The Navy and Government in Early Modern France*, 24, 40, 50, 58, 62, 76. The strengthening of the French admiral's authority appears to have been the reverse of the trend in England at the beginning of the seventeenth century. There, the admiralty's jurisdiction was in decline amid competition from other local maritime courts and common law courts. See J. H. Baker, *An Introduction to English Legal History*, 2nd ed. (London: Butterworths, 1979), 106-8; Frederic R. Sanborn, *Origins of Early English Maritime Law* (New York: Century, 1930), 303; A. T. Carter, *History of English Legal Institutions* (London: Butterworths, 1902), 172, 173-74.

52. L-A. Boiteux, *Richelieu, grand maître de la navigation et du commerce de France* (Paris: Ozanne, 1955), 67. On the various licenses Condé issued as viceroy, see Emile Gosselin, *Nouvelles Glanes historiques normandes* (Rouen, 1873), 34, 38-39. As Condé and Montmorency were brothers-in-law, it is possible that this purchase was also part of a shuffling of maritime interests among allied houses.

53. This aggressive action had its dignified, ceremonial corollary in New France. Upon the arrival of Champlain and Montmorency's commissioners in the spring of 1620, a Récollet performed Mass and Montmorency's and Champlain's commissions were read aloud before the habitation's residents. See *Works*, 5: 6-7.
54. *Nouv. docs.*, 406. Although notarial acts such as the compromise of 1620 were designed to prevent lawsuits, they could also hide a party's true intentions, thereby precipitating a suit; in this case, Montmorency wished to remove the CRSM from trade to New France. See Carrier, "Virtuosité procédurière," 66.
55. For the two sides' positions, see *Nouv. docs.*, 417-19.
56. On that company's history, see "Lettres patentes par Louis XIII pour la première Compagnie des Indes Orientales," 2 July 1615, in Jacques du Fresne de Francheville, *Histoire de la Compagnie des Indes* (Paris, 1746), 162-66; Philippe Haudrère, *La Compagnie française des Indes au XVIIIe siècle* (Paris: Indes savantes, 2005), 1: 19-23; James, *The Navy and Government in Early Modern France*, 41-42.
57. *Nouv. docs.*, 408. When the Company of New France was established in 1627, it followed the same practice; the intendant of the company and the colony presided over its assemblies.
58. In 1625, for example, the Huguenot duc de Soubise captured a royal fleet on its way to free Christian slaves in Barbary and took the Atlantic islands of Ré and Oléron. The latter were retaken by French royal forces only with the help of Dutch ships. See Victor-L. Tapié, *France in the Age of Louis XIII and Richelieu*, trans. D. McN. Lockie, 2nd ed. (Cambridge: Cambridge University Press, 1984), 148.
59. Henri Hauser, *La Pensée et l'action économiques du Cardinal de Richelieu* (Paris: Presses Universitaires de France, 1944), 54-56; Tapié, *France in the Age of Louis XIII and Richelieu*, 141-42; Robin Briggs, "Richelieu and Reform: Rhetoric and Political Reality," in Joseph Bergin and Laurence Brockliss, eds., *Richelieu and His Age* (Oxford: Clarendon, 1992), 86; James, *The Navy and Government in Early Modern France*, 43-46.
60. See, for example, Bibliothèque nationale de France (hereafter BnF), département de manuscrits (hereafter dépt. de ms.), fonds nouvelles acquisitions françaises, vol. 7287, fo. 24v-5, "Mémoire pour l'establissement du commerce en France," n.d.; Antoine de Montchrétien, *Traité de l'économie politique* (Paris, 1615), 249-51.
61. For the two companies' contracts, see LAC (Ottawa), C11A, correspondance générale (hereafter corresp. gén.), "Edit du roi pour l'établissement de la Compagnie des Cent-Associés," July 1626 ; "Contrat de la Compagnie du Morbihan ou des Cent Associés," in Pierre Grillon, ed., *Les Papiers de Richelieu*, vol. 1 (1624-1626) (Paris: Pedone, 1975), 305; LAC (Ottawa), Collection Dupuy, vol. 318, "Contrat fait par Monsieur Le Cardinal de Richelieu comme Surintendant général du Commerce avec une compagnie de Flamens [sic] et autres associés," 19 May 1626.
62. The Estates registered the edict in January 1628. The Compagnie de Morbihan was definitively abandoned in 1628. See Gervais Carpin, *Le Réseau du Canada: Étude du mode migratoire de la France vers la Nouvelle-France (1628-1662)* (Paris: Presses de l'Université de Paris-Sorbonne, 2001), 55 and 55 n. 39, 57, 58 n. 55; Kenneth M. Dunkley, "Trading Companies and Privilege in Richelieu's France: The Hundred Associates of Morbihan," *Proceedings of the Third Annual Meeting of the French Colonial Historical Society* (1978): 5-9. The Compagnie de la Nacelle enjoyed no more success than the Compagnie de Morbihan. It, too, encountered considerable opposition, particularly due to its strategy of recruiting foreigners, specifically Flemish, to develop industry and commerce in France. The

company continued until at least March 1627, when Richelieu was preparing its edict to bring before the parlements once more. See Boiteux, *Richelieu, grand maître*, 100-101; *Les Papiers de Richelieu*, 2: 124-25.

63. BnF, dept. de ms., Cinq Cents de Colbert, vol. 203, "Lettres patentes de création de la charge de Grand Maître Chef et surintendant général de la navigation et commerce de France et provision d'icelle en faveur de Monsieur le Cardinal de Richelieu en octobre 1626," fo. 203. Parlements were as reluctant to register these letters patent as they had been with the Compagnie de Morbihan edict. While the sovereign court of Brittany registered them in April 1627, they recognized only Richelieu's powers to grant licenses for overseas voyages and to oversee the coastguards. See Boiteux, *Richelieu, grand maître*, 103; Carpin, *Le Réseau du Canada*, 72.
64. Boiteux, *Richelieu, grand maître*, 146. I follow recent historiography on Richelieu that argues that, far from initiating a revolution in government practices, he worked pragmatically within existing institutions and traditional structures of authority. Maritime oversight was not transformed into a modern bureaucracy but, instead, maintained continuity with earlier methods. Among these works, see Briggs, "Richelieu and Reform," 71-97; David Parrott, *Richelieu's Army: War, Government, and Society in France, 1624-1642* (Cambridge: Cambridge University Press, 2001); James, *The Navy and Government in Early Modern France*. For the more traditional view of Richelieu as a reformer with a coherent, long-term, and wide-ranging program, see Tapié, *France in the Age of Louis XIII and Richelieu*; J. H. Elliott, *Richelieu and Olivares* (Cambridge: Cambridge University Press, 1984); Pierre Castagnos, *Richelieu face à la mer* (Rennes, Brittany: Editions Ouest-France, 1989).
65. LAC (Ottawa), Série E, Conseil d'Etat du Roi, vol. 95b, fo. 123, 15 March 1628; my translation. For the original order to the CNF, see vol. 95a, fo. 95, 26 January 1628.
66. See, for example, LAC (Ottawa), Série E, Conseil d'Etat du Roi, vol. 95b, fo. 311, 30 March 1628; LAC (Ottawa), V6, Conseil privé, c. 91, no. 29, 19 July 1633. Article 6 of the CNF's contract proclaimed the revocation of "all gifts made of the said lands, parts or portions thereof." See "Acte pour l'établissement de la Compagnie des cent Associés pour le commerce du Canada . . . le 29 Avril, 1627," 4.
67. For the terms of compensation, see BnF, dépt. de ms., fonds français, vol. 16738, fo. 44-67, 27 August 1634; LAC (Ottawa), MC, vol.. I, étude XVI, no. 72, 23 February 1636. The money owed de Caen and his associates was included in the company's statement of debts in 1642. See LAC (Ottawa), C11A, corresp. gén., fo. 195-209v, "Etat général des debtes passives de la Compagnie générale de la Nouvelle France," 1641-1642. In coming to a compromise out of court, de Caen and the CNF associates chose the preferred resolution to disputes for the majority of litigants in the period. See Carrier, "Virtuosité procédurière," 63; Kagan, *Lawsuits and Litigants in Castile*, 93.
68. Apart from Montmorency himself, de Caen had at least one well-placed ally at the Admiralty of France, the sieur de Saint Martin, lieutenant general of the admiralty in Paris, who became a guarantor for him in an agreement with the other associates of the Company of Montmorency in 1626. See LAC (Ottawa), MC, vol. CI, étude CV, no. 267, 31 March 1626; LAC (Ottawa), Série E, Conseil d'Etat du Roi, vol. 87a, fo. 41, 4 April 1626. The CNF suggested in the course of its defense that de Caen had only received trading privileges "by the favor of certain people who were close to seigneur Montmorency." LAC (Ottawa), Collection Margry, vol. 9269, fo. 276, 16 August 1629. On Richelieu's desire for control over the company, see Carpin, *Le Réseau du Canada*, 78.

69. Indeed, the most prominent associates were clients of Richelieu, among them Isaac and Claude de Razilly, Isaac Martin, sieur de Mauvoy, Philippe de Longvilliers, sieur de Poincy, Sebastien Cramoisy, Gabriel Lattaignant, and Louis Houel. Some of these men engaged in more than one company under the cardinal. See Carpin, *Le Réseau du Canada*, 63-64, 73, 98; Castagnos, *Richelieu face à la mer*, 129-41. Among the royal officials in the CNF were the controller-general of finances, the Marquis d'Effiat, and the intendant of the navy, Martin de Mauvoy. For the full membership list, see Appendix A in Trudel, *Histoire de la Nouvelle France*, vol. 3, part 1: 415-25.
70. "Articles et conventions de société et compagnie du 7 mai 1627," in *Édits, ordonnances royaux*, article 26; Carpin, *Le Réseau du Canada*, 88.
71. On the importance of Montmorency's example to Richelieu, see Boiteux, *Richelieu, grand maître*, 79-80. It is worth observing that the trajectory from proprietors to large companies in New France is different from that of its Anglo-American neighbors. One of the conclusions drawn from the crisis in Virginia in the early 1620s was that joint-stock companies were not appropriate for such an enterprise, inaugurating a period of proprietary and royal government. See Wesley Frank Craven, *Dissolution of the Virginia Company: The Failure of a Colonial Experiment* (Gloucester, MA: Peter Smith, 1964), chaps. 9, 10; Tomlins, "Law's Empire," 34-36.
72. All three of the main ports in the New France trade—Rouen, La Rochelle, and Saint-Malo—were free ports, exempt from duties on imports and exports; the first two were also permitted to engage in the spice trade. See André Lespagnol, *Messieurs de Saint-Malo: Une élite négociante au temps de Louis XIV* (Rennes: Presses Universitaires de Rennes, 1997), 1: 43; Etienne Trocmé, "La Rochelle protestante," in Marcel Delafosse, ed., *Histoire de La Rochelle* (Toulouse: Privat, 1985) 107-9; Gayle Brunelle, *New World Merchants of Rouen, 1559-1630*, vol. 16 of Sixteenth-Century Essays and Studies (Ann Arbor, MI: Edward's Brothers, 1991), 33.
73. LAC (Ottawa), Série E, Conseil d'Etat du Roi, vol. 79a, f. 386, 27 June 1624.
74. LAC (Ottawa) Série C11D, fol. 52-7, "Lettre patente pour l'enregistrement des pouvoirs et commissions donnés au Sieur de Monts," 29 janvier 1605; Jean Liebel, *Pierre Dugua sieur de Mons fondateur de Québec* (Paris: Le Croît vif, 1999), 166. The Parlement of Rouen had also protested; although registration occurred sometime after January 1605, the precise date is unknown.
75. Trudel, *Histoire de la Nouvelle France*, 2: 66; Liebel, *Pierre Dugua, sieur de Mons*, 166.
76. Belated and conditional registrations were also features of later letters patent. See, for example, LAC (Ottawa), Série E. Conseil d'Etat du Roi, vol. 95a, fo. 95, 26 January 1628; Archives départementales de Seine Maritime (hereafter ADSM), 1B 981, Parlement de Rouen, 14 December 1613; *Nouv. docs.*, 267-70, esp. 270. Provinces also used their oversight in other areas to voice their opposition. In 1605, de Monts had to appear twice before the royal council to request the release of his furs from customs officials in Normandy. See *Nouv. docs.*, 94 n. 3, 101; "King's declaration concerning the exemption of New France merchandise from customs," 8 February 1605, in Marc Lescarbot, *History of New France*, ed. H. P. Biggar (Toronto: Champlain Society, 1907-1914 [based on 1618 ed.]), 1: 223-26; Robert Le Blant, "Henri IV et le Canada," *Revue de Pau et du Béarn* 12 (1984-85): 51; Trudel, *Histoire de la Nouvelle France*, 2: 65-66. On the application of royal edicts to all parts of the kingdom in theory, see Olivier-Martin, *Histoire du droit français*, 345-46.
77. Quotation from a decree of the royal council (date unknown) in Archives municipales de Saint-Malo (hereafter Arch. mun. de Saint-Malo), register 6, 26 March 1609; my

translation. Denoting a "vested right or privilege," liberty of trade would confer status rather than remove all claims. Although the concept of free trade appeared to put merchants of all ports on an equal footing, Saint-Malo sought to advance its own traders at the expense of other ports' through an emphasis on its long history with North America and its customary rights. See Thomas J. Schaeper, "Colonial Trade Policies Late in the Reign of Louis XIV," *Revue française d'Histoire d'Outre-Mer* 67, nos. 3/4 (1980): 210-11.

78. Arch. mun. de Saint-Malo, register 6, 26 March 1609; my translation. On the community of inhabitants of Saint-Malo, see Lespagnol, *Messieurs de Saint-Malo*, 1: 44-46.

79. *Nouv. docs.*, 191-93. For the progression of suits in this case, see also *Nouv. docs.*, 210-11, 231, 303-4, 336; Arch. mun. de Saint-Malo, register 6, 22 November 1612. There was no admiralty in Saint-Malo until 1681; there was, however, probably a representative of the Admiralty of France in the port at this time.

80. The kingdom of France was divided into *pays d'état,* which had provincial estates made up of the three orders in the province, and *pays d'élection,* which had no such representation and for whom taxes were decided upon by the king without consultation. On the role of the estates in the protection of provincial customs, see Olivier-Martin, *Histoire du droit français*, 392-97.

81. *Relation originale du voyage de Jacques Cartier au Canada en 1534: documents inédits sur Jacques Cartier et le Canada*, ed. H. Michelant and A. Ramé (Paris: Librairie Tross, 1867), 46. All documents cited in this collection are my translation. See also *Nouv. docs.*, 372 n. 3.

82. The Estates of Brittany in turn instructed their syndic and deputies in Paris to "defend there with all their power," which stretched the case into 1619. *Documents inédits*, 47-49; see also resolutions to the same effect 23 October 1618 and 3 October 1619, 49-51; Jean Berenger, "Les Etats de Bretagne et la colonisation nord-américaine," *Etudes canadiennes-Canadian Studies* 17 (December 1984): 13.

83. The exact date of the council's ruling in favor of the CRSM is unknown. Berenger suggests that it occurred as early as 27 May 1617, but documents in *Documents inédits* show that this was merely the date of the company's request. The case had not yet been resolved by November of that year. See Berenger, "Les Etats de Bretagne et la colonisation nord-américaine," 13; *Documents inédits*, 47-49; *Nouv. docs.*, 371-72.

84. For examples of each side's requests in their favored jurisdictions, see ADSM, 1B 981, Parlement de Rouen, 25 June 1633 (1) and (2). One of many disputes over jurisdiction occurred in 1614-1615 in which the CRSM requested an order for the Rochelais to appear before the Admiralty of Rouen and the latter responded with a like order for company associates to appear before the council. In January 1615, the royal council ordered both parties before the admiralty. See *Nouv. docs.*, 340-43. On the manipulation of jurisdictions by opposing parties, see Parker, "Sovereignty, Absolutism, and the Function of Law," 58.

There appears to have been a striking contrast between the metropolitan legal jurisdictions involved in English overseas disputes and French ones. Whereas parties in the latter frequently came before local admiralty courts, the English admiralty's jurisdiction did not extend—in theory at least—to colonies but was limited to the sea itself. Contemporary disputes that I have examined seem to uphold this fact: factional conflicts within the Virginia Company, for example, drove disputants to the king and the Privy Council. In addition to metropolitan appeals, companies in the American colonies had their own general courts, a practice not seen in French America. See Craven, *Dissolution of the Virginia Company*, 119, 123, 140, 251; Andrews, *Trade, Plunder, and Settlement*, 325.

85. ADSM, 1B 981, Parlement de Rouen, 25 June 1633 (2); LAC (Ottawa), V6, Conseil privé, carton 52, no. 42, "Arrêt ordonnant que les differends entre les deux parties seront procédés à l'admirauté de Rouen et en appel au Parlement de Rouen," 11 March 1625; my translation. On the strength of local and regional legal institutions, see Tomlins, "Law's Empire," 39. On the practice of favoring one jurisdiction over another, see Carrier, "Virtuosité procédurière," 95.
86. Carrier, "Virtuosité procédurière," 96.

PART II

Political and Religious Imagination

4

Aspects of Legal Pluralism in the Ottoman Empire

KAREN BARKEY

Introduction

Empires, considered as political formations that incorporate colonized peoples within multiple legal jurisdictions that draw on diverse forms of law, offer prime examples of the practice of legal pluralism. I understand the term "legal pluralism," following John Griffiths's definition, as referring to a situation in which "the sovereign commands different bodies of law for different groups of the population varying by ethnicity, religion, nationality, or geography, and [. . .] the parallel legal regimes are all dependent on the state legal system."[1] Empires were forced to deal with this plurality because of the manner in which they expanded, incorporating and accommodating local cultures at different times and under different circumstances in a piecemeal way. Multiple economic arrangements, fragmented monetary systems, and legal plurality were simple facts of life in many premodern empires thanks to their histories of conquest and politics of domination. This lack of unity often allowed imperial systems to function more pragmatically but also made them vulnerable to competition and conflict. Did legal pluralism, then, lead to intercommunal violence or to accommodation among groups? How did empires manage the diversity of legal systems they incorporated? On the one hand, we could hypothesize that multiple, uncoordinated, and diverse bodies of law create potential for conflict among groups and individuals and with the state. On the other hand, we could also argue that multiple legal systems provide space for flexibility, pragmatic decision making, and a measure of freedom that can encourage adaptation and peaceful coexistence. This is an especially important issue in the contemporary world, where community-based legal systems are flourishing to challenge unified state legal systems. Comparisons across time have to be treated carefully, however, since historically legal pluralism operated within quite different political systems from those we observe today.

The Ottoman Empire presents an important case of legal pluralism that has not been sufficiently studied, especially in comparative perspective. Thanks to their modes of expansion, the contemporaneous Ottoman, Habsburg, and Russian empires were all legally plural societies. The Habsburgs adopted the independent courts of the national groups they incorporated, while the Russians, in ways that resembled Ottoman practice, maintained an umbrella Russian Law, promulgated by the emperor, that applied to the entire population. They nevertheless allowed local customs and jurisdictions to exist side by side with Russian imperial law. According to Jane Burbank, "Russian imperial law accommodated particular social institutions extant in the population, did not homogenize them, but legalized them selectively within the whole opus of imperial legislation. The law recognized and incorporated particularity, and retained its claim to be the ultimate source of justice."[2]

This chapter examines the sources and institutions of legal pluralism in the Ottoman Empire to argue that the Ottomans used legal pluralism to assimilate non-Muslims into a hegemonic Islamic court system while keeping interreligious peace and tolerance. Ottoman legal pluralism was never an uncoordinated and unbound set of laws emanating from different communities; it was a carefully choreographed legal pluralism coordinated by the center. Consequently, as we shall see, whenever non-Muslim Ottoman subjects had the option of choosing among various legal jurisdictions, they made their very real legal choices in light of the cultural hegemonic messages and meanings embedded in the Ottoman court system, which encouraged particular legal preferences. These messages articulated and modulated the tension between the non-Muslim community courts and the central government's representative, the *kadi* courts. In the last instance, Ottoman Islamic law could dominate the entire system without sacrificing the perception among non-Muslim subjects that they, too, had fair access to justice.

Many scholars of the Ottoman Empire have depicted the different layers of legal complexity, the tension and accommodation between religious and secular law, and the relative autonomy of non-Muslim communities in legal matters. They have highlighted the special status that the "Peoples of the Book," Jews and Christians, enjoyed under Islamic rule, since the Pact of Umar, attributed to the second Caliph, who ruled from 634 to 644. According to this pact, non-Muslims consented to enduring a series of discriminatory acts in return for protection and a measure of autonomy in their personal affairs. As this set of arrangements was reenacted through Islamic empires, including the Ottoman Empire, one of its most important facets became the practical legal autonomy that each non-Muslim community acquired to maintain its own religious tribunals with jurisdiction over personal law, while Islamic law remained predominant in criminal matters. It was long assumed that members of each religious community in the empire visited and used their own religious courts and that they led, in effect, parallel and unconnected lives. Studies of court records, however, have shown otherwise. They have exposed the degree to which the *shari'a* court was an important hub for Muslim and non-Muslim communities alike, and demonstrated that legal pluralism did not, in actual practice, reflect a simple and clean differentiation of groups along religious lines, but was in fact much more complex, multilayered, and, therefore, consequential for relations among communities within the empire.[3] Ottoman legal institutions, I argue, made the most of the fact that the pact of Umar, whether intentionally or not, provided Jews and Christians with more jurisdictional venues, and therefore more legal choices.

We need a better history of several aspects of legal pluralism in the Ottoman Empire that takes into account this more complex picture in order to explain why the legal politics of the empire was important. What did it entail in its daily practice and what were its implications for imperial society and interreligious, intercommunal life in the empire? We also have to interrogate the questions of empire and legal pluralism more comparatively, as they bear both on interconnected legal understandings of diversity and on wider political effects. In this paper, I explore legal pluralism as it functioned in the Ottoman Empire from its inception to the late eighteenth century, before the gradual incorporation of European law and the late-nineteenth- and early-twentieth-century transition to the Republic of Turkey and its new secular and civil law.

I argue, to reiterate and extend my earlier claim, that the particular legal order of the Ottoman Empire powerfully contributed to a political culture of diversity and toleration in that it provided communities and actors with choices even though, in the end, they were choosing the hegemonic court. Accordingly, it is very plausible that legal pluralism was a tool for the management of diversity. That is, the legal pluralism that was practiced in the Ottoman imperial space, in the juxtaposition of state, religious, and community laws, produced a compromise that integrated different legal systems—Islamic, indigenous, and even foreign—while allowing forum shopping between community courts and encouraging a preference for the hegemonic court system. But it existed at the state's discretion—enacted, challenged, used, and manipulated for state-society accommodation.

In order to make this argument, I rely on Bourdieu's notion of field, arguing that within the legal politics of the empire we need to pay attention to the composition of a relational field among the state, the court, and community actors that chose to utilize the court. The field, a configuration of relations, as Bourdieu describes it, incorporates rules of the game, actors, their habitus (their learned ways of behaving), and their capital (mostly the varied resources they have).[4] It is in this social arena that we should consider the politics and needs of the imperial state, the different court systems, and the autonomy and knowledge of countless sets of actors and the established patterns by which people pursued resources. According to Bourdieu, it is in this field that the state is able to exert symbolic violence, by which he means that the state "incarnates itself simultaneously in objectivity, in the form of specific organizational structures and mechanisms, and in subjectivity, in the form of mental structures and categories of perception and thought."[5]

In identifying key characteristics of the legal field in the Ottoman Empire, we should keep in mind that legal pluralism, first, operated within a larger Ottoman state-society system strongly dominated by Islamic institutions emerging from a state Islam that established how multiple religious and secular jurisdictions would engage one another. That is, although many different and competing legal jurisdictions existed, they operated according to a particular understanding of state Islam that ordered legal relations within the empire. Since, however, Islamic law did not directly guide procedure in every legal jurisdiction within the empire, we understand that the particular brand of Ottoman legal pluralism lies somewhere between the extremes of imperial legal regimes identified by Lauren Benton—between multicentric, truly plural imperial and colonial regimes, such as fifteenth-century Spain, and state-dominated legal regimes, such as the British Empire, where European law held supreme sway.[6]

Second, legal pluralism in the Ottoman Empire, with its semi-autonomous community religious courts, operated nevertheless within the boundaries of a "state law" that concentrated and circulated combined coercive and symbolic power in and through the Islamic court system. Yet within this institutional context, the actual workings of pluralism were dependent on the interaction of court personnel, religious leaders, and those actors, Muslims and non-Muslims, who used the courts. It is in this relational field that I think we will find answers to how legal pluralism helped non-Muslims find alternative venues for their day-to-day dealings and conflicts, alternatives that frequently afforded a desirable escape from the grip of their own community leaders, who often responded to situations of contested hegemony by being harsh and unyielding. This same tension serves to demonstrate that non-Muslim communities simultaneously supported Ottoman state law and confronted it in order to establish the parameters of their power in the local community. A similar tension probably arises in contemporary cases of legal pluralism when community members and their religious and cultural leaders confront the state.

Let me further clarify my point: legal pluralism in the Ottoman Empire was closely linked with the role of Islam. Yet Islam was never a source of "legal centralism" in the empire; that is, the fact that the *shari'a* (religious law) never dominated as a single source of law was very important for the imperial state and society. It follows that in order to study legal pluralism in the Ottoman Empire, we must first place Islam in its proper position within Ottoman imperial society. We must understand the role of Islam in statecraft and its limited jurisdiction vis-à-vis the state. The state in the Ottoman Empire almost always retained the power to impose its own ends on learned religious men, who were organized as an arm of the government. Islam's blueprint for ruling non-Muslim communities by allowing them practical legal autonomy to maintain their own religious tribunals with jurisdiction over personal law further contributed to the complexity of the Ottoman legal field. In order better to understand how Ottoman legal pluralism was managed so that potential conflict within and between religious communities contributed in the end to strengthen the stability of the Islamic state, I will examine in turn three pieces of the Ottoman legal puzzle: the role of Islam in the system of Ottoman legal institutions, the influence of Ottoman diversity on their particular ordering, and interactions among actors within the legal field that ordered society and organized its various parameters.

Islam in the Ottoman Empire

The Ottoman state represents one particularly powerful relationship between the state and religion. The imperial state, although hardly neutral on the question of religion, was nevertheless able to incorporate and control religion and to balance the majority religion against other existing religions as well as manage its internal denominations. In this sense, Ottoman Islam, like other Islamic empires, was good at recognizing different forms of belief thanks to the pact of Umar. But the Ottoman state achieved something more than that. We should emphasize, on the one hand, that the Ottoman state was not a theocracy insofar as neither the *shari'a* nor the *ulema* (religious learned men) directed the state. On the other hand, the Ottoman state was not a religiously "neutral" state, since Islam supplied a portion of its legitimacy. In the words of Ocak, "Ottoman Islam bestowed sacredness on the concept of sovereignty and, at the same time, performed an active function by providing a means of governing."[7] Ottoman Islam was primarily a political Islam, subordinated to the state and used, in turn, to develop state institutions and administer various state functions. Whereas many Christian realms experienced a perennial struggle between the Crown and the Church, the supremacy of the state in Muslim polities neutralized this potential source of struggle and lowered the tension between religious and secular state law. Therefore the intense struggle that arose in western European states and their colonies between secular and ecclesiastical legal and social forces did not materialize in the Ottoman case.[8]

Islam shared the limelight in the Ottoman Empire with "secular" *kanun* (dynastic law), and this "state law" was, at its core, plural. It was a composite of religious and sultanic, regional and territorial law pragmatically bound together and separated in response to the needs of particular situations. Islam, no doubt, contributed a large part of the empire's identity, especially after Selim I (1512-1520) conquered large swaths of Muslim territory. Yet we must be sensitive to the internal limitations of the Ottoman state's claim to be Islamic, since Islam was not ideationally, legally, or institutionally dominant in the empire. We cannot fully explain both the Ottoman Empire's identity and all of its basic structures on the basis of Islam, especially if we follow the Weberian tradition in considering religion to be complex, varied, and assembled from a combination of institutional and ideational structures.[9] Religion in the empire was a set of ideas, institutions, and practices that provided a worldview within which actors lived, believed, and interpreted their lives.

The reasons why Islam was not institutionally dominant can be summarized analytically, despite their complexity. First, Islam was tamed within the Ottoman Empire mostly because the empire's founders carefully balanced the state's relations with it from early on, using the Greek-Byzantine imperial model as an example. Further, the Ottomans did not emerge as a ruling group along with the strict establishment of a formal body of Islamic law. Rather, initial decision making was based on the sultan and his immediate associates, the *yasa*, or Turkish traditions of Central Asia, and customary law, in the sense of a repertoire of local knowledge about how to conduct everyday matters. Second, Ottoman justice based on both *shari'a* and *kanun* was exercised by the religious and administrative authorities of the empire, and the two legal traditions were welded together or separated out of local necessity.[10] The Ottomans understood *shari'a* according to the conventions of their time as a guide to apply God's will refracted through the interpretations of competing schools of Islamic learning. *Shari'a* was mainly applied in prescribed fields, such as family and personal law.[11] Since the fields of land tenure, criminal law, and taxation were much less developed in the *shari'a*, the *kanun* was preferred for dealing with such cases. In fact, there are many places where the *kanun* simply reiterates *shari'a* law, but we also find independent and separate rulings. One scholar of Ottoman Islam puts it in the following manner: "It [*kanun*] is a confirmation of the *shari'a*, but also, in a sense, a violation of it, in as much as the *shari'a* is God-given."[12] In everyday practice *kanun* and *shari'a* worked together to address the circumstances at hand and find the best available path to peace, security, and justice. Third, the particular construction of the Ottoman state was such that it maintained and nurtured an important separation between religion as an institution and religion as a system of meanings and relations that gave coherence to a community of faith. Religion as an institution helped to administer the empire. Religion as a system of beliefs provided the tools for everyday practice. The two were not entirely separate; they were connected most obviously in the person of the magistrate (*kadi*), the religious official versed in both religious and secular law.

Islam could be publicly proclaimed as the great universal religion that bound the empire together and provided legitimacy to the imperial ruling house. Yet it could also be confined in institutions shaped by actual conditions in the empire and its rulers' aspiration to maintain supremacy in all matters. In what Serif Mardin has called the "empiricism of Ottoman secular officialdom," Ottoman rulers embarked on a bid to build a religious elite and an educational system that would be controlled by the state.[13] Religion functioned as an institution of the state, and its practitioners emerged as state officials. Religion had been subjugated to the state. But the state had also acquired the most well-organized bureaucratic machinery in the Islamic world. Although the early sultans Mehmed II (1451-1481), Beyazıd II (1481-1512), and Selim I (1512-1520) had harnessed Islam in the course of accommodating to the natural balance of the imperial population and their needs, Sultan Süleyman the Law Giver (1520-1566) applied himself expressly to reshaping the institutions of Islam in order to expand the physical and intellectual capacity of the *medreses* and increase the numbers of students. First, the Ottomans were distinguished by creating a sophisticated group of learned scholars to represent Sunnî Islam, particularly of the Hanafi School. But second, the expanding empire demanded more administrative power and therefore also more and better-educated magistrates to represent the state throughout the empire. Under Süleyman, they reached every corner of the imperial lands. Given that they depended on state rewards for their livelihoods and their careers, these men were fully integrated into the state and acted to maintain it in both its aspects as a religious Islamic state and as a secular bureaucratic state.

The court and the magistrate became the main representatives of state hegemony at the local level. The magistrate exerted symbolic domination that was manifested objectively in the day-to-day administration of his jurisdiction and subjectively in the mental structures of Islamic domination and the perception of justice. The central authority clearly demanded that, in judicial matters, the decisions of the *kadi* be followed by governors and police officers. Rarely were *kadi* decisions overturned by higher-ranking religious officials; the authority to overrule the *kadi* rested with the sultan. Imbued with state power, this center of religious and administrative life in every locality of the empire was the site where state law, *shari'a*, and customary law were combined and interpreted, and, consequently, it was the hub of state-society relations. As we shall see, the *kadi* court also became the court of choice for non-Muslims. The local magistrate became the intermediary between state and folk, between high culture and folk culture, and between literate society and illiterate understandings of religion. Administrators of the empire, *kadıs* were also entrusted with maintaining basic moral and cultural unity by applying religious sultanic law in their roles both as judges and as *medrese* teachers. They were bred and educated in the religious *medreses*, and then spent time in retraining, becoming expert in secular and regional law. They were sent out into the provinces and cities of the empire as men *of* the empire, representing much more than Islam as they adjudicated according to the *shari'a* and sultanic law. They tied the state to the people, embodying the unity between center and periphery. As a result, they could not just be religious men; they had to be religious men of the center. In this sense the mixture they represented would have seemed odd to a medieval Catholic man. For the common folk, the Ottoman administrator represented both Islam *and* the state.

In the routines of daily court practice, the *kadıs* reproduced the demands of the *shari'a*: that they watch over the lives of those who were of Islamic faith. They both watched for transgressions of Islamic precepts and helped define the parameters of Islamic practice. That is, they performed Islamic practice, and even though they ruled in practical religious and in local customary terms, they still represented the institution of Islam and connected people to the broader religion and its forms of thinking. When common folk came to court asking for justice between adversaries, and the *kadı* ruled as the representative of the sultan, all members of the community were reenacting a very old traditional Islamic concept of the just ruler. Beyond the performance side of this relationship, the fact that the religious official and the religious court offered to the inhabitants of a region resolution, clarification, support, and relief focused the people on religion and its day-to-day signs and symbols. Yet this resolution was achieved anew on each occasion, drawn from Islamic law, but combined with customary law in a bundle arranged according to the learning of the individual judge.

The power of the judge was significant not because he represented Islam but because he represented the state and a particular synthesis of various legal systems. He did have some latitude to act on behalf of the sultans, although certainly less than what Weber articulated in his notion of *kadi* justice. Weber argued that the Islamic system was neither rational nor predictable and that the *kadi* had unlimited discretion.[14] By contrast, according to Halil Inalcik, the individual judge had collections of sultanic law at his disposal, and he also recorded legislative orders broadcast from the center in his official registers. Given these sultanic laws and the continual dissemination of new legislative orders, Inalcik argues that Ottoman law was always changing, developing, and never stagnant.[15] Most important, however, was the fact that *kadis* ruled on behalf of the center; they upheld the law, but they were clearly concerned that their judgments agree with rulings from the center. They fulfilled the mission of the state.[16]

Ottoman Diversity

The concurrent operation of Islamic law, secular law, and customary law in the *kadi* courts certainly complicated the legal field, although they were available to the subjects of the empire only through the mediation of the *kadi*, not as entirely separate bodies of law that could be chosen by litigants themselves. A further complication of the Ottoman legal system, one that did, in fact, offer opportunities for litigants to choose the venue in which their cases would be heard, arose from the fact of diverse populations within the empire and the main strategy the Ottoman state devised for managing them. This layer of legal complication emerged in the form of communal legal autonomy and the resulting availability of community-based religious courts for the non-Muslims of the empire. At a basic level, diversity was organized along the simple Islamic blueprint inherited from earlier Islamic empires, but the Ottoman state and its courts elaborated their own very effective and consequential manner of managing non-Muslim communities. The Ottoman state organized and administered a system of religious and communal rule that instituted religious boundaries, thus explicitly marking difference and division with parallel administrative structures, yet maintaining a cohesive and tolerant imperial society by taking advantage of the spaces for movement created by the peculiar relationships among those structures. Imperial indirect rule vis-à-vis religious communities produced the *millet* system, a loose administrative set of central-local arrangements for each community that provided the basic script for multireligious rule. *Millet* allowed for the simultaneous division of communities and their integration into the state, and, like other indirect forms of rule, permitted intermediaries, who, as a result, had a real stake in the maintenance of the status quo, to administer internally autonomous self-regulating religious communities. The combined effects of top-down pressure from state authorities and bottom-up enthusiasm for peace and order from intermediaries from the subject populations provided the key to many centuries of Ottoman pluralism.

The basic normative guidelines by which Muslim and non-Muslim communities were incorporated into Ottoman society came to the Ottomans from other Islamic empires that drew on Islamic law. Accordingly, Islam pervaded Ottoman society and became the primary marker of inclusion into the political community.[17] But Islam also dictated a relationship between a Muslim state and non-Muslim "Peoples of the Book," that is, Jews and Christians. According to the pact of Umar, which I mentioned earlier in this chapter, non-Muslims would be protected and could practice their own religion, preserve their own places of worship, and, to a large extent, run their own affairs as long as they recognized the political superiority of Islam. The immediate public markers of the boundaries among Muslims, Jews, and Christians were codes of conduct, rules, and regulations regarding dress, housing, and transportation. Despite frequent references to physical markers of difference such as clothing, colors, height of residence, and ownership of slaves, the sultanate did not fully enforce such regulations.[18]

The sultans, especially Mehmed II, supplemented the role of Islam in establishing the simple rules of multireligious living by forging the *millet* semiformal concords that were periodically renewed by the religious communities of the empire. These arrangements entailed minimal innovation, since they adopted the existing authority structures of each community and thereby provided them with significant legal autonomy and authority. In the interests of maintaining continuity in the midst of institutional adaptation, wherever there was already a strong community organization and/or a strong ecclesiastical hierarchy, the central state recognized these institutions as the representative structures for each community. For example, the conqueror of Constantinople, Mehmed II, quickly acknowledged not only the ecclesiastical but also the administrative power of the Greek Orthodox Patriarchate, and so enlisted the Church to administer an ethnically and linguistically diverse population that followed Orthodox Christian practice. The Jewish communities subjected to the Ottomans were much smaller, primarily urban, and scattered across the empire. They followed no existing overarching rabbinical authority, but a looser assembly of religious and lay leaders, and had to be administered differently from the Orthodox population when the initial centralized model failed. Instead, Jewish communities were finally incorporated into the empire's administrative structures as individual self-regulating units with lay or religious leaders acting as intermediaries. In each of these encounters, the facts on the ground, the relations between state and religious communities, and the interests of each community's leaders helped shape the rules of governance. Yet each of the arrangements consistently ensured the independence of *millet* communities in personal and family legal matters, entrusting each group to its own religious courts.[19] In treating the other religious communities, the Ottomans believed, possibly under the influence of the division of labor between religious and *kanun* law in the Muslim courts, that each community ought to have a religious set of rulings on family and personal matters.

Once *millet* arrangements were agreed upon, they were maintained by religious or secular intermediaries from each community, enforced by incentives and punishments. As the key brokers between the state and the *millets*, these intermediaries strategically behaved as boundary managers, maintaining peace and order by actively and efficiently monitoring relations across religious and community lines. Fearon and Laitin, in their work on issues of interethnic peace, call such arrangements "institutionalized in-group policing," where leaders successfully police not only activity within their communities but also transactions among communities.[20] In order to keep intergroup relations from blowing up into large-scale ethnic conflict, the state empowered intermediaries, whether religious or secular leaders, to monitor internal community affairs in return for continued benefits and autonomy. Community leaders who maintained peace and paid their dues on time would be rewarded with continued appointment and increased opportunities for wealth. Leaders whose communities were embroiled in violence or who were unable to collect taxes lost their livelihoods and, quite often, their heads.

State Islam and *millet* arrangements combined to forge the patterns of diversity in the empire. Separation and difference were institutionalized, and community leaders were expected to manage the boundaries in order to enforce separation. Legal pluralism, the practice of allowing multiple legal forums, nevertheless provided one mode of movement among categories, creating new tensions that contributed to social cohesion by relaxing to a calculated degree the rule of separation. No doubt individuals of different religions and ethnicities mingled and traded with each other. Yet it was the production of a legal regime in which members of different religious communities not only maintained their agency within their own communities but were also given a legal choice that could take them across religious boundaries that made difference and diversity a success. This particular combination gave the Ottoman state the ability to control and order diversity to its own benefit.

Ottoman Legal Pluralism

We can look at the history of Ottoman legal pluralism, understand its antecedents in the great Muslim empires, and discuss the role played by each of the legal traditions of the empire without capturing how and to what effect the subjects of the empire utilized those multiple, sometimes-interconnected legal traditions. If legal pluralism is to be understood as an advantage for maintaining diversity and coexistence, then we must be able to see how this transpired in the choices made by Ottoman subjects and in the results of those choices. We would expect that specific conflicts and tensions were diffused by subjects having access to multiple court systems, and that Ottoman subjects chose a legal forum based on knowledge of the various legal traditions, especially of their comparative advantages, as well as on knowledge about the quality of justice meted out by particular court magistrates or ecclesiastical leaders. That is, we need to analyze relations among actors within the legal field. Knowing, ourselves, the basic outlines of the legal system that the Ottoman state elaborated to meet the demands both of state Islam and of the fact of diversity, we can now turn to this task.

I claimed earlier in my chapter that the pact of Umar effectively created more choices of legal venue for non-Muslim subjects of an Islamic empire, and that the Ottomans took advantage of this situation to promote stability in the empire. Let me spell out more clearly the options available in the Ottoman legal system. In this legally plural system, Jews and Christians were able, naturally, to use their own courts for personal and family legal matters (recall that criminal matters were restricted to the *kadi* courts), but they also had the option of choosing to litigate in the Islamic courts. Any case that pitted Muslims against non-Muslims was subject to Islamic law, but whenever Jews and Christians litigated among themselves or against one another, they were free to choose either their own or the dominant Islamic jurisdiction.[21] By contrast, we could say that Muslims were more limited, choosing sometimes between the *kadi* court and the governor's court, although the literature is not clear on the status of this latter choice. Marcus, in his study of Aleppo in the eighteenth century, finds that Muslims unhappy with the *kadi* court justice would go to the governor's court. He argues that the governor's jurisdiction extended to issues that normally entered the purview of the *kadi*.[22] Every group also possessed more informal spaces of communal adjudication based on community self-governance, tribal structures, and community elders, among other sources.

The first and most important conclusion of many studies on court records shows that there was a marked level of assimilation of non-Muslims in general into the Muslim courts. Jewish and Christian courts were set up to provide each of the *millet* communities with access to its own laws. Their courts provided an essential service in drafting and drawing up legal documents such as deeds, contracts, wills, and other agreements that defined relationships among members of the same religious community, but that would also be valid in the larger Islamic and Ottoman world. Every Jewish community had a law court operating according to Jewish law and equipped to assist Jewish members of the community in meeting all kinds of social and economic contingencies.[23] Orthodox Christians had their ecclesiastical courts, presided over by metropolitans, bishops, and other religious leaders, and based solely on canon law.[24]

Despite these resources, non-Muslims frequently chose to litigate in Muslim court. This was true in many areas of the empire, especially large cosmopolitan centers of trade, whether western Anatolian seaports or the cities in the Arab provinces of the empire. Numerous studies for Kayseri, Cyprus, Aleppo, Damascus, Sofia, and other cities demonstrate this with reliable evidence. Moreover, non-Muslim women, in particular, found protection and relief in the Islamic courts, which were more moderate in divorce and inheritance matters than the courts in their own communities. The availability of multiple religious jurisdictions allowed for forum shopping, permitting individuals to search for rulings more to their own advantage. The *kadi* courts overwhelmingly provided better rulings at least until the eighteenth century. The court thus became a tool for incorporation and assimilation by encouraging non-Muslims to engage directly with specifically Ottoman institutions. To the degree that Islamic courts favored non-Muslims in their rulings and provided them with just rule and equal treatment, incorporation and assimilation would be promoted. The reverse movement of Muslims into non-Muslim courts was rarely observed. Some scholars mention that when Jews and Muslims were in property disputes, Muslims would sometimes go to the Jewish court in order to show respect for Jewish religious obligations. Marcus refers to a Jewish judge in late-eighteenth-century Aleppo, Ephraim Laniado, who recounts that such gestures of respect commonly occurred in his court.[25] This could not, however, have been a generalized practice, since Muslims who went to Jewish or Christian court could be accused of apostasy.

Why did non-Muslims use *kadi* courts? Besides the fact that *kadi* courts themselves were a specifically Ottoman amalgam of legal traditions and practices (religious, secular, and customary), there were routine and nonroutine reasons for choosing a legal venue outside of their religious communities. Routine visits to Muslim courts occurred regularly in order to accomplish a number of legal tasks, from establishing a binding agreement or recording a financial transaction to registering land ownership and making property transfers. By registering transactions and agreements in the Islamic courts, Christians and Jews protected themselves against potential challenges from Muslims to their deeds and claims. In such cases, especially when claims were not contested, it is easy to understand why non-Muslims frequented Islamic courts. It is much more difficult to explain why Jewish and Christian subjects of the empire chose Muslim courts for private community and personal matters that fell squarely under the jurisdiction of their own court systems. Historians of Jewish and Christian communities in the Ottoman Empire have not yet offered satisfactory solutions.[26]

Some scholars argue that it was rational for non-Muslims to go to Muslim court; others argue that in many localities non-Muslims did not have easy access to their own religious institutions. Others still focus on internal struggles within non-Muslim communities between religious leaders, determined to follow their own interests in maintaining the boundaries of the community, and subjects who had rebelliously resolved to seek their own advantage outside the community. I argue, once again, that when we examine actors' legal choices within a larger relational legal field, we can see that their actions were motivated not merely by free choice and rational interest. They reveal a response to internalized cultural messages that encouraged them to prefer their status as Ottoman subjects to their religious community loyalties, contributing, in effect, to imperial stability by affirming their belief that the imperial government dispensed religiously tolerant justice through its *kadi* courts. Non-Muslim actors evaluated the quality of justice in the *kadi* courts not only on the basis of their immediate advantage but also on the basis of their hegemonic "universality," a quality missing, by design, from their own community courts.

Among earlier studies of non-Muslims in the Islamic courts, Timur Kuran focuses on an economic argument to find that, until the eighteenth century,

Jews considered that they derived more benefit from using the Islamic legal notion of partnership even when their partners were Jewish, since the Islamic *mudaraba* offered advantages over the Talmudic *isqa* in matters of flexibility and risk management.[27] He also finds that Jews often incurred steeper costs (in fees and in litigation time) in their own courts than in the Islamic court. He not only explains why Jews used Muslim courts and Muslim economic practices up to the eighteenth century but also demonstrates that when it became more favorable to switch to European practices and make use of European consular courts after the eighteenth century, they eagerly did so. The intrusion of the Western legal system into an already plural legal order increased the choices non-Muslims had, giving them yet another opportunity—in this case, to register their business partnerships in Western contractual forms. In each instance, the non-Muslim economic actor chose the legal order that would maximize and protect economic rewards.[28] Muslims, by contrast, lacked the same privileges to use Western legal structures and faced, as a result, a disadvantage in trade. By means both of forum shopping in the early centuries of the Ottoman Empire and, in later centuries, of opportunities to use Western contracts, non-Muslims benefited from the fluidity in the empire's plural legal politics.

A different line of argument has focused on the social benefits of using Muslim courts. Christians, Bruce Masters finds, were likely to use Muslim courts to initiate divorce proceedings against their spouses. Christian women were particularly likely to use the Muslim courts to divorce their husbands. They did this most often by converting to Islam and then asking for divorce, although sometimes it was possible to proceed without conversion.[29] Najwa Al-Qattan, writing on eighteenth- and nineteenth-century Damascus, finds that Islamic courts were much more lenient than their Jewish or Orthodox Christian counterparts in marriage, divorce, and inheritance cases. Jewish women came to *shari'a* courts "to obtain a share of their patrimony, denied them in Jewish law."[30] Christians preferred Muslim dowry rules and divorce laws, while Jews preferred Muslim provisions for support after divorce and various other legal protections, and by choosing Muslim courts, these non-Muslim women obtained rights that were otherwise unavailable to them. Women chose to use Islamic courts for these proceedings even when, as in most of these cases, their husbands did not contest their claims. Rossitsa Gradeva tells us that "Christians never stopped turning to the *sheriat* courts for a wide range of cases, including those dealing with subjects that were the exclusive competence of the bishops. Indeed, sometimes it was the Christian clerics themselves who sought the intervention of the Ottoman authorities and the *kadi* court in the settlement of their relations with other Christians."[31]

Ronald Jennings finds, in his examination of sixteenth-century court records in Cyprus, no indication that Christians used their own courts, but the records show clearly their widespread use of Muslim courts.[32]

There is nothing controversial in following legal actors' calculations of economic and social benefits, but they need to be considered in the larger context of a relational legal field that expressly provided the flexibility and openness for members of non-Muslim communities to maneuver within it. This multilayered and complex legal field would not have worked without a particular understanding of the state, the court, and the actors embedded in it. In this social field, agency, cultural capital (a sort of knowledge of the different sets of law that comprised the system), and interests coincided to make the larger systemic ordering of different religious communities function smoothly. In the legal field, the state maintained its interest in interreligious peace and coexistence, claimed openness to non-Muslims and to various heterodoxies within Islam (at least initially), and claimed the traditional Islamic notion of justice as the cornerstone of its rule.[33]

The court remained the center for distributing justice and, as I emphasized earlier, was imbued with the symbolic power of the state as the representative of the state in the locality. The court maintained order and justice and, despite the discriminatory aspects of *shari'a*, implemented the law without regard for the religious identity of the subjects who stood before it. Al-Qattan even maintains that, according to the Hanafi School, the *kadis* were obligated to apply the law as if non-Muslim litigants were Muslim.[34] As we might expect, then, many studies of Islamic court rulings find that Jews and Christians often won cases against their Muslim opponents when they had cause and when they produced the appropriate evidence. Al-Qattan, once again, argues more generally that the Ottoman Empire's Muslim courts were known for their broad leveling effect and that their judges enjoyed the reputation of providing men and women from every background a fair hearing and a just decision even when they faced men, political elites, and the wealthy. That is, "the material in the *sijill* indicates that the court was not the arena for the practice of extra-legal or illegal discrimination, despite the *shari'a* theoretical discrimination, for example against *dhimmis* and women. Furthermore, the court often provided weaker individuals with legal protection against those who were tempted to use religion, gender or ignorance of the law to reap undue advantage."[35]

Although community leaders could relatively easily control intracommunity relations and conflicts, it was far more difficult to avoid the escalation of intercommunal struggles, especially between Christians and Jews, into unmistakable public cases once a conflict had begun. While Jews mostly preferred to live in Muslim neighborhoods and avoided Christian—especially Greek—locales for fear of abuse, relations between Jews and Christians were difficult to monitor and restrict in major cities like Salonica and Istanbul. In such places, relations were regulated by a highly stylized and controlled set of customs. For example, when a Christian and a Jew entered a relationship, especially in business, they eagerly applied to the Islamic court in order to register it, since this ensured that their transaction would be honored. Relations between these two non-Muslim communities were sometimes so tense that litigants were afraid of the consequences of using their own courts and, instead, sought impartial treatment in the Muslim courts.[36] Blood libels, when Jews were accused of using Christian blood to make their Passover bread, were merely one instance of conflicted relations between the two communities. Given the gravity of such accusations and their potential for violent conflict, Mehmed II had already issued a *ferman* asking the *kadıs* of the realm to refer such cases to the Divan, the imperial court. Despite the reissue of this *ferman*, local *kadis* preferred to keep such matters within their jurisdictions, perhaps in the belief that they were also fulfilling some sort of intercommunal policing function. The important point is that, more often than not, all the leaders concerned carefully monitored such cases to avoid a spiraling public confrontation. Such behavior on the part of rabbis and lay leaders in the Jewish community is especially evident in the Jewish community's rabbinical *responsa* literature.[37]

The *kadi*, as the representative of the state and of Ottoman Islam, had an interest in upholding state demands by deploying, in his judgments, the various legal traditions of the empire, combining religious and secular as well as local customary law to make sense of the context, the particular case, and a ruling appropriate to the situation. His task of balancing, and perhaps synthesizing, these systems of law also implied a duty to recognize instances where local punishments might be too harsh or too lenient and to defend the correct practice from the point of view of the Ottoman center. In seventeenth-century Bulgarian villages, for example, customary laws allowed routine physical abuse of spouses, whereas both ecclesiastical and, especially, *shari'a* courts considered abuse as grounds for divorce. Knowing this fact about both courts, abused wives among the Christians were nevertheless drawn to Islamic courts. The Muslim court's attraction was based on its message of power and domination but also on its practice of justice.[38] When ecclesiastical courts did not respond, litigants went to *kadi* courts as a way of exerting pressure on their own courts. Eirene, for example, a young woman who persistently asked for divorce from her husband because he beat her, was refused by the metropolitan and the clergy. She then obtained separation from her husband in the Ottoman court, but returned to the ecclesiastical court and finally succeeded in having her divorce recognized by the authorities in her own community.[39]

Within the relational field, the knowledge the *kadi* wielded by the nature of his position was impressively matched in the leaders of non-Muslim communities and the various litigants, who were often regular members of their communities. Contact between court systems bred knowledge. In each of the non-Muslim communities, the legal executives (rabbis, judges, or ecclesiastical court officials) were forced to study and become fully conversant with Ottoman law in order to make sure that the members of their communities did not commit offenses serious enough to harm relations between the communities and the authorities.[40] But litigants were also well-versed in the body of laws and the comparative advantages offered by different jurisdictions of the legal system, so that their choices were informed, as against Weber's characterization of *kadi* justice, with a measure of predictability.[41] Al-Qattan argues that the Damascus litigants, "by availing themselves of the courts in pursuit of personal interests . . . demonstrated an impressive knowledge of Islamic legal practice, an acceptance of shared cultural-legal norms, and a pragmatic outlook on marital and familial affairs."[42] In this way, the links in the legal order were much more intricate and complexly subordinated than a definition of legal pluralism that simply emphasizes parallel systems would suggest.

Furthermore, men and women, Muslims and non-Muslims came to the Islamic court on their own volition. Whether they were registering a deed, protecting their rights, initiating divorce proceedings, claiming their inheritance, or resolving a transaction that had turned sour, these men and women came to court to demand their rights. This tradition of making claims in the Islamic court was so important that subjects of the empire sometimes incurred serious hardship just to reach the court and make their demands known.[43] The symbolic justice of the court system encouraged strong individual decision making and concomitant action to attain goals. This appears even more significant when we consider the frequent cases of non-Muslims bringing their Muslim associates to *shari'a* courts for redress. There are many cases in which female relatives of deceased Christian and Jewish merchants brought their fathers' and husbands' Muslim trading partners to court in order to receive their fair share of an inheritance or business stake. That non-Muslim women did not feel threatened by coming to *shari'a* court to litigate against a member of the dominant group indicates that they assumed that the court would reliably render justice, but it also demonstrates the power of agency they possessed under the Ottoman legal system.

Non-Muslim religious leaders often provided the main opposition to the opportunities provided to members of their communities. The state employed legal pluralism as part of its arsenal to dominate non-Muslim communities by constructing a system that reflected Islam's openness to assimilation and conversion. The court, thanks to its prestigious local position and even-handed practice, was the conveyer belt for assimilation. Unsurprisingly, the Islamic court's attraction for non-Muslims was the bane of non-Muslim community leaders' existence. The tension between domination and autonomy in the Ottoman *millet* system was articulated in part in intracommunal struggles between religious leaders and their flock. Community leaders, especially religious authorities in their role as intermediaries between the Ottoman state and the non-Muslim peoples, had a keen interest in maintaining authority over their people and keeping their communities together. In many ways, this was a general phenomenon for indigenous religious leaders subjected to colonial domination. Benton highlights the degree to which the Muslim leadership of the Iberian Peninsula during the long Reconquista lacked tools for living under Christian subjugation, and shows the manner in which they adapted, while both their own positions and the status of Islamic law declined over time. The core contradiction in the legal field for leaders caught in this particular structural position requires them, as intermediaries, simultaneously to maintain their own community's law and to yield to the law of the imperial power.[44]

The religious hierarchy worked hard to maintain the *millet* boundaries set by the state, not only because it sustained itself through ecclesiastical taxes on its domains and their population but also because it saw the community's interests best preserved by the arrangement they had forged with the Ottoman state. Such leaders were always interested in maintaining a community of the faithful for financial as well as religious reasons. The literature attests to the fact that the most important struggles between patriarchs or rabbis and their constituencies were related to preserving the community's monopoly over its members' basic religious functions. For example, rabbis in numerous *responsas* demanded that Jews be married in Jewish court rather than in the *kadı* court; ecclesiastical courts struggled to maintain marriages that had been dissolved at the *kadı* court. The rabbis threatened, and the patriarchs excommunicated their people and prohibited them burial in Christian cemeteries.[45]

Religious leaders attempted to restrict their community members from using the dominant legal institutions of the country for many reasons. Both rabbis and patriarchs believed in the superiority of their indigenous laws. Rabbis wanted members to respect Jewish law; more importantly, they maintained restrictions in order to avoid decisions that contravened Jewish law. Rabbis voiced their fear of assimilation and conversion, since they felt that the more Jews resorted to the Islamic courts, the more likely they were to become assimilated. Rabbis often made concessions in an effort to keep their communities from disintegrating.[46] Shmuelevitz reports that rabbis in the Jewish courts often restricted Jewish litigants' access to the Islamic courts because they wanted to maintain the Jewish community's good reputation and were concerned to conceal intracommunity struggles that showed the community's uglier side. When infractions by Jews came to light, rabbis were unsure whether to report them to the authorities, since they feared both for the community and for the individuals involved. False accusations were also a significant object of fear, especially when the community as a whole was likely to suffer punishment on the basis of Jews' denunciations of one another in the *kadi* court. When a Jew harmed his own community in such a way, he was severely punished. Christian leaders must have shared this common strategy for survival by concealing intracommunity conflicts from a dominant foreign power. Furthermore, religious leaders simply sought to protect their people from the harsh conditions of Ottoman prisons.

In the Balkans, the representatives of official Orthodox Christian ecclesiastical law struggled to maintain predominance over popular law and, more importantly, over Islamic law. Metropolitan and Episcopal courts in the provinces, and the patriarchal court in Istanbul, worked hard to apply patriarchal law in Orthodox Christian communities. They not only believed in its sanctity but also abhorred interference from the conqueror's laws, especially in matters internal to the community, like family and inheritance law. The *kadi* court, for example, frequently approved a temporary type of marriage between Christian women and Muslim men, or even just between Christians. For the ecclesiastical courts, however, this form of marriage endangered not only individual Christian souls but the soul of the whole Christian community. Ecclesiastical courts imposed harsh penalties to keep these marriages from occurring.[47] Kermeli sees these struggles as part of a continuous struggle between the Church and the central administration: "On the one hand, the administration recognized the Church with limited judicial rights; on the other, it was not willing to limit the individual judicial freedom of its subjects to submit to the arbitration body of their choice."[48] In that sense, she says that the Church had no legal autonomy; legal autonomy was granted to the metropolitans by the sultans, without abrogating the rights of the local Ottoman powers.

That the leaders of these *millet* communities were struggling against Ottoman rule makes intuitive sense. Yet examining legal pluralism helps us see unmistakably some of the forms their struggles took. To the leadership, their people were slipping away and becoming assimilated into the dominant culture, threatening the dissolution of everything they believed in. To the members of the *millet* communities, it was only logical to adapt, to participate, to assimilate, and to make ample use of the resources provided by the dominant culture. For most of the history of Ottoman imperial domination, community leaders maintained religious and ethnic boundaries, although the opposing pressures to assimilate and convert were, perhaps unexpectedly, what made coexistence in separate communities viable.

With the European incursion in the eighteenth century and the influence of European contract law on the Ottoman legal system, the whole legal field began to shift, disrupting precisely the hegemonic cultural messages of the Ottoman court system. At the same time, a new world system of ideas was also spreading though Europe into the non-Muslim communities of the Ottoman Empire. The introduction of consular courts followed greater European-Ottoman commercial engagement and the development of larger and more intense relationships that demanded new forms of protection and negotiation. The earlier Ottoman openness expressed through Capitulations provided the initial set-up for increasing European penetration not only of trade, traders, and consuls but also of legal systems and, fatefully, new forms of ethnic and national self-understanding. European consular courts, among many other channels, helped introduce nationalist thinking into Ottoman society, injecting serious doubts, especially among non-Muslim subjects, about Ottoman "universalism" and Ottoman forms of domination and cultural hegemony. Accordingly, in choosing consular courts, non-Muslim actors not only looked after their economic interests but also began to conceive of their communities in more ethnic or national terms, outside of the *millet* system, and in relation to other states with affinities to their own "nations." The introduction of consular courts coincided with the rise of a new ethnic and national leadership from within the *millets*, prepared to oppose both the Ottoman rulers and the old leaders in their own religious communities, especially the old ecclesiastical and rabbinical leadership that resisted any change that would erode their positions of power.

Conclusion

Legal pluralism, then, functioned as long as jurisdictional forums were both open and available, but also required that religious leaders clearly maintain and monitor the boundaries of their communities. In this sense, legal pluralism operated in a social field where the tensions of living with difference were experienced at the level of non-Muslim communities between members who were pulled toward the dominant institutions of the state and community leaders who pulled them back toward their own jurisdictions. This tension operated where knowledge of the law and the court systems was widely shared and where state control played a key role. Pluralism offered space and flexibility for Ottoman subjects to engage in positive ways with the dominant state, while boundary maintenance through in-group policing kept contention from spilling beyond boundaries and, even more importantly for the state, kept cross-community struggles under control. Yet the most important conclusion about legal pluralism in the Ottoman Empire is that given the spread of a hegemonic cultural field, it was a successful tool for social management of diversity. It prevailed as long as state strategies to control and to build power relations gave up some domination at the level of the communities, but managed to reinforce hegemony by providing freedom of access to judicial institutions at the level of the individual.

This struggle is also embedded in modern cases of legal pluralism wherever community legal rights and individual rights to exit clash and will do so more as legal pluralism is extended. In contemporary nation-states where modern states strive for control by pushing a single official structure of laws, diverse local communities adjust by maintaining their own cultural and religious-legal identities and laws. In some cases the legal claims of certain religious minorities are already in place; in others they are not. In post-Ottoman Turkey, the secularization of law left similar pockets of Muslim law that communities use to fulfill their personal and communal requirements. As legal pluralism spreads, the issue will become increasingly one that was real in the Ottoman Empire but was managed by a strong state and a strong court system. That is, the ability for individual members of religious communities to exit and seek secular ruling in family and private matters will become harder.

NOTES

1. John Griffiths, "What Is Legal Pluralism?" *Journal of Legal Pluralism* 24 (1986): 5-8. Also cited in Sally Engle Merry, "Legal Pluralism," *Law & Society Review* 22, no. 5 (1988): 871.
2. Jane Burbank, "Rights, Courts, and Citizenship: Law and Belonging in the Russian Empire," prepared for workshop on "Citizenship, Nationality, and the State in Imperial Russia and the Soviet Union," Davis Center for Russian Studies, Harvard University, March 27-28, 2003, p. 4.
3. Haim Gerber, *State, Society, and Law in Islam: Ottoman Law in Comparative Perspective* (Albany: State University of New York Press, 1994); Rossitsa Gradeva, "Orthodox Christians in the Kadi Courts: The Practice of the Sofia Court, Seventeenth Century," *Islamic Law and Society* 4, no. 1 (1977): 37-69; Najwa Al-Qattan, "Litigants and Neighbors: The Communal Topography of Ottoman Damascus," *Comparative Studies in Society and History* 44, no. 3

(2002): 511-33; Najwa Al-Qattan. "Dhimmis in the Muslim Court: Legal Autonomy and Religious Discrimination," *International Journal of Middle East Studies* 31, no. 3 (1999): 429-44. These are just a sampling of relevant recent works. I will refer to others later in the chapter.

4. Pierre Bourdieu and Loic J. D. Wacquant, *An Invitation to Reflexive Sociology* (Chicago: University of Chicago Press, 1992), 94-96.
5. Pierre Bourdieu, Loic J. D. Wacquant, and Samar Farage, "Rethinking the State: Genesis and Structure of the Bureaucratic Field," *Sociological Theory* 12, no. 1 (March 1994): 4-5.
6. Lauren Benton, *Law and Colonial Cultures: Legal Regimes in World History, 1400-1900* (Cambridge: Cambridge University Press, 2002).
7. Ahmet Yaşar Ocak, "Islam in the Ottoman Empire: A Sociological Framework for a New Interpretation," *International Journal of Turkish Studies* (2003): 188.
8. Lauren Benton's analysis of Spanish domination in the Americas shows the clash between religious and secular law, the clash between the state and the Church, and the inability of the state to establish more effective jurisdiction over indigenous people.
9. Here, I wholeheartedly agree with Halil Berktay, who argues that the Western scholarly tradition and its followers have erroneously identified the Islamic tradition as the key component for explaining every aspect of the empire. See his "Studying 'Relations' or Studying Common Problems in Comparative Perspective," in Bartolomé Benassar and Robert Sauzet, eds., *Chrétiens et Musulmans à la Renaissance: Actes du 37e Colloque International du CESR* (Paris: Honoré Champion Editeur, 1998), 313-15.
10. Haim Gerber, *Islamic Law and Culture, 1600–1840*, Studies in Islamic Law and Society 9 (Leiden: Brill, 1999).
11. Ocak, "Islam in the Ottoman Empire," 189.
12. Gerber, *State, Society, and Law in Islam*, 63.
13. Serif Mardin, "Religion and Secularism in Turkey," in Ali Kazancıgil and Ergun Özbudun, eds., *Ataturk: Founder of a Modern State* (Hamden, CT: Archon Books, 1981), 192-95.
14. Max Weber, *Economy and Society* (Berkeley: University of California Press, 1968).
15. Halil Inalcik, *The Ottoman Empire: The Classical Age, 1300-1600* (New Rochelle, NY: Aristide Caratzas, 1973), 75.
16. The importance of religion would increase steadily after the seventeenth century, along with the rise of a class of connected and powerful religious leaders who believed in carving out an oppositional position vis-à-vis the state. Over time, reforming sultans would gain control once again over the religious establishment, bring in European law, and pave the way for the establishment in modern Turkey of a secular state.
17. Benjamin Braude and Bernard Lewis, eds., *Christians and Jews in the Ottoman Empire: The Functioning of a Plural Society* (New York: Holmes & Meier, 1982), 1-34; C. E. Bosworth, "The Concept of Dhimma in Early Islam," in *Christians and Jews in the Ottoman Empire*, 37-51; Bruce Masters, *Christians and Jews in the Ottoman Arab World: The Roots of Sectarianism* (Cambridge: Cambridge University Press, 2001), 17- 40.
18. Minna Rozen, *A History of the Jewish Community in Istanbul: The Formative Years, 1453–1566* (Leiden: Brill, 2002), 21.
19. Karen Barkey, *Empire of Difference: The Ottomans in Comparative Perspective* (Cambridge: Cambridge University Press, 2008).
20. James D. Fearon and David D. Laitin, "Explaining Interethnic Cooperation," *American Political Science Review* 90 (1996): 715–35.
21. Bernard Lewis, ed., *Islam*, vol. 2 (New York: Walker, 1974); Mark R. Cohen, *Under the Crescent and Cross: The Jews in the Middle Ages* (Princeton, NJ: Princeton University Press,

1994); Timur Kuran, "The Economic Ascent of the Middle East's Religious Minorities: The Role of Islamic Legal Pluralism," *Journal of Legal Studies* 33, no. 2 (June 2004): 475-515.

22. Abraham Marcus, *The Middle East on the Eve of Modernity: Aleppo in the Eighteenth Century* (New York: Columbia University Press, 1989), 107-8.
23. Aryeh Shmuelevitz, *The Jews of the Ottoman Empire in the Late Fifteenth and the Sixteenth Centuries: Administrative, Economic, Legal, and Social Relations as Reflected in the Responsa* (Leiden: Brill, 1984); Morris Goodblatt, *Jewish Life in Turkey in the XVIth Century as Reflected in the Legal Writings of Samuel de Medina* (New York: Jewish Theological Seminary of America, 1952).
24. N. J. Pantazopoulos, *Church and Law in the Balkan Peninsula during the Ottoman Rule*, Hidryma Meletōn Chersonēsou tou Haimou 92 (Thessaloniki: Institute for Balkan Studies, 1967); Peter Sugar, *Southeastern Europe under Ottoman Rule, 1354–1804* (Seattle: University of Washington Press, 1977).
25. Marcus, *The Middle East on the Eve of Modernity*, 108.
26. Joseph Hacker, "Jewish Autonomy in the Ottoman Empire: Its Scope and Limits; Jewish Courts from the Sixteenth to the Eighteenth Centuries," in Avigdor Levy, eds., *The Jews of the Ottoman Empire* (Princeton, NJ: Princeton University Press, 1994); Shmuelevitz, *The Jews of the Ottoman Empire.*
27. Kuran, "The Economic Ascent of the Middle East's Religious Minorities," 475-515.
28. Ibid.
29. Bruce Masters, *Christians and Jews in the Ottoman Arab World: The Roots of Sectarianism* (Cambridge: Cambridge University Press, 2001), 34-35.
30. Al-Qattan, "Dhimmis in the Muslim Court," 433.
31. Gradeva, "Orthodox Christians in the Kadi Courts," 46.
32. Ronald C. Jennings, *Christians and Muslims in Ottoman Cyprus and the Mediterranean World, 1571-1640* (New York: New York University Press, 1998).
33. Cornell Fleischer, "Royal Authority, Dynastic Cyclism, and 'Ibn Khaldunism' in Sixteenth-Century Ottoman Letters," *Journal of Asian and African Studies* 18, no. 3-4 (1983): 201.
34. Al-Qattan, "Dhimmis in the Muslim Court," 438.
35. Ibid., 436.
36. Ibid., 46.
37. Esther Benbassa and Aron Rodrigue, *Sephardi Jewry: A History of the Judeo-Spanish Community, 14th–20th Centuries* (Berkeley: University of California Press, 2000), 18.
38. This does not mean that there were no corrupt or ineffectual judges. We know there were numerous cases of corruption, since the people complained and the state took action to remove many corrupt individuals. Yet it must be acknowledged that, in many instances and in different regions of the empire, honest judges were doing their job. We should also admit, however, that we have no way of accounting for region-wide or empire-wide practices. See Ahmet Mumcu, *Osmanli Devletinde Rusvet* (Ankara, 1969) and Gerber, *State, Society, and Law.*
39. Eugenia Kermeli, "The Right to Choice: Ottoman Justice vis-à-vis Ecclesiastical and Communal Justice in the Balkans, Seventeenth–Nineteenth Centuries," in A. Christmann and R. Gleave, eds., *Studies in Islamic Law: A Festchrift to Colin Imber,* supplement 23, *Journal of Semitic Studies*, (September 2007): 165-210, in 190-91.
40. Shmuelevitz, *The Jews of the Ottoman Empire*, 38-40, reports that that the fifteenth- and sixteenth-century rabbis demonstrate in the *responsas* he read that they were fully conversant with secular and Islamic law.

41. Gerber, *State, Society, and Law*, 177.
42. Al-Qattan, "Dhimmis in the Muslim Court," 433.
43. Karen Barkey, *Bandits and Bureaucrats: The Ottoman Route to State Centralization* (Ithaca, NY: Cornell University Press, 1994).
44. Benton, *Law and Colonial Cultures*, 33-41.
45. The best sources on these disciplinary actions are Shmuelevitz for the Jewish community and Pantazopoulos for the Greek Orthodox community.
46. Shmuelevitz, *The Jews of the Ottoman Empire*, 68-69.
47. John C. Alexander, "Law of the Conqueror (The Ottoman State) and Law of the Conquered (The Orthodox Church): The Case of Marriage and Divorce," *International Congress of Historical Sciences* 16 (1985): 369-71.
48. Kermeli, "The Right to Choice," 176.

5

Reconstructing Early Modern Notions of Legal Pluralism

RICHARD J. ROSS AND PHILIP J. STERN

Early modern Europeans knew that they lived in a legally plural world.[1] But how exactly did they think about it? Our essay seeks to get at this question by reconstructing some of the ideological frameworks, vocabularies, and concepts that early modern Europeans used when defining what we might call "legal pluralism," advocating for it, or contesting it.

At the outset, it is important to distinguish among the various ways in which scholars have come to use the term "legal pluralism." "Weak" legal pluralism exists where there may be multiple institutions at the "central" level of government—such as a "constitutionalist" form of mixed government—or different jurisdictions for specific territories or social groups, which nonetheless remain more or less under the hierarchical supervision of a larger state or empire. Examples of this include the Ottoman *millet* system and twentieth-century European colonial regimes in India and Africa. Most early modern Europeans would have agreed that a wide range of jurisdictions—from towns to seigneurial fiefs to guilds to merchant associations and so forth—could exercise legal authority with the approval of the ruler, who empowered and limited them. Bodin, Hobbes, and other advocates of thoroughgoing state sovereignty and legal centralism accepted and expected this form of "weak" pluralism but remained apprehensive of it. By contrast, "strong" pluralism exists where multiple legal orders govern over common spaces or peoples yet are not part of a single, clearly hierarchical "system" under a coordinating authority.[2] This "strong" version of legal pluralism is our quarry. We want to know under what conditions, and why, some early modern theorists supposed that jurisdictions could exercise authority in their own right rather than as delegates of a superintending ruler?

Early modern Europeans wrote much about the powers and precedence of jurisdictions vis-à-vis competitors.[3] And they amply discussed the problem of overlapping jurisdictions, divisible sovereignty, and the interaction of public and private political authority. But unlike present-day scholars, they did not set out to write about "legal pluralism" per se. Nor have modern scholars tended to connect these discourses to the practices of early modern legal pluralism. Nonetheless, support for legal pluralism could be found in a range of early modern discussions that were *about* something else: for instance, in debates over the right of resistance, the divine right of rulers, and customs; in historical work on the ancient Jewish commonwealth; in theological disputes over which precepts "bind conscience"; in "jurisdictional" conceptions of the family as a "little commonwealth"; and in writings on political economy in a rapidly globalizing world.[4] While aiming at other objectives, each of these intellectual pursuits offered grounds, if sometimes tacitly or inadvertently, for justifying plural legal orders. Although early modern Europeans did not group these discourses under the rubric of "legal pluralism," they were frequently conjoined in practice. Resistance theorists drew on accounts of the ancient Republic of the Hebrews, political economists looked to the idea of the social contract, and so forth. Reconstructing the relationship of these discourses to the problem of early modern legal pluralism is the central ambition of our essay.

Examining these discussions challenges a history of early modern political thought that tends to focus on "centralizing" discourses, whether absolutist or constitutionalist, within a teleology of modern state formation. We also enrich a history of legal pluralism that is preoccupied less with its foundations in theory than with its origins in the messy pragmatisms of rule. Seen from this vantage point, the history of early modern legal pluralism is not simply about the tension between forward-looking centralizing theorists and resistant, pluralistic conditions "on the ground." It is, rather, a far more complicated debate in which one can find advocates for both pluralism and centralism, in theory and in practice, both often arising out of shared sets of questions and controversies.

I. Legal Pluralism in Early Modern Europe: Competing Narratives

Historians typically recognize that early modern European states maintained a marked degree of legal pluralism. Many European polities were "composite" states built out of jurisdictions with dissimilar constitutions and a multiplicity of legitimate governing institutions.[5] They enforced intricately detailed special law regimes of customs applicable to specific geographical areas and social statuses. Within and among these states were royal, local, ecclesiastical, and seigniorial jurisdictions exercising a variety of forms of law, which together produced a complexity that some contemporaries likened to a labyrinth. Since many of the essays in this volume explore the plural legal orders of overseas settlements, it is worth pausing to examine critically the underlying assumption of this work: that a generous legal pluralism characterized early modern European polities and that colonial and overseas encounters generated an even more complex and pluralistic legal order. We agree that this is true. But why it is true—and how contemporaries thought and theorized about it—is far more interesting than commonly supposed.

In an era marked by war, religious strife, and civil conflict, there was a growing discomfort among many early modern political theorists with Europe's medieval inheritance of polities that were flexible, composite, and legally plural. The period witnessed an efflorescence of writings advocating more centralized forms of sovereignty in which, as an ideal type, a state was "sovereign" if its authority was final and absolute, subject to no other human will, and entitled to supervise the institutions and groups contained within it.[6] This particular definition of sovereignty arose as a political ideal and guide to constitutional reform rather than as a description of lived experience in early modern Europe. Of course, as prescriptive rather than descriptive enterprises, these efforts to generate more monolithic notions of sovereign power were not themselves monolithic. Some thinkers insisted that sovereignty might reside only in a king, while others allowed it in either a king, an aristocracy, a popular assembly, or a compound state (mixing monarchy and representative institutions). Some saw monarchical power as divinely ordained; others saw it as deriving from some form of social compact. Some extended state sovereignty over the governance of the church, while others confined it to the civil realm so as not to unduly subordinate ecclesiastical to temporal jurisdiction. Despite the complexity of sovereignty theory and its divergence from actual political practice, historians looking for the intellectual origins of the modern legal centralism commonly find it in a line of late-sixteenth- and seventeenth-century thinkers running from Bodin through Suárez, Grotius, Hobbes, and Pufendorf. These figures tend to be treated as elaborating upon Bodin's famous portrait of the ideal early modern sovereign state—one containing a host of cities, inferior magistrates, colleges, and corporations, each enforcing diverse rules and customs, yet all subordinate to a ruler whose permission allowed them to exercise jurisdiction and whose laws and power limited the range of their acceptable activities.[7]

The practices of early modern states kept pace with this emerging theory. Crown institutions—such as Castilian *audiencias* and *corregidores*, and English justices of the peace and royal courts and commissions—curtailed or more intensely scrutinized municipal, occupational, and seigneurial jurisdictions. Monarchs issued far more edicts to regulate society from the center, developed standing bureaucracies and more intensive networks of revenue collection, encouraged reliance on Roman law, Crown tribunals, and learned lawyers, and pressed for codification or judicial pruning of customs—all of which decreased local variation in norms and procedures.[8] Post-Reformation confession building transferred jurisdiction over family life, education, and social welfare to state institutions and reduced the privileges of nobles, clerics, and cities in the name of religious uniformity.[9] Viewed from our modern world, early modern Europe may seem like a cacophony of pluralistic jurisdictions, but compared to just centuries earlier, what stands out is not the pluralism of early modern European states but all of these concerted attempts to diminish it.

This, however, is not the only story one might tell. There are two different ways of contesting this account that once again make early modern European legal pluralism appear generous. First, we can highlight the attributes of early modern European society that preserved and perhaps even expanded plural legal orders in the face of centralizing pressures. In this view, legal pluralism was not the dying remnants of something once more vital but an essential feature of the social organization of politics. The state was so dependent on provincial magnates, local notables, and corporations that its very operation assumed pluralism and, in certain ways, the expansion of its ambitions further entrenched pluralism. Although some officials such as French *intendants* owed their power to the Crown and served at its pleasure, most did not, from provincial and local estates and feudal lords to guilds and urban corporations. State endeavors commonly succeeded if they worked through rather than against these powerholders, who needed to be recruited into alliances with the Crown. Officials nominally under the king often did not behave as his servant out of a sense of aristocratic independence or because they supposed themselves irremovable except for cause. An increasing number bought their offices and obtained the right to pass these to heirs even if sacrificing the interests of the king to their own or to their community's advantage. Over the course of the seventeenth century, Castilian and French monarchs desperate for revenue accelerated the sale of offices and jurisdictions and committed the Crown to their protection. In order to obtain support on matters ranging from taxation and foreign affairs to religious and economic policy, kings took to granting magnates, cities, and estates further jurisdictional rights and legal privileges such as exemptions from the law of the realm through the use of special customs. The political logic of centralizing states thus left monarchs with little choice but to protect, and in places enhance, some measure of jurisdictional pluralism (even while, elsewhere on the balance sheet, Crown councils and tribunals more intensely scrutinized seigneurial and municipal jurisdictions and customary law).[10] When centralization did happen, it was often not a top-down enterprise but rather an unintended consequence of localities drawing on central authority for their own particular purposes, which could at the same time further solidify jurisdictional diversity.[11] In this view, pluralism was not merely a vulnerable inheritance. It was a political foundation of "centralizing" states, a currency traded for a political or economic *quid pro quo*.

Another strategy for emphasizing the robustness of early modern pluralism is to focus not on practice but, as we do, on ideology. Historians of political thought preoccupied with the rise of the modern state have lavished attention on discourses of sovereignty and its more thoroughgoing variant of "absolutism"—the power of rulers to be "absolved" from obedience to human law and institutional restraints. The frequent invocation of Bodin, Suárez, Grotius, Hobbes, and Pufendorf as the founding theorists of sovereignty and legal centralism creates the impression that pluralistic thinking was impoverished or on the wane. But workaday legal pluralism did not struggle against a predominantly hostile intellectual climate. Many discourses supported pluralism. And the most emphatic theorists of a powerful singular sovereign were often responding to intellectual projects that valorized pluralism, and even at times left space in their own work for pluralistic understandings of the polity.

II. Ways of Talking about Legal Pluralism in Early Modern Europe

A. Civic Pluralism: Contract Theory, Right of Resistance, and Custom

Early modern theorists of sovereignty commonly emphasized a downward-flowing model of authority. Magistrates received jurisdiction not from their community but from the "fountain" of the king. They were his "servants" in that they followed his policies and operated within his administrative structure, even if he did not typically intervene in ordinary judicature.[12] But some key bodies of early modern political thought on the origins and limits of political and legal authority—those concerning the right of resistance, the compact theory of the state, the divine empowerment of inferior magistrates, and popular validation of customs—could be configured to deny the downward flowing model of authority intrinsic to legal centralism. Historians have typically read texts on these matters in order to understand, say, the relationship between religious and political thought or the repertoire of arguments for limiting kingship or dividing government at its center. Entering from another direction, we will explore how these bodies of thought upheld forms of legal pluralism.

Medieval and early modern jurists and theologians widely assumed that in the distant past the people enjoyed a sovereign power out of which emerged the state and the authority of the ruler. But on what terms? Sovereignty theories in the tradition of Bodin contended that the people had fully and unconditionally alienated its power to the ruler, making him the master of the state and of lesser jurisdictions within it. In opposition, those wishing to restrain the ruler, such as Hugo Grotius, held that the people through a long-distant compact had not alienated power but had delegated it to the commonwealth subject to conditions.[13] The people as a whole stood above the ruler, who for all his dignity and power served as the "minister" of the state rather than its master. Some pushed these premises far enough to infer a right of resistance. The sixteenth-century Huguenot theorists Theodore Beza and Philippe du Plessis Mornay were among the most prominent, writing amid continuous French religious conflict that invited royal overreaching. They reasoned that the people could correct and, in extreme cases, remove their ruler if he violated divine and natural precepts or the laws that his predecessors agreed to respect in the compact that established their authority. However, it was not the people, as individuals, who should raise their hand against their king; this would have invited anarchy. Rather, they must act collectively through the magistrates of the kingdom, provinces, and towns, who represented them.[14] By emphasizing the role of magistrates and their jurisdictions rather than the people *per se*, such arguments implicitly built a case for legal pluralism.

The Huguenots expanded upon Calvin, who allowed resistance by inferior magistrates only when a polity gave them explicit constitutional permission, as with the ephors of Sparta and the tribunes of the Roman republic.[15] Beza and de Mornay generalized this right of resistance to vest it in all magistrates empowered to command in war and administer justice, from nobles and patricians to elected officers of towns and members of diets and parliaments. There was thus a vision of popular resistance to monarchy that comprehended corporate groups or local officials as the proper venue for action. But if these officials were not specifically authorized by the realm's constitution to restrain the ruler in the manner of tribunes and ephors, what was their warrant? The Huguenot theorists contended that the authority of lesser magistrates did not flow downward from the king but upward from the people through the compact that established the commonwealth. Inferior magistrates served the kingdom rather than the king and held their jurisdictions, in Beza's words, "not of the sovereign but of the sovereignty."[16] In order to protect the people and the compact against violations by the king, they needed to scrutinize him free of his oversight. Mornay's *Vindiciae Contra Tyrannos* (1579) at several points likened inferior magistrates to "judges" of the king "who are obliged to pass judgment on him according to the law."[17] Since magistrates might disagree with each other, selected duchies or towns might resist the king, while others did not. The legalistic metaphors of "judgment" along with the centrifugal possibilities in the right of resistance led to support for legal pluralism. This was, in theory, a legal regime where lesser magistrates reached legal conclusions in contradiction to the king and even to each other and where they exercised authority in their own right rather than as controllable delegates of the Crown.[18] Although Huguenots expected only occasional resistance, their system depended on continual scrutiny by numerous jurisdictions of the king's fidelity to law.

Certain variants of social contract theory reinforced this notion. The more famous and common accounts of the passage from state of nature to a commonwealth ended with ruler sovereignty and legal centralism, not pluralism. These depicted a compact or series of compacts by which individuals or families in the state of nature formed a polity and alienated their sovereignty to a ruler in a process managed by natural law. After the creation of the state, only the family and commonwealth retained their honored status as entities grounded in natural law. Villages, corporations, and lower jurisdictions were seen as creatures of positive law rather than of nature.[19] The commonwealth allowed them jurisdiction as its sufferance and regulated them to avoid *imperium in imperio*, or "state within a state."[20] In opposition to this position was German Calvinist jurist Johannes Althusius, whose prominent alternative reading of state formation brought out its pluralist and constitutionalist possibilities. Althusius's *Politica* (1604) and the writers influenced by him depicted the commonwealth as emerging from the association of lesser political and social units through a progression of compacts of ever greater scope. Families contracted to form local communities and fellowships (autonomous corporate bodies with privileges of self-government, such as guilds or associations of clergy). Fellowships, villages, and towns fashioned provinces, which in turn created the commonwealth. The compact of union that fashioned the state bound together not individuals, as was the case with conventional accounts of ruler sovereignty, but lower units.

In one sense, Althusius was a right of resistance theorist who shared common ground with the Huguenots Beza and Mornay. Yet Althusius's ideal state went even further in offering support to legal pluralism. His estates, elders, patricians, and electors, like the lesser magistrates of Beza and Mornay, could exercise legal judgment independent of the ruler and of each other when assessing whether the "supreme magistrate" had so exceeded his just authority as to provoke nullification of his orders, armed resistance, or secession of provinces or cities from the realm.[21] Yet Althusius's "ephors" would make their judgments within a bottom-up, natural-law-associational state dissimilar from the kingdom assumed by the Huguenots. For all the importance of the Huguenots' lesser magistrates as initiators of resistance, they did not themselves form the commonwealth; they served it. By contrast, Althusius's families, fellowships, villages, towns, and provinces were the progenitors of the state rather than its subordinates.[22] These lower units ceded only such powers as were necessary for the existence of higher associations, otherwise retaining their independent authority and jurisdiction. They administered their own "special laws" as a matter of right, albeit within boundaries established by the compacts creating the commonwealth. The sovereignty that Althusius's ideal polity kept ever among the people was, in practice, shared among the higher and lower associations in a system of plural rule.[23] As a result, legal pluralism was not just the foundation of a Huguenot-style right of resistance to be invoked in exceptional times. Rather, it served as a core constitutive principle of the state, visible in its daily routines.

A third way to support legal pluralism was to contest the assumption that God upheld more absolutist forms of sovereignty. Divine right theorists, drawing on the New Testament's declaration that the "powers that be are ordained of God" (Romans 13:1), contended that rulers obtained their authority directly from the Lord. As a result, sovereigns were not answerable to the church, the estates and nobility of the realm, or their people.[24] Inferior magistrates exercised only such limited, revocable, and supervised jurisdiction as their divinely empowered sovereign allowed them in a legally centralist state. In opposition, those who would restrict the sovereign ruler and sustain legal pluralism advanced a contrary interpretation of Romans 13. Did not lesser magistrates stand alongside rulers as "powers" that were "ordained of God"? And if their authority came directly from the Lord rather than as a concession from the sovereign, were they not entitled to reach legal conclusions opposed to the ruler and, in extreme cases, to resist him? Like the argument from popular sovereignty and political compacts, this interpretation of Romans 13 led to a pluralistic conclusion. Both strategies cast inferior magistrates as more than the mere delegates of the ruler by connecting their right of contrary legal judgment and resistance to the original source of authority in the commonwealth. But the theocratic approach identified that source as God rather than the community.[25] In this formulation, it was the magistrate's conscience rather than the original compact between the people and their ruler that determined just rule. Consider in this respect Scottish presbyterian Samuel Rutherford's *Lex, Rex* (1644), published to justify opposition to the high royalism of Charles I in the early stages of the English Civil War. Kings, Rutherford admitted, exceeded inferior magistrates in dignity and appointed them to office. Notwithstanding this "external call," judges were no less "the immediate vicars of God than the king." For subjects, the "resisting of the inferior magistrate in his lawful commandments is the resisting of God's ordinance." And both the king and magistrate must, upon God's command, follow their consciences in judicature. Because "judging is an act of conscience, as one man's conscience cannot properly be a deputy for another man's conscience, so neither can an inferior judge . . . be a deputy for a king." The magistrate does not impose sentence at the behest of the king. The "judgment is God's" (Deut. 1:17). As agents of the Lord, the king and judge differ by "more and less only," not by "nature" or "essence."[26] Rutherford's formulations at once denied the ruler his pretensions of being the supreme, final interpreter of law and secured lesser magistrates a divinely empowered jurisdiction in their own right.

Custom provided a fourth foundation for legal pluralism. To be sure, prescription could be domesticated within a legal centralist framework. Bodin insisted that a custom "has no force but by sufferance, and so long as it pleases the sovereign prince."[27] The Bodinian sovereign expected the villages and trades of his commonwealth to live by a wide variety of usages provided that none threatened to constrain him against his will and each drew its power to bind as law not from the people who created it but from the approval of the Crown. Yet these commitments came under strain when applied to a working early modern European legal system. Because the king's officials and judges could never actually know, let alone endorse, the thousands of evolving customs particular to localities and occupations, systems of legal theory that began with Bodin's pronouncements inadvertently drifted towards a *de facto* pluralism. Francisco Suárez's *De Legibus* (1612), for example, asserted forthrightly that the authority of the prince "is necessary to give force" to a custom.[28] The monarch may revoke customs and prohibit their introduction.[29] But as Suárez amplified the principles for recognizing and validating custom in a nearly hundred-page-long chapter on the subject, the qualifications and exceptions began. The consent of a king was irrelevant in a popular commonwealth where the people possess "supreme legislative authority." Here the "sovereign is the whole commonwealth, and so, if a custom is accepted by such a people, the consent is necessarily given by the sovereign, since in this case the two are identical."[30] In a monarchal state, the king need not give actual consent to customs; a "tacit" permission sufficed.[31] Suárez stretched the meaning of "tacit" to make royal concurrence ever more distant and nominal. The monarch's consent might take the form of silence, as when he knows of a custom and "does not check it." Or he might enact "a law to the effect that a custom which contains such and such conditions shall be valid."[32] Cities, merchant communities, and other organizations might receive preapproval to form customs. This permission would be "continuously available" so that the "prince need not have particular knowledge of a custom" introduced in the future.[33] Since it was "practically impossible that all customs should come to the knowledge of the prince," Suárez insisted on the legal validity of reasonable usages that lasted through the prescriptive period without ever coming to the attention of the monarch or his officials.[34] The king could later nullify such customs, should he ever hear of them. Complicating the picture further, Suárez acknowledged that changed circumstances could, unbeknownst to the king, alter the terms of customs or eliminate them entirely.[35]

But those who wished to regulate social life and empower jurisdictions without or against the ruler's approval needed more than the extensive *de facto* legal pluralism that theorists like Suárez allowed in the wide, dark shadow of tacit consent. The identification of custom with the "will of the people" in English common law and Continental Roman/civil law and in popular politics provided them with a strong foundation for a pluralistic theory of custom.[36] But this commonplace could make custom support legal pluralism for a variety of reasons depending on the prevailing legitimation of political authority. To begin with, suppose one assumed that an originally sovereign people had in the distant past transferred power to a ruler and his successors. Did they thus alienate their power to authorize customs? Suárez recognized that the people could "give force and efficacy" to their own customs "while they still retained the sovereign power." But once they "handed over that power to the prince, the force of custom will mainly depend upon his consent."[37] To be sure, Suárez admitted, other writers objected that "when the people transferred their power to the prince, they did not give it up entirely, but . . . surrendered it . . . in such a way as always to reserve to themselves the power of introducing customs."[38] And here was the crucial point: what were the conditions of this long-ago compact? Political writers who acknowledged the theoretical possibility that the people in a given polity might have surrendered the power to authorize custom commonly insisted that their ancestors had retained this privilege in their ancient contract establishing government. Richard Hooker observed in the *Laws of Ecclesiastical Polity* that monarchies "which were first instituted by agreement" arose from "articles of compact . . . clean worn out of knowledge." Nonetheless, some of the terms could be inferred. As he and John Selden insisted, the current constitution of a country, its laws and usages, bore the trace of the compact that established the polity.[39] The king of England was no Bodinian sovereign validating customs by his will since their polity respected the binding force of immemorial custom upon the Crown. In sixteenth- and early-seventeenth-century France, the Crown represented by lawyers engaged in a series of negotiations with the assemblies of particular towns and provinces in order to redact and publish custumals. Donald Kelley has likened this century-long process to "a kind of ceremonial reenactment of the original social compact."[40] The people's power to authorize customs—and the resulting legal pluralism—could be defended as a surviving remnant of their ancestors' original sovereignty.

Even a sovereign, by right of conquest rather than compact, could be limited from below by custom, as it evolved over time. A monarch who took power through conquest enjoyed plenary power to impose law by his will.[41] He made no compact with an originally sovereign people, who therefore could not claim a continuing right to validate customs. But that right could evolve, ironically, through custom itself. Hooker argued that the slow accretion of laws and customs collectively constitute an "after-agreement" that limits royal power "in kingdoms . . . whose ancient predecessors were by violence and force made subject."[42] Edward Coke believed that William I conquered England in 1066 but chose not to alter fundamentally its law. But imagine if William's successors had desired to rule by fiat. In Johann Sommerville's interpretation of Coke, the jurist contended that "in the course of time absolute rule became subject to *customary* limitations."[43] The people's right to validate customs, although denied by the subjugation of conquest, could later emerge through the long-standing exercise and tacit acceptance of the practice. And what of God? Kings who looked to the Lord as the source of their power neither necessarily extinguished nor supported the people's privilege of binding monarchs through custom. Absolutists read the divine right of the king as grounds for loosening him from the restraints of law and custom and making their validity dependent on his will. But an alternative, "community-centered" view assumed that God empowered government in general, but human societies determined the state's particular form and its ground rules for making law and validating custom. Coke saw no contradiction in celebrating the power of the judiciary to pronounce the common customs of the realm that constrained an unwilling king, while simultaneously glorifying that king as the "Lord's anointed" under "God and none other."[44] Opponents of overreaching Stuart royal power in the 1640s insisted that Romans 13 created no obstacle to the people of England's power to create customs that limited the sovereignty of the Crown.[45] Indeed, as Conrad Russell observed, jurists who stressed the consonance of the common law with God's precepts elevated the realm's common customs so they enjoyed a "divine right of the law."[46]

Whatever the theoretical basis for them, customs that could bind a commonwealth without the Crown's approval profoundly supported legal pluralism. Customs did more than provide rules governing private conduct in localities and trades—creating rights to take firewood from a forest or procedures for resolving miners' and merchants' disputes. More deeply, basic rules of government and numerous jurisdictions crisscrossing early modern states emerged through prescription rather than through the positive enactment of monarchs or meetings of the estates. In late-sixteenth- and seventeenth-century France, many legal theorists pointed to custom as the source of "fundamental laws" limiting the king's power to alienate territories of the realm or devise the Crown to females.[47] English lawyers and politicians outside of high royalist circles went further. For them custom served as the foundation not only of numerous urban corporations and manorial, seigniorial, and commercial courts but of the "courses" of royal tribunals and the privileges of Parliament. Matthew Hale believed that the common law, itself the general custom of the realm, gave to the rules and governmental institutions arising from custom "the force and efficacy of their obligation."[48] As early modern rulers drew on discourses of sovereignty, divine right, and contract to justify programs of political centralization and legal uniformity, advocates for the rights of the estates and for group, local, and corporate interests reinterpreted custom to meet these new ideological challenges. They made it a better theorized resource for upholding a plural legal order.

B. Godly Pluralism: Laws "Binding in Conscience" and the Republic of the Hebrews

If a foundation for pluralism could be found in a reinterpretation of compact, custom, and popular sovereignty, so too could it be located in that other great exemplar for politics and law: the Bible. Consider once more, but from another angle, Romans 13. The fifth verse of that chapter commands obedience to law "not only for wrath, but also for conscience sake." Catholics and Protestants alike interpreted the verse to mean that disobedience to divine precepts and to some, but not all, human laws imperiled the soul in the afterlife. A substantial early modern theological/juristic literature arose explaining how to tell the difference between ordinances that merely imposed a penalty on earth ("penal laws") and those that bound conscience so as to put the soul at risk in case of violation.[49] The Catholic Thomist variant of this tradition, more elaborate than its Protestant cousin, laid out an especially formidable array of categories and distinctions to guide the uncertain Christian. Laws imposed by human rulers obligated conscience only if they were "just," a concept defined in various ways.[50] Violation of a just law, if unrepented, constituted either a mortal sin (threatening damnation) or a venial sin (bringing a term in purgatory).[51] A complicated set of tests distinguished one from the other. To know the difference between mortal and venial sins, theologians and jurists looked to the inherent gravity of the offense and the circumstances under which it was committed; the cardinal virtues harmed by the misdeed; the subjective intent of the legislator (Did he mean his ordinance to offer "counsel" or to obligate as a "true law"?); and the subjective intent of the wrongdoer (Did he or she act out of heedlessness or contempt?).[52] Dozens of treatises, Catholic and Protestant, applied their respective frameworks to particular cases. They earnestly discussed the extent to which conscience was bound by laws that, say, laid taxes or fixed prices,[53] imposed such severe burdens as to threaten livelihood and life,[54] or appeared to lapse on account of desuetude, contrary custom, or a new ruler's interpretive fancies.[55] And on and on.

European learning on binding in conscience became further complicated in the New World through engagement with indigenous peoples and the innovations of colonial governance. Juan de Solórzano Pereira's *Política Indiana* (1648), for example, asked under what conditions the policies of the Spanish empire—the reduction of Indians into towns, the conduct of *visitas* and *residencias*, and the collection of customs—implicated the "*fuero* [jurisdictional competence] of conscience" as well as temporal jurisdictions.[56] Solórzano Pereira, like any number of treatise writers in Europe, contributed to the creation of a map of legal pluralism. They discussed conscience in jurisdictional language. They disputed whether the internal *fuero* of conscience or merely the external *fuero* of secular governance had jurisdiction over given behaviors. And they quarreled about which precepts were merely counsels or penal laws leaving conscience unaffected, and which entered into the jurisdiction of conscience and bound it under penalty of venial or mortal sin. Beyond the conflict of ecclesiastical and state jurisdictions that underlay early modern plural orders was an additional, often overlooked, layer of pluralism generated by the highly disputed relation of law(s) to the afterlife. This was a layer of vital importance to early modern Christians.

Turning to biblical history, Christian Hebraists' efforts to reconstruct the ancient "Republic of the Hebrews" offered yet another potential justification for pluralistic authority within a state. From the mid-sixteenth-century forward, a series of Christian scholars began writing histories of Israelite society and government, capitalizing on greater familiarity with Hebrew and with Jewish sources from Josephus and the Talmud through Maimonides and rabbinic commentaries. Some surveyed the ancient Jewish past from Abraham through the destruction of the Second Temple. Others deployed selected episodes to advance political programs. Far more than their medieval predecessors, the early modern Christian Hebraists drew on the Hebrew Bible as a resource in legal and political disputes. They "secularized" ancient Jewish history in the restricted sense that they described the Hebrews' government and law with the same categories deployed to analyze contemporary and classical "profane" states.[57] Surveying the changing division of power among the Israelite tribes, cities, judges, prophets, kings, captains, and Sanhedrin, the Christian Hebraists asked questions whose answers could be crafted in terms familiar to early modern political analysts. What was the relationship of the "civil" and "ecclesiastical" realms in the Republic of the Hebrews? Was that state best described as a monarchy, aristocracy, democracy, or mixed government? Did its tribal and local jurisdictions rule by right or through the concession of their superiors?

If the ancient Israelites could now be placed next to their Greek, Roman, and Egyptian neighbors and beside contemporary polities for the purposes of political comparison, there was one crucial difference. The Hebrews lived in the only commonwealth designed personally by God. Grotius, Hobbes, and other early modern intellectuals echoed first-century Jewish historian Josephus's depiction of ancient Israel as a "theocracy," a polity where the Lord ruled as king and legislator.[58] Christian Hebraists commonly described the Jews' commonwealth, before its corruptions in its final stages, as the "best" or "highest" state.[59] To be sure, contemporary Christians were not bound by the Israelites' institutions and legal system.[60] Yet these carried a touch of God's authority, particularly among biblically minded political elites in the Netherlands and England and among advanced Protestants. The Israelite commonwealth became a polemical resource as controversialists held it up as an ideal in a wide range of disputes over issues as various as republicanism, land reform, tithes, the right of resistance, and church governance.

When it came to legal pluralism, biblical history and law as usual allowed conflicting readings. A legal centralist could cite scripture for his purpose. Bodin described the ancient Israelite commonwealth as a monarchy governed first by Moses, then by captains under the "grace of God," and, after Saul, by a series of Jewish and foreign kings. Against Josephus's influential depiction of the Sanhedrin as an "aristocratical government," Bodin contended that it "had no sovereign power and it was no optimacy." Diminishing its role left behind a monarchical sovereign, a suitable precedent for Bodin's ideal state.[61] Hobbes viewed Moses as the first sovereign prince of Israel. Like all princes, Moses' authority "must be grounded on the consent of the people." In a strained interpretation of Exodus 20:18-19, Hobbes perceived the Israelites, unnerved by the thunder and lightning raging upon Sinai, promising obedience to Moses. As founder of the commonwealth, Moses "needs have sovereign power" over both civil and ecclesiastical affairs, an authority not divided with "Aaron, nor the people, nor any aristocracy of the chief princes." A holy leviathan arose in the shadow of Sinai. Its unchallenged sovereignty, established by compact, descended to a succession of high priests and, later, kings.[62]

Few readings of the Hebrew commonwealth found legal centralism in such a stark fashion. More commonly, scholars acknowledged the significant jurisdictional differentiation in ancient Israel. The work of Lancelot Andrewes, Peter Cunaeus, Thomas Goodwin, Hugo Grotius, James Harrington, Moses Lowman, and Carlo Sigonio provide a composite picture of the situation before the Babylonian captivity.[63] Sigonio aptly summarized the common observation that the "government of the Hebrews was in a sense divided into three parts. The first was composed of the entire people, that is, the twelve tribes; the second, of the individual tribes themselves; and the third, of the individual towns within each of the tribes." The Israelite state at the national level split legislative and judicial power among a people's assembly, the elders (or Sanhedrin), and a principal ruler (the judge in the years between Joshua and Saul and, later, the kings or high priests). The Sanhedrin legislated in both the civil and religious realms and interpreted all laws; offered pardons; consented to taxes; chose or acclaimed kings; called the people's assembly into session; judged false prophets; and exercised appellate jurisdiction over all lower tribunals. The high priest oversaw hierarchically organized lower orders of lesser priests and Levites. Each tribe was led by a phylarch who commanded its military and supervised a tribal judiciary. He and the heads of families of his tribe formed a council (or senate). Each major town had its "own senate, which decided matters that were especially important to the community" and appointed urban courts.[64] The federalist division of authority among the towns, tribes, and Israelite state, and the distribution of power among the ruler, senate/council, and courts within each layer, could be portrayed in a legal centralist light. Grotius insisted that the Sanhedrin was "endowed with the supreme power to administer the republic and that all other civil authorities were subservient to it and, as it were, derived from it."[65]

Yet the marked jurisdictional differentiation in God's commonwealth could as easily lead to pluralist conclusions. Early modern right of resistance theorists took this the furthest. They envisioned tribal chiefs and the seventy elders of the Sanhedrin as "ephors" empowered to restrain and, if necessary, remove kings who strayed from the terms of the covenant between God and the people and rulers of Israel. Some of the rebellions and usurpations depicted in the Old Testament could be interpreted in this spirit.[66] Resistance, which presupposed that elders and tribal chiefs might judge the ruler and each other, was an extreme form of pluralism. The more typical inference was that the Republic of Hebrews created multiple jurisdictions with uncertain boundaries and unclear divisions of responsibility, which invited clashes among authorities and allowed creative manipulation. Consider: kings could not direct the sentences of lower court magistrates, who could judge as they wished, barring corruption or ignorance. Nor could kings remove cases from the Sanhedrin. Inferior magistrates judged on behalf of the Lord, not in the service of kings or the Sanhedrin, despite its appellate jurisdiction.[67] The regular tribunals from cities up through tribes and the Sanhedrin had no monopoly on providing justice. Prophets rode circuit and held assizes.[68] The assembly (or "congregation") of Israel irregularly exercised criminal and civil jurisdiction.[69] Kings judged the people alone or, at their discretion, in combination with elders and priests.[70] The interpretation of religious law and the management of sacred rites was split ambiguously among kings, priests, and the Sanhedrin.[71] The Hebrew constitution provided opportunities for forum shopping. Jethro, in order to relieve Moses of some burdens of government, advised him to send routine judicial cases to rulers of thousands, hundreds, fifties, and tens. Lowman speculated that the system gave "persons liberty to choose before whom their cause should be heard" so that they might be "satisfied in choosing their own judge."[72] In the mature judicial system of the settled land of Israel, litigants could not insist, by right, that judges in their town hear their case. They approached the chief judge in the city with their dispute, who might introduce it to the court or send the petitioner to another, nearby town. If refused there, the litigant might seek justice in the lower courts of Jerusalem or, if necessary, at the Sanhedrin itself. Jewish sources explained this procedure as a way for judges to turn away disputes raising legal issues so complicated or obscure as to exceed their learning. But as recounted in bare form by the Christian Hebraists, the system offered no little possibility for tactical manipulation by judges and litigants alike.[73] For all of Grotius's assurances about the superintending authority of the Sanhedrin, the federalist division among the towns, tribes, and central state and the simultaneous vesting of administrative and juridical authority in rulers, councils, and judges at each level suggested that the collisions among plural jurisdictions in the turbulent Hebrew commonwealth were no less frequent than in the polities of early modern European states.

Several Christian Hebraist authors insisted that a single sovereign did not rule over the Republic of the Hebrews. But they disagreed on why. Some explicitly divided sovereignty. For Rutherford, kings were the head of the commonwealth, but the phylarchs and fathers of the leading tribal families were "parts of the head."[74] Harrington split sovereign power among the Sanhedrin and representatives of the people of Israel (the "congregation of the Lord").[75] Baruch Spinoza, an excommunicated Jew writing in dialogue with the Christian Hebraists, contended that "after Moses' death no one exercised all the functions of a sovereign. The management of affairs was not entirely in the hands of one man, or one council, or the people." The tribes divided oversight of public business, he concluded, obscurely.[76] More radically, Moses Lowman made (human) sovereignty an inapplicable concept in the Hebrew commonwealth. For Bodin and those in his debt, the essence of sovereignty was the power to make law without the consent of another ruler.[77] But this "was a right Jehovah reserved to himself." God insisted that no human ruler could add to or diminish from the precepts he revealed to the Jews (Deut. 12:32). Though the rulers of Israel might make "by-laws," they lacked the "proper legislative authority" that was the essence of sovereignty.[78]

Further complicating the uncertain sovereignty and jurisdictional tangle of the Hebrew commonwealth were the prophets. Spinoza ingeniously laid out how they served as both a check on rulers and a source of acute political confusion. Appearing intermittently, prophets could win the "supreme right to command in the name of God" if the commonwealth accepted their claim to represent the will of the Lord. But such judgments were uncertain and a touch opportunistic. If "the people were oppressed, such prophets could easily gain support, and by signs of no great significance they could convince the people of whatever they wished. On the other hand, if the government were properly conducted," the ruler would have little difficulty in executing the would-be prophet as a pretender. Recalling how Samuel had transferred the right to rule from Saul to David, kings regarded prophets as, potentially, an "empire within their empire."[79] God, architect of the Republic of the Hebrews, had set up a commonwealth where overlapping jurisdictions exercising power in their own right rather than at the sufferance of an earthly sovereign intermittently experienced challenges to their normal rivalries by the totalistic claims of prophets who may or may not speak for heaven. All of this left the impression that the Lord was no Bodinian.

C. Oikonomic Pluralism: The Family and Political Economy

If the Republic of the Hebrews was one model for good government and political authority, the well-managed family was another. Early modern theorists commonly drew on the classical Greek notion of *oikonomia*, or prudent housekeeping, to link two ideas usually separated in the modern world: management of the family and its economy, and stewardship of the commonwealth's production and commerce.

Contemporary social theorists creating models of pluralism have spent much time debating whether the family should be regarded as a lawmaking entity.[80] Historians of plural legal orders in early modern Europe and its overseas empires tend to give the family little space in their portraits of colliding legislators and jurisdictions. But early modern discussions of the household could support pluralism insofar as the family was analogized to a jurisdiction or form of government. To be sure, some theorists limited the metaphor by pointing out the family's limited scope of competence in comparison to the state. The family was, to Suárez, an "imperfect community" lacking the Aristotelian ideal of self-sufficiency. The wife, children, and servants stood as inferiors of the paterfamilias rather than as agents who united to compose a political body.[81] And as English bishop Robert Sanderson pointed out, the father's "mastership" neither extended to the wider community nor included the power to kill, banish, or imprison.[82] Yet with these limitations in mind, jurists and divines continually likened the family to a "little commonwealth" and the father to the head of a "government" enjoying "coercive power" and "legislative" authority. Sanderson asserted that the "command of a father is as much a rule of action to the son as the law of a ruler is to the subject."[83] His nonconformist contemporary Richard Baxter added that as "the several justices in the counties do govern as officers of the king, so every magistrate and master of the family do govern as an officer of God."[84] This notion of the family as a kind of jurisdiction mattered greatly in an early modern world where the household head mediated between the polity and his dependents (wife, children, apprentices, and servants), who had little direct access to state officials.[85]

The family's "natural" status reinforced its jurisdictional authority. It was conventional to assume that the father's authority over the family descended from God and nature. His powers of government were not a concession by the state.[86] In addition, social compact theories commonly treated the family as the only jurisdiction other than the commonwealth directly grounded in nature.[87] Unlike many other jurisdictions and corporate bodies, the family did not receive authority by delegation from the ruler. The family existed in the state of nature and preserved its natural status after the formation of the commonwealth. It, not the individual, was also often the unit that contracted with others to form the state. The natural status of the family did not, of course, shield it from regulation by the state or community when the household head failed to support, discipline, and educate his dependents.[88] But the family's foundation in nature did create a presumption in favor of maximizing fatherly control and limiting others' ability to intervene in his autonomy, a presumption that rested as much on perceptions of the natural rights of the household head as on judgments about practicality. English theologian Jeremy Taylor explained that the father's "natural power is entire, absolute, and unlimited, except where the law of God or of nations does intervene." In only a limited number of extreme cases, from child abuse to lack of support, did the state's law allow children to approach a judge and "complain: because in all other things he [the child] is entirely under his father's power."[89]

Some theologians maintained that the family head, employing his natural authority, could bind the conscience of his dependents. Family government no less than the state needed tools adequate to secure obedience. "Compulsion without the power to obligate in conscience," wrote Suárez, "is either morally impossible, because a just compulsion presumes guilt, . . . or very insufficient."[90] Catholics and Protestants alike assumed that violations of the "commands of parents" were a "sin against God" that, if unrepented, put the soul at risk.[91] Theorists weighing contrary demands on conscience went so far as to debate when allegiance to the natural authority of the family trumped the duty of submission to the commonwealth. The day-to-day activities of modern and early modern families, from child care and education to discipline and labor, bear a certain resemblance. But the conceptualization of the early modern family—as a semi-autonomous jurisdiction grounded in nature with the power to bind conscience—lent support to strong legal pluralism in a way that its contemporary successor does not match.

What gave the family such a pride of place in early modern political theory was not just its form as a natural and divinely ordained unit, but its function as the most fundamental site for good management. A great many early modern political theorists extrapolated their vision of the state from their understanding of the family as the foundational unit of society. The relationship between the family and the commonwealth was thus both a historical one—commonwealths derived their power from family, and, as Robert Filmer argued, monarchs their authority from the first father, Adam—and a metaphorical one: good husbandry was an exemplar of good government.[92] Thus, if it was not a far leap from the household to the state, there was an even more natural connection to be made between the *oikos* (household) and economy. The early-seventeenth-century political economist Gerard de Malynes, for example, reasoned that just as a father should make sure more goods and money came into his household than went out, "the prince," who was "the father of the common-wealth," was responsible for maintaining a positive balance of trade with other states.[93]

In what ways did political economy, this vehicle for thinking about the extended *oikos*, support plural legal orders? Much like early modern political theory, which has tended anachronistically to be associated with a pathway toward state centralism, early modern thought about commerce is often generalized under the rubric of "mercantilism": a supposedly complementary trend, in which the economy served the aggrandizement of powerful states, and vice versa, no less in the colonial world than in Europe. Certainly, some "mercantilist" thought did underscore assertions of power at the center, from sumptuary laws to Navigation Acts to claims of sovereignty over the seas.[94] Moreover, much thought on political economy, like that of Malynes, had at its core a divine right or social contract theory of sovereignty.[95]

Still, like political thought on the problem of sovereignty, such arguments trended equally in the opposite direction, toward a language of overlapping, rival, and coexisting venues of legal authority. Early modern theorists often imagined economic activity as something not to be captured but rather *governed*. It was not always clear to them that the state was the best equipped or most legally appropriate body to do that governing. Many early modern political economists supported legal pluralism by arguing that successful and safe commerce required a variety of forms of legitimate government over merchants and markets besides the national state, from venerable bodies politic (like municipalities and magistrates) to new ones (like joint-stock companies). They also contended that features of economic life such as money and credit were in their own ways sites of government.

Towns, parishes, manors, and market franchises had long served as a primary site for governing economic behavior. Yet the great transformations in early modern economic relations prompted even more urgent thought about the authority of jurisdictions apart from the central state that regulated those relations. In England, towns and cities grew more powerful because of rising population coupled with rapid urbanization. The legal and financial transformations occasioned by the Reformation and the dissolution of the monasteries not only furthered the ambitions of the Henrician Crown but encouraged the expansion of municipal authority, as boroughs scrambled to fill the void left behind by the decline of monastic, ecclesiastical, and manorial jurisdictions.[96] Meanwhile, growing commerce and credit networks were drawing more people and their business from the country to the cities, and particularly to their courts, which, as Craig Muldrew has shown, grew ever more popular as venues both for town dwellers and for those in the countryside, even as courts at the center grew as well.[97] The authority of local officials remained robust and often in tension with one another and the central state, not least because of their role in governing trade, commerce, and "private" life.[98] As Phil Withington has put it, "Hobbes"—who so famously excoriated municipal corporations as parasites in the bowels of the body politic—"was not criticising a chimera."[99]

Growing global commerce and pressing commercial and fiscal problems—such as the expansion of credit, or currency exchange and debasement—prompted thought that could easily underscore a pluralistic foundation for political society.[100] Many theorists who grappled with the problem of trade offered a range of arguments reinforcing both traditional and novel self-regulating mercantile institutions.[101] These arguments continued to see local commerce as rooted in the guilds, associations, and municipal councils and courts that were the most immediate place for the regulation of economic life. Commercial health was in this sense understood in the humanist mode: rooted in a republican notion of citizenship, intimately connected not to monarchy or state *per se* but to the fundamental unit of the *civitas* and *polis*.[102] It was almost a cliché to view municipal corporations and like jurisdictions as overlapping and even rival forms of "commonwealth," "publick state," and "republic."[103]

Moreover, even for an absolutist like Malynes or his interlocutor Edward Misselden, the world of commerce itself seemed to bind and limit monarchs. Not only were the market and merchants governed by a divine, natural law, which good human law ought to imitate, but mercantile practice generated its own customary law "approved by the authoritie of all Kingdomes and Commonweales, and not a Law established by the Soveraigntie of any Prince." This so-called *lex mercatoria* arose from a variety of sources: natural law, law of the sea, and the customs of mercantile life. Even divinely ordained monarchs, Malynes implied, could not alter it and were obligated to uphold it. *Lex mercatoria* treated money, though authorized by princes, as having a moral autonomy of its own: a "*Publica Mensura*," the product of a social contract that "by common consent" was "the rule and square to set a price unto all things, and the right and true judges of them."[104] Meanwhile, in its transnational dimensions, the law merchant as a form of customary law put restrictions on monarchs, demanding that they respect the rights of hospitality and free passage of strangers. The *lex mercatoria* was thus a sort of self-constituting legal regime: it was employed by mercantile courts, guided merchants' self-regulation, and in theory defined a consistency in a transnational legal order that was unaffected by variability in state law.[105]

The law merchant, of course, was primarily concerned with overseas trade, whose massive growth posed a particular challenge to centralizing theories of sovereignty. While many saw the companies that engaged in trade as ultimately subordinate to the monarchies and republics that chartered them, this was not always an easy position to sustain for companies and mercantile networks that did their business at great distances from the realm and often in the world beyond Christendom. After all, the very meanings of "to commerce" and "to traffic" were not just to trade, but to have relations with other people, making them inherently social and political acts that required government.[106] Though companies and corporate colonies were commonly chartered by the Crown, these charters were founded on European models—such as the manorial duchy or municipal corporation—that granted recipients significant customary rights and great autonomy and jurisdiction. These expansive forms of self-government acted as restraints on the monarch.[107] So did the languages used to describe these bodies. Grotius envisioned the Dutch East India Company, for which he advocated tirelessly, as occupying a space as both a corporation and a republic, fitting it within a larger theory that liberally allowed both company and state to exercise violence and jurisdiction, especially on the seas.[108] Meanwhile, theorists sliced, diced, and reorganized familiar political and economic ideologies to accommodate the novel conditions of overseas expansion. Jurists in England and abroad liberally mixed sources of common, civil, and natural law, principles of equity, and the law of nations as they tried to comprehend European authority in the extra-Christian world. This in turn authorized a particular form of legal pluralism, as proprietors and companies governed trade, and as a variety of litigants moved across imperial jurisdictions and among legal venues, from Mayor's Courts to Admiralty Courts, seeking those that could best accommodate their needs.[109]

The potential for legal pluralism found in the practices of overseas companies, however, did not simply rest in the legal lineages of their charters but in the theories behind early modern trade itself. While some humanist thought was deeply apprehensive of expanding commerce, other thinkers steeped in that tradition, such as Botero, Vitoria, and their English acolytes, valorized a union of commerce and colonization that required accommodation of various forms of jurisdiction, including indigenous systems of law.[110] Yet even within an "imperial system," the political economy of empire could generate a robust form of pluralism. Even for someone like Josiah Child, so often said to be tightly connected to Stuart absolutist ambitions, overseas trade required law and government, but such regulation was not necessarily vested in the Crown. Instead Child and others, like Charles Davenant, envisioned trade, especially in the world beyond Europe, as necessarily governed by a "mixt Assembly of Noblemen, Gentlemen, and Merchants," councils dedicated to the "common good," which often took the form of governments of joint-stock companies. Such discourses could find support as far back as the Roman republic, but were drawn most immediately from the Dutch, whose republican models of trade many late-seventeenth-century English writers admired.[111]

To be sure, there were many who supported a far more centralized notion of colonial commerce, which, like political theory, came in two broad variants. One, already mentioned, we tend to call "mercantilism," and paralleled absolutist valorization of Crown authority. A second, which tracked with "constitutionalist" thought, mixed government, and the power of Parliament and "public," advocated for a free colonial trade, excoriated "monopolies," and looked suspiciously on corporations as "the common wealth being made private," in the words of Robert Kayll, an early East India Company critic.[112] Likewise, there were various forms of what we might call, metaphorically, "weak" pluralism of political economy, in which merchants, attorneys, and intellectuals served as counselors to the monarch—a role Patrick Collinson has likened to that of modern think-tanks—or that defended overseas trading corporations as a service to Crown and "commonwealth."[113] Yet others offered a far more expansive vision of the commercial and colonial corporation, as bodies politic in themselves: very real forms of government apart from that Crown that established courts, councils, legislatures, cities, and even other nested, pluralistic jurisdictional forms. Companies, proprietors, and the forts, factories, and colonies they erected claimed jurisdiction over people and borders as they moved in and out of nebulous spaces. The East India Company treated the entirety of the eastern hemisphere as a zone in which *it*, rather than the Crown or Parliament, exercised final say over English people, places, and things.[114] For its advocates, what modern historians have understood in statist terms as a purely economic category of "monopoly" was in fact a form of jurisdiction that, much like the chartered boroughs of the English provinces, provided another forum for governance over traffic. Discourses about the role and responsibilities of "traffick" with the extra-European world gave rise to concepts of divisible state sovereignty, which were both rooted in older European discourses and ironically willed away by modern interpreters as unimportant anachronisms or "anomalies."[115]

In sum, early modern economic thinkers tended to see the market as something that required governing, but they did not always agree on who it was that should do that governing. While some advocated a centralist model that fed into state formation, others explored how burgeoning overseas trade and legal pluralism reinforced one another. They called for a variety of forms of overseas activity, decentralized and locally flexible legal systems, and different ways of governing the market that were specific to time and place—something we might, in essence, understand as a political-economic theory of legal pluralism.

This theory, which along with the jurisdictional conception of the family was a part of *oikonomic* pluralism, stood amid the variety of discourses that we have encompassed under the headings of godly and civic pluralism. In early modern political thought, legal pluralism was everywhere, partly as a defense of tradition and the status quo and partly as a response to new challenges. In all of these discourses, pluralism and centralism did not simply square off as antagonists. They both arose out of similar problems and were articulated in related vocabularies. Seen in this way, the emergence of modern states and empires may not necessarily be the triumph of centralism over pluralism, but rather yet another point in the perennial tussle between these two interlinked discursive poles. The dialogue between pluralism and centralism became even more complicated as Europeans expanded to the world overseas. This, though, is another story.

NOTES

1. For help and advice, the authors would like to thank Amitai Aviram, Edward Balleisen, Lauren Benton, Jacqueline Ross, Julia Rudolph, and participants in the University of Illinois College of Law Research Incubator, the Van Leer Institute workshop, the Hebrew University Legal History workshop, and the Triangle Global British History and Legal History workshops.
2. John Griffiths, "What Is Legal Pluralism?" *Journal of Legal Pluralism and Unofficial Law* 24 (1986): 5-8, 12.
3. One thinks of the flood of tracts championing Crown as against ecclesiastical tribunals, or seigneurial courts as against urban ones, and on and on.
4. This list, of course, is not exhaustive. Other intellectual projects, such as histories of the Christian church and of the republics of classical antiquity, would be worth further exploration.
5. J. H. Elliott, "A Europe of Composite Monarchies," *Past and Present* 137 (1992): 48-71.
6. F. N. Hinsley, *Sovereignty*, 2nd ed. (Cambridge: Cambridge University Press, 1986), 26; James J. Sheehan, "The Problem of Sovereignty in European History," *American Historical Review* 111 (2006): 2.
7. Jean Bodin, *The Six Books of a Commonweal*, ed. Kenneth D. McRae (Cambridge, MA: Harvard University Press, 1962), 49-50, 156-57, 365, 372; Francisco Suárez, *Tratado de las Leyes y de Dios Legislador [De Legibus ac Deo Legislatore]*, trans. José Ramón Eguillor Muniozguren (Madrid: Instituto de Estudios Politicos, 1967), 2: 226-27, 230-32 [Book III, chapter 9, §§5, 16-21]; Hugo Grotius, *The Rights of War and Peace*, ed. Richard Tuck (Indianapolis: Liberty Fund, 2005), 1: 257-77 [Book I, chapter 3, §§6-9]; Samuel Pufendorf, *De*

Jure Naturae et Gentium Libri Octo, trans. C. H. and W. A. Oldfather (Oxford: Clarendon, 1934 [1668 ed.]), 2: 1010-22 [Book 7, chapter 4].

8. Gerald Strauss, *Law, Resistance, and the State: The Opposition to Roman Law in Reformation Germany* (Princeton, NJ: Princeton University Press, 1986), 71-92, 136; John Miller, ed., *Absolutism in Seventeenth-Century Europe* (New York: St. Martin's, 1990), 3-4; Richard L. Kagan, *Lawsuits and Litigants in Castile, 1500-1700* (Chapel Hill: University of North Carolina Press, 1981), 211; David Parker, "Sovereignty, Absolutism, and the Function of Law in Seventeenth-Century France," *Past and Present* 122 (1989): 40, 43; Michael Braddick, *The Nerves of State: Taxation and the Financing of the English State, 1558-1714* (Manchester, UK: Manchester University Press, 1996).
9. Heinz Schilling, "Confessional Europe," in *Handbook of European History, 1400-1600: Late Middle Ages, Renaissance, and Reformation*, ed. Thomas A. Brady, Heiko A. Oberman, and James D. Tracy (New York: Brill, 1995), 2: 641-81; Ute Lotz-Heumann, "The Concept of 'Confessionalization': A Historiographical Paradigm in Dispute," *Memoria y Civilizacion* 4 (2001): 93-114.
10. See, e.g., Julia Adams, *The Familial State: Ruling Families and Merchant Capitalism in Early Modern Europe* (Ithaca, NY: Cornell University Press, 2005), 109-11; Julian H. Franklin, *Jean Bodin and the Rise of Absolutist Theory* (Cambridge: Cambridge University Press, 1973), 2-6; Nicholas Henshall, *The Myth of Absolutism: Change and Continuity in Early Modern European Monarchy* (New York: Longman, 1992), 9-10; Kagan, *Lawsuits and Litigants in Castile*, 211, 226, 234; Roger Mettam, "France," in Miller, ed., *Absolutism*, 43; Parker, "Sovereignty, Absolutism," 65, 71; I. A. A. Thompson, "Castile," in Miller, ed., *Absolutism*, 88-94, 96-97.
11. Michael J. Braddick, *State Formation in Early Modern England* (Cambridge: Cambridge University Press, 2000); Paul Halliday, *Dismembering the Body Politic: Partisan Politics in England's Towns, 1650-1730* (Cambridge: Cambridge University Press, 1998).
12. Chancellor Ellesmere, "Discourse concerning the Royal Prerogative" (c. 1604), in Louis A. Knafla, ed., *Law and Politics in Jacobean England: The Tracts of Lord Chancellor Ellesmere* (Cambridge: Cambridge University Press, 1977), 198; Bishop Robert Sanderson, *Bishop Sanderson's Lectures on Conscience and Human Law: Delivered in the Divinity School at Oxford,* trans. Chr. Wordsworth (Lincoln, 1877 [MS, 1647]), 155-56, 201-3, 223-24.
13. Martin Van Gelderen, "The State and Its Rivals in Early-Modern Europe," in *States and Citizens: History, Theory, Prospects*, ed. Quentin Skinner and Bo Strath (Cambridge: Cambridge University Press, 2003), 79-96.
14. Theodore Beza, "Right of Magistrates" (1574), in *Constitutionalism and Resistance in the Sixteenth Century*, ed. Julian H. Franklin (New York: Pegasus, 1969), 108-9, 111, 114, 130; Philippe du Plessis Mornay, *Vindiciae Contra Tyrannos* (1579), in *Constitutionalism and Resistance*, 146, 149-56, 151-56, 161, 179, 181, 190-91, 196-97. See generally Howell A. Lloyd, "Constitutionalism," *The Cambridge History of Political Thought, 1450-1700*, ed. J. H. Burns (Cambridge: Cambridge University Press, 1991), 260-63; Otto von Gierke, *The Development of Political Theory*, trans. Bernard Freyd (New York: Howard Fertig, 1966), 93-94, 97, 155-57; Quentin Skinner, *The Foundations of Modern Political Thought* (Cambridge: Cambridge University Press, 1978), 2: 320-26, 329-34, 337-44.
15. Julian Franklin, "Introduction," in *Constitutionalism and Resistance*, 31.
16. Beza, "*Magistrates*," 111.
17. Mornay, *Vindiciae*, 196.

18. Beza, "Magistrates," 110-12; Mornay, *Vindiciae*, 149-53, 185-86, 190-91, 196-97 (quotation on p. 196). Richard R. Benert, "Inferior Magistrates in Sixteenth-Century Political Thought" (Ph.D. dissertation, University of Minnesota, 1967), 162-95, 350.
19. Otto von Gierke, *Natural Law and the Theory of Society, 1500 to 1800*, trans. Ernest Barker (Boston: Beacon, 1960), 63-64.
20. For one example, see Pufendorf, *De Jure Naturae*, 2: 995-97 [Book 7, chapter 2, §§21, 22].
21. Johannes Althusius, *The Politics of Johannes Althusius*, trans. Frederick S. Carney (Boston: Beacon, 1964 [1614 ed.]), 93-101, 62, 95, 185-92.
22. "For families, cities, and provinces existed by nature prior to realms, and gave birth to them." Althusius, *Politics*, 61.
23. Althusius, *Politics*, chapters 2-18 and 38, and esp. pp. 5, 61-62, 65, 67-68. See generally Gierke, *Natural Law and the Theory of Society*, 35-40, 63-64, 70-75, 164; Thomas O. Hueglin, *Early Modern Concepts for a Late Modern World: Althusius on Community and Federalism* (Waterloo, Canada: Wilfrid Laurier University Press, 1999), 4-5; and Stanley Parry, "The Political Science of Johannes Althusius" (Ph.D. dissertation, Yale University, 1953), 471-73, 488.
24. Johann Sommerville, *Royalists and Patriots: Politics and Ideology, 1603-1640*, 2nd ed. (London: Longman, 1999), 10-13, 23-24, 35-41, 54. Cf. Glenn Burgess, "The Divine Right of Kings Reconsidered," *English Historical Review* 425 (1992): 837-61. Among many possible examples, consider Richard Mocket, *God and the King* (London, 1616), 36-45, 55-57.
25. These two possibilities—God and the community—are analytically separate and need not be united. Early Lutherans and Calvin pointed to divine rather than communal authority as the reason why inferior magistrates might (cautiously) set themselves against their ruler. In the generations after Calvin, the Reformed tradition fused both arguments. Skinner, *Foundations*, 2: 324; Benert, "Inferior Magistrates," 52, 106-8.
26. Samuel Rutherford, *Lex, Rex* (London, 1644), 159-62, 165, 168, 176, 253, 350-51. See generally Conrad Russell, "Divine Rights in the Early Seventeenth Century," in *Public Duty and Private Conscience in Seventeenth-Century England*, ed. John Morrill, Paul Slack, and Daniel Woolf (Oxford: Clarendon, 1992), 101-20, esp. 106.
27. Bodin, *Commonweal*, 161. See also Thomas Hobbes, *Leviathan* (1651), ed. Richard Tuck (Cambridge: Cambridge University Press, 1991), 184.
28. Suárez, *De Legibus*, in *Selections from Three Works of Francisco Suárez*, trans. Gwladys L. Williams, Ammi Brown, and John Waldron (Oxford: Clarendon, 1944), 2: 520, 553 [Book VII, chapter 9, §2, and Book VII, chapter 13, §1].
29. Id. at 2: 556 [Book VII, chapter 13, §5].
30. Id. at 2: 553 [Book VII, chapter 13, §1].
31. Id. at 2: 462 [Book VII, chapter 3]. Tacit consent "is regarded as of equal effect with explicit consent." Id. at 2: 560 [Book VII, chapter 13, §12].
32. Id. at 2: 556-57 [Book VII, chapter 13, §6].
33. Id. at 2: 525-26, 553-54 [Book VII, chapter 9, §11; and Book VII, chapter 13, §2].
34. Id. at 2: 557-58 [Book VII, chapter 13, §§7, 8].
35. Id. at 2: 631-32 [Book 7, chapter 20, §1]. Book 8 of *De Legibus* considers for approximately two hundred pages the individual and communal privileges that may arise with only the most nominal approval of the Crown. This greatly enhances the *de facto* pluralism established by geographically specific customs.
36. See, e.g., *The Digest of Justinian*, ed. Theodor Mommsen and Paul Krueger, trans. Alan Watson (Philadelphia: University of Pennsylvania Press, 1985), 1: 13 [Digest I.iii.32]; John

P. Dawson, "The Codification of French Customs," *Michigan Law Review* 38 (1940): 791-92; Strauss, *Law, Resistance, and the State*, 98-99; James Q. Whitman, "Why Did the Revolutionary Lawyers Confuse Custom and Reason?" *University of Chicago Law Review* 58 (1991): 1332 (and sources cited).

37. Suárez, *Legibus*, in *Selections*, 2: 555 [Book VII, chapter 13, §4]. More precisely, in a monarchical state, a valid custom requires the consent of the people who generate the usage *plus* the consent of the king. Suárez termed the latter the "efficient cause" that makes the custom legally binding. Id. at 2: 577 [Book VII, chapter 16, §1]. See also Jeremy Taylor, *Ductor Dubitantium; or, The Rule of Conscience* (London, 1660), 2: 429-30 [Book III, chapter 6, §6].
38. Suárez, *Legibus*, in *Selections*, 2: 556 [Book VII, chapter 13, §5].
39. Richard Hooker, *The Folger Library Edition of the Works of Richard Hooker*, ed. W. Speed Hill (Cambridge, MA: Harvard University Press, 1981), 3: 340 [Book VIII, chapter 2, §11 (MS, c. late 1590s; printed, 1648)]. On Selden, see Richard Tuck, *Natural Rights Theories: Their Origin and Development* (Cambridge: Cambridge University Press, 1979), 97-100. Suárez acknowledged the possibility that the people might validate their own customs without royal assent. In some polities, the royal power may be limited by agreement, as "when the monarchy is not absolute, but partly democratic. Yet this is not the usual situation." Suárez, *Legibus*, in *Selections*, 2: 556 [Book VII, chapter 13, §5]. In Suárez's view, Castile was the norm, Hooker's and Selden's England the exception.
40. To be sure, royal commissioners directed the process of redaction, and the final custumal was promulgated in the king's name. But local assemblies retained control over the process and resolved disputed points by majority vote. The "formal vote of local assemblies was the essential medium for translating the custom of the neighborhood into codified 'law.'" Dawson, "Codification of the French Customs," 774-80, 788-94 (quotation on p. 791); Peter Stein, *Roman Law in European History* (Cambridge: Cambridge University Press, 1999), 83; Donald R. Kelley, *The Human Measure: Social Thought in the Western Legal Tradition* (Cambridge, MA: Harvard University Press, 1990), 203.
41. See, e.g., Robert Mason, Speech in House of Commons (May 22, 1628), in Robert C. Johnson, et al., eds., *Commons Debates, 1628* (New Haven. CT: Yale University Press, 1977), 3: 528.
42. Hooker, *Works*, 3: 340 [Book VIII, chapter 2, §11]. Hooker's argument goes beyond the typical English constitutionalist claim that William the Conqueror "swore to observe" the already existing laws of the realm. Edward Coke, "Preface," *Coke's Reports* (London, 1826), part 8, p. iv. Hooker suggests that long-observed customs could come to bind a conquering monarchy even when it had not affirmatively agreed to respect municipal law in the immediate aftermath of victory.
43. Sommerville, *Royalists*, 67.
44. Coke, *Speech and Charge [at the Norwich Assizes]* (London, 1607), C1[v]; *Caudrey's Case*, in *Coke's Reports* (London, 1826), Part 5, 21a.
45. Charles Herle, *A Fuller Answer to a Treatise Written by Doctor Ferne, Entitled, The Resolving of Conscience upon This Question* (London, 1642), 6, 22-23; Philip Hunton, *A Treatise of Monarchy* (London, 1643), 2-3, 6, 32, 38. I owe the phrase "community-centered view" to Corinne Comstock Weston and Janelle Renfrow Greenberg, *Subjects and Sovereigns: The Grand Controversy over Legal Sovereignty in Stuart England* (Cambridge: Cambridge University Press, 1981), 2.
46. Russell, "Divine Rights," 109, 111.

47. Lloyd, "Constitutionalism," 262, 270; William Farr Church, *Constitutional Thought in Sixteenth-Century France: A Study in the Evolution of Ideas* (Cambridge, MA: Harvard University Press, 1941), 83-93.
48. Matthew Hale, *History of the Common Law of England*, ed. Charles M. Grey (Chicago, 1971 [1713]), 16-18 (quotation on p. 18); *Lane's Case* (Common Pleas 1586), in *Coke's Reports* (London, 1826), part 3, 16b-17a; Speeches of Thomas Wentworth and William Hakewill to the House of Commons (Dec. 15 and 17, 1621), in Wallace Notestein, Francis Helen Relf, and Hartley Simpson, eds., *Commons Debates, 1621* (New Haven, CT: Yale University Press, 1935), 6: 239, 243. Edward Coke's *The Fourth Part of the Institutes of the Laws of England* (reprinted, Buffalo, NY: Hein, 1986 [1644]) made clear how many English courts owed their origins and procedures in part or in whole to prescription. A few, of many, examples include court of equity in Exchequer Chamber (p. 118), judiciary of County Palatine of Chester (211-12), royal franchise of Ely (219), Courts of the Stanneries in Cornwall and Devon (229), and the court of equity of the Council of Wales (242).
49. See, e.g., William Perkins, *A Discourse of Conscience* (1608 ed.), in *William Perkins, 1558-1602, English Puritanist: His Pioneer Works on Casuistry*, ed. Thomas F. Merrill (Nieuwkoop: De Graaf , 1966), 36-37; William Ames, *Conscience with the Power and Cases Thereof* (London, 1639), 168-69; Suárez, *Legibus*, 3: 468-72 [Book 5, chapter 4].
50. A law might be unjust if it contravened a natural or divine precept; furthered a ruler's greed or vainglory rather than the common good; exceeded the power committed to the lawmaker; or imposed unequal burdens on the community. Thomas Aquinas, *Summa Theologica*, Q96, article 4; Domingo De Soto, *De Iustitia et Iure [De la Justicia y del Derecho]*, trans. P. Marcelino González Ordóñez (Madrid: Instituto de Estudios Políticos, 1967-68), 1: 50, 55, 71-72 [Book 1, Question 6, Articles 4 and 8]; Robert Bellarmine, *De Laicis; or, The Treatise on Civil Government*, trans. Kathleen E. Murphy (New York: Fordham University Press, 1928), 46-47.
51. Protestants denied the distinction between venial and mortal sin. They held that all unrepented violations of human laws that bound conscience constituted a mortal sin, although some sins were worse on account of circumstances. Perkins, *Discourse*, 12; John Davenant, *A Treatise on Justification; or, The Disputatio de Justitia Habituali et Actuali, Together with Translations of the "Determinationes" of the Same Author*, trans. Rev. Josiah Allport (London, 1844-46), 1: 343-44; Jeremy Taylor, *Unum Necessarium; or, The Doctrine and Practice of Repentance* (London, 1655), 112-21.
52. De Soto, *De Iustitia*, 1: 50-57, and 3: 420-22, 425-26, 486-88, 503; Fernando Vázquez Menchaca, *Controversiarum Illustrium Aliarumque Usu Frequentium Libri Tres*, trans. Fidel Rodríguez Alcalde (Valladolid: Talleres Tipográficos "Cuesta," 1931-33), 2: 189-90 [Book 1, chapter 29]; Francisco de Vitoria, *Political Writings*, ed. Anthony Pagden and Jeremy Lawrance (Cambridge: Cambridge University Press, 1991), 179; Bellarmine, *Laicis*, 47, 52; Suárez, *Legibus*, 2:, 291, 295 [Book 3, chapter 22, §§ 2, 12], 2: 302-6, 313-14 [Book 3, chapter 25-27], 3: 467-71 [Book 5, chapters 3 and 4].
53. Jeremy Taylor, *Ductor Dubitantium; or, The Rule of Conscience* (London, 1660), 2: 124-30; Suárez, *Legibus*, 3: 467 [Book 5, chapter 3, §10], 3: 545-55 [Book 5, chapter 18], 3: 559-64 [Book 5, chapter 20].
54. Taylor, *Ductor Dubitantium*, 2: 15-16, 26-28.
55. Richard Baxter, *A Christian Directory; or, A Sum of Practical Cases of Conscience* (London, 1673), 4: 37-38; Taylor, *Ductor Dubitantium*, 2: 14, 23, 398-431; Ames, *Conscience*, 168; De Soto, *De Iustitia*, 1: 71-73 [Book 1, Question 6, Article 8].

56. Juan de Solórzano Pereira, *Política Indiana* (reprinted, Madrid: Fundación José Antonio de Castro, 1996 [1648]), 478 [Book II, chapter 21, §43]; 521 [Book II, chapter 24, §35]; 2106-7 [Book V, chapter 11, §46]; and 2374-75 [Book VI, chapter 9, §16, 18, 19]. For additional examples—on failure to pay tribute to the Crown and to *encomenderos*, and on the improper distribution of *encomiendas* without regard to merit—see *Política*, 436 [Book II, chapter 19, §7]; 742 [Book III, chapter 8, §7].
57. For this paragraph and the next, see generally Guido Bartolucci, "The Influence of Carlo Sigonio's 'De Republica Hebraeorum' on Hugo Grotius' 'De Republica Emendanda,'" *Hebraic Political Studies* 2 (2007): 193-210; Guido Bartolucci, "Carlo Sigonio and the Respublica Hebraeorum: A Reevaluation," *Hebraic Political Studies* 3 (2008): 19-59; Frank Edward Manuel, *The Broken Staff: Judaism through Christian Eyes* (Cambridge, MA: Harvard University Press, 1992), 115-28; Eric Nelson, *The Hebrew Republic: Jewish Sources and the Transformation of European Political Thought* (Cambridge, MA: Harvard University Press, 2010); Fania Oz-Salzberger, "The Jewish Roots of Western Freedom," *Azure* 13 (2002): 88-132; and Adam Sutcliffe, *Judaism and Enlightenment* (Cambridge: Cambridge University Press, 2004), 26-38, 42-57.
58. Hugo Grotius, "De Republica Emendanda [On the Emendation of the Dutch Polity]," in *Grotiana*, n.s., 5 (1984 [MS, c.1600]): 67-69; Hobbes, *Leviathan*, 281, 324, 357; Althusius, *Politics*, 90. Many Christian Hebraists believed that God's theocracy ended when the Israelites demanded a king, thereby rejecting the Lord's institutions in favor of rule by a man. See, e.g., Beza, "Magistrates," 116; Grotius, "Emendanda," 83, 89-91; Carlo Sigonio, *The Hebrew Republic*, trans. Peter Wyetzner (Jerusalem: Shalem, 2010 [1582]), 27.
59. See, e.g., Mornay, *Vindiciae*, 163; Althusius, preface to third edition (1614), in *Politics*, 10.
60. On the challenges involved in deciding what elements of Old Testament law bound early modern Christians, see Richard J. Ross, "Distinguishing Eternal from Transient Law: Natural Law and the Judicial Laws of Moses," *Past and Present* 217 (2012): 79-115.
61. Bodin, *Commonweal*, 719-20. See also Mocket's *God and the King*, 47-49, which argued that the priests were strictly subservient to the king as a way of combating the common opinion that the priests in the Sanhedrin enjoyed the power to judge the king.
62. Hobbes, *Leviathan*, 324-31 [chapter 40].
63. The paragraphs below draw on Lancelot Andrewes, "A Summary View of the Government Both of the Old and New Testament," in *Certain Brief Treatises Written by Learned Men concerning the Ancient and Modern Government of the Church* (Oxford, 1641), 7-22; Petrus Cunaeus, *The Hebrew Republic*, trans. Peter Wyetzner (Jerusalem: Shalem, 2006 [1617]), 47-58; Thomas Goodwin, *Moses and Aaron: Civil and Ecclesiastical Rites Used by the Ancient Hebrews* (London, 1628), 219-36; Grotius, "Emendanda," 93-105; James Harrington, *The Art of Lawgiving* (London, 1659), 2: 1-52; Moses Lowman, *A Dissertation on the Civil Government of the Hebrews* (London, 1740), 61-80, 125-90; Sigonio, *Hebrew Republic*, 29, 227-36. See also Algernon Sidney, *Discourses concerning Government*, ed. Thomas G. West (Indianapolis: Liberty Fund, 1996 [1698]), 127-28.
64. Quotation from Sigonio, *Hebrew Republic*, 29.
65. Grotius, "Emendanda," 105. Sigonio claimed that the tribes and cities could not establish tribunals without the approval of the Sanhedrin and "on the condition that the courts of each region would be subordinate to the great court of their superiors that met in Jerusalem." Sigonio, *Hebrew Republic*, 248.
66. Althusius, *Politics*, 90, 95, 111; Beza, "Magistrates," 104, 110-13, 118; Mornay, *Vindiciae*, 143-47, 149-50, 152, 158-59, 180-81.

67. Harrington, *Lawgiving*, 1: 10, 35; Rutherford, *Lex, Rex*, 159-62; Sigonio, *Hebrew Republic*, 242.
68. Goodwin, *Moses*, 236.
69. Lowman, *Dissertation*, 145-48.
70. Sigonio, *Hebrew Republic*, 277.
71. Cunaeus, *Hebrew Republic*, 58; Hugo Grotius, *De Imperio Summarum Potestatum circa Sacra [English and Latin]*, trans. Harm-Jan Van Dam (Leiden: Brill, 2001), 193 [chapter 2, §5]. Thomas Goodwin, advancing a minority view, found separate ecclesiastical and civil courts. Goodwin, *Moses*, 219-21. Most Christian Hebraists denied that the Israelite commonwealth maintained independent ecclesiastical jurisdictions. Nelson, *Hebrew Republic*, 88-137; G. J. Toomer, *John Selden: A Life in Scholarship* (Oxford: Oxford University Press, 2009), 747, 760.
72. Lowman, *Dissertation*, 163.
73. Sigonio, *Hebrew Republic*, 244-45; and see 370, notes 158 and 160. By contrast, Selden downplayed the discretion in the appellate system if judges in a lower court "decided that a case was too difficult for them to decide." Toomer, *Selden*, 765.
74. Rutherford, *Lex, Rex*, 172.
75. Harrington, *Lawgiving*, 2: 51.
76. Baruch Spinoza, *Tractatus Theologico-Politicus* (1670), in *Spinoza: Complete Works*, trans. Samuel Shirley (Indianapolis: Liberty Fund, 2002), 544.
77. Bodin, *Commonweal*, 159.
78. Lowman, *Dissertation*, 128-29. "Among the Hebrews the *majestas imperii*, the authority of government, was in the first place to be considered in Jehovah himself as King of Israel." Id. at 254.
79. Spinoza, *Tractatus*, 546, 551. Other authors noted that the Sanhedrin had the right to judge the credentials of prophets. Cunaeus, *Hebrew Republic*, 50; Toomer, *Selden*, 767.
80. See, e.g., Brian Z. Tamanaha, "The Folly of the Social Scientific Concept of Legal Pluralism," *Journal of Law and Society* 20 (1993): 205, 211; Tamanaha, "A Non-Essentialist Concept of Legal Pluralism," *Journal of Law and Society* 27 (2000): 304, 313, 316; and Sally Engle Merry, "Legal Pluralism," *Law and Society Review* 22 (1988): 870-71, 878-79.
81. Suárez, *Legibus*, in *Selections*, 2: 87 [Book I, chapter 6, §20]. Women did lead households, though rarely. For the sake of streamlined language, we will refer to family heads as "fathers."
82. Sanderson, *Lectures on Conscience*, 198-200.
83. See, respectively, William Gouge, *Of Domestical Duties* (London, 1622), 18; Suárez, *De Legibus*, in *Tratado*, 2: 288 [Book III, chapter 21, §8]; and Sanderson, *Lectures on Conscience*, 198.
84. Baxter, *Christian Directory*, 2: 512.
85. Carole Shammas, *A History of Household Government in America* (Charlottesville: University of Virginia Press, 2002), xiii.
86. See, e.g., Suárez, *De Legibus*, in *Tratado*, 2: 300 [Book III, chapter 24, §3]; Taylor, *Ductor Dubitantium*, 2: 363; Baxter, *Christian Directory*, 2: 550.
87. Gierke, *Natural Law and Theory of Society*, 63-64.
88. For British North America, see John Demos, *A Little Commonwealth: Family Life in Plymouth Colony* (New York: Oxford University Press, 1970); Mary Beth Norton, *Founding Mothers and Fathers: Gendered Power and the Forming of American Society* (New York: Knopf, 1996); and Shammas, *Household Government*.

89. Taylor, *Ductor Dubitantium*, 2: 388, 376. In addition to the father's "natural" power over the family, he enjoyed a "political" power established by civil law, which the state was more capable of extending or restricting. Id. at 2: 389.
90. Suárez, *De Legibus*, in *Tratado*, 2: 288 [Book 3, chapter 21, § 8].
91. Catholic sources include Bellarmine, *Laicis*, 46; Suárez, *De Legibus*, in *Tratado*, 2: 288 [Book 3, chapter 21, § 8], and 2: 300 [Book 3, chapter 24, § 3]; cf. Vázquez Menchaca, *Controversiarum Illustrium*, 2: 187 [Book 1, chapter 29]. For the Protestants: William Fenner, *The Soul's Looking Glass* (Cambridge, 1640), 268-69, 296-97; Sanderson, *Lectures on Conscience*, 125, 198; Taylor, *Ductor Dubitantium*, 2: 9, 359-63; and Baxter, *Christian Directory*, 4: 38 (the quotations in the text are from Baxter).
92. Gordon Schochet, *Patriarchalism in Political Thought: The Authoritarian Family and Political Speculation and Attitudes Especially in Seventeenth-Century England* (Oxford: Blackwell, 1975). Though the omnipresence of the metaphor by no means meant that everyone agreed on its meanings or implications. Rachel Weil, *Political Passions: Gender, the Family, and Political Argument in England, 1680-1714* (Manchester: Manchester University Press, 1999).
93. Gerard Malynes, *Consuetudo, vel lex mercatoria; or, The Ancient Law-Merchant* (London, 1622), 60.
94. Thomas Wemyss Fulton, *The Sovereignty of the Sea: An Historical Account of the Claims of England to the Dominion of the British Seas and the Evolution of the Territorial Waters* (Edinburgh: Blackwood, 1911), 6.
95. Malynes, *Lex Mercatoria*, 2; Andrea Finkelstein, *The Harmony and the Balance: An Intellectual History of Seventeenth-Century English Economic Thought* (Ann Arbor: University of Michigan Press, 2000), 37-39.
96. Robert Tittler, *Townspeople and Nation: English Urban Experience, 1540-1640* (Stanford, CA: Stanford University Press, 2001); Paul Slack, *From Reformation to Improvement: Public Welfare in Early Modern England* (Oxford: Clarendon, 1999); E. A. Wrigley, *Poverty, Progress, and Population* (Cambridge: Cambridge University Press, 2004), 284.
97. Halliday, *Dismembering the Body Politic*, 37; Craig Muldrew, "Rural Credit, Market Areas, and Legal Institutions in the Countryside in England, 1550-1700," in Christopher Brooks and Michael Lobban, eds., *Communities and Courts in Britain, 1150-1900* (London: Hambledon, 1997), 160, 177; Muldrew, *Economy of Obligation: The Culture of Credit and Social Relations in Early Modern England* (Basingstoke, UK: Palgrave, 1998), 104-6, 210-21, 337.
98. See, e.g., Robert Tittler, *Architecture and Power: The Town Hall and the English Urban Community c. 1500-1640* (Oxford: Clarendon, 1991); Zoë A. Schneider, *The King's Bench: Bailiwick Magistrates and Local Governance in Normandy, 1670-1740* (Rochester, NY: University of Rochester Press, 2008); Julie Hardwick, *Family Business: Litigation and the Political Economies of Daily Life in Early Modern France* (Oxford: Oxford University Press, 2008).
99. Phil Withington, *The Politics of Commonwealth: Citizens and Freemen in Early Modern England* (Cambridge: Cambridge University Press, 2005), 12.
100. On the problem of credit, see particularly Muldrew, *Economy of Obligation*, and Carl Wennerlind, *Casualties of Credit: The English Financial Revolution, 1620-1720* (Cambridge, MA: Harvard University Press, 2011).

101. Amalia Kessler, *A Revolution in Commerce: The Parisian Merchant Court and the Rise of Commercial Society in Eighteenth-Century France* (New Haven, CT: Yale University Press, 2007).
102. See, for example, Giovanni Botero, *A Treatise, concerning the Causes of the Magnificencie and Greatnes of Cities* (London, 1606); Lewes Roberts, *The Merchants Mappe of Commerce Wherein, the Universall Manner and Matter of Trade, Is Compendiously Handled* (London, 1638).
103. Withington, *The Politics of Commonwealth*, 12, 25-26; Patrick Collinson, "De Republica Anglorum; or, History with the Politics Put Back" (Inaugural Lecture, University of Cambridge, 9 November 1989) in Collinson, ed., *Elizabethan Essays* (London: Hambledon, 1994), 16; Mark Goldie, "The Unacknowledged Republic: Officeholding in Early Modern England," in Tim Harris, ed., *The Politics of the Excluded, c. 1500-1850* (Basingstoke, UK: Palgrave, 2001), 176.
104. Malynes, *Lex Mercatoria*, 5-6, 59; Finkelstein, *Harmony and the Balance*, 43.
105. Mary Elizabeth Basile, et al., eds., *Lex Mercatoria and Legal Pluralism: A Late Thirteenth-Century Treatise and Its Afterlife* (Cambridge, MA: Ames Foundation, 1998); Brian Tamanaha, "Understanding Legal Pluralism: Past to Present, Local to Global," *Sydney Law Review* 30 (2008): 375-411; Peter Mazzacano, "The Lex Mercatoria as Autonomous Law" (September 27, 2008), CLEA 2008 Meetings Paper; CLPE Research Paper No. 29/2008. Available at SSRN: http://ssrn.com/abstract=1137629.
106. Withington, *Politics of Commonwealth*, 128; Philip J. Stern, *The Company-State: Corporate Sovereignty and the Early Modern Foundations of the British Empire in India* (New York: Oxford University Press, 2011).
107. See, e.g., Vicki Hsueh, *Hybrid Constitutions: Challenging Legacies of Law, Privilege, and Culture in Colonial America* (Durham, NC: Duke University, 2010).
108. Eric Michael Wilson, *The Savage Republic: De Indis of Hugo Grotius, Republicanism, and Dutch Hegemony within the Early Modern World-System* (Leiden: Martinus Nijhoff, 2008), 9, 139.
109. Lauren Benton, "Legalities of the Sea in Gentili's *Hispanica Advocatio*," in Benedict Kingsbury and Benjamin Straumann, eds., *The Roman Foundations of the Law of Nations: Alberico Gentili and the Justice of Empire* (Oxford: Oxford University Press, 2010); see also Lauren Benton, *A Search for Sovereignty: Law and Geography in European Empires, 1400-1900* (Cambridge: Cambridge University Press, 2010).
110. Andrew Fitzmaurice, "The Ideology of Early Modern Colonisation," *History Compass* (2004): 6, 9
111. Philopatris, *A Treatise Wherein Is Demonstrated That the East-India Trade Is the Most National of Foreign Trades* (London, 1681), 2; Josiah Child, *A New Discourse of Trade, Wherein Are Recommended Several Weighty Points relating to Companies of Merchants* (London, 1694), 106, 110; W. A., *An Apology for the East-India Company* (London, 1690), 6; Charles Davenant, *An Essay on the East-India-Trade* (London, 1696), 6, 10; Finkelstein, *Harmony and the Balance*, 17-18, 223, 228, 337 n. 51. See also Philip J. Stern, "Corporate Virtue: The Languages of Empire in Early Modern British Asia," *Renaissance Studies* 26, no. 4 (2012): 510-30.
112. David Harris Sacks, "The Countervailing of Benefits: Monopoly, Liberty, and Benevolence in Elizabethan England," in Dale Hoak, ed., *Tudor Political Culture* (Cambridge: Cambridge University Press, 1995); Phil Withington, *Society in Early*

Modern England: The Vernacular Origins of Some Powerful Ideas (Cambridge, MA: Polity, 2010), 230.

113. Patrick Collinson, "Puritans, Men of Business, and Elizabethan Parliaments," (J. E. Neale Memorial Lecture, November 1987) in Patrick Collinson, ed., *Elizabethan Essays* (London: Hambledon, 1994), 7; Miles Ogborn, *Indian Ink: Script and Print in the Making of the East India Company* (Chicago, 2006), 115-17.
114. See Stern, *Company-State,* chap. 2.
115. Edward Keene, *Beyond the Anarchical Society: Grotius, Colonialism, and Order in World Politics* (Cambridge: Cambridge University Press, 2002), 2-3, 40-96; Tuck, ed., *Rights of War and Peace.*

6

Between Justice and Economics

"Indians" and Reformism in Eighteenth-Century Spanish Imperial Thought

BRIAN P. OWENSBY

By the mid-eighteenth century, Spain's gathering crisis was plain for all to see. Kings Felipe V (1714-1746) and Fernando VI (1746-1759) understood that the props of power were weakening under the weight of inter-imperial competition. Bullion flows from the mines at Potosí had slowed dramatically in preceding decades. Self-dealing in the New World had undermined revenue collection; smuggling and piracy had broken the *flota* system. Such concerns were hardly new. From the late seventeenth century, Spanish *arbitristas* had been calling for reforms to government, economy, and society in order to replenish the royal fisc and reestablish Spanish power in the face of growing challenges from the French and the British.[1] Dynastic transition from Hapsburgs to Bourbons during the War of Succession between 1701 and 1714 had stripped the Spanish monarchy of its European holdings (Naples, the Spanish Netherlands, Sardinia, Milan, Minorca, Sicily, and Gibralter) and left it with a tenuous hold on transatlantic trade. Sustained attacks on conciliar government by the new Bourbon regime and limited influence over day-to-day rule in the Indies were restricting the Crown's ability to respond robustly to new challenges.

Policy makers were beginning to ask anxious questions about the fate of empire. Between 1720 and 1740, reformers conceptualized the matter as fundamentally one of transatlantic trade.[2] Others began to wonder whether perhaps the problem went beyond commodity flows. To such thinkers, a reform of conditions and structures in the Indies seemed to provide the only long-term answer to the dilemmas of Spanish power and dominion. Yet, there was a growing sentiment that the very foundations of governance in the Indies prevented Spain from making the most of the region's vast wealth. The New World was too distant and had become too autonomous of royal authority to be a reliable engine for generating revenue. Something had to change.

In the early 1740s, a white paper entitled *Nuevo sistema de gobierno económico para la América* advanced a series of proposals to make the Indies more profitable to the Spanish Crown.[3] Not published until 1789, when it was attributed to José Campillo y Cosío, its prescriptions became a touchstone and lightning rod for reformist thought through the reigns of Fernando VI, Carlos III, and beyond.[4] Despite its title, the *Nuevo sistema* is decidedly unsystematic. It covers a variety of topics, such as the Crown's overreliance on mining, the advantage of greater emphasis on agriculture and manufacturing, the need for roads and canals, the importance of trade, both internal and transoceanic. In arguing for reform, it looks to foreign examples, not so much to copy British colonialism or Colbertian mercantilism as to emulate a pragmatic and unashamedly "economic" rather than "political" spirit.

The limited historiography on the *Nuevo sistema* has targeted the impractibility of its proposals in relation to an emergent Atlantic capitalism that came to be dominated by the British.[5] It has been less common to note that the heart of the reforms advanced in the *Nuevo sistema* sought to recast the relationship between indigenous subjects and the Crown: The chief goal of a "new system" must be to "make the Indian vassals useful and advantageous" to Spain.[6] Under Hapsburg rule, royal jurisdiction and the king's justice had been the foundation of governance. The *Nuevo sistema* said little about justice, instead focusing on how indigenous vassals might contribute to "economic government" as producers and consumers. This view signaled a critical change regarding the role of "Indians" in Spanish imperial thought.[7]

There is no better way of parsing the implications of this shift than by juxtaposing the *Nuevo sistema* to paired manuscripts from the same period, the *Representación verdadera y exclamación* and *Breve y compendiosa satisfacción* of 1749, widely attributed to Fray Calixto de San José Túpac Inca.[8] Fray Calixto was a rare *mestizo* member of the Franciscan order. Son of a Spanish father, he claimed direct descent from the last Inca through his Indian mother. We do not know whether Fray Calixto actually penned these documents, though the author wrote from his experience as an indigenous Andean, claiming to speak for the "entire Indian nation" and for all "American Indians" in the New World. Like Felipe Guamán Poma de Ayala's *Nueva crónica y buen gobierno* of circa 1615, the *Representación verdadera* and *Breve satisfacción* directly addressed the king.[9] These documents proposed a dramatic expansion of indigenous vassals' ability to represent themselves within a social order premised on the monarch's role as ultimate judge of disputes among the members of an inclusive and hierarchical social order oriented to the common good and royal justice. While some have heard in these document a rebellious tenor, they were similar to the *Nuevo sistema* in diagnosing a large problem and offering a remedy that would protect Indians in a changing context, respect royal authority, and advance the Crown's interests.

My goal in setting these documents against one another is twofold. First, I seek to illuminate the political-philosophical difficulties faced by the Spanish monarchy at the dawn of Bourbon efforts to reform imperial rule. Second, I argue that their differing depictions of indigenous people represent a crack in the philosophical foundations of Spanish rule and the practice of legal pluralism in the New World. The tensions between the *Nuevo sistema* and the *Representación/Satisfacción* are early evidence that the moral, religious, and juridical bases of the legality indigenous vassals had relied upon during two centuries of Spanish rule were beginning to buckle under the weight of the idea that "the principles of the good economy of the state" were eroding the impulse to justice, the instinct to compromise, and the shared willingness to premise social order on a negotiated rather than absolute obedience to royal law.

Hapsburg Rule in the New World

Spanish conquest of the New World's indigenous polities in the sixteenth century advanced chiefly by decapitating centralized political structures. In Mexico and in the Andean highlands, Spanish conquistadores defeated dominant groups by force of arms (with the aid of indigenous allies), by political maneuver (in the context of internal strife among indigenous groups), by cultural displacement (through evangelization), and ultimately by disease (the hecatomb suffered by native populations between 1521 and roughly 1620). No facet of indigenous life remained unaffected. Survival became the great challenge for indigenous rulers and ordinary people following initial contact. Worlds that had known remarkable cultural and political unity during the preceding century fissured, along old and new fault lines.[10]

Spain's dominion over its new realms was hardly assured. The Mexican capital of Tenochtitlan had fallen by 1521, but resistance continued in the Andes until the 1570s. At the same time, the Spanish king faced political challenges from newly entitled conquistadores. Fearing the rise of a landed aristocracy, Carlos V had opted for *encomiendas*—access to native labor, with a reciprocal obligation to evangelize the natives—over outright land grants to reward those who had fought for new terrains and subdued new peoples. Early on there were signs that the *encomienda* by itself might not restrain the cupidity of those who aspired to local power. In Peru, *encomenderos* opposed a royal edict abolishing the *encomienda* in the 1540s, killing the viceroy to reinforce their point. Hearing of this, the Mexican viceroy prudently set the king's order aside. Clearly, royal authority in the New World would be a sharply contested matter.

The Crown did not altogether lack a model for confronting these challenges. Medieval understandings of government dating to the Iberian Reconquista emphasized obligations over rights and moral and juridical functions over the power to control things.[11] Spain had long experience balancing competing demands of autonomous regions and peoples.[12] In the New World, Spanish kings faced different challenges from other Old World European monarchies, whose most pressing concern during the sixteenth and early seventeenth centuries was to keep religious difference from tearing societies apart. In America, the Spanish Crown sought to incorporate conquered peoples, evangelize them, and put them to work as tributaries. This was not domination pure and simple. As of the 1550s, the New World's indigenous people were considered royal vassals, obligated to render tribute but entitled to the same justice as the king's other subjects.[13] Justice, in turn, was rooted in the idea of *buen gobierno*, good government, understood as balancing the competing demands of diverse elements of a society divided into mutually reinforcing corporations oriented to the *bien común*, or common good. The king's job was to ensure the conditions by which the public weal of collectives and individuals could be secured against threats to order and tranquility. Vassals were to seek their interests within the limits of the common good and obey just laws enacted by the king.

Nothing was more inimical to public order and tranquility than when private interests overran their boundaries to factionalism and the pursuit of individual gain. Society was understood in terms of *civitas*, the human community established by God, within which each individual could seek perfection with the help of others, according to a hierarchical arrangement connecting lowest to highest.[14] Law, good government by another name, was ordained to the "service of God and to the common good of our people," according to *Las Siete Partidas*, the Spanish legal code dating back to the thirteenth century.[15] In concrete terms, members of the community, *ciudadanos* or citizens, formed a single body known as the *república*, which varied by estate and within which individuals were free men who by conscience bore a primary obligation to the common good.[16] There was no naïve assumption that all would in fact confine their ambitions to the limits of the common good. Quite the opposite. "It is natural for the powerful to oppress the poor," noted a legal treatise written in Peru in the early seventeenth century.[17] This, stated *Las Siete Partidas,* was why the king needed to "restrain the proud and stengthen the humble," for the humble were likely to "suffer wrong or violence from others more powerful than they."[18]

These ideas were solidly in place as Spain met the problem of how to govern America. Applying them to a novel situation was another matter. Historical experience in balancing geographically and historically distinct regions in the Iberian peninsula had limited relevance in the New World. The central challenge was how to incorporate vanquished peoples distributed across new territories and cultural milieux. Eliding natives' own understandings of geographical, historical, and linguistic distinctness, Spanish law created the *república de indios* in order to protect the indigenous people from predatory Spaniards, who now became members of the *república de españoles*. Natives would be "*indios*," a legal category premised on ethnic rather than geographical or historical difference.[19] Members of the *república de indios* were obliged to pay tribute. They were also to be "protected as people who are more miserable and of less defense" in the rough and tumble world of the Americas.[20] As a result, "*indio*" became a corporate identity with standing before the law, enabling individuals and communities to bring their grievances before local, royal, and ecclesiastical judges. They did so according to an open-ended logic of overlapping, cross-cutting, at times competing jurisdictions—legal pluralism in the parlance of our day.[21]

This arrangement served the Crown's interest in several ways. Tribute provided a stream of revenue. It also incorporated the Indians into the Spanish empire as vassals, rather than leaving them to be enslaved by *encomenderos* and, later, landowners. Initially, this restrained aristocratic pretensions of conquistadores motivated chiefly by private interest, because indigenous communities were able to defend their land at law, rather than simply watch it pass to local Spaniards.[22] Just as Spanish kings faced a different situation from their counterparts in Europe, so the indigenous people of the New World confronted a different problem from European common people: Their concern was not for the overweening power of the monarchy but for the unchecked power of local Spaniards who saw in royal law an impediment to the advancement of private interests, particularly access to Indian labor as the ultimate source of wealth. From this perspective, the problem for indigenous people was that the king was so far away and his laws so easily ignored or circumvented by those who saw the common good and obedience to law as an inconvenience.

As with other corporations, native communities had the right to self-government. Indian *pueblos* were required to elect new governing officials on a yearly basis. Local *gobernadores* and councils were the first tier of the system of royal justice, though any Indian could appeal directly to the viceroy, who represented the king's original jurisdiction in any matter regarding his vassals. There was nothing automatic about outcomes of litigation. The king was far away and local Spaniards, often in league with officials who acted as "less than reliable instruments of royal authority," frequently had their way, despite the law. These circumstances created a permanent atmosphere of negotiation and maneuver between the king and his vassals divided between the two American *repúblicas*.[23] Laws did not impose themselves so much as they effected a delicate balance between protection and exploitation of indigenous people. Precisely because local power could be so nakedly asserted, the common good expressed through justice served as an antipower against those acting from private motive. As a result, local power and a chastened royal absolutism coexisted, forcing all actors to operate from a shared need to compromise and accommodate.[24]

This impulse to concession deeply marked the law's role in public life. Legality was not a matter of abstract elaborations.[25] A 1612 primer for law students pointed out that there can be no "universal rule for everyone," "for what else does human fragility do than produce varied facts and a diversity of circumstances, which are what inform instances and exceptions"? "Generality" breeds "uncertainty," continued the primer, whereas attention to the concrete case ensured justice in light of actuality.[26] Juan de Solórzano y Pereira, jurist and former magistrate in Peru, reiterated the point in his *Política indiana* of 1648-49: No single rule could "take the measure of all cases . . . because these alter and vary, according to the difference and variation of their quality and circumstance."[27] In effect, Hapsburg law was anchored in the idea that "man is the axis of political and juridical organization, as opposed to the depersonalization that would come later, when rationalism put its confidence in reason," leaving "vast spaces for particular dispositions, privileges, exceptions and discretion."[28]

This understanding of legality and its relation to justice was part and parcel of a principled rejection of Bodin's theory of sovereignty, with its insistence on the divine right of kings and concern for "reasons of state." For sixteenth-century neo-Thomist treatise writers, such as Suárez, Luis de Molina, and others, Spanish kings bore a relationship to the divine, but owed an obligation to society, from which they derived legitimacy. Sovereignty ultimately rested with the people as a collective—the *civitas* ordained by God—an idea that survived through the eighteenth century to the independence period at the beginning of the nineteenth century.[29] The king's obligation to dispense justice grounded a reciprocal social pact and constituted the lifeblood of good government and the common good.[30] This was why Spanish political thinkers through the seventeenth century resisted Bodinnian notions regarding "reasons of state": The state, even the monarch, was secondary to justice in the grand scheme of things.[31]

For nearly two hundred years, from the fall of Tenochtitlan to the dynastic change from Hapsburgs to Bourbons in 1700, this flexible matrix of principle and practice bore the institutional weight of Spanish rule in the New World.[32] The infrequency of rebellions in a place lacking a standing army or a permanent constabulary suggests that the matrix was widely accepted. Indeed, the *repúblicas* remained a legal reality long after they had become social fiction.[33] Premised on the simultaneous protection and exploitation of native peoples, the practices of negotiated rule became *costumbre*, enshrined and established custom, especially within native villages, a principle prizing "conservation" over change.[34] Indigenous litigants, like litigants more generally, shopped for judges, appealed to different jursidictions, and navigated law as a network of options for pursuing interests, expressing grievances, asserting rights, and engaging power. This is precisely what came under increasing pressure from roughly 1740, as Bourbon monarchs, their advisers, and even their subjects began to debate the meaning of "good government" in light of new concerns.

Toward a "New System"

Bourbon victory in the War of Succession did not immediately push Hapsburg forces to the margins of political and economic debate. Despite early-eighteenth-century proposals to revive the *flota* system—because the "actual state of commerce between Spain and the Indies" had led to Spanish "decline"—by 1740 the arrangements governing transatlantic trade remained improvised and uncoordinated, putting Spain at a disadvantage vis-à-vis European competitors and deepening its domestic crisis.[35] For some, "the Indies" were the problem: Spain bore the expense of governing the New World while its competitors enjoyed the advantages of freer trade, because the Crown lacked effective control over the exchange of goods between old world and new.

It was in this context that the *Nuevo sistema de gobierno económico para la América* appeared in the early 1740s. As a diagnosis of Spain's woes, the *Nuevo sistema* did little more than gather and coagulate ideas that had been flowing from the pens of reformist royal bureaucrats since the 1720s.[36] Its significance lies in its framing a critique of established interests—especially those of Cádiz merchants—and asserting the centrality of the New World in reestablishing Spanish economic might. Instead of focusing on contraband and venal royal officials, the *Nuevo sistema* sought to reconceptualize Spain's imperial system by looking to larger isssues of economic structure and performance, including the colonial elites' "fixation" (Stein) on mining, the shortcomings of agriculture, and particularly the role of indigenous people, "the great Treasure of Spain."[37]

At the core of the *Nuevo sistema's* approach is the idea that the "public good" depended on putting land and people to adequate use. On this point the manuscript was unequivocal: "The good of the republic consisting chiefly in the cultivation of the land and the employment of men, which are the real power and solid wealth of every nation, these are the two goals that deserve primary attention."[38] The *Nuevo sistema* raised other critical issues—the need for internal markets, improved transportation systems, less cumbersome taxation schemes, and a revamped transatlantic trade policy—but these were secondary to land and people. Of these two, the *Nuevo sistema* left no doubt that people, which in the New World meant indigenous people, were the first priority. As the manuscript notes in a concluding summary, "There are two chief points to which, in substance, the new system of economic government can be distilled. The first, to make the Indians useful and beneficial vassals."[39]

This proposition reflected a deep shift in thinking regarding the relationship between subjects and the king. Where under Hapsburg rule, the king had been responsible for dispensing justice to secure the common good and maintain order as part of a reciprocal relationship between subjects and monarch, the *Nuevo sistema* argued that the Crown's primary responsibility consisted in making the Indians *útiles* ("useful"). This word itself was not new. Solórzano y Pereira, in his *Política indiana* of 1648-49, understood *utilidad* (utility) in relation to the *bien común* (common good), as opposed to the "pernicious poison" of "the private utility of each person." Thus, "in the republic what may be best for each individual should not be considered, but instead what is of common benefit and utility for all."[40] Solórzano's views carried great weight in officialdom and became the basis for the *Recopilación* of 1680-81, the legal compendium that represented the clearest statement of New World law to the late eighteenth century.

The *Nuevo sistema* employed the words "*útiles*" and "*utilidad*" to different effect. The emerging understanding relied on a clear separation between politics and economics: "In the Indies, as in other places, there are two components to government, the political and the economic." Though *Nuevo sistema* does not give a definition for "political" or "politics," the *Diccionario de autoridades* published by the Royal Spanish Academy between 1726 and 1739 indicates the widely accepted tenor of the word: "Politics" meant "the government of the Republic, which treats and orders the things that touch on the *Policía*, conservation and good conduct of men." This necessarily implied "observance of the laws and ordinances established for the better government of [cities and republics]." Economic government, according to the *Nuevo sistema*, meant "good order, the arrangement of commerce, the means of civilly employing men, the cultivation of lands and the bettering of its products and, in the last analysis, all that which leads to securing the greatest benefit and utility of a country [*país*]": "Political government should so arrange itself as not to oppose the measures of the New System."[41]

This distinction between politics and economics was a relatively novel one. Covarrubias's *Tesoro* of 1611/1674 contained no entry for "economy" or its variants. The *Diccionario de autoridades* offered a definition for "economics" (*economía*) but limited it to the older notion of administering a household, with no sense that land and men needed to be *arranged* to ensure "the greatest benefit and utility of a country."[42] *Utilidad* is still in play in the *Nuevo sistema's* formulation, though pointing to the "country" as an abstraction that omits any reference to its own composition, rather than to the diverse aggregation of people and groups within a hierarchically arranged republic governed by the king's justice in light of the common good. Indeed, the *Nuevo sistema* refers only once to "common good." There are several references to "the public good," usually as a stand-alone phrase and otherwise in relation to "the country" or "the State." In one instance, the manuscript refers to "good politics and reasons of state."[43] It alludes to "order," but emphasizes commerce, the employment of men, and the productivity of land, which, taken together, spell out the meaning of "utility."

This characterization treated "economic government" as separate from other aspects of the organization of large human communities.[44] Under Hapsburg rule, "justice" ensured each thing its proper place in a harmonized social arrangement premised on the "common good." Individuals and groups were free to compete within a field of overlapping jursidictions and legal regimes—legal pluralism—so long as their actions did not undermine the king's ultimate authority or power. Under the new circumstances of eighteenth-century imperial crisis, justice had been distorted in two ways: Spaniards, including "*políticos superficiales*," often sought to "deflect the will of the king," while Indians responded by bringing too many lawsuits.[45] The situation had become too "political." The only solution was to subordinate politics to economics: If "the political" is mentioned, "it will only be in passing," for it is far more important to clarify the "fundamental principles of the good economy of the state."[46] In effect, the unending project of harmonization should yield to the idea that social organization was better oriented to notions of "wealth, power and prosperity" in an abstract future.[47]

Beneath this change in emphasis lay a new conceptualization of the role of indigenous people in the empire. Under the Hapsburgs, law and justice had sought to insulate indigenous people from abuse, so they could pay tribute, perform their status as vassals, and contribute to the common good. By contrast, the *Nuevo sistema* insisted that Indians become effective producers of exportable commodities and eager consumers of imported manufactured goods from Spain. To this end, they would receive land and be guaranteed "the full and peaceful possession of all of the fruits of their labors" against the abuses of Spanish landowners and employers.[48] New Indian yeomen would be moved by the "ambition for convenience and splendor, which is almost natural in everyone" and "the mother of industry."[49] Until now, the king's indigenous vassals had not been able to aspire to that which motivated other men to great effort. Once this changed, argued the *Nuevo sistema*, Spain would surpass England, where five million "free and property-owning men" working six thousand leagues produced four times what twenty- to twenty-five million slaves drew from one hundred thousand leagues for the Spanish monarch.[50]

For production and consumption to have this mutually reinforcing effect, commerce needed to be freer, especially among the Indians.[51] The key, according to the *Nuevo sistema*, was for indigenous producers to trade among themselves and with others in the "competition between seller and buyer." This meant ending the "connections and confabulations" perpetuated by "our American Spaniards," who treated the Indians without dignity and had no idea of trade beyond "monopoly."[52] Linking property rights, consumption, and commerce would put Indians and Spaniards on a more equal footing. There would be no further need for African slavery, that "improper and cruel commerce in human kind," and indigenous people would play an integral economic role in sustaining Spanish power in the inter-imperial system.[53]

The author of the *Nuevo sistema* did not imagine reform would come easily. Perhaps he knew of the *Diccionario de autoridades*' entry for "*político*," or had read Saavedra Fajardo's *Empresa* 53, quoted there: "Once greed has been fattened on public goods, it seeks to fatten itself on private goods, as a result of which the entire purpose of *political* arrangements, which consists in the conservation of the good of each person, is undermined."[54] Attitudes among New World Spaniards were deeply entrenched, and a frontal assault on local Spanish power holders, the manuscript suspected, would not succeed. Instead, the Indians needed to take up the challenges of property, consumption, and commerce. In doing so they would force Spaniards to accept a restructured economic system. The "abuse" of Indians by Spaniards was not only "contrary to all laws of justice, charity and even of humanity, but also destructive of the new economic system."[55] In short, "justice" was to be secondary to the proposition that Indians were first and foremost producers and consumers in a reformed economic environment. To this end, the *Nuevo sistema* advanced four basic (quite radical) policy proposals regarding the Indians: that they take individual ownership of land; that they learn to work with greater eagerness; that they adopt Spanish dress and language; and that they participate more fully in trade.

The first of these anticipated deep reforms to the colonial property regime. Too much land lay unused or underutilized. According to the manuscript, Spaniards owned huge tracts of land but either failed to exploit them or cultivated them using Indians and African slaves, who lacked incentive to work hard, since they could not enjoy the fruits of their labors. Far better for the Crown to distribute unused or underutilized lands to the Indians themselves—"other, more useful vassals"—so that they might gain the "hope of reward and recompense" that animates industriousness in other men.[56] Crucially, individuals rather than communities were the targets of such grants. Indians receiving lands would be encouraged in their "early progress" with the promise of greater "prizes" for those who proved worthy. This, notes the *Nuevo sistema*, is a maxim held by all "wise nations" with regard to "their individuals."[57] The manuscript ignores the effects such a program might have on Indian communities that had held and worked land communally throughout the period of Spanish rule.

Even when land was properly distributed, it could not be assumed that indigenous yeomen would enthusiastically take up the hoe. It was true, admitted the *Nuevo sistema*, that Indians often failed to work hard, though not because they were naturally lazy: They simply lacked the proper incentive. Even so, a natural desire for "convenience and splendor" might not ensure industriousness, given their "smallness of spirit," their "opposition to work," and their affinity for the "monstrous liberties of idleness."[58] As a result, the Crown should "galvanize them by all means," even relieving them of tribute obligations that tended to compete with other work.[59] Indian women, known for their "idleness" and "leisure," were not exempt. The "general good" demanded that they too be inclined to "application and separate themselves from idleness."[60]

As soon as the Indians gained financial means through their work, the Crown should persuade them to adopt Spanish dress and to speak only Spanish. This would be "useful" to the new economic government and would increase commerce generally. Proper policy and the "vigor and sweetness of their treatment" would convince them to leave their own dress behind.

Indian *caciques* who owned land, or those who had a "lucrative employment," could be required to dress in the Spanish manner, setting an example for others. Another means of encouraging this change, according to the *Nuevo sistema*, was to allow those who dressed like Spaniards to enter public places, including churches, by the same door as Spaniards and to allow them to join the same brotherhoods as Spaniards. At the same time, those who performed "vile" jobs should be prohibited from wearing Spanish dress, with the hope that the "horror" of "vileness" would dissuade the more respectable people from continuing to dress in the Indian manner.[61] Encouraging the Indians to speak only Spanish would hasten this process, though here, too, states the *Nuevo sistema*, the Crown needed to introduce change "with sweetness and gentleness."[62]

Finally, the Crown should ensure the Indians' participation in trade. Indians employed in commerce should be treated as Spanish masters treated Spanish servants. Their duties should be spelled out and their salaries and eating arrangements negotiated annually as the only means to end the "tyranny" in which Spaniards had held Indians in their employ.[63] The Crown should establish markets, fairs, and "other grand functions," so that people would see the best people dressed in the Spanish way and hear them speaking Spanish among themselves and to others. Seeing what money can bring would develop the Indians' desire for new things, for the "longing" to look good is, "of all the passions among men and women, the strongest."[64] To enable indigenous people to consume more readily, the Crown should adopt financial reforms. Letters of credit should be introduced so that goods could find their way more easily to market. A copper currency should be instituted—since silver was beyond the means of many—so that even the poor could buy things. In this way, the whole Indian population would develop a desire for appearances, "the richest mine for the State, since from it springs the desire to possess."[65]

These proposals spelled out a new relationship between Indian subjects and government. Again and again, the *Nuevo sistema* speaks of "good reasons of state" rather than of the king's obligation to justice vis-à-vis his indigenous vassals.[66] The language of vassalage remained, though repeated references to "reasons and interests of state" signal an altered sense of the monarch's chief responsibility, now to the "good economy of the State" and what is "useful to the State" rather than to justice as the guarantor of harmony in the republic.[67] People, their labor and their consumption, are now "the true treasure of the State," objects of anxious expectation, programmatic attention, and active manipulation by planners and bureaucrats, rather than subjects of good government and bearers of a right to justice and to relative autonomy in day-to-day life. In this new understanding, "well governed commerce is the principal nerve of the State, and the blood that imparts vigor and increase to the entire body of the Monarchy" by "enriching the State and the Treasury."[68] The Indians must therefore be made to participate in trade, for otherwise Spain would be a country of the poor, that is, "poor for the State, because without consumers, no one will buy, no one will sell, nor is there commerce, nor circulation of money, nor rights for the Sovereign."[69]

In response to those who claimed that the Indians lacked the intelligence to bear the weight of such expectations, the *Nuevo sistema* argued that in a monarchy not everyone need be of great talent. A few must know how to command the Indians "to their own good and to that of the State." The indigenous mass needed only "corporeal strength and the docility to allow themselves to be governed." Thus, what is assumed to be the "great nullity" of the Indians is in fact a "very special advantage, useful and beneficial for many things."[70] Whereas from the earliest times the rationality of indigenous people had been in question, it had always been framed as a problem. In the *Nuevo sistema* their supposed incapacity for self-government is now a boon, if harnessed to the new economic vision. This view implies that the Indians were to have virtually no political role in a reformed Spanish empire. They were to be laborers, consumers, and traders, not members of self-governing communities, litigants, good Christians, and tribute payers. The manuscript is careful not to tread on their "liberty"—to land and to their persons—which had been safeguarded since the sixteenth century. But now the system itself, rather than the law and the king's justice, would protect them: "With the implementation of the New System, they will enjoy all of the privileges that nature conferred on them in their liberty, and which the imperious domination of men has taken from them."[71]

This assumes that Spaniards and Indians alike would readily accede to the dictates of a more interventionist "State" and a more competitive "economy." Yet the mansucript does not discuss how New World Spaniards, entrenched in local privilege, might seek to thwart change and perpetuate their "empire" over the Indians, or how Indians might resist them. In the arrangement envisioned by the *Nuevo sistema*, the recourse to justice through law and litigation would no longer be the touchstone of order. A tolerance for the diversity of circumstances and outcomes, the idea that "it is useful to apply a law to each cause," rather than seek a "universal rule for everyone," were now "small things" of secondary importance to "great matters" of state.[72] In the *Nuevo sistema*, the Indians' ability to negotiate inequality across a system of cross-cutting jurisdictions, backed by the king's responsibility to compensate for power differentials by dispensing justice, had yielded to the idea that the unconscious operations of the system itself could hold abuses in check.

"So Many Kings in the Indies"

The author of the *Nuevo sistema* was hardly alone in regarding the future of Spanish imperial rule in the New World with anxiety. In 1749 two Spanish naval officers, Jorge Juan y Santacilia and Antonio Ulloa, who had spent nearly a decade in the northern Andes between 1735 and 1745, presented a document called *Noticias secretas de América* to secretary of state Marqués de Ensenada. Though Juan and Ulloa were accompanying La Condamine's scientific expedition, Ensenada had commissioned the two officers to write a "secret report" on the state of affairs in Peru, with special attention to problems of imperial governance.[73]

Juan's and Ulloa's reflections were withering.[74] They chronicled the unrelenting greed of Spaniards in the Andean highlands, which had led to the "unhappiness" of the natives. From the "disorder of the curates," the "extortion of the *corregidores,*" and the "bad treatment" to which they were subject, indigenous people effectively lived in "slavery." *Criollos* referred constantly to the Indians' "incapacity to govern themselves," though the Incan past demonstrated this to be a false view, concluded Juan and Ulloa. The truth was that the Indians could not fulfill their role as proper tributaries because they lacked justice. Those who governed Peru thought of justice as "risible and purely ideal, without utility in the republic." Such people almost did not "recognize themselves as vassals since each thinks of himself as a [small] sovereign" subject only to his "own will," thereby undermining the common good.[75]

The *Noticias secretas* make clear that Juan and Ulloa still thought of indigenous people in terms of their reciprocal relationship to the king, their entitlement to justice, and their shared commitment to the common good. The problems of America boiled down to the fact that *criollos*, Spaniards, *mestizos* (mixed-race people), and even some Indians thought of themselves first as interest-seeking individuals. Juan and Ulloa conveyed their dismay sarcastically:

> Peru displays to the eyes of those who govern it [certain great attractions]; with the flattering trickery of despotic authority, Peru offers the greatest scope of action, figured in the great ostentation of power; with the magnet of precious metals, it whets desire and greed; and so attractive are such people that it charms, captivates and applauds those who do not deserve it. In these three circumstances consists all of the poison which oppresses and kills good government in those kingdoms.[76]

Divergent political premises aside, both the *Noticias secretas* and the *Nuevo sistema* revealed a fretful uncertainty regarding Spain's colonial dominance in light of its increasingly tenuous position in Europe's inter-imperial system. In both documents, the treatment and role of the indigenous people lay at the center of diagnoses and proposed reforms. This was no less true of the *Representación verdadera y exclamación* and *Breve y compendiosa satisfacción* of 1749, though the vision animating them bespeaks a profoundly different understanding of the problem faced by indigenous people—and solutions to it.[77]

The *Representación verdadera y exclamación* (True Representation and Exclamation) takes biblical form—with chapter five of the Book of Jeremiah and the last chapter of the Lamentations as backdrop. It opens by appealing to the royal conscience, rather than strictly to the king's reason:

> Oh Lord, . . . oh Emperor of the Indies, merciful, very Catholic and very Christian! . . . Remember what has befallen us in more than two centuries of opprobrium; attend and see the affronts against us: our heritage (Jeremiah cried with all of his People) and your Christian People in the Indies clamor and cry, and tell you their lament as follows.

From this beginning, which figured King Fernando VI's relationship to the Indians as that of Yahweh to the Isrealites, the manuscript broadens to an "exclamation" of the "entire Indian nation" and asks for a "remedy to remove them from the offensive, vituperous and opprobrious circumstance in which they have been for two hundred years."[78]

The text begins by noting that the Indians of the New World are "pupils and orphans without a father" and asks Fernando why he does not honor his "obedient, yielding, gentle and humble children": It seems we have no father, because "Christian Spaniards" mistreat us, even though the Indians are Christians too. How have we been "exiled" from the honor that accords to "your sons and vassals?" asks the *Representación*. Extending the theme, the text notes that "our mothers"—the churches and cathedrals of the Indies—are "widows," because Spaniards "possess" them and think of the Indians as "renters" who enter only for reasons of "convenience and temporal gain," which could not be further from the truth.[79] For we Indians must "drink our tears, which is our constant water, buying it with our wages, because we must pay, because they mistreat us until we must cry; we must buy, oh!, the wood on which we are crucified, the wood with which we are burned and consumed." We must suffer the curates and priests who administer the "pure waters of Grace but only in exchange for our sweat and tears and work," leaving us "dry and parched of knowledge."[80]

The issue, according to the *Representación*, was that the Indians were forced to answer to too many masters focused on their own economic gain. From the viceroy and judges of the *audiencia* to local judges and magistrates to *corregidores* and governors to priests and ecclesiastical judges, the number of people seeking to live by the "labor and sweat of the Indians" was infinite. This, writes the author of the *Representación*, is what most anguishes us. Your servants and vassals "become our kings and lords, and we have as many kings as you send judges to administer justice." They act as our "absolute owners, overturning the laws, acting on whim, enriching themselves at the expense of your Indians. There is no one to redeem us from their hands," though we too are your loyal subjects.[81] Even the African slaves, "vile and servile" men who are not your vassals, mistreat us. A slave could travel to Spain, whereas the most noble Indian lacks "the free will" to come before your majesty and show you his "wounds." Look, Lord, and you will see that "you have and we have so many kings in the Indies." *Criollos*, Spaniards, African slaves, *mestizos, mulatos*—all are your servants but "all are our masters, even though you alone, Lord, are our Lord."[82]

In raising this clamor, the *Representación* advanced a fundamental and familiar point. Justice belonged to the entire community of men and order demanded that each member of the community subordinate private interests to common ends by obeying rational propositions embodied in law. The ruler, acting as lawmaker and the supreme judge, was charged with the care of the whole people. Thus, ruler and subjects alike could ensure justice by acting according to the dictates of conscience, premised on a voluntary submission to God in light of the common good.[83]

From this perspective, the problem for the king's indigenous subjects was that too many *criollos*, Spaniards, and even Indian office holders were acting as rulers unto themselves. Each had become a sovereign (as Juan and Ulloa had put it) and the benefit of life in *civitas* was being lost to the free pursuit of individual interest. By striving "more slugglishly for the common good," individuals had created a situation in which "each one attends to it as if it were his own."[84] With too many kings, there could be no real political community. As Solórzano had noted from his experience in mid-seventeenth-century Peru, "if everyone were given license to proceed according to their free will, liberty would perish in liberty and . . . the republic would sink."[85] For the author of the *Representación*, the source of this scourge was obvious—greed and the New World's distance from the throne, a diagnosis shared with the *Noticias secretas*.

The difference between the two documents is that the *Representación* proposed a remedy reflecting the Indians' two centuries of life under Spanish rule. It did not simply harken to a bygone, supposedly golden age. In some ways, the Indians' plight since conquest had always been what it was at the mid-eighteenth century—a vulnerability to the whims of the powerful. Previous kings had sought to protect indigenous subjects through laws designed to restrain private actors and blunt their worst abuses. But now even the king's judges could not be counted on, as evidenced by the "violent, hard, cruel, tyrannical government the ministers of the king have invented, distinct from everything practiced in other Catholic kingdoms and quite other than the king's intention." It was as though the Indians cannot "speak or treat with [the king], since he is hidden from them, occluded and behind veils, and it is only on faith that they know themselves to have a king." As a result, stated the *Representación*, royal laws are not observed, because those who "do not want good for us know how to interpret them against us."[86]

The answer to this dilemma was to cut the "Gordian knot" by allowing the Indians to have their own judges and advocates, chosen by Indian nobles and appointed by the king.[87] These judges should be free to travel to Spain and present their grievances, just as the Spaniards do. For "your Indian vassals are equal to your Spanish vassals, the nobles the same as nobles and *hidalgos*, and the rest according to their general estate."[88] In this way, all would enjoy "your royal magnificence, since we all serve your royal crown" and the Indians, who "sweat treasure in paying their tribute" would learn "the literature and politics of court" so that they can stand before the throne.[89] If Indian advocates are properly trained, they will be able to give account of whether the royal will is enforced. This was hardly a novel idea, noted the *Representación*. In 1733, King Felipe V had commanded that there be two Indian *procuradores* (legal advocates) at each *audiencia* and advocates in other cities of the Indies. Little had come of this, but only because "when something is ordered to benefit the Indians it is not enforced and is even turned against us" so that "the doors for seeking justice have been closed to us."[90] Yet only if the Indians have protectors will his majesty know whether the justice God ordains and the royal conscience demands actually prevails in the Indies.[91] And only then will the king know he has loyal subjects in the New World who obey the law, as should all good vassals. As the processions organized by Indian leaders in Lima in February 1748 to celebrate Fernando VI's coronation (which had taken place in Spain in mid-1746) attest, noted the *Representación*, the Indians have always surpassed "what your Spanish vassals have done, and even those of the ancient Roman triumphs and of all the nations."[92]

A second part of the argument to the king, *Breve y compendiosa satisfacción* (Brief and Compendious Satisfaction), argued that the Indians should be allowed to join ecclesiastical orders and the priesthood. No law had ever barred the Indians from being monks, nuns, or secular clergy. They had not been able to do so "because that is how the Spaniards want it."[93] It is no argument against indigenous people that they are not literate, because Spaniards have "impeded all the avenues of knowledge" and denied them the opportunity to master "latinity and other literary faculties."[94] Spaniards claim that it "is a great offense" for an Indian to defend himself and that knowledge itself is a "grave crime": "The ignorance of the Indian is, for the Spaniard, a virtue, profit and convenience" (as the *Nuevo sistema* had made clear).[95] The remedy was for the king to allow indigenous vassals to study in schools such as the Colegio de San Martín in Cuzco. This would allow them to bring grievances before the king and ensure their religious faith, since they would not be distracted by the "bad example" Spaniards have set since conquest.[96]

The problem went deeper still. Since conquest, stated the *Satisfacción*, Indians have lived a "political life in cities and villages throughout the kingdom" and have sought to live "unified with the Spaniards" as "one people and one nation."[97] Yet the children of Spaniards and Indians are deemed different and called "*mestizos*," a "vulgarity" that bespeaks philosophical error, since "true philosophy or wisdom says that all men are one, and all are sons of Adam, whether they are Spaniards, Indians, Frenchmen, etcetera": "[I]n the essential we are all of the same substance."[98] Why in Spain and elsewhere, asks the *Satisfacción*, has this term not been used in referring to men born of different nations? Chiefly because learned men have seen it as an "odious" cause of "discord and schisms." So why is it used in the New World? Spaniards claim that *mestizos* are neither Spanish nor Indian, but rather a "mixture of the two nations."[99] Yet nothing about Indian blood "infects, contaminates or incapacitates the Indians," insists the *Satisfacción*, since it is "clean and very noble."[100] Moreover, the Spanish have no one for their daughters to marry. This could be resolved if the Spaniards and the Indians were to "love one another, marrying and making a single people and nation, given that they are Catholic Christians, under one law, vassals of a single lord, governed by the same laws . . . and everyone together, as your Majesty commands."[101]

The benefits of this "Christian politics" would be great. Royal officials would be spared the burden of domination that leaves Spain in such "infamy" in the eyes of other nations. The practice of excluding the Indians from positions of authority, claimed the *Satisfacción*, derives from the idea that sovereigns who seek absolute power over their provinces must exclude from office all those who dwelt there before conquest. As a result, no one trusts anyone, "factions among subjects and vassals of a prince" have been fomented, and the "condemned maxims of Machiavellianism" have come to govern the Indies. Those who are "zealous for the good of the republic are pruned away and exiled" in favor of a "tyranny of the powerful," and there is no "compassion for the life and property of the vassals."[102] This is precisely what has happened with the king's Indian vassals, concludes the *Satisfacción*, and there is no one to speak for them.

Having registered this bill of particulars regarding bad government in the Indies, the *Satisfacción* proceeds to a list of practical remedies the Crown might adopt. It begins by asking that the "Christian laws and canons of the Holy Mother Roman Catholic church" and all royal decrees be enforced throughout the kingdom, even older ones that had fallen into abeyance. It suggests that the king lift the ban impeding Indians and their representatives from traveling to Spain. The Indians should be protected in their land and be able to engage freely in commerce. They should be allowed to administer assets of their own hospitals, manage tribute collection, and govern their own communities without interference from Spaniards or others. The king should open the schools to the Indians, so that they can learn to read, write, calculate, and study the sciences. They should be admitted to religious and secular organizations on the same footing as others and be able to serve in important positions, such as bishoprics and as protectors of Indians. To ensure their advancement, the king should order an end to all labor drafts and personal service. Spanish *corregidores*, who have extorted the Indians for two hundred years, should be "absolutely and totally removed" and Indian judges should be put in their place, subject only to the king and the viceroys in secular matters, and bishops in religious ones. Finally, the king should create a new tribunal, independent of the viceroys and *audiencias*, made up of people concerned for the "weak," as the Indians are. For it was people "adverse and powerful" who had put the Indians into so miserable a state. In effect, the *Satisfacción* was asking the king to establish a new jurisdiction that would allow the Indians to protect themselves against abuses more readily and enable them to pay tribute in a timely manner. If these things were done, the foundations of the kingdom would be restored with "stones solid and unified, ordered and placed to strengthen one another, like vassals in mutual love and concord, which along with God's love, will bring eternal peace in the kingdoms of Spain, consisting of happy rule, made fast by reason and crowned by the enforcement of the laws."[103]

Conclusion

At this early stage of debates over how to confront growing challenges to imperial rule, the *Nuevo sistema* and the *Representación/Satisfacción* shared a sense of what was wrong: The Crown was losing or had lost effective administration of the New World, largely because it could not protect its indigenous vassals from abuse. Put another way, the balance between public and private that had enabled Indians to establish a modus vivendi with local power holders through the operations of law had been upset. Royal officers, Spaniards generally and many others acting out of private motive and with no regard for the common good, deprived the Crown of revenues and oppressed the Indians. A common diagnosis did not lead to any agreement on what to do. The *Nuevo sistema* rejected a straight-up attack on Spanish privilege in the New World. The power of local actors to skirt the law and evade legal remedies was great, and the Crown's ability to enforce its will small. The only answer was for a more directive state to treat the Indians as objects of "economic government." With opportunities to accumulate and acquire, Indians would force Spaniards to compete economically. The system would be largely self-correcting and would require only that the "State" ensure the liberties of commerce and trade and galvanize the indigenous people to greater industry. The *Representación/Satisfacción* proposed a different solution: Strengthen the Indians' hand in seeking justice by giving them their own judges and their own advocates, thereby enabling them to reach the king with their grievances. This would bolster royal law, because the Indians would continue to act as loyal vassals—paying tribute, ensuring good government, and becoming fuller members of the empire's community of peoples. Within a greater sphere of action regarding local political conditions, Indians (and *mestizos*) would rescue the imperial *civitas* by shoring up the pact between the kingdom and its king against the "tyranny of the powerful."[104]

Taken together, these texts bespeak the weakening of law and legal pluralism as economic interests gained traction in a social and political system that had assumed the primacy of jurisdiction in the arrangement of human communities.[105] Though the *républica* system dated back to the sixteenth century, Indians had always inhabited the interstices of the New World's legal and administrative structures. They had found some measure of protection there, so long as willingness to enforce royal law acted as a checkrein on the pursuit of private advantage. A plural system had depended on the hegemony of the common good and justice in political discourse—in the sense that few were in a position to question them as the *summa bona* of social existence. This was less and less the case with the advance of the eighteenth century. The *Nuevo sistema* responded by yielding the field to economics, proposing a homeostatic system that would largely police and correct itself.[106] The Indians might remain vassals in name, but as economic factors their political participation would be minimal. In the world envisioned by the *Nuevo sistema*, they were less subjects of empire than objects of state and factors in the market. The *Representación/Satisfacción* responded to this uncompensated economic objectification by calling for a jurisdictional solution: Indians who complained of abuse should be able to reach the king directly. "Jurisdictional jockeying"—a hallmark of legal pluralism—would not cease.[107] But under this proposal, the king's indigenous vassals would begin all legal proceedings from within their own jurisdiction, just as other corporate entities did in the Spanish legal world. In essence, recognized principles of governance would be stretched and reformed to suit a new age, but the idea of justice as the ground of human community would remain.

Nothing was written in stone at this point, and these two documents are but instances of larger processes that unfolded more fully in following decades. Perhaps what we can say is that this was a moment of ideological superposition regarding the empire's fate as a polity. We know which of these visions of large, diverse human communities won out over the latter decades of the eighteenth—and the nineteenth century—and not only in the New World. Notions of *civitas*, reciprocity, justice, and the common good animated by the practices of legal pluralism did not vanish entirely in the face of economic imperatives. They remained free-floating particles of political culture in Latin America, especially among indigenous and other vulnerable people, long after the Bourbon reforms and the ideological liberalism of independent republics had displaced them.

Accounts of the Spanish empire have tended to confine discussion of the Bourbon reforms to the period after 1750, and especially after the Seven Years' War. The *Nuevo sistema* and the *Representación/Satisfacción* remind us that before midcentury there were other axes of debate that mirrored legal, philosophical, and political concerns just beginning to be expressed in the Atlantic. Perhaps this is why the proposals appear to have had little direct impact in the policy circles from which subsequent reforms emerged. On one hand, a willingness to confront large questions may have wilted in the face of later emergency. On the other, their diagnoses were too damning and their proposals too radical to stand.[108] This was particularly true of the *Representación/Satisfacción*. Vassals claiming rights at law in a negotiated and plural legal world did not square with the growing sense within the Spanish empire that economics—commerce, trade, production, and consumption—might be the weapon of choice in the arena of inter-imperial competition and an emergent global capitalism.[109]

NOTES

I have benefited from the incisive comments of Lauren Benton and Richard Ross in completing the manuscript. I thank them for their insight and patience. I am also grateful to the members of the Latin America History Workshop at Northwestern University, who generously read and discussed the manuscript while there was still time to change it. Any errors of commission or omission are entirely mine.

1. J. H. Elliot, *Empires of the Atlantic World: Britain and Spain in America, 1492-1830* (New Haven, CT: Yale University Press, 2003); Stanley J. Stein and Barbara H. Stein, *Silver, Trade, and War: Spain and America in the Making of Early Modern Europe* (Baltimore, MD: Johns Hopkins University Press, 2000).
2. Stein and Stein, *Silver*, 200-230.
3. Joseph Del Campillo y Cosío, *Nuevo sistema de gobierno económico para la América. Con los males y daños que le causa el que hoy tiene, de los que participa copiosamente España; y remedios universales para que la primera tenga considerables ventajas, y la segunda mayores intereses* (Madrid, 1789). This manuscript, submitted to King Felipe V before the interventions of Campomanes, Floridablanca, Antonio de Ulloa, Esquilache, and Gálvez in policy debates, has long been of disputed authorship. See Luis Navarro García, "Campillo y el *Nuevo sistema*: Una atribución dudosa," *Temas Americanistas* 2 (1983): 22-29; Luis Navarro García, "El falso Campillo y el reformismo borbónico," *Temas Americanistas* 12 (1995): 5-14; Stein and Stein, *Silver*, 221-26.
4. Miguel Artola, "Campillo y las reformas de Carlos III," *Revista de Indias* 12 (1952): 685-714; Stein and Stein, *Silver*, 231-59; Stanley J. Stein and Barbara H. Stein, *Apogee of Empire: Spain and New Spain in the Age of Charles III, 1759-1789* (Baltimore, MD: Johns Hopkins University Press, 2003); Josefina Cintrón Tiryakian, "Campillo's Pragmatic New System: A Mercantile and Utilitarian Approach to Indian Reform in Spanish Colonies of the Eighteenth Century," *History of Political Economy* 10, no. 2 (1978): 233-57.
5. Elliott, *Empires*; Jane Burbank and Frederick Cooper, *Empires in World History: Power and the Politics of Difference* (Princeton, NJ: Princeton University Press, 2010), 235-40; Stein and Stein, *Apogee*; Frederick Cooper, *Colonialism in Question: Theory, Knowledge, History* (Berkeley: University of California Press, 2005), 178-79; Emma Rothschild, "Global Commerce and the Question of Sovereignty in the Eighteenth-Century Provinces," *Modern Intellectual History* 1, no. 1 (2004): 3-25.
6. Campillo y Cosio, *Nuevo sistema*, 303.
7. One that carried over to the new republics emerging from the wars of independence in the early nineteenth century. Tiryakian, "Campillo's Pragmatic," 254-57.
8. The full titles are *Representación verdadera y exclamación rendida y lamentable , que toda la nación indiana hizo a la majestad del Señor Rey de las Españas y Emperador de las Indias, el Señor Don Fernando VI, pidiendo los atienda y remedie, sacándolos del afrentoso vituperio y oprobio en que están mas had de doscientos años. Exclamación de los indios americanos, usando para ella de la misma que hizo el Profesta Jeremías a Dios en el Cap. 5 y último de sus Lamentaciones* and *Breve y compendiosa satisfacción a las razoens que tiene la nación española en mantener el error de no admitir a la nobilísima y muy limpia nación de los indios americanos, y a los mestizos y descendientes de los indios, a las religiones de frailes y de monjas, y a las dignidades eclesiásticas y seculares.* They have been published as *Clamor de los Indios Americanos*, ed. F. Eduardo Osorio C. (Mérida, Venezuela, 1993) (hereafter *Clamor*). See also Jorge Bernales Ballesteros, "Fray Calixto de San José Tupac Inca, Procurador de Indios y la 'Exclamación' reivindicalista de 1750," *Historia y Cultura* 3: 5-18. Alcira Dueñas

raises the possibility of collective authorship among a few Franciscans: Fray Antonio Garro, Fray Isidoro de Cala, and possibly others. See Alcira Dueñas, *Indians and Mestizos in the "Lettered City": Reshaping Justice, Social Hierarchy, and Political Culture in Colonial Peru* (Boulder: University Press of Colorado, 2010), 71,

9. Dueñas, *Indians*, 71-78.
10. See Charles Gibson, *The Aztecs under Spanish Rule: A History of the Indians in the Valley of Mexico, 1519-1810* (Stanford, CA: Stanford University Press, 1964); Nancy Farriss, *Maya Society under Colonial Rule: The Collective Enterprise of Survival* (Princeton, NJ: Princeton University Press, 1984); Steve J. Stern, *Peru's Indian Peoples and the Challenge of Spanish Conquest: Huamanga to 1640* (Madison: University of Wisconsin Press, 1993); Brooke Larson, *Cochabamba, 1550-1900: Colonialism and Agrarian Transformation in Bolivia* (Durham, NC: Duke University Press, 1999).
11. Michel Senellart, *Les Arts de gouverner: Du regimen mediéval au concept de gouvernement* (Paris: Seuil, col. Des Travaux, 1995), 20-30, 67-83.
12. Luis Weckman, *The Medieval Heritage of Mexico* (New York: Fordham University Press, 1991).
13. Lewis Hanke, *The Spanish Struggle for Justice in the Conquest of America* (New York: Little, Brown, 1965); *All Mankind Is One: A Study of the Disputation between Bartolomé de las Casas and Juan Ginés Sepúlveda on the Religious and Intellectual Capacity of the American Indians* (Dekalb: Northern Illinois University Press, 1974).
14. Aquinas, *The Political Ideas of St. Thomas Aquinas*, ed. D. Bigongiari (New York: Free Press, 1997), 175-76, 178-79, 182, 185.
15. R. Burns, ed., *Las Siete Partidas* (Philadelphia: University of Pennsylvania Press, 2001), 2: 271-72 (2.1.5).
16. Juan Solórzano y Pereira, *Política indiana* (Madrid: Biblioteca Castro, 1996), 1: 219 (2.5.6), 1: 232 (2.6.6), 1: 381 (2.16.33).
17. Juan de Hevia Bolaños, *Curia philipica* (Valladolid: Lex Nova, 1989), 1: 150.
18. Burns, *Partidas*, 3: 710 (3.18.41); Solórzano y Pereira, *Política*, 2: 1176 (3.32.46).
19. Brian P. Owensby, *Empire of Law and Indian Justice in Colonial Mexico* (Stanford, CA: Stanford University Press, 2008), 25. The *república* system was not made of whole cloth by a single royal decree; rather, it was the result of independent decrees that over time created a penumbra of protections favoring the Indians against abuse.
20. R. Konetske, ed., *Colección de documentos para la historia de la formación social de hispanoamérica, 1493-1810* (Madrid: CSIC, 1953), 1: 528. "Miserable," here, is a legal tag referring to the wretchedness and vulnerability of those who lacked power in a patriarchal social order. See Owensby, *Empire of Law*, 55-56; Lauren Benton, *Law and Colonial Cultures: Legal Regimes in World History, 1400-1900* (New York: Cambridge University Press, 2002), 42-44.
21. Benton, *Law and Colonial Cultures*, 2-3.
22. Of course, there was no end of abuse and it was frequently said in the sixteenth century that the situation of Indians in *encomienda* was barely distinguishable from that of slaves. Legally, they remained free people and ultimately the legal system gave them some space and tools with which to operate.
23. Annick Lempérière, *Entre Dieu et le Roi, La République. Mexico, XVIe-XIXe siècle* (Paris: Belles Lettres, 2004), 70.
24. Lempérière, *Entre Dieu*, 71, 99. Benton, *Law and Colonial Cultures*, 27.
25. Victor Tau Anzoateguí, *Casuismo y sistema: indagación histórica sobre el espíritu del derecho indiano* (Buenos Aires: IIHD, 1992).

26. Francisco Bermúdez de Pedraza, *Arte legal para estudiar la jursiprudencia* (Salamanca, 1612), 135.
27. Solórzano y Pereira, *Política*, 2: 941 (3.20.22), 3: 2092 (5.11.5).
28. Tau Anzoateguí, *Casuismo*, 468, 569.
29. Francisco Xavier Guerra, "The Spanish American Tradition of Representation and Its European Roots," *Journal of Latin American Studies* 26 (1994): 1-35.
30. See Alfonso García-Gallo, "El pactismo en el reino de Castilla y su proyección en América," in *El pactismo en la historia de España*. Simposio celebrado los días 24-26 de abril 1978 en el Insituto de España, Madrid, 1980. Brian P Owensby, "Pacto entre rey lejano y súbditos indígenas. Justicia, legalidad y política en Nueva España, siglo XVII," *Historia Mexicana* 61, no. 1 (2011): 59-106.
31. Lempérière, *Entre Dieu*, 67-68.
32. Colin MacLachlan first used the word "matrix" to describe the philosophy of Spanish rule in the New World. MacLachlan, *Spain's Empire in the New World: The Role of Ideas in Institutional and Social Change (*Berkeley: University of California Press, 1988), 67.
33. Solórzano y Pereira, *Política*, 1: 230 (2.6.1).
34. José Antonio Maravall, *La cultura del Barroco: Análisis de una estructura histórica* (Barcelona: Ariel, 1975), 271-72.
35. See, e.g., Juan de Legarra, "Representación a SM sobre el estado actual de los Comercios de España e Indias. Con expresión de las causas de que proviene su decadencia, y medios para reestablecer, reintegrando en el uso de ellos a los Españoles," included in "Comercios de España e Indias" (1719), Colección Sempere y Guarinos, Biblioteca de la Real Academia de la Historia (Madrid), Ms. 4666. See also José del Campillo y Cosío, *Lo que hay de más y lo que hay de menos en España para que sea lo que debet eser y no lo que es* (Madrid, 1898), 20. See also Stein and Stein, *Silver*, 169-72.
36. There has been much debate about whether Campillo or Melchor Macanaz wrote the *Nuevo sistema*. The 1789 version contains an *exordio* supposedly signed by Campillo in 1743 and with a reference to *Lo que hay de más*. Stein and Stein conclude that Macanaz was the author. Few would hold fast any longer to the proposition that it was indisputably Campillo, though not all would agree that it was Macanaz. Stein and Stein, *Silver*, 221-26. According to Stein and Stein, the manuscript was found among Macanaz's papers and published under Campillo's name only in 1789. This is why they treat the *Nuevo sistema* as of a piece with Macanaz's *Discurso sobre América española* of the same period. Navarro García has also argued that Campillo was not the author of the *Nuevo sistema*. See note 4 above. See also Tiryakian, "Campillo's Pragmatic," which treats the manuscript as Campillo's work.
37. *Nuevo sistema*, 54. Pagination is as follows: unless otherwise indicated, all page cites are to the portion of the text after the table of contents, which ends at page 32 in the 1789 version. The text then runs from page 1 to page 297.
38. *Nuevo sistema*, 83.
39. *Nuevo sistema*, 284.
40. Solórzano y Pereira, *Política*, 1: 218 (2.5.1), 3: 2194 (5.15.22), 2: 1178 (3.32.50).
41. Real Academía Española, *Diccionario de autoridades* (1726-39), http://www.fsanmillan.es/biblioteca/biblioteca.jsp?pagina=1&cadena=Diccionario+de+Autoridades®istro=10&orden=titulo. *Nuevo sistema*, 3, 41. See generally, Karl Polanyi, *The Great Transformation: The Political and Economic Origins of Our Time* (Boston: Beacon, 1957), 71.
42. *Diccionario de autoridades*, http://www.fsanmillan.es/biblioteca/biblioteca.jsp?pagina=1&cadena=Diccionario+de+Autoridades®istro=10&orden=titulo. See also, Sebastian de

Covarrubias Orozco, *Tesoro de la lengua castellana or espannola* (1611, 1674), http://bib.cervantesvirtual.com/servlet/SirveObras/80250529545703831976613/index.htm. This is not the place for a full treatment of the etymologies of such key terms as "*política*" and "*economía*" and related usages, including "*administración*" and "*gobierno*" (and their variants).

43. *Nuevo sistema*, 65-66, 68, 104, 174.
44. I do not want to overdraw this contrast. At several points, the *Nuevo sistema* lumps politics and economics together, though even then it makes clear that "political government" should not oppose the New System. *Nuevo sistema*, 41.
45. *Nuevo sistema*, 183.
46. *Nuevo sistema*, 4.
47. *Nuevo sistema*, 60-61.
48. *Nuevo sistema*, 86.
49. *Nuevo sistema*, 131.
50. *Nuevo sistema*, 85-86.
51. *Nuevo sistema*, 172-73.
52. *Nuevo sistema*, 279-80.
53. *Nuevo sistema*, 121.
54. *Diccionario de autoridades*, vol. 5, p. 312, quoting Saavedra Fajardo's *Empresa* 53.
55. *Nuevo sistema*, 108.
56. *Nuevo sistema*, 108-9.
57. *Nuevo sistema*, 109.
58. *Nuevo sistema*, 109, 123. This discourse regarding idleness among the Indians was not a strictly colonial phenomenon. Very similar language was being used in Spain at this time to describe the work habits of Spanish peasants. See Ruth Mackay, *Lazy, Improvident People: Myth and Reality in the Writing of Spanish History* (Ithaca, NY: Cornell University Press, 2006), especially chapters 3 and 4.
59. *Nuevo sistema*, 123.
60. *Nuevo sistema*, 121-22.
61. *Nuevo sistema*, 124-28
62. *Nuevo sistema*, 137.
63. *Nuevo sistema*, 229-30.
64. *Nuevo sistema*, 140-41.
65. *Nuevo sistema*, 141.
66. *Nuevo sistema*, 103, 115, 174, 185, 243.
67. *Nuevo sistema*, 4, 166, 261.
68. *Nuevo sistema*, 18, 155.
69. *Nuevo sistema*, 118.
70. *Nuevo sistema*, 91-92.
71. *Nuevo sistema*, 21 (in Exordio II).
72. *Nuevo sistema*, 42.
73. Kenneth Andrien, "The *Noticias secretas de América* and the Construction of a Governing Ideology for the Spanish American Empire," *Colonial Latin Ameican Review* 7, no. 2 (1998): 1751-92. See also, Luis J. Ramos Gómez, *Época, genesis y texto de las "Noticias secretas de América," de Jorge Juan y Antonio de Ulloa (1735-1745)* (Madrid: CSIC, 1985), 2 vols. (hereafter *Noticias secretas).* Ramos Gómez's study is an exhaustive comparison of the various versions of the text. The London 1826 version in English was the first actually published

in any language. See Andrien, "The *Noticias secretas*." In 1748, Juan and Ulloa did publish their multivolume *Relación histórica de viage a la America meridional* (Madrid: Fundación Universitaria Española, 1978) describing their decade in the Andes. See Neil Safier, *Measuring the New World: Enlightenment Science and South America* (Chicago: University of Chicago Press, 2008), chapter 4; Jorge Cañazres Esguerra, *How to Write the History of the New World: Histories, Epistemologies, and Identities in the Eighteenth-Century Atlantic World* (Stanford, CA: Stanford University Press, 2001), 247.

74. They were not alone in this. Don Vincente Morachimo, an Andean noble who spent several years at court in Madrid in the 1720s presenting the grievances of Indians to King Felipe V (and to King Luis I, during his brief reign in 1724) and the Council of the Indies, wrote a "Manifiesto de agravios y vejaciones" in the early 1730s detailing the abuse of indigenous people at the hands of *corregidores*, priests, and other Spaniards. The "Manifiesto" was later paired with Juan's and Ulloa's secret report as describing conditions in the Andes. See Dueñas, *Indians and Mestizos*, 62-65.
75. Ramos Gómez, *Noticias secretas*, 2: 192-93, 351, 352, 357.
76. Ramos Gómez, *Noticias secretas*, 2: 357.
77. The *Representación verdadera* and the *Breve y compendiosa satisfacción* emerged from "cross-currents of native and clerical discourses . . . in the colonial world of Peru stemming from the pedagogical relationship between Indian nobility and religious mentors." According to Dueñas, "Andean discourses borrowed heavily from the literary imagery and narrative styles of the missional epistolary genre to which the writers were exposed." Dueñas, *Indians and Mestizos*, 137. Fray Calixto spent a decade as a Franciscan mission aide in Tarma and Cusco during the 1720s and 1730s. He was hardly an isolated case, and Dueñas argues that the *Representación* was a collective writing, in keeping with Andean notions of authorship and activism, part of a larger project that sought to resituate Andeans in colonial society. Dueñas, *Indians and Mestizos*, 73.
78. *Clamor*, 65 (1-1v), 63. Parenthetical references are to the pagination of the original manuscript.
79. *Clamor*, 66 (2v-3).
80. *Clamor*, 67 (2v-3).
81. *Clamor*, 68 (3v-4).
82. *Clamor*, 68 (3v-4, 4-4v) and 73 (8-8v).
83. Aquinas, *The Political Ideas*, xxi.
84. Aquinas, *The Political Ideas*, 185.
85. Solórzano y Pereira, *Política*, 1: 241 (2.6.42).
86. *Clamor*, 75 (9-9v, 9v-10), 80 (13v-14).
87. *Clamor*, 81 (14v-15).
88. *Clamor*, 76 (10v-11).
89. *Clamor*, 79 (12v-13).
90. *Clamor*, 74 (8v-9).
91. *Clamor*, 79 (12v-13).
92. *Clamor*, 72-73 (7v-8).
93. *Clamor*, 85 (16-16v).
94. *Clamor*, 89 (19-19v).
95. *Clamor*, 89 (19-19v).
96. *Clamor*, 89 (19v-20), 115 (40-40v), 117 (42-42v).
97. *Clamor*, 117 (42-42v).

98. *Clamor,* 103 (30v-31).
99. *Clamor,* 105 (32v-33).
100. *Clamor,* 105 (32v-33).
101. *Clamor,* 119 (44-44v).
102. *Clamor,* 122 (47-47v).
103. *Clamor,* 126-28 (50v-52v).
104. See Owensby, "Pacto"; García Gallo, "El pactismo." *Clamor,* 122 (47-47v).
105. To understand precisely what was changing and how requires much more research at the local and regional levels.
106. This was not yet the "invisible hand," but it did look in that direction nearly two decades before Adam Smith announced it. Adam Smith, *The Theory of Moral Sentiments,* I.IV.10 (1759); *An Inquiry into the Nature and Causes of the Wealth of Nations,* I.72, I.73, IV.2.9 (1776) (both available online at http://www.econlib.org/library). It is worth noting as well that the view espoused in the *Nuevo sistema* predated the writings of the French physiocrats. Quesnay's *Tableau économique* theorizing the circulation of money and wealth was published in 1759 and Turgot's *Reflections sur la formation et distribution de la richesse* (Reflections on the Generation and Distribution of Wealth), with its argument in favor of irreducible self-interest and the freedom of trade, did not appear until the late 1760s.
107. See Benton, *Law and Colonial Cultures,* 3.
108. The subsequent history of the *Representación/Satisfacción* and their supposed author speaks volumes. After receiving the manuscript from the Franciscans, and after the 1750 conspiracy to assassinate the viceroy in Lima had come to light and the Huarochirí rebellion had exploded that same year, King Fernando VI called for an investigation of the charges made in it. Viceroy Conde de Superunda in Lima did as asked and then summarily banished Fray Calixto for his supposed role in writing the two inflammatory manuscripts. Dueñas, *Indians and Mestizos,* 183. The viceroy linked the manuscript to the conspiracy and rebellion. Dueñas, *Indians and Mestizos,* 71.
109. I am in complete agreement with Benton that our focus needs to be on "the conditions and conflicts" that constituted the global economy. Benton, *Law and Colonial Cultures,* 24. I would want us to be equally attentive to differences and similarities within that environment. On ideological changes within the empire during the latter half of the eighteenth century, see generally, Gabriel B. Paquette, *Enlightenment, Governance, and Reform in Spain and Its Empire, 1759-1808* (New York: Palgrave Macmillan, 2008). For a challenging new interpretation of capitalism from the perspective of the regional and global history of the Bajío, see John Tutino, *Making a New World: Founding Capitalism in the Bajío and Spanish North America* (Durham, NC: Duke University Press, 2011).

PART III

Constructing Imperial Jurisdiction

7

Magistrates in Empire

Convicts, Slaves, and the Remaking of the Plural Legal Order in the British Empire

LAUREN BENTON AND LISA FORD

In early January, 1790, the *Duke of Leicester* approached an unsettled coast on the sparsely populated island of Barbuda in the West Indies, and offloaded forty-eight men and five women before sailing away.[1] The stranded passengers told locals they had signed contracts of indenture and were on their way to Philadelphia when the ship had strayed off course. Residents took pity on the castaways and transported them to the town of St. John's, on Antigua, where they were given food and shelter. The charitable islanders were surprised a few weeks later by news that the *Duke of Leicester* had attempted to land a second group of passengers at Anguilla, where the mate confessed to officials that the ship was carrying convicts from Ireland, with instructions to dump them on uninhabited coasts near British settlements in the West Indies. The "great uneasiness and alarm" of Antigua residents as they contemplated having "a set of desperate wretches left at large" among them prompted urgent attempts to reembark the convicts and led Thomas Shirley, the captain general, to exhort London officials to block any future attempts to send convicts to the islands.[2]

London officials did not regard the convicts with the same terror. Official concern focused instead on a different source of disorder: the authority that local elites were seeking to assume over an imperial process. Lord Grenville, the home secretary, ordered Shirley in no uncertain terms to block local legislative efforts in Antigua to outlaw future shipments of convicts.

No act or law "should be allowed to pass *in any of the colonies* for inflicting penalties on persons who might, under the King's authority, convey thither persons of that description."[3] Colonial anxieties about men without masters—fears intensified by deep worries about the rebelliousness of slaves—had come face to face with a newly acute metropolitan preoccupation with the center's power to assign, regulate, or remove legal prerogatives in the colonies.

Antigua was one of many sites within the British Empire where conflicts over the nature and scope of middling authorities came to occupy a dominant place in legal politics in the early nineteenth century. Such conflicts brought a set of colonies with diverse systems and legal orders into a single conversation about the imperial constitution. As it had been in Antigua, the presence in the colonies of legally subordinate men and women came increasingly to be described as a constitutional challenge rooted in a permanent threat to order, one that appeared different in the eyes of colonial elites and imperial officials. In British colonies from New South Wales to the West Indies, elites perceived threats to order as flowing from two related conditions: a surfeit of power over them by middling officials and the ungovernability of groups of subordinates such as convicts, slaves, servants, and vagrants. At the imperial center, officials perceived disorder differently—as a species of legal pluralism generated chiefly by an excess of autonomy that colonial elites and delegated legal authorities enjoyed. Colonial claims to independent legal authority over subordinates stood as an obstacle to effective imperial command.

In reining in powers wielded by planters and other privileged men, imperial officials hoped to transform a jumble of offices into an administrative system that would do the bidding of the imperial center, whether by regulating violence on distant settler frontiers or by interposing the colonial state between masters and slaves. United by a devotion to hierarchy but often divided by different visions of jurisdictional order, colonial elites parried attempts at imperial control while also generating disputes that prompted intervention. At the heart of this wide-ranging struggle over imperial order lay a shared concern with jurisdiction and a language of law that linked the centers and the peripheries of empire vertically and horizontally.

Jurisdictional politics had long plagued imperial administration. The difference in the early-nineteenth-century British Empire lay in the way such conflicts propelled ambitious reform projects designed precisely to reorder legal pluralism in the empire. In particular, metropolitan and local fears about bureaucracy and order came to focus on the reform of colonial magistracies in the nineteenth century. As representatives of local elites and as law keepers charged with preserving the king's peace in the colonies, magistrates were in some respects obvious targets in a struggle over imperial order. In sites of unfree labor, their pivotal role in regulating the exercise of masters' jurisdiction over slaves and convicts subjected magistrates to both imperial and local scrutiny. This chapter uses two case studies—from the Leeward Islands and New South Wales—to investigate how conversations about magisterial failure or abuse of power generated sustained and transformative debates over configurations of authority after 1800, not only in unfree labor colonies but throughout the British Empire. These debates culminated in the transformation of magisterial offices in the 1820s, one strand of a broader project of legal experimentation and reform that altered the shape of the plural legal order.

Magistrates, Masters, and Slaves in the Leeward Islands

On January 23, 1810, Edward Huggins and his two sons ordered two drivers to flog about thirty enslaved men and women in the public marketplace on the island of Nevis. The severe punishment of so many slaves drew a small crowd. John Burke would testify later that he began to record the number of lashes, "being under the impression that the country would take up the business." Burke counted 115, 65, 47, 165, 242, 212, 181, 59, and 187 lashes for men, and he tallied 110, 58, 97, 212, 291, 83, 49, 68, 89, and 56 lashes for women. He noted the names of magistrates present at the scene who had done nothing to stop the floggings or protest their severity.[4]

The beatings occurred in the context of heightened attention to the treatment of slaves in the British West Indies. In debates leading up to the 1807 abolition of the slave trade, abolitionists had drawn attention to the "arbitrary" or unchecked power of slave masters to discipline and punish slaves.[5] One of the arguments in favor of abolition of the trade was that it would force planters to improve their treatment of slaves, whose value would rise when they could not be replaced. For their part, many planters endorsed the goal of "amelioration" of the conditions suffered by slaves, having recognized that only self-regulation would stave off tightening metropolitan controls. In 1787, two absentee West Indian planters sponsored a House of Commons resolution calling on colonial legislatures to pass measures in order to improve the condition of slaves and "to secure to them throughout all the British West India Islands, the certain, immediate, and active protection of the Law."[6] The General Assembly and Council in the Leeward Islands held a rare meeting on St. Christopher's in 1798 to pass the Leeward Islands Slave Amelioration Act.[7] Similar legislation had passed in Jamaica, the empire's premiere sugar-producing colony, nearly a decade before.[8]

In this context, it is not surprising that the public punishment of Huggins's slaves sharply divided slave owners on Nevis. The Nevis Assembly passed a resolution a week after the event condemning Edward Huggins for inflicting punishments so severe that they constituted "an act of barbarity, altogether unprecedented in this Island."[9] Although Huggins was wealthy and well connected—he had recently purchased a large sugar estate and his son-in-law was president of the Council of Nevis—he was indicted by a grand jury in March for violating the Amelioration Act by punishing "several of his negroes in a very cruel manner in the public market-place."[10] Between the time of the indictment and the trial in May, Huggins's allies found a way to stack the petit jury with Huggins's allies, and he was acquitted after a trial featuring planter testimony for both prosecution and defense.[11]

Huggins's acquittal by a biased jury was the stuff of scandal.[12] The case also raised deeper questions about whether a system staffed by locals could ever act impartially. The grand jury had recognized this challenge in announcing plans to indict seven magistrates, including one of Huggins's sons, "for suffering Edward Huggins senior to correct his negroes" in a way contrary to the Amelioration Act.[13] Though a month later it prepared a detailed indictment only for Huggins—apparently concluding that the magistrates could be accused of a crime only if Huggins was found guilty—attempts to bring the magistrates to account did not end there. When word of Huggins's acquittal reached London, the Earl of Liverpool instructed the Leeward Islands' new governor, Hugh Elliot, to gather and send all documents from the case and "to bring to justice any of the parties" implicated in the act, including "any magistrates or other officers who may have been so criminally negligent of their public duties as to have witnessed, or forborne to interfere . . . in . . . so disgraceful a scene."[14] Nearly a year after Huggins was acquitted, London continued to badger Elliot about removing the magistrates from office.[15]

Attention to the magistrates' actions reflected a widespread concern with the capacity of local legal institutions to define and limit the scope of masters' authority to punish slaves. Slave owners also understood the controversy in these terms. In Huggins's defense at trial, one of his sons testified at length about the "acts of riot and rebellion" engaged in by the estate's slaves. Slave rebellion seemed a clear and present danger in the aftermath of the Haitian revolution. In the weeks before the public flogging, groups of Huggins's slaves had run away; they had failed to report in the fields for work on several days; and on one occasion, they had armed themselves with sticks and dispersed only when Huggins's son threatened to shoot them. The most immediate act prompting the punishment was the slaves' refusal to carry dung out to the fields at night—work explicitly banned by the Amelioration

Act. Huggins's son claimed that the public floggings had been necessary "to deter other slaves from similar conduct" on other estates.[16] Defense witnesses confirmed that, given evidence of the slaves' rebelliousness, the punishments had been mild. In a statement he wished to have transmitted to officials in London, Huggins cited what for him was the basic principle excusing his actions: the law "entrusted to the master the power of correcting his slave."[17] From Huggins's point of view, he was the first line of defense against slave rebellion, and the role of watching magistrates was to support, not to undermine, him in this duty.

Behind the issue of authority over planters' prerogatives to judge and punish slave wrongs lay still broader questions about the proper structure of legal administration in the empire. Commentary on the case focused in part on the dearth of trained legal personnel in the islands. One critic from Nevis subjected himself to a libel charge by writing a letter to the *St. Christopher Gazette* calling the chief justice "an habitual drunkard, often intoxicated on the Bench" and insinuating that other slaves had died on the Huggins estate without any investigation.[18] Governor Elliot echoed such attacks. White society in the West Indies, he asserted, was composed of "managers, overseers, self-created lawyers, self-educated physicians, and adventurous merchants," a motley group given to corruption and without the education or training to staff responsibly the government and court:

> To collect from such a state of society, men fit to be legislators, judges or jurymen, is perfectly impracticable. Individual interest—personal influence—animosity of party feuds, weigh down the scale of justice, and divert the course of legislative authority into acts of arbitrary and unjustifiable power, cloaked under the semblance, and dignified with the name, of constitutional acts.[19]

Elliot proposed that the best response to the Huggins case would be for the islands to adopt the standard included in the Jamaica Consolidated Act, by which inflicting more than thirty-nine lashes on a slave was defined as a crime. Such a standard had apparently been rejected in Nevis because colonial planters viewed the measure as "too great an interference with the authority of the proprietor."[20] London officials and Governor Elliot could only recommend that such a measure be taken up in the self-governing colonies of the Leeward Islands. Beyond instructing Elliot to remove the magistrates who had stood by when Huggins's slaves were punished, Whitehall could direct him only to proceed with his planned "inquiry into the state of the civil and judicial institutions of each Island."[21]

Elliot did not get very far with this inquiry before another case emerged involving planter cruelty and magisterial indifference. Emboldened by the controversy over the Huggins trial, planters from the Virgin Islands sailed to Antigua to report that a wealthy planter on Tortola, Arthur Hodge, had killed and maimed slaves on his estate over a period of several years. The accusations were prompted as much by local feuding as they were by concern for Hodge's slaves, but they hit their mark. Elliot traveled to Tortola with the solicitor-general to oversee the prosecution. Writing to his wife, Elliot called the charges against Hodge "more dreadful than any I ever heard of within the limits of the British Empire."[22] The gruesome details that emerged in the investigation and trial of Hodge indicated that he was responsible for the death of perhaps a dozen slaves and the torture of many others over an eight-year span. Hodge was tried for the murder of Prosper, a slave who had been so severely beaten after taking a mango from Hodge's property that he died from his wounds. Although planters had occasionally before been convicted on charges of cruel treatment of slaves in the Leeward Islands, the result in Hodge's case was unprecedented in the West Indies: he was found guilty and hanged.[23] In refusing the jury's recommendation for mercy, Elliot reasoned that even if pardoned for the murder of Prosper, Hodge would have been found guilty of causing the death of other slaves.

As in Nevis, the Tortola trial prompted pledges and recommendations about the reform of colonial legal practices. Writing a year after the Huggins case and less than a month after Hodge's hanging, Elliot reported that whereas legal appointments on the islands had too often been guided by personal interests and connections, he had installed a new system for appointing magistrates. He hoped that this measure would result in "reorganizing the Government of a Colony, which has of late afforded many examples of disorder and tumult."[24] At the same time, reports were being penned in Tortola by an estate manager, Abraham Mendes Belisario, who by his own admission was seeking to position himself for an appointment as an agent of some kind for the imperial government.[25] Belisario echoed Elliot's analysis in stating confidently that the tragedy of the Hodge case lay in a lack of sufficient magisterial oversight. "Owners should not be allowed to be Judge and Party to the same cause," he wrote. Magistrates should be permitted to hear and credit the testimony of slaves about the violence of whites or free persons and should be required to approve severe punishments of slaves. Belisario also suggested that registries of slaves be created "with the names of Owners annexed" and sent to England each year, "that a resident Commissioner be appointed for the specific purpose of watching over the protection of the

Slave," and that better records be kept of slaves "liberated" from intercepted slave-trading ships and apprenticed out by local vice-admiralty courts. Just one of these measures, he argued—a registry for slaves—would have allowed officials to discover Hodge's acts of brutality much sooner by tracking the decline in the slave population on his estate.[26]

Belisario and Elliot were probably aware that both slave registries and more stringent legal control of masters were emerging as key strands of abolitionist advocacy at home. The campaign for a registration scheme for slaves in the West Indies was led by James Stephen Sr., a member of William Wilberforce's inner circle. Since 1802 Stephen had been insisting that only Parliament could impose a measure of effective regulation of the "strange and unprecedented relation between master and slave," the legality of which rested wholly "on a kind of lex non scripta, or custom" in the colonies that remained relatively untouched by tepid colonial legislation.[27] According to Stephen, colonial reforms had produced only "mock laws" that left masters' rights to punish slaves largely intact and denied slaves the capacity to testify, blocking meaningful legal redress against a master's cruelty.[28] Registries constituted a basic step toward opening this private jurisdiction to public scrutiny.[29] Stephen was unable to get legislation passed to establish slave registries in all slave colonies, but his efforts led directly to an Order in Council in March 1812 to create a registry in Trinidad. As a conquered colony with no local assembly to deflect directives from the metropole, Trinidad represented a likely site for experiments in the imperial regulation of slavery.[30]

Both as a matter of strategy and as part of a shift toward a vision of emancipation, abolitionists like Stephen increasingly but cautiously supported broader legislation to contain the "discretionary private powers" responsible for "the largest share of the miseries of slavery."[31] In 1802, Stephen worried that "the interference of the magistrate" might provoke "bad passions" in West Indian masters; by 1824, he was signaling the urgent need for summary and criminal jurisdiction over slave masters.[32] The concern with law and with local officials in the colonies inflected other attempts at greater legal oversight. A turn toward a more systematic approach to the review of colonial legislation was initiated when James Stephen Jr. took his father's cause to the heart of the Colonial Office as legal counsel in 1813.[33] In this capacity, he scrutinized Caribbean labor legislation for repugnancy and recommended disallowance of any acts that failed to regulate the abuse of slaves by their masters.[34]

By 1824, magistrates occupied center stage in imperial efforts to reorder slave colonies. The 1824 Order in Council established a slave code for the Island of Trinidad—confirming its role as the legal laboratory of the empire.

This code was intended to serve as a model to press the Leeward Islands, and other self-governing slave colonies, to interpose magisterial jurisdiction between masters and slaves. The lynchpin of the new code was a magisterial office: the Protector of Slaves. Based on a position that had already existed in Spanish Trinidad, the office was now remodeled as a weapon of the British Empire against both slave masters and complicit magistrates.[35] In lifting the office from its Spanish context and adapting it for new purposes, British reformers were removing the Protector from any association with the institution's roots in the jurisdictional claims of the Catholic Church to protect classes of legally disadvantaged persons.[36] The Protector's job was to investigate disputes between masters and slaves, to take the part of slaves in civil suits or criminal prosecutions, and to report minutely to the secretary of state on the relationships of masters and slaves.[37]

The office of Protector of Slaves in Trinidad never functioned in precisely the way its architects imagined. Layered on top of not just Spanish institutions but also a system of three criminal courts created by an Order in Council of 1822, the new office introduced procedures that did not mesh smoothly with the preexisting court system. Because the office was one of a magistrate, the Protector was not regarded by island judges initially as having the capacity to prosecute under the island's laws.[38] The introduction of the new office also did little to create an impartial system since most judges, and most of the commandants charged with investigating and reporting cases from around the island to the Protector, continued to be drawn from the ranks of slaveholders.[39] The reports sent by the Protector's office detailed cases not just of complaints by slaves but also of punishments of slaves. The act of recording punishments was supposed to deter cruel treatment, but the practice also reaffirmed the legal relation at the heart of slavery: the power of masters over slaves. Even the core business of protection served local as well as metropolitan concepts of order in Trinidad. While Protectors spent much of their time "attending to and deciding upon the complaints proffered by slaves against their owners and others," imperial officials were often dismayed by protectors' and even the royal governor's collaboration in punishing many of the slaves who had brought forward complaints.[40]

In colonies like Nevis and Tortola, meanwhile, the Trinidad experiment served only as a model and a warning; imperial power to reorder masters and slaves in self-governing colonies was hotly contested in the decades after the American Revolution.[41] Self-governing colonies were sent the ordinance and were instructed to adapt and amend it to suit local circumstances, but very few established a protector of slaves. Most local governments chose instead to invest local magistrates with increased powers and duties to regulate the relationship between masters and slaves.[42] Lazarus-Black reminds us not to dismiss such efforts as insignificant for slaves, who managed to use available avenues of complaint; women in particular appealed to magistrates for protection and did so often in groups, no doubt to avoid individual retaliation.[43]

In both the West Indies and London, colonial authorities were represented as acting both to preserve the worst practices associated with slavery and to shelter the empire from anarchy. To supporters of Huggins, the magistrates' function was to protect planter prerogatives and help to shore up their authority before potentially rebellious slaves; for critics of Huggins, magistrates' local connections spelled corruption, but the office, if rescued from its compromised position, held the secret to effective reform. Replicating the contradiction of painting magistrates as agents of entrenched injustice and as enforcers of standards of justice, London officials advocated holding magistrates accountable for failing to stop the punishment of Huggins's slaves while overlooking the chronic negligence of Tortola magistrates in ignoring Hodge's much longer and more brutal reign of terror. Abolitionists also viewed the enhanced authority of magistrates as one prop of a broader policy of gradual reform—one about which they expressed strikingly little optimism, given the obstacle of local assemblies in self-governing colonies and the implausibility, even at the empire's center, of legislating radical reforms such as the recognition of slave testimony.[44] Within fifteen years of the trial of Huggins and Hodge, the magistracy formed the heart of efforts from center and periphery to order masters and slaves in the British Empire. Their centrality reflected more than a desire to exercise jurisdiction over masters. As middling officials tied both to their locality and the imperial center, magistrates remained uncertain, but increasingly important, members of a new imperial hierarchy. In this respect, the slaveholding colonies shared in a much wider reform agenda based on the administration of very local justice.

Magistrates, Masters, and Convicts in New South Wales

In August of 1822, Sydney exploded in acrimony when Dr. Henry Grattan Douglass, a magistrate, was accused of having his way with his assigned servant, a beautiful, nineteen-year-old convict woman called Ann Rumsby. If guilty of having a sexual relationship with his female servant, Douglass would not have been the first master in New South Wales to be so.[45] Extramarital sex between convict women and free men had been ubiquitous in the early decades of the colony.[46] Ann Rumsby's case, however, was elevated by its context into a colossal scandal. The rumor became a scandal because Ann Rumsby had a besotted protector. Ship's surgeon Dr. James Hall had developed an unhealthy interest in her physical and moral well-being on their voyage out from England.[47] He trumpeted Rumsby's allegations that she would be ruined if she remained in Dr. Douglass's household widely, to the magistrate, Reverend Samuel Marsden, to Judge Advocate John Wylde, and to the governor. The circumstances were also scandalous because Dr. Douglass was the superintendant of the Female Factory—an institution designed to save female convicts from inevitable moral profligacy by removing them from private service.[48] He had apparently taken Rumsby on his own authority from the Factory to his household—a move that, given her good looks, suggested nefarious intentions on his part.[49] Rumsby's situation appeared worse because Douglass was a married man of considerable social status, so could not and would not provide her with the benefits of social and financial mobility enjoyed by many female assigned convicts before her. It was probably beyond his power to do so in any case, as, by 1822, local high society was closing its doors against emancipated convicts generally and fallen women in particular.[50]

Ann Rumsby's virtue was not the only thing at stake in this scandal, however. Like Huggins and Hodge, Dr. Douglass had provoked the ire of some local elites, notably a coterie of fellow magistrates on the Parramatta Bench who had much to gain from excluding convicts and emancipists from social and political life in the colony. The friends and family of these so-called exclusivists had deposed the imperious Governor Bligh, charmed the imperial commission of enquiry headed by Commissioner Bigge into supporting their agenda, prompted the recall of the pro-emancipist Governor Macquarie, and were in the process of plotting the demise of Governor Brisbane.[51] In contrast, Dr. Douglass had been close to the pro-emancipist Macquarie regime; Macquarie had given him the triple honor of being superintendent of the government hospital, superintendent of the Female Factory, and a magistrate. He had since ingratiated himself with Governor Brisbane, regularly attending his home after Brisbane's arrival in the colony in 1821. Douglass was a natural target in these circumstances.

When he refused to alleviate suspicion by sending Rumsby back to the Female Factory, Douglass goaded the Parramatta Bench into action. Marsden, with fellow magistrates and exclusivists Hannibal McArthur, John Palper, George Palmer, and John Blaxland, publicly denounced "the great impropriety of . . . [Douglass's] conduct towards them" and refused to sit on the bench with him in future.[52] They also issued a summons, demanding that Douglass answer the criminal allegations made against him. Douglass refused to attend the proceedings. Instead, he asked the governor to intercede in the affair, by interviewing Ann Rumsby himself and publicly exonerating Douglass. The bench retaliated by summoning Rumsby to testify before them. She refused to verify allegations made against her master by Dr. Hall, claiming that she merely objected to Douglass's attempts to marry her off to a convict named Bragge. The bench then convicted her of perjury and sentenced her to secondary transportation to the penal colony at Port Macquarie. Governor Brisbane demanded that the magistrates retract their refusal to act with Douglass or submit their resignations. At a public meeting attended by some of the most important office holders in the colony—including the judge advocate (John Wylde) and the judge of the Supreme Court of Civil Judicature (Barron Field)—the magistrates resolved to defy the governor. They were duly removed from office.[53]

Douglass responded to these very public indignities in kind. Mobilizing his own magisterial jurisdiction, he charged Parramatta exclusivist Reverend Samuel Marsden with letting his convicts work for wages in contravention of a government order—a common practice in the colony. When Marsden refused to pay his fine, Douglass and cronies ordered the sheriff to seize his piano. The whole mess appeared to end in 1822 in the unconditional pardon of Ann Rumsby, the dismissal of Douglass's five antagonists from the magistracy, and two successful lawsuits—one to vindicate Douglass's reputation, and the other to restore Marsden to his piano. A toxic stew of animosity bubbled away for a number of years thereafter, however, reemerging in mutual, public accusations that Douglass and Marsden had used their magisterial jurisdiction to torture convicts who came before the Parramatta Bench. Needless to say, the furor was minutely described in despatches to London.

This colonial scandal grew out of local concern about the jurisdiction of masters over convict women in their households. It also reflected the stirring of broader anxieties about the assignment system, whereby property in the services of convict labor was transferred from the New South Wales government to private masters for the term of a convict's sentence. Hall's complaint against Douglass was just one of a variety of allegations of wrongdoing by masters, magistrates, and master-magistrates circulating in local papers and in letters to London in the 1820s—many of which drew parallels between the New South Wales assignment system and horrifying accounts of colonial slavery.[54] Chief Justice Forbes wrote a series of private letters and public opinions that made clear the legal links between masters in New South Wales and the Caribbean. He noted that assigned servants were "considered, and treated" as slaves in the colony and that private assignment offered no incentive to masters to assist in the reform of convict laborers. The tendency of masters to oppose every indulgence to convicts had contributed, Forbes thought, to recent increases in crime.[55] The parallels between assignment and slavery were reiterated by James Stephen Jr. from his perch as legal counsel in the Colonial Office in London. He advocated broad colonial jurisdiction to revoke assignments in order to prevent assignee masters from exercising the power of slaveholders.[56] By the 1830s, stories of torture, virtual enslavement, and sexual exploitation by masters were being gathered and published by advocates of free settlement and former antislavery activists in order to bring an end to both the transportation and the assignment of convicts throughout the British Empire.[57]

In the short term, the Rumsby case was experienced as a crisis of magisterial jurisdiction to manage convict masters in the colony.[58] Magistrates on both sides of the Rumsby scandal demonstrated the breadth of power and the lack of accountability that had accrued to the New South Wales magistracy since settlement in 1788. The convicted majority in New South Wales, like the slave majority in Britain's African and Caribbean colonies, formed the bedrock of the local labor system. A succession of autocratic naval and military governors (acting without supervision or properly constituted legislative authority) had balanced public order with private assignment by expanding magisterial jurisdiction.[59] By the time Commissioner Bigge arrived in 1819 to diagnose the convict system, single magistrates had power to administer severe, summary discipline to convicts for all wrongs not punishable by death and to withdraw convicts from private service for a variety of ill-defined reasons ranging from a master's cruelty to a convict's complicity with the state.[60] In short, magistrates had aggregated an enormous array of powers to keep order, many of them inconsistent with the laws of Great Britain and its empire.[61]

These powers became controversial in the 1820s for a number of reasons. First, the magistracy had become a key institution in the struggle between emancipated convicts and exclusivist free settlers. Macquarie had elevated several emancipists to the magistracy during his tenure as governor—a move that contributed to his removal from office when Commissioner Bigge took the part of exclusivists on this issue.[62] Second, magistrates increasingly used their powers either to thwart the governor or to pursue private ends.[63] In Ann Rumsby's case they showed both that they were willing to use their supervisory jurisdiction to arbitrarily deprive their enemies of servants and that they were unreliable protectors of convicts against abusive masters.[64] In his long opinion on the controversy commissioned by Wilmot Horton, James

Stephen Jr. described Rumsby's conviction for perjury as "repugnant to the clearest maxims both of Law and of moral Justice."[65]

The mistreatment of Ann Rumsby coincided with local and metropolitan concern about the New South Wales magistracy's use of excessive violence in convict discipline. In his 1822 report, Commissioner Bigge had very subtly criticized the excessive powers of magistrates to punish convicts.[66] Douglass's and Marsden's mutual accusations of convict torture in the aftermath of the Rumsby affair added lurid detail to Bigge's insinuations.[67] The dispute prompted Governor Brisbane's 1825 enquiry into the magistracy, which catalogued the widespread practice of illegal punishment in the colony for the scandalization of local elites and the British Parliament.[68] In his private letters to Wilmot Horton, meanwhile, Chief Justice Forbes described the deep corruption of local magistrates who "were accustomed . . . as justices of the public peace, to punish their own servants for breach of merely private duty, by sentencing them to public punishment."[69] His Supreme Court intervened repeatedly to control magisterial profligacy, at the request of a growing coterie of irate colonists.[70] Scrutiny of the magistracy was also augmented by the advent of the free press in the colony. From its first publication in 1826, the Sydney *Monitor* in particular made a mission of cataloguing magisterial abuses of power and transmitting them to London.[71]

As in the Leeward Islands, scandal about the power of masters over convict servants in New South Wales revealed deep flaws in the operation of the magistracy. These flaws were experienced as sources of disorder by New South Wales elites, even as they vied for control of local offices and political institutions. Meanwhile, James Stephen Jr., the Colonial Office, and the Imperial Parliament regarded the arbitrary use of magisterial jurisdiction in New South Wales as a threat to imperial order. The viability of the convict system and its capacity both to punish and to reform convicts depended simultaneously on the magistracy's power and its accountability to empire.

The intermingling of local with metropolitan concern about controlling the magistracy is evident in the checkered half-decade of imperial legislation reforming the judicial institutions of New South Wales. Even as it moved to give New South Wales the rudiments of self-governance in 1823, the Imperial Parliament acted to regulate (but not to diminish) magisterial power in the colony. The New South Wales Act 1823 (4 Geo. 4, c.96) s 19 limited the power of single magistrates over convicts by vesting jurisdiction over convict discipline in a Court of Quarter Sessions, at the same time as it confirmed the power of the new court to punish convicts summarily for all noncapital offenses. The Transportation Act 1825 (Imp) (6 Geo. IV. c. 69) responded to panicked local predictions about mayhem and murder resulting from s 19 by investing Quarter Sessions jurisdiction in one or more magistrates so long as they were sitting more than one week or twenty miles away from a duly established court.[72] Further, while s 8 of Peel's Transportation Act 1824 (Imp) (5 Geo. 4, c 84) limited the power of the governor to interfere with the property of assignee masters in convict service, the Australian Courts Act 1828 (Imp) (9 Geo. 4, c 83, s 9) reinstated the power of the governor, through magistrates, to revoke assignment and grant full or conditional pardons in order to better serve convict reformation.[73]

Local governments used several strategies to bring the magistracy into line. They tried, first, to tie the New South Wales magistracy more securely to government. Brisbane's dismissal of the Parramatta magistrates in 1822 responded to growing concern in Sydney about the hostility of magistrates to the colonial government. Often against the wishes of the miserly Colonial Office, Brisbane and his successors also advocated the expanded use of paid magistrates in New South Wales to break the corrupting nexus between magistrates and their neighbors. Stipendiary magistrates, like salaried magistrate-protectors in the slave colonies, were tied to the government by salary and patronage. They were deployed first in Sydney and then to troublesome districts where local magistrate-masters were implicated in either frontier violence or widespread abuse of convicts.[74] The magistrates were understood by some frontier elites in particular as servants of Sydney constituting a threat to local autonomy.[75]

Local legislation also struggled to strike the right balance between broad magisterial power to order convicts and the potential abuse of magisterial discretion. Legislation passed by various governors after 1824 variously limited the capacity of individual magistrates to punish convicts with more than fifty lashes, excused their former abuses, and radically expanded their jurisdiction.[76] The last trend culminated decisively in the passing of iterations of the notorious Bushranging Acts between 1830 and 1852.[77] These acts gave extraordinary jurisdiction to constables to detain, and magistrates to imprison, people reasonably suspected of being bushrangers who could not prove their freedom on demand. The acts became a flashpoint for further controversy about arbitrary magisterial power over free settlers and convicts.[78] While some members of the local judiciary expressed deep concern over the repugnancy of such acts in English Law, local elites (with metropolitan acquiescence) defended them as a necessary response to convict disorder.[79]

Magisterial power in New South Wales had always been the lynchpin of the convict system. Ann Rumsby's case in 1822 showed its potential also to transgress newly policed norms of governance both in the colony and in the empire at large. Profligate masters and their magistrate-foes misused the office to pursue personal, moral, and political ends. Their contests ensured that the magistracy was the object of reform in the 1820s. Reform from both the Imperial Parliament and the new local legislative council did not diminish the power of the magistracy; their measures sought to control it. The colony may have received the rudiments of self-government and independent superior courts in this decade, but by 1830 magistrates empowered and controlled by the empire and the local legislature held more sway than ever over the lives of convicts and free people in the colony.

Conclusion

Historians have often treated nineteenth-century comparisons of convicts to slaves as a rhetorical stroke intended for political effect.[80] Because the nature of the captivity of slaves and their degree of legal incapacity were singular within the empire, it has seemed implausible that contemporaries viewed convicts, servants, or other subordinated workers as truly parallel to slaves.[81] The main point of intersection between slavery and convict transportation appeared to lie in the schemes of resettlement of freed captives and transported felons in West Africa at the end of the eighteenth century.[82] Even comparative studies of systems of subordinated labor have analyzed the legal similarities of slaves and convicts in relation mainly to broader processes of the construction of sovereignty.[83]

What happens, though, when instead of comparing slaves and convicts, we compare the capacity of colonial magistrates to control convict and slave masters? From this point of view, there is striking continuity in the legal context of the two labor systems and in the impetus for their reform. The empowerment of magistrates to order masters of slaves or convicts emerges, too, as the pivotal focus of contemporary conflicts. Whether in London, the Caribbean, or the Antipodes, contests of the mastery over masters used similar language and mechanisms of law. Huggins's defiance was cast by all as a deficit of magistrates' legal responsibility first, and of his own immoral cruelty second. Likewise, Rumsby's mistreatment by a variety of magistrates, including her master, was blamed both on her legal vulnerability as a convict and on the legal unaccountability of her assailants. Even the vile Hodge had been sustained and protected—and ultimately brought down—by local mechanisms of legal order activated by rival factions.

These legal contests emerging from unfree labor systems focused as much or more on magistrates and middling officials as they did on the legal capacities of convicts or slaves. The project of streamlining even the most local of jurisdictional orders married concerns about disorder in colonial peripheries and the imperial center. Even as moral reformers sought to remove legal disabilities from slaves and to increase those of transported convicts, they focused their efforts on enhancing and controlling the authority of magistrates to order both unfree laborers and their masters. Reformers recognized that the terms and conditions of subordination could be altered by regulating the legal prerogatives of those with the power to judge and punish. Whether or not they were moralists, imperial policymakers sought increasingly to bring middling officials, masters, and unfree laborers within their purview by altering the scope of colonial jurisdiction. Their key strategy here was to articulate the jurisdiction and duties of magistrates more clearly, and to hold those officials accountable when they failed to keep metropolitan notions of the king's peace.

Imperial efforts to erode the private jurisdiction of masters, on the one hand, and to bring magistrates into prominence within the legal order, on the other, formed two strategies in a much larger agenda to create a connected legal order out of the panoply of colonies and interests that accrued to Britain after half a century of global conflict. This agenda turned on a new metropolitan resolve to intervene in colonial life. The British Parliament, the King in Council, and the Colonial Office emerged from the American Revolution cautious about regulating the legislative powers of their old, corporate colonies in the Caribbean but otherwise curiously unabashed in their determination to participate in colonial governance. This interest reflected intensified inter-imperial conflict, which prompted a new preoccupation with both cost cutting and intra-imperial chains of command. Global conflict also caused new constitutional diversity. Britain conquered, ceded, and settled colonies from Canada to Africa in the late eighteenth and early nineteenth century, with different legal systems and constitutional standing and with varied capacities to make their own laws. The constitutional fragility of these new colonies emboldened swelling ranks of reformers in London to test the transformative power of imperial proclamations and legislation.[84]

The result was a new emphasis on cataloguing difference and fostering legislative and judicial uniformity.[85] In this larger constitutional project, the magistracy took center stage. Imperial records from the period are littered with briefly sustained legal experiments in erecting middling authorities, from the office of Protectors of Slaves and of Aborigines in slave and settler colonies to the instatement of resident magistrates and consuls in trading ports and settlements beyond the formal boundaries of the empire. The incomplete implementation of many such experiments—and their relative brevity—remind us that we are not observing a neat transition from private to public authority, or a simple conflict between a constitutionalism of liberty and a constitutionalism of command.[86] Efforts to interpose middling officials and to hold them accountable sometimes prompted colonial elites and imperial officials to invoke both notions of British liberty and the rule of law.

Campaigns to impose delegated legal authorities to restrict some local prerogatives could also work to erect new protections for private authority, as when slaveholders benefited from greater clarity about their title to slaves or their rights to inflict measured punishments, or when controls on convict assignment paralleled tighter enforcement of a more generalized master-servant law.[87] At times, then, metropolitan reforms bolstered the strategies of colonial elites concerned about ordering subordinates and protecting their own rights. When local elites proposed new rigor in the magistracy, they often did so with an eye to buttressing their prerogatives and muting metropolitan objections to them. Their vision of imperial order included hierarchy, but it was hierarchy of a much looser kind that still suspended within it the protected jurisdictions of the master's authority. While colonies proved adept at staving off incursions on their power by cultivating the loyalty of magistrates, local legislation from New South Wales to Jamaica in the 1820s also records an expansion in the jurisdiction of local magistracies over free masters and subordinate populations. Whether "order" or "disorder" applied as labels to new configurations of the plural legal order was a matter of timing, and of perspective.

This pan-imperial context ensured that the jurisdictional politics produced by magistrates and masters in the Leeward Islands and New South Wales between 1810 and 1830 fed quickly and directly into constitutional debates about the scope of legal authority of middling officials and their relation to imperial sovereignty. If this conjuncture has gone largely unnoticed by historians, the oversight is partly explained by its presentation as a jumble of controversies over individual cases, a set of disjointed projects of legal reform, and seemingly unrelated calls for altering magisterial power in constitutionally fragile peripheries.[88] Across the early decades of the nineteenth century, magistrates emerged as both the problem and the answer within the jurisdictional puzzle of the colonial legal order. Understanding the politics of legal pluralism in the empire at the beginning of the nineteenth century depends on reconstructing the history of such projects, and on tracing the peculiar colonial conflicts and singular cases that helped to produce them.

NOTES

1. The authors would like to thank Richard Ross for comments on a draft. Parts of the research for the chapter were supported under Australian Research Council's Discovery Projects funding scheme, project number DP110103832, under Lisa Ford's direction. We thank Doris Sher for her research work in Hugh Elliot's papers in the National Library of Scotland.
2. A plan of shipping them back to Ireland in the *Duke of Leicester* faltered after the ship sailed to St. Martin's and the Dutch inhabitants prepared to seize the vessel for payment of the captain's debts. Officials next appealed without success to the British naval commander in the region, but he refused to transport the convicts back to Ireland in a British naval vessel. Shirley could soon report that thirty of the convicts had been sent as indentured servants to United States ports, while three—as if offering proof of the dangers posed by the release of a group of felons—were tried and convicted in Antigua for stealing watches and a silver altar plate. The National Archives (UK), Records of the Colonial Office (TNA, CO) 152/70.
3. TNA, CO 152/69, f. 40. Emphasis added.
4. "No. 4, in Letter from Governor Elliot to the Earl of Liverpool, 25 November, 1810," House of Commons, "Papers relating to the West Indies: viz. correspondence relating to punishments inflicted on certain Negro slaves, in the island of Nevis; and to prosecutions in consequence," May 1811 (hereafter "Papers relating to the West Indies: Nevis"), 23.
5. On the links between debates about abolition and about slave punishment, see especially Diana Paton, *No Bond but the Law: Punishment, Race, and Gender in Jamaican State Formation, 1780-1870* (Durham, NC: Duke University Press, 2004), 4-5. On discourse about petty despotism at the turn of the nineteenth century, see Lauren Benton, "Just Despots: The Cultural Construction of Imperial Constitutionalism," in *Law, Culture, and the Humanities*, forthcoming.
6. David Barry Gaspar, "Ameliorating Slavery: The Leeward Island Slave Act of 1798," in Robert L. Paquette and Stanley L. Engerman, eds., *The Lesser Antilles in the Age of European Expansion* (Gainesville: University Press of Florida, 1996), 241-58, 242. It is interesting to note that the act followed a wave of legislation in the Leeward Islands focused on controlling slaves and protecting masters' prerogatives. That legislation had included provisions for the trial by magistrates of slaves accused of serious crimes. Elsa Goveia, *Slave Society in the British Leeward Islands at the End of the Eighteenth Century* (New Haven, CT: Yale University Press, 1965), 176.
7. "An Act more effectually to provide for the Support, and to extend certain Regulations for the Protection of Slaves, to promote and encourage their Increase, and generally to meliorate their Condition," *The laws of the island of Antigua: consisting of the acts of the Leeward Islands, commencing 8th November 1690, ending 21st April 1798; and the acts of Antigua, commencing 10th April 1668, ending 7th May 1804*, vol. 1 (London: Samuel Bagster, 1805), no. 36, 20-43. It was often referred to as the Melioration Act.
8. The Jamaica Consolidated Slave Act had passed in that colony in 1787.
9. "No. 3, in Letter from Governor Elliot to the Earl of Liverpool, 25 November, 1810," House of Commons, "Papers relating to the West Indies: Nevis," 19.
10. To the outrage of critics, the jury was selected by drawing cards with the names of eligible jurors from a previously arranged deck; the panel included friends of the

defendant, his overseer, and the overseer of his son-in-law's estate. "No. 6, in Letter from Governor Elliot to the Earl of Liverpool, 25 November, 1810," House of Commons, "Papers relating to the West Indies: Nevis," 25. There is some evidence that an impartial grand jury might have indicted Huggins for murder. However, the grand jury included several of his sons, and critics of Huggins asserted later that a sympathetic coroner had failed to investigate whether a female slave named Fanny had died as the result of the beating she received.

11. "Letter from J. W. Tobin to Governor Elliot, Nevis, September 7, 1810," TNA, CO 152/96, No. 7.
12. On colonial scandals, and another case involving punishment in the West Indies, see James Epstein, "Politics of Colonial Sensation: The Trial of Thomas Picton and the Cause of Louisa Calderon," *American Historical Review* 112, no. 3 (2007): 712–41.
13. "No. 6, in Letter from Governor Elliot to the Earl of Liverpool, 25 November, 1810," House of Commons, "Papers relating to the West Indies: Nevis," 25.
14. "Letter from the Earl of Liverpool, to Governor Elliot; 20 September 1810," House of Commons, "Papers relating to the West Indies: Nevis," 1.
15. "Letter from the Earl of Liverpool, to Governor Elliot, 12 April, 1811," House of Commons, "Papers relating to the West Indies: Nevis," 2.
16. "No. 7, Letter from Governor Elliot to the Earl of Liverpool, 25 November, 1810," House of Commons, "Papers relating to the West Indies: Nevis," 31.
17. "No. 10, Letter from Governor Elliot to the Earl of Liverpool, 25 November, 1810," House of Commons, "Papers relating to the West Indies: Nevis," 36.
18. "Letter from J. W. Tobin to Governor Elliot, 7 September, 1810," TNA, CO 152/96. Tobin also complained that two of the people on the jury had conducted the flawed inquest in the case, including "one of the Magistrates who, with unconcern beheld the flogging in the market place" and that most of the lawyers appearing in the trial were "men overwhelmed by debt." An extract of the letter was printed in the *London Chronicle,* prompting complaints to Elliot by the chief justices of St. Christopher and Nevis and one of the lawyers present at the trial who defended his advanced training in law. House of Commons, "Papers Relating to the West Indies, viz. Letters to Governor Elliot from Mr. Garrett, Mrs. Weekes and Mr. Peterson, January, 1812."
19. "Letter from Governor Elliot, to the Earl of Liverpool, 21 November 1810," House of Commons, "Papers relating to the West Indies: Nevis," 13.
20. "No. 4, Letter from Governor Elliot, to the Earl of Liverpool, 21 November 1810," House of Commons, "Papers relating to the West Indies: Nevis," 14
21. "Letter from the Earl of Liverpool, to Governor Elliot, 12 April, 1811," House of Commons, "Papers relating to the West Indies: Nevis," 2.
22. National Library of Scotland, MS 12960, 190-93.
23. On the trial of Arthur Hodge, see Lauren Benton, "This Melancholy Labyrinth: The Trial of Arthur Hodge and the Boundaries of Imperial Law," *Alabama Law Review* 64 (2012): 91-122. Three planters had been tried and found guilty for severe mistreatment of slaves in St. Christopher's between 1784 and 1786. Abolitionists argued that the resulting fines for the guilty planters did not conform to the punishments required for the crimes under the island's laws. Speaking about the insincere and ineffective self-regulation by planters in the House of Commons, Wilberforce pointed especially to the St. Christopher's case of William Herbert, a planter convicted only of "immoderate correction" for lacerating the

mouth of a six-year-old slave so severely that he nearly died. "Debate on Mr. Wilberforce's Motion for the Abolition of the Slave Trade, 3 April 1797," in W. Cobbett, ed., *The Parliamentary History of England,* vol. 33, 1382.

24. "Despatch 42, Tortola, 15 May, 1811," TNA, CO 152/97.
25. Abraham Mendes Belisario was a Sephardic Jewish merchant who had made, then lost, a fortune in Jamaica before being contracted in London to embark again for the West Indies and manage an estate in Tortola.
26. "Accounts required to be furnished by the Governors of West Indies Islands, relative to the treatment of slaves, 2 July 1811," TNA, CO 152/100.
27. James Stephen, *The Crisis of the Sugar Colonies: An Inquiry into the Objects and Probable Effects of the French Expedition to the West Indies; and Their Connection with the Colonial Interests of the British Empire* (London: J. Hatchard, 1802), 137, no. ±.
28. James Stephen, *Reasons for Establishing a Registry of Slaves in the British Colonies: Being a Report of a Committee of the African Institution* (London, African Institution, 1815), 36.
29. See Stephen, *Reasons for Establishing a Registry,* 6.
30. When Britain took over the island from Spain, the acquisition prompted sharp debate in London about whether Britain should end or continue slavery on the island. Stephen characterized Trinidad as a site for "an experiment of unspeakable importance to mankind." Stephen, *Crisis of the Sugar Colonies,* 186. On Trinidad as a place of experimentation, see also James Epstein, *Scandal of Colonial Rule: Power and Subversion in the British Atlantic during the Age of Revolution* (Cambridge: Cambridge University Press, 2012), ch. 3.
31. Stephen, *Reasons for Registry,* 7.
32. Stephen, *Reasons for Registry,* 7, James Stephen Sr., *The Slavery of the British West India Colonies Delineated, as It Exists Both in Law and Practice, and Compared with the Slavery of Other Countries, Antient and Modern,* vol. 1 (London: Butterworth, 1824), 12, 15, 24-26, 302.
33. Stephen's career spanned key decades in the development of British colonial legal policy. He at first served part-time in the role of legal counsel; his permanent appointment came in 1825. Stephen acquired the additional title of permanent undersecretary in 1836, and he remained in the position until 1846. Paul Knaplund, *James Stephen and the British Colonial System, 1812-1847* (Madison: University of Wisconsin Press, 1953).
34. M. K. Banton, "The Colonial Office, 1820-1955: Constantly the Subject of Small Struggles," in Douglas Hay and Paul Craven, eds., *Masters, Servants, and Magistrates in Britain and the Empire, 1562-1955* (Chapel Hill: University of North Carolina Press, 2004), 254; D. B. Swinfen, *Imperial Control of Colonial Legislation, 1813–1865: A Study of British Policy towards Colonial Legislative Powers* (Oxford: Clarendon, 1970), 41, 60; Russell Smandych, "'To Soften the Extreme Rigor of Their Bondage': James Stephen's Attempt to Reform the Criminal Slave Laws of the West Indies, 1813-1833," *Law and History Review* 23, no. 3: 537-88, especially 551-54.
35. Mary Turner, "The British Caribbean, 1823-1838: The Transition from Slave to Free Legal Status," in Douglas Hay and Paul Craven, eds., *Masters, Servants, and Magistrates in Britain and the Empire, 1652-1955* (Chapel Hill: University of North Carolina Press, 2004), 306.

36. For an overview of the Spanish legal basis for the office and the 1824 Code, see Claudius Fergus, "The 'Siete Partidas': A Framework for Philanthropy and Coercion during the Amelioration Experiment in Trinidad, 1823-34," *Caribbean Studies* 36, no. 1 (2008): 85-90.
37. Order in Council, 10 March 1824, enclosed in "No. 1, Letter from Earl of Bathurst to Sir Ralph Woodward, 25 March 1824," House of Commons, "Papers in Explanation of Measures for Melioration of Condition of Slave Population in W. Indies and S. America," 1825, 124-38.
38. For an overview of jurisdictional problems, see Noel Titus, *The Amelioration and Abolition of Slavery in Trinidad, 1812-1813* (Bloomington, IN: Authorhouse, 2009), 10-12, and Fergus, "The 'Siete Partidas,'" 85-88.
39. This tendency was increased when an amending Order in Council returned summary jurisdiction over slave complaints to "*Alcaldes* of the *Cabildo*, including the Chief of Police," Fergus, "The 'Siete Partidas,'" 87.
40. TNA, CO 300/19, f. 355. For an example of imperial concern about the punishment of slaves for unfounded complaints to the Protector in the Cape Colony, see "Secretary Huskisson to Lt. Governor Bourke, 28 September 1827," House of Commons, "Protectors of Slaves Reports . . . ," 12 June 1829 , 108. Jurisdiction to punish slaves for wrongful accusations was severely truncated by LXXII of the Order in Council of 2 February 1830, enclosed in "No 13: Letter from Sir George Murray to Major-general Grant, 4 February 1830," House of Commons, "Papers in Explanation of Measures adopted for Melioration of Condition of Slave Population in H.M. Possessions in W. Indies, S. America, Cape of Good Hope and Mauritius," 16 July 1830, 104. Though it occurred before the establishment of the Protector of the Slaves, an 1822 case is instructive. It resulted from a complaint by two slaves against their owner for a murder of another slave and brought before the Spanish office of the Syndic Procurador of the Cabildo. Governor Woodford ordered both slaves severely lashed for bringing a false complaint. There was no trial, and Woodford cited Spanish laws in asserting that slaves had only very narrow grounds of complaint against their masters (Titus, *The Amelioration and Abolition of Slavery in Trinidad*, 11).
41. Stephen noted that Britain had legislated for the colonies in many ways in the past, and he discounted the argument that the prerogative had been renounced after the American Revolution. Stephen, *Reasons for Establishing a Registry*, 103; and see Claude Levy, "Barbados: The Last Years of Slavery, 1822-33," *Journal of Negro History* 44, no. 4 (1959): 308-45; Melanie Newton, "The King v. Robert James, a Slave, for Rape: Inequality, Gender, and British Slave Amelioration, 1823-1834," *Comparative Studies in Society and History* 47, no. 3 (July 2005): 583-610.
42. Manchester to Bathurst, 13 November 1826, and *An Act to Alter and Amend the Slave Law of This Island*, 1827, *Amelioration, West Indies*, 1827, Part 1, 59-106.
43. Mindie Lazarus-Black, "Slaves, Masters, and Magistrates: Law and the Politics of Resistance in the British Caribbean, 1736-1834," in Mindie Lazarus-Black and Susan F. Hirsch, eds., *Contested States: Law, Hegemony, and Resistance* (New York: Routledge. 1994), 252-81.
44. Goveia remarks that the problem of meaningful legal reform appeared, even to abolitionists, to be "insoluble." Elsa V. Goveia, *Slave Society in the British Leeward Islands at the End of the Eighteenth Century* (New Haven, CT: Yale University Press, 1965), 190.

45. See generally Kirsten McKenzie, *Scandal in the Colonies: Sydney and Cape Town, 1820-1850* (Fitzroy: Melbourne University Press, 2005), 145-46.
46. J. B. Hirst, *Convict Society and Its Enemies* (Sydney: Allen & Unwin, 1983), 70-72; Robert Hughes, *The Fatal Shore: The Epic of Australia's Founding* (New York: Vintage, 1988), 161-62; McKenzie, *Scandal in the Colonies*, 50.
47. Stephen to Wilmot Horton, 2 September 1824, *Historical Records of Australia* (*HRA*), IV: I (Australia: Parliamentary Library Committee, 1922), 565. See also, Brisbane to Bathurst, 6 September 1822, *HRA*, I:X, 744-75.
48. Macquarie to Castlereagh, 30 April 1810, *Historical Records of New South Wales* (*HRNSW*) 7 (Sydney, 1901), 340, cited in Annette Salt, *These Outcast Women: The Parramatta Female Factory, 1821-1848* (Sydney: Hale & Iremonger, 1984), 39 n. 49.
49. Brisbane to Bathurst, 6 September 1822, *HRA*, I:X, 745; Stephen to Wilmot Horton, 2 September 1824, *HRA*, IV:I, 557.
50. Carol Liston, "The Damned Whore and the Public Man: Sarah Wentworth," in Penny Russell, ed., *For Richer, for Poorer: Early Colonial Marriages* (Melbourne: Melbourne University Press, 1993), 114-34; McKenzie, *Scandal in the Colonies*, 146.
51. See Bigge, Report of the Commissioner of Enquiry into the State of the Colony in New South Wales, 1822, House of Commons Parliamentary Papers, 156 (Bigge Report). See John Kennedy McLaughlin, "The Magistracy in New South Wales, 1788-1850," Master of Laws, University of Sydney, 1973; David Neal, *The Rule of Law in a Penal Colony* (Cambridge: Cambridge University Press, 1991), 269-70; John Ritchie, *Punishment and Profit: The Reports of Commissioner John Bigge on the Colonies of New South Wales and van Diemen's Land, 1822–1823; Their Origins, Nature, and Significance* (Melbourne: Heinemann, 1970), 114-20.
52. Brisbane to Bathurst, 6 September 1822, *HRA*, I:X, 747; Stephen to Wilmot Horton, 2 September 1824, *HRA*, IV:I, 560.
53. Stephen to Wilmot Horton, 2 September 1824, *HRA*, IV:I, 560-63.
54. See McKenzie, *Scandal in the Colonies*, 143-47; Hirst, *Convict Society and Its Enemies*, 173.
55. Forbes to Wilmot Horton, 6 Feb. 1825, in John Michael Bennett, ed., *Some Papers of Sir Francis Forbes: First Chief Justice in Australia* (Sydney: Parliament of New South Wales, 1998), 53.
56. Stephen to Wilmot Horton, 27 March 1825, *HRA*, IV:I, 607-9.
57. House of Commons, "Report from the Select Committee on Transportation; together with the minutes of evidence, appendix, and index," 1837; see also Hirst, *Convict Society and Its Enemies*, 20-27.
58. Hilary Golder, *High and Responsible Office: A History of the NSW Magistracy* (Sydney: Sydney University Press), 31-33.
59. As Stephen Jr. noted, New South Wales governors had made law without submitting it for review between 1806 and 1823 when the colony received legislative authority and a local legislative council: Stephen to Horton, 29 November 1823, *HRA*, IV:I, 525-26. This meant that New South Wales was a colony that had "no law at all which can properly be recognised as such": Knaplund, *James Stephen and the British Colonial System*, 40 n. 9.
60. Magisterial duties are mentioned on nearly every page of the Bigge Report: see, e.g., "Bigge Report," at 18, 74-118 (regarding the administration of assigned convicts). On the

powers of the early magistracy generally, see McLaughlin, "The Magistracy in New South Wales," chapters 2-4; Neal, *The Rule of Law in a Penal Colony*, 61-84.

61. Stephen to Hay, 16 August 1825, *HRA*, IV:I, 617-618.
62. Golder, *High and Responsible Office*, 18-19.
63. The extended controversy between Judge Field and Edward Eagar before the Parramatta Bench provides a particularly good example: "Papers relating to the case of Eagar v Field" in Macquarie to Bathurst, 1 September 1820, *HRA*, I:X, 354-64.
64. The arbitrary power of magistrates to take servants away from private masters underpinned one of the most puzzling outcomes of the Bigge Report in 1822: Transportation Act 1824 (5 Geo. IV. c.84) s 8, which reasserted a master's "property in the services of their convicts" subject only to the governor's right to give convicts unconditional pardons.
65. Stephen to Wilmot Horton, 2 September 1824, *HRA*, IV:I, 564.
66. "Bigge Report," at 55; McLaughlin, "The Magistracy in New South Wales," 245.
67. *Sydney Gazette*, 18 August 1828, 2. See also C. H. Currey, *Sir Francis Forbes* (Sydney: Angus & Robertson, 1968), 154-55; Hirst, *Convict Society and Its Enemies*, 175.
68. "Return to an address of the Honourable the House of Commons, dated 17 April 1826; for copies of papers relating to the conduct of magistrates in New South Wales, in directing the infliction of punishments upon prisoners in that colony," House of Commons, 1826.
69. Forbes to Wilmot Horton, 6 Feb. 1825, in Bennett, ed., *Some Papers of Sir Francis Forbes*, 53.
70. *R. v. Gillman*, 1824 (magistrate prosecuted for misusing a search warrant); *Adams v. Dawson*, 1827 (damages of fifty pounds awarded against magistrate for falsely imprisoning one of his employees at the Australian Agricultural Company); *Cokely v. Simpson*, 1831 (magistrate fined for illegally detaining and punishing a convict whose term had expired); *Broadbear and wife v. McArthur et al.*, 1827 (damages of eighty pounds awarded against three magistrates for maliciously convicting and falsely imprisoning a convict for leaving her position at the Orphan School): all available on *Decisions of the Superior Courts of New South Wales*, Macquarie University, http://www.law.mq.edu.au/scnsw. See also McLaughlin, "The Magistracy in New South Wales," 245–46; Golder, *High and Responsible Office*, 32–34.
71. See, for example, *The Monitor*, 22 September 1826, 7, which publicizes descriptions of magistrates at Sydney, Parramatta, Windsor, Penrith, Liverpool, and Campbell Town "passing indefinite and irregular sentences, and causing punishments to be inflicted contrary to law."
72. Note the ambiguity of Australian Courts Act 1828 (Imp) (9 Geo. IV. c. 83) on this point. See Golder, *High and Responsible Office*, 36; McLaughlin, "The Magistracy in New South Wales," 263-67.
73. For controversy over the meaning of both of these sections, see, for example, "Forbes' Convict Assignment Opinion," in Darling to Goderich, 8 November 1827, *HRA*, I:XIII, 608-12; *Ex parte Wardell and Wentworth*, 1827; *In re Jane New*, 1829: all available on *Decisions of the Superior Courts of New South Wales*, Macquarie University, http://www.law.mq.edu.au/scnsw. See also Darling to Bathurst, 1 March 1827, *HRA*, I:XIII, 138; Darling to Goderich, 8 November 1827, *HRA*, I:XIII, 606-12; Forbes to Horton, 6 March 1827, *HRA*, IV:I, 696; Forbes to Hay,

12 November 1827, *HRA*, IV:I, 748. See generally, Currey, *Sir Francis Forbes*, 244-47.

74. Michael Quinlan, "Australia, 1788–1902: A Workingman's Paradise?" in Douglas Hay and Paul Craven, eds., *Masters, Servants, and Magistrates in Britain and the Empire, 1562–1955* (Chapel Hill: University of North Carolina Press, 2004), 222, 237.
75. Golder, *High and Responsible Office*, 28.
76. E.g., Justices Indemnity Act 1825 (NSW) (6 Geo. 4, No. 18); Summary Jurisdiction Act 1832 (NSW) (3 Wm. No. 3) s 16.
77. Robbers and Housebreakers Act 1830 (NSW) (11 Geo. 4, No. 10); Transported Offenders and Suspected Robbers Apprehension Act 1834 (NSW) (5 Wm 4, No. 9).
78. E.g., *Cokely v. Simpson*, 1831: available on *Decisions of the Superior Courts of New South Wales*, Macquarie University, http://www.law.mq.edu.au/scnsw. See also *The Australian*, 6 June 1834.
79. *R. v. Elliot*, 1823: available on *Decisions of the Superior Courts of New South Wales*, Macquarie University, http://www.law.mq.edu.au/scnsw; Burton to Bourke, 25 August 1834, *HRA*, 1:XVII, 524-33.
80. See, e.g., Hirst, *Convict Society and Its Enemies*, 173–74; Neal, *The Rule of Law in a Penal Colony*, 170-72; David Brion Davis, "Looking at Slavery from Broader Perspectives," *The American Historical Review* 105, no. 2 (2000): 452-66.
81. Seymour Drescher recognizes that the comparison was more than rhetorical but focuses on the relative cost-benefit analysis by Europeans of European servitude and slavery as labor systems while emphasizing the "legal distance" maintained between the metropole and colonies. *Abolition: A History of Slavery and Antislavery* (New York: Cambridge University Press, 2009), 47-57, 58.
82. Christopher Leslie Brown, *Moral Capital: Foundations of British Abolitionism* (Chapel Hill: University of North Carolina Press, 2006), 278-79; Deirdre Coleman, *Romantic Colonization and British Anti-Slavery* (Cambridge: Cambridge University Press, 2005).
83. Benton compares slavery and convict labor systems in studying martial law and the imperial constitution, and Ford notes the similarities of the role played by the legal categories of slaves and convicts in analyzing jurisdictional conflicts in Georgia and New South Wales. Lauren Benton, *A Search for Sovereignty: Law and Geography in European Empires, 1400-1900* (Cambridge: Cambridge University Press, 2010), chapter 4; Lisa Ford, *Settler Sovereignty: Jurisdiction and Indigenous People in America and Australia, 1788–1836* (Cambridge, MA: Harvard University Press, 2010), 4-9.
84. A further impetus flowed from the upsurge in British adventuring within and beyond the boundaries of empire, a trend that confronted imperial officials with the need to discipline and protect British subjects. See, e.g., Elizabeth Kolsky, *Colonial Justice in British India* (Cambridge: Cambridge University Press, 2010).
85. Lauren A. Benton, *Law and Colonial Cultures: Legal Regimes in World History, 1400–1900* (New York: Cambridge University Press, 2002), 12; Lisa Ford, *Settler Sovereignty*, 4.
86. John Phillip Reid, *Constitutional History of the American Revolution* (Madison: University of Wisconsin Press, 1995), xiii.
87. Douglas Hay and Paul Craven, "Introduction," in Douglas Hay and Paul Craven, eds., *Masters, Servants, and Magistrates in Britain and the Empire, 1562–1955* (Chapel Hill: University of North Carolina Press, 2004), 26, 34.

88. It is interesting to note that the conjuncture did not go unnoticed by an older set of historians of imperial administration who traced shifts at the center without paying much attention to metropolitan policy's connections to colonial legal politics (e.g., Swinfen, *Imperial Control of Colonial Legislation*). A notable recent exception to the synchronicities of imperial policy who is not limited by a metropolitan-centered view is P. G. Marshall (*The Making and Unmaking of Empires: Britain, India, and America c.1750-1783* [Oxford: Oxford University Press, 2007]).

8

"Seeking the Water of Baptism"

Fugitive Slaves and Imperial Jurisdiction in the Early Modern Caribbean

LINDA M. RUPERT

In 1702 thirty-one fugitive slaves arrived on the Caribbean coast of Venezuela from the small Dutch island of Curaçao, located just forty miles due north.[1] Local authorities quickly captured them and sold them in a public auction. This generated protests from the representative of the French Guinea Company, which then held the *asiento de negros* (the contract that allowed foreigners to provide slaves to Spanish America). He claimed that the company had exclusive rights to sell slaves in Venezuela. Meanwhile, the captain of the local free black militia interceded on behalf of the slaves, citing two previous *reales cédulas* (royal decrees) that gave freedom to runaway slaves who arrived in Spanish America from the colonies of rival powers. When Venezuelan authorities remained intransigent, he took the case to the Audiencia of Santo Domingo on the island of Hispaniola, over five hundred miles to the north, which then had jurisdiction over the Province of Venezuela. There, he argued that the runaways had "risked their lives in search of liberty and Spiritual Peace, for the good of their souls" and so should be freed. The Audiencia concurred. It issued a royal provision, dated 7 June 1704, which manumitted the fugitives, annulled their previous sale, and ordered that they be given land in Venezuela.[2]

These were not the first runaway slaves to arrive in Venezuela from Curaçao. Nor would they be the last. Throughout the eighteenth century at least a thousand fugitives made the short journey across the calm waters that separated the tiny Dutch island from the extensive Spanish American mainland.[3] Their migration was not unique. Around the Caribbean slaves regularly fled to freedom across imperial boundaries. Spanish America was a particularly attractive magnet, due to a combination of colonial realities and imperial actions. The royal provision that the Audiencia of Santo Domingo issued in 1704 was not a one-time proclamation. Nor were the royal decrees cited by the captain of Venezuela's free black militia. From the late seventeenth century through the first half of the eighteenth, Spanish authorities issued well over a dozen royal decrees, orders, and provisions aimed at attracting runaway slaves from the colonies of rival European powers. Offering freedom to these fugitives was an innovative solution that helped the Crown consolidate its often tenuous jurisdiction over problematic areas, although it frequently went against the interests of local colonial officials and denizens. The enslaved emigrants had their own interests, although they often became caught up in the power dynamics between imperial and colonial authorities, and sometimes became pawns in interimperial politics.

The Spanish royal decrees granting freedom to fugitives from rival realms, and slaves' responses to the opportunities these created, raise several issues related to the legal complexity of early modern empires. First and foremost, this material brings colonial American slavery squarely into the discussion of legal pluralism. How did slavery intersect with issues of imperial sovereignty and jurisdiction? How did the creation of legal spheres of enslavement and freedom help to expand and clarify jurisdictions and to legitimate state sovereignty? Much of the analysis of legal regimes in colonial American slave societies has focused on the stark dichotomy between draconian legal codes and forms of slave resistance, framed as a clash between formal and informal normative orders.[4] The material analyzed here, however, provides a different perspective, one in which the interests of enslaved people seeking freedom intersected with the Spanish Crown's efforts to consolidate its jurisdiction. More broadly, the evidence requires us to reframe our understanding of the role of seemingly marginal colonial areas and peoples in the larger imperial project. The relevant Spanish royal decrees were designed to extend the Crown's control over specific colonial areas that were outside effective imperial jurisdiction. They did this by recasting members of one of the region's most marginal and elusive groups, fugitive slaves who crossed imperial boundaries, as full-fledged colonial actors in the service of larger imperial interests. Whether this was a coherent policy rooted in imperial philosophy, or an ad hoc response to unfolding colonial realities, or (most likely) a combination of the two, remains open to debate. Finally, this material provides insight into the multifaceted transimperial and intercolonial connections that characterized the early modern Caribbean and complicated the effective exercise of imperial sovereignty.

Transimperial Marronage in the Circum-Caribbean

The Spanish Crown issued its earliest royal decrees related to intercolonial marronage in March and May 1680. They applied to the sparsely inhabited island of Trinidad, just off the northeastern coast of South America.[5] Almost identical in wording, the two decrees ordered “that all blacks who came directly seeking baptism from whichever of the foreign nations that occupy the lands of the King, be declared free”; specifically mentioned the Windward Islands, Martinique, St. Vincent, and Grenada as sources for the fugitives; and expressly excluded Curaçao and any territories that were under Spanish control. The Crown further ordered that runaways who had arrived in previous years and had been kept enslaved “have their liberty restored.” In spite of the geographic restrictions, the decrees left open the possibility for a wider application, declaring that “freedom be granted to all those blacks who came seeking faith from any of the foreign countries which occupy territories in this Kingdom,” but not to those who lived under the jurisdiction of the Spanish Crown, “nor those who came under license for the benefit of my domains.” (The latter apparently was a reference to slaves who had been brought to Spanish American colonies through the *asiento de negros.*) Those who had come to the island “in search of baptism” should be freed retroactively.[6]

While it is not clear what effect these decrees had in sparsely settled Trinidad, their repercussions were felt throughout the circum-Caribbean for decades to come. These were just the first of several such pronouncements. Over the next century the Spanish Crown issued at least a dozen similar royal decrees, as well as various other related decrees, orders, and provisions, offering freedom to fugitive slaves who arrived in Spanish America from the colonies of its (usually Protestant) European rivals.[7] Like the 1680 *reales cédulas*, many of them specifically mentioned conversion to Roman Catholicism and/or baptism as a condition for freedom. Most applied to specific source areas and destinations, although they also were cited as precedent for the manumission of slaves in other parts of the Spanish American empire. Subsequently, slaves found freedom not only by escaping from the Leeward Islands to Trinidad but also by traveling from British South Carolina and Georgia to Florida, from Danish St. Thomas, Dutch St. Eustatius, and the

British leeward islands to Puerto Rico, from French to Spanish Hispaniola, from Jamaica to Cuba, from English outposts in Belize to Guatemala and Honduras, and from the Dutch ABC islands (Aruba, Bonaire, and Curaçao) and the Wild Coast of South America to Venezuela.[8] Several of these routes were overland—from British to Spanish settlements in North and Central America, from the Guyanas through the jungle to Venezuela, and from French Saint Domingue across the mountains to Spanish Santo Domingo. The rest were maritime routes. All the destinations were relatively marginal parts of the Spanish empire, thinly populated, and regularly visited by pirates, privateers, and smugglers, whose activities threatened Spanish economic hegemony.[9]

Intercolonial marronage in all of these areas, and throughout the Americas, predated the Spanish decrees, and it remained somewhat independent of them. Spanish America was not the only magnet for border-crossing fugitives. Marronage always has coexisted with slavery. Some runaways ignored political boundaries in making their escape; others intentionally sought safety in areas of so-called free soil.[10] Places where borders were difficult to demarcate or downright disputed proved especially attractive to and beneficial for fugitives who sought to elude the reach of authority. One such region was the Wild Coast of South America, the littoral between the Orinoco and Amazon deltas on the continent's northeastern coast, where dense jungle and cartographic confusion provided opportunities for flight between the colonies of all five major European overseas empires.[11] Geography also facilitated marronage between the small islands of the eastern Caribbean, many of which were within sight of each other and thus formed what some geographers have conceptualized as a continent-like continuum connected by the sea, even when they fell under the jurisdiction of rival empires.[12] Maritime marronage was especially common in the Caribbean, offering physical distance from owners and additional logistical challenges to capture. Vessels that traveled regularly on well-established trade routes provided convenient means to escape.[13] Seaports were an especially strong magnet, providing employment and a degree of anonymity for foreign-born fugitives who arrived on board ship. By the mid-eighteenth century ports around the Caribbean and beyond had significant populations of enslaved and free people of color.[14] It was in this wider context that the Spanish Crown issued the various royal decrees.

By the mid-eighteenth century there was a patchwork of royal decrees and provisions that applied to specific areas around the Americas. These added another element of attraction for would-be fugitives who contemplated moving beyond imperial borders. Word inevitably spread along Caribbean exchange circuits that legal freedom could be had in certain parts of Spanish America. The Spanish decrees boosted the appeal of existing escape routes and no doubt influenced the routes of at least some slaves. Given that intercolonial marronage already existed in all these areas, the decrees were at least partly an imperial response to happenings on the ground (and at sea) in the colonies. They were part of a wider policy toward, and they provided a legal framework for, the thorny issue of Spanish jurisdiction in outlying areas of the circum-Caribbean. The Crown thus took advantage of an existing situation and turned it to further imperial advantage. Slaves, in turn, took advantage of the situation for their own purposes, and they did not always behave as the Crown might have envisioned. Between these two were middle sectors, including colonial authorities, clergy, notaries, and court officials, all of whom participated in enforcing the decrees to some degree. Their own interests did not always coincide with those of either the Crown or the fugitives. The actions of one of the most marginalized groups of colonial denizens and the collaboration of intermediary groups thus helped to shape Spanish policy and strengthen jurisdiction in these relatively marginal areas.

As the eighteenth century progressed, royal advisors were well aware that slaves were fleeing regularly to many Spanish territories across the Americas.[15] The Crown eventually took another step toward developing a more integrated overall policy on the issue. In 1750 the Crown issued its most extensive royal decree to date related to the problem of intercolonial marronage. Citing the precedent of various previous decrees that it had promulgated in 1680, 1693, 1733, and 1740, the Crown now proclaimed a much more blanket and extensive emancipation, declaring that "henceforth and forever all black slaves of both sexes who come from English and Dutch colonies to seek refuge (whether in times of peace or of war) in my domains to embrace our Holy Catholic Faith shall be free."[16] Such freedom was to be automatic and irrevocable. "With the fact of having arrived in my domains they must become free, and cannot under any pretext be resold or returned to slavery," according to the decree. The case that precipitated the decree apparently was the arrival in the Cuban port of Santiago de Cuba of three fugitives from Jamaica, who had come "with the same motive of embracing our Holy Catholic Faith." This decree provided a further impetus to intercolonial marronage, especially from British and Dutch possessions.

The royal decree of 1750 did not apply to the French colonies. However, since at least the late seventeenth century, slaves regularly crossed the mountainous border between French Saint Domingue and Spanish Santo Domingo on Hispaniola, drawing the attention of authorities on both sides of the political divide. This was an area of imperial contention. The Spanish did not recognize French possession of the western half of the island until the Treaty of Rijswijk in 1697, although there had been French settlements there since the mid-1500s. Exact lines of jurisdiction through the rugged terrain remained tenuous at best. As early as 1679, authorities in the capital of Santo Domingo noted the relatively large number of French fugitives who resided there, many of whom lived in a state of de facto freedom.[17] "Those who have fled from owners who are not my subjects, in search of their liberty should be given it," the Crown ordered local authorities one year later (just months after the royal decrees freeing slaves who arrived in Trinidad).[18] Subsequently, the governor of Santo Domingo freed seventy French fugitives and used them to found the town of San Lorenzo de los Negros de Mina. In 1688 he conscripted some of them into the local militia.[19]

Apparently marronage increased in the first two decades of the eighteenth century, although the overall numbers probably remained low. As runaways continued to arrive, Spanish policy vacillated, no doubt reflecting changing imperial alliances. In 1722 the Council of the Indies ordered that those fugitives who could be found easily be rounded up and returned to their owners in Saint Domingue.[20] Seven years later the Crown's advisors noted that this had resulted in improved relations with the French.[21] By 1740, as marronage continued from Saint Domingue, the town of San Lorenzo had grown to two hundred inhabitants, although local authorities and slaveholders repeatedly called for its destruction, claiming that it was a den of thieves and vagabonds.[22] The Crown finally issued a *real cédula* on the topic in 1764. Expressing concern about the many people from Saint Domingue who "wander fugitive in the countryside having no fixed abode, living with no Christian moorings," and noting that such rootless people could not easily be caught or returned to their unidentified owners, the Crown declared that "the restitution of said blacks is out of the question," and ordered that local authorities "leave them in the liberty which they now enjoy," with the hope that they would embrace Christianity and become productive rural laborers.[23] Apparently there was no pretense here of requiring either conversion or baptism as a condition for their freedom. This may have been due at least in part to the fact that most French slaveholders were Roman Catholic and would have expected nominal profession of faith by their chattel (although it is doubtful that many invested significant time instructing them in the finer points of that religion).

In contrast, documentation related to intercolonial marronage to Spanish Florida is permeated with references to conversion and baptism. As elsewhere, fugitives began arriving in the seventeenth century, and they helped shape Spanish colonial policy for the area even before there were any relevant decrees. The arrival of the first recorded group, ten people, in 1688 triggered extensive correspondence between local and imperial authorities. The runaways claimed that "they came only to become Christian and seeking holy Baptism and protection from Your Majesty," according to a missive local authorities sent to the Crown.[24] In response, the Crown issued a *real cédula* dated 7 November 1693, which granted freedom to these runaways, "who fled on the pretext of being baptized."[25] This wording seemed to leave open at least the possibility that conversion might be somewhat of a convenient ruse. This royal decree apparently did not guarantee freedom to subsequent fugitives, however.[26] Nor did it appear to spark widespread marronage. The next group that formally sought freedom did not arrive until 1724.[27] Although they specifically referenced the 1693 *real cédula*, the governor sold them at public auction, claiming that the decree only had applied to the original group, and that he dared not risk the wrath of the British.[28] The governor appealed to the Crown for guidance in resolving the case. The issue dragged on for at least six years, and came to include cases of other runaways who had arrived in the meantime.

The matter to decide was now one of wider policy.[29] Was the 1693 royal decree a one-time provision, or did it represent a more comprehensive response to marronage from the British colonies? How should the Crown take into account past and developing approaches to the same matter elsewhere in the region? In 1731 the Council of the Indies in Madrid recommended that the fugitives be allowed to stay, that their British owners not be compensated, and that future arrivals be treated similarly.[30] With this last point, the council clearly intended to establish a broader policy. The council also made extensive reference to the situation in Hispaniola. It noted that ongoing marronage from Saint Domingue had caused significant problems with the French, who had suffered economically from the uncompensated loss of labor; that the subsequent policy of restitution had done much to improve relations between the two Catholic powers; and that luring slaves from English colonies to Florida would cause similar economic hardship to the Protestant English.

The religious element remained front and center in the council's deliberations. Noting that the original group of ten fugitives had come to Florida "seeking the Water of Baptism," it recommended that the most recent arrivals be allowed to stay "in the event that they embrace the Catholic faith."[31] However, the council also left open the possibility that some conversions might be bogus, that when slaves "express a desire to become Christian" this might on occasion "be simulated only so that they will not be returned."[32] Nevertheless, it opined that the people who had brought the case not be returned to their owners because they would then "live in the domain of Heretic Owners, enemies of the Catholic Church, lacking the faith received in Baptism."[33] In 1733 the Spanish Crown issued two *reales cédulas* that granted freedom to all fugitives who arrived in Florida and converted to Roman Catholicism.[34] Those who had first brought the case did not obtain their freedom until 1738, however, almost half a century after the original group of ten had been freed.[35] That same year the governor established the town of Gracia Real de Santa Teresa de Mose to serve both as a home for the fugitives and as a buffer to protect St. Augustine from British attack.[36] As Jane Landers has observed, "who better to serve as an advanced warning system than grateful ex-slaves carrying arms?"[37] The ex-slaves had their own agendas. Landers has called them "diplomats" and "pragmatists," noting that, besides assisting short-handed local authorities, "their own interests were clearly served by fighting those that would seek to return them to chattel slavery."[38]

Intercolonial Networks and Overlapping Jurisdictions

Marronage from Curaçao to Venezuela was particularly robust, and it is especially well documented in Dutch and Spanish colonial archives. It predated any relevant Spanish decrees or proclamations, increased significantly in the eighteenth century, and continued well after the royal decrees were rescinded. Authorities on both the island and the mainland commented on the problem as early as 1638, just four years after the Dutch had seized the small, arid island from the Spanish.[39] In mid-1644 several blacks and mulattos tried to escape on a makeshift raft but were apprehended before they could sail away.[40] Ten years later a black man successfully paddled away in a canoe.[41] By 1657 attempts at marronage had become so common that the island governor complained that all seaworthy vessels had to be chained securely at night.[42] Women as well as men occasionally fled. In 1688 four black women attempted to journey to the mainland, accompanied by a Sephardic Jewish woman and a crew of three Spanish-speaking sailors, but they were drowned when their vessel capsized.[43] Even in these early years authorities and runaways alike were aware that the fugitives played into wider imperial power dynamics. The group of slaves whom Dutch authorities captured in 1644, for example, intended "to go to the mainland to reveal . . . the weakness of the fort" to the Spanish, according to the island governor.[44]

By the end of the seventeenth century slaves were escaping regularly from the Dutch island to the nearby Spanish mainland. Fugitives both built on and further developed regional integration between two areas that had close geographic ties and deep historical connections but that belonged to two separate and rival imperial spheres. The inhabitants of Curaçao and Venezuela created an integrated intercolonial space, one that transcended political demarcations and was formed by interconnected and overlapping physical, economic, cultural, and religious geographies.[45] Close links between the peoples of the island and the mainland dated from pre-Columbian times, continued during Spanish tenure of the island (1499-1634), and were further strengthened after the Dutch West India Company (WIC) took Curaçao in 1634.[46] The particular characteristics of colonialism in each place, and the interface between the two, shaped ongoing contact between inhabitants across the imperial divide. They provide a context for interpreting marronage and the corresponding imperial response.

By the last quarter of the seventeenth century tiny, arid Curaçao had become an entrepôt of the Dutch West India Company, a major colonial center in the Dutch Atlantic system.[47] The Amsterdam Chamber of the Company controlled the island's administration and also oversaw large-scale, transatlantic commerce. The bustling port city of Willemstad, located on a large, natural deepwater harbor on the sheltered southern coast, was the hub of the island's economy. People of African descent, enslaved and free, were the majority of the island's population and dominated Willemstad's labor force. Most dock workers and sailors were black; they kept the port running and the ships sailing. By the early eighteenth century two-thirds of all of Curaçao's seafarers were of African descent.[48] The nearby Spanish American mainland was a particularly attractive market for Curaçaoan traders, easily accessible by boat and inhabited by eager trade partners due to ongoing Spanish neglect. The Province of Venezuela, especially, became Willemstad's economic hinterland. The area, known variously to contemporaries as the Coast of Caracas (the Caribbean littoral) and Tierra Firme (encompassing inland areas as well as the coast), was one of what John TePaske has called the "vital peripheries" of the Spanish empire, areas that were central to the wider imperial project even though they were not primary, wealth-producing colonies like Mexico and Peru.[49] In spite of imperial prohibitions, smuggling was widespread throughout Tierra Firme and drew in participants from across the socioeconomic spectrum.[50]

Although the Dutch had ousted the Spanish from political and economic control of Curaçao in 1634, they were less successful in the religious realm. The island remained under the jurisdiction of the Roman Catholic Church in Venezuela, first the Bishopric of Coro and, after 1637, that of Caracas.[51] The Dutch, who largely were uninterested in converting slaves in their domain, tacitly allowed this situation to continue through the late eighteenth century. They even permitted itinerant priests to visit regularly from Spanish America. Clergy crossed the porous imperial divide to evangelize semi-clandestinely, even as Curaçaoan traders were crossing in the other direction to trade illicitly.[52] As a result, by the end of the seventeenth century the majority of slaves and free people of color on the island were Roman Catholic, a status quo that continued throughout the eighteenth century.[53]

Imperial control was exercised in markedly different ways in Dutch Curaçao and Spanish Venezuela.[54] This shaped the character of intercolonial relations, including marronage. Dutch control over Curaçao was tight and focused. The small island, with the majority of its population concentrated in one compact port city, was relatively easy to govern. The WIC controlled both island administration and the trade-based economy. By the last quarter of the seventeenth century the Dutch empire was more dependent on far-flung commercial networks than on territorial control, with nodal points such as Curaçao serving as anchors around the Atlantic and beyond.[55] The Province of Venezuela, in contrast, was a vast territory, its exact parameters unclear, much of its population outside the effective control of imperial management. Throughout the eighteenth century Venezuela ping-ponged back and forth between the jurisdiction of the Audiencia of Santo Domingo, located on Hispaniola five hundred miles to the north, and the Viceroyalty of Nueva Granada, an enormous area encompassing all of northern South America from the Orinoco Delta on the shores of the Atlantic westward to Panama and the Pacific coast.[56] Neither arrangement proved tenable for effectively governing the province. The resulting confusion gave an exceptional degree of independence to local authorities, while also facilitating contraband trade and marronage, both internally and with traders from other imperial spheres.

Intercolonial commerce created a well-integrated economic zone between Curaçao and Venezuela, especially after the Dutch declared the island a free port (the Caribbean's first) in 1675. By the second half of the eighteenth century, trade with Tierra Firme made up at least half of Curaçao's registered shipping.[57] Entire areas of Venezuela had much closer economic ties to the Dutch island than to Spain.[58] However, intercolonial trade was strictly against Spanish imperial policy, and traders faced stiff sanctions and even imprisonment if they were caught by authorities.[59] Certain coastal areas were particular magnets for smuggling. One was Coro, located on the narrow eastern base of the Paraguaná Peninsula, a straight sail downwind and down-current from Curaçao. Another was the Barlovento area east of Caracas. Not coincidentally, both areas also attracted fugitive slaves, who found transport on board the sailing vessels that engaged in contraband. Entire areas of Tierra Firme remained chronically short of labor, adding a local incentive to fugitives, who found ample employment opportunities in Tierra Firme, often as smugglers.

Enslaved Africans were an important commodity in intercolonial commerce. Curaçao was the main Dutch transshipment center for slaves to Spanish America, both via the *asiento de negros* and through a parallel clandestine commerce in human cargo. Between 1651 and 1700 the island received some eighty thousand slaves from Africa.[60] Most were re-exported to Venezuela. Smuggling slaves created a dilemma for Spanish authorities and a conflict of interest between those on the ground, whose job it was to enforce imperial policy in the face of local realities, and those across the Atlantic, who only had to conceptualize it. While Venezuelans were acutely aware of the area's labor shortage, and were eager to purchase slaves regardless of their provenance, the Crown was concerned primarily with defending the integrity of its economic system, which strictly prohibited colonies from having commercial intercourse with merchants from rival powers, regardless of local needs.

Venezuela's chronic labor shortage, combined with local authorities' tolerance of smuggling, prompted the first royal decrees related to the movement of slaves from Curaçao to Tierra Firme. Between 1685 and 1705 the Spanish Crown issued four royal decrees aimed at addressing the problem of so-called blacks of bad entry (*negros de mala entrada*), by granting freedom to any slave on the mainland whose owner could not show a legitimate bill of purchase.[61] The 1689 decree specifically mentioned "the fraud which was committed" by the *asiento*-holders (who used Curaçao as a transshipment point), and noted that the trade often served as an entry point for contraband goods.[62] It is not clear whether any slaves actually were manumitted as a result, however.

By the turn of the century the problem of slaves smuggling themselves from Curaçao to Tierra Firme was also growing. Apparently the first large group of fugitives arrived in 1690, fourteen hungry, thirsty, half-naked people who complained of food shortages and abusive treatment on the desert island. Although Dutch authorities demanded their return, at least several successfully eluded capture by fleeing into the interior, assisted by local blacks. There is no indication that any of them appealed to the terms of the 1680 *reales cédulas* or that they had any contact with the judicial system.[63] By the time the next known group of thirty-one fugitives arrived in 1702 (the case discussed at the beginning of this chapter), the geopolitical context had changed markedly. With the outbreak of the War of the Spanish

Succession, the plight of Afro-Curaçaoans became entangled in geopolitics.[64] Spain and the Netherlands were now enemies, and the *asiento de negros* was in the hands of the French, who were now allies of the Spanish. In considering what to do with the foreign fugitives, the Audiencia of Santo Domingo was not particularly sympathetic to French interests, however, having been forced to accept the division of Hispaniola just a few years before.[65] Citing the 1697 *real cédula* that had freed French fugitives in Santo Domingo, the Audiencia issued a royal provision dated 7 June 1704, which gave the Curaçaoans both freedom and land, so they could "found a town and till the soil," and required that they "bear arms for the defense of the Royal Crown against all enemies who arrive in these ports." It further ordered that all fugitives from Curaçao, including those currently living in Caracas and around the countryside, "be rounded up and assembled in a new town." Locals who had purchased runaways were entitled to just compensation.[66] The Audiencia's decision pleased neither the French representatives of the *asiento*, who lost valuable revenue, nor white landowners in Tierra Firme, who lost much-needed labor. The Afro-Curaçaoans had their own interests, individually as well as collectively. Not all of them stayed together. Some settled in Caracas, where sixteen joined the free black militia.[67] Others became part of existing maroon communities around the Venezuelan countryside.[68]

Given the Crown's ongoing attempts to stem the contraband slave trade, and the perennial labor shortage, the temptation to enslave the runaways proved too attractive to resist. Local landowners were eager to keep the fugitives in bondage and set them to work on lands that produced agricultural commodities such as cacao (from which chocolate is produced) for smuggling circuits. Venezuelan authorities thus largely ignored the 1704 proclamation and continued to auction off Afro-Curaçaoans who arrived, in direct violation of the Crown's orders.[69] At least seventeen Afro-Curaçaoan fugitives were captured and resold in Coro in 1708 and 1709.[70] When a large group of runaways was seized in 1711, some of their compatriots traveled to Caracas to petition the governor to make good on the Crown's promise of freedom and land.[71] Lack of compliance remained an ongoing problem, however. The Audiencia of Santo Domingo issued at least two more royal provisions, dated 26 January 1711 and 11 March 1720, ordering the governor of Caracas to comply with the terms of the original 1704 directive.[72] Apparently these, too, were ignored. In the late 1720s a free black man named Juan Hilario Bueno petitioned authorities in Coro for the terms of the royal provisions to be applied, requesting that "all the blacks who have fled the island of Curaçao to this jurisdiction be given freedom."[73]

In 1721 the governor of Caracas authorized the head of the free black militia, Juan del Rosario Blanco, to round up fugitive slaves and found the town of Curiepe in the Barlovento area east of Caracas.[74] One-quarter of the town's original inhabitants were Curaçaoan.[75] Many of them and their descendants were conscripted into the town's free black militia, as had been ordered by the original royal provision of 1704.[76] All the settlers received land, on which most of them planted cacao, the most lucrative contraband commodity.[77] Curiepe's inhabitants regularly traded with foreigners who arrived, many of them from Curaçao.[78] Afro-Curaçaoans and their descendants found ample opportunities in Curiepe. For example, a woman named Juana Isabel Curazao, who fled the island in 1729, acquired her freedom and a small plot of land in Curiepe, on which she planted cacao trees. Curiepe was not without its conflicts, however. Local free blacks and those who traced their roots to Curaçao were embroiled in extensive battles over land ownership rights. As world demand for cacao skyrocketed in the second half of the eighteenth century, free blacks found their holdings increasingly challenged by white elites. By the 1760s Juana Isabel's heir, a free black woman named Ana María Motete, lost half of her holdings (now numbering one thousand trees) after a lengthy court case.[79]

By the mid-eighteenth century slaves were fleeing Curaçao in unprecedented numbers.[80] The Dutch West India Company compiled a detailed list of 585 Curaçaoan slaves who escaped to Tierra Firme between 1729 and 1774, with their names, owners, ages, skills, and likely destinations in Venezuela.[81] They included eighty-nine women, among them many seamstresses and vendors. Most of the male fugitives were skilled tradesmen: carpenters, masons, artisans, and eighty-two seafarers. The overwhelming majority of them went to Coro. Marronage from Curaçao to Tierra Firme apparently increased significantly in the second half of the century, spurred no doubt at least in part by the 1750 *real cédula*. Venezuelan historian Ramón Aizpurua has documented an average of twenty-two fugitives per year, over a thousand total, and has calculated that this represented a cost in lost labor of over fifty-eight thousand pesos for their Curaçaoan owners.[82] Given these numbers, the 1750 Spanish royal decree granting blanket freedom to fugitives who arrived from English and Dutch colonies may well have had a greater impact in Curaçao and Venezuela than anywhere else in the Americas.

Venezuelan archives contain dozens of cases of foreign fugitives who petitioned for their freedom, often on the basis of their supposed recent conversion and baptism in Tierra Firme. The overwhelming majority of these cases involved runaways from Curaçao at midcentury. In a typical case, in 1753 Juan Joseph obtained his freedom "for having embraced the

Catholic faith."[83] Women and children, as well as men, appear often in the records. Not all successful legal cases that were brought by Curaçaoan fugitives cited religious freedom as justification for manumission. For example, between 1738 and 1743 María Francisca de Nieto petitioned for freedom for herself and her three children, Antonio, Gabriela, and Susana, claiming they all had been free in Curaçao.[84] However, many petitioners explicitly cited conversion and baptism in Venezuela as the rationale for their right to freedom, and they often used similar phrases that echoed the specific wording of the relevant Spanish decrees or proclamations. Some fugitives used especially flowery language. In September 1746 Juan Lorenzo Rodríguez presented a case as to why he should not be included among the possessions of his Venezuelan owner, using a style and language that are found in many of the cases:

> Having been raised in the land of heretics, in the service of God and in the Light of His Holy Law, and in order to assure my salvation and to have more frequent access to the Holy Sacraments of Penitence and the Eucharist, of which spiritual sustenance I was deprived on said island of Curaçao on many occasions, which by the motivation of my conscience I wanted to receive . . . I determined with certain risk to my life to flee from the servitude in which I found myself.[85]

Some petitioners adjusted their testimonies, perhaps as they became versed in the nuances of the developing Spanish policy, and possibly with coaching from priests, notaries, or others who were knowledgeable about the relevant royal decrees. Such was the case with three brothers who had fled from Curaçao in the late 1730s and were jailed for several years in Caracas while they petitioned for their freedom. In their early declarations all three men testified that "before their flight they already professed the Apostolic Roman Catholic faith," at which point local authorities recommended that they be returned to the island. Given the fact that by then most Afro-Curaçaoans were Roman Catholic, due to regular visits by priests from Spanish America, this testimony rings true. However, they modified their original story in subsequent testimony, insisting that they came to Venezuela "in search of Christianity and spiritual peace, in order not to be among infidels." The tactic proved successful. Two of them were freed in March 1746; the fate of the third is not clear.[86]

Three men who arrived in a small boat in Coro in 1739 were baptized (perhaps not for the first time) by a local parish priest in the town of Tocuyo six months before they began their formal petition for freedom.[87]

Their legal case repeatedly cited several relevant *reales cédulas*, including both of the ones from 1680. These royal decrees were reproduced in their entirety (including the phrases that specifically excluded Curaçao) in the court documents.[88] The men's testimonies are filled with religious rhetoric. All three used virtually identical language to report that they had left the island "to seek the Water of Baptism and the faith of Jesus Christ." They further testified that in Curaçao they were "practicing a religion against our will, desiring to be instructed in the mysteries of the holy Catholic faith" and that "finding ourselves on said island enslaved to our Dutch and Jewish owners, and living unfaithfully with no spiritual attention whatsoever because we lack Holy Baptism," they were now making this petition "to save our souls." It is not clear whether they themselves were so well versed in the intricacies of the decrees and the corresponding religious language or whether (more likely) they were being coached. The document authorizing their freedom in 1742 cited as justification both the 1680 royal decrees and the fact that they had provided evidence of having been baptized in Venezuela.

Whether or not they pursued legal cases, fugitives from Curaçao found a degree of freedom and began new lives in Venezuela. Some scattered throughout the countryside, following the patterns of maroons within Venezuela.[89] Others settled in cities, especially the capital of Caracas.[90] Several areas, like Curiepe, had clearly identifiable communities of Afro-Curaçaoans. Coro, almost due south of Curaçao, attracted the greatest number of Curaçaoan fugitives. By the 1790s there were over four hundred Afro-Curaçaoans living in the area, most of them in the rural settlements of Macuquita and Santa María de la Chapa, not far from the town.[91] Others lived in Coro's urban neighborhood of Guinea.[92] If most of these migrants led a life of relative obscurity, some made a name for themselves. No doubt the best known intercolonial fugitive—revered in the folklore of Venezuela and Curaçao alike—is José Caridad Gonzalez, who was accused of being one of the masterminds of an aborted uprising of slaves and free blacks that broke out in Coro in May 1795. Earlier, after fleeing the island and settling in the town of Coro, Gonzalez helped other fugitives procure land. He traveled frequently to Caracas and even to Spain to represent their interests before the Crown.[93]

In spite of the large numbers of Afro-Curaçaoans who successfully started new lives in Tierra Firme, the journey was not without its perils. The usually calm waters occasionally turned turbulent, sometimes with fatal results. In 1688 four women perished while fleeing the island on board a small sailing vessel.[94] Sometimes shipmates turned traitorous, as happened to a black man and a mulatto in 1751 as they traveled across the waters in a small canoe in the company of a freeman, who tried to sell them to the crew of a passing schooner.[95] Not all the fugitives from Curaçao became free. Some were reenslaved in Venezuela; some, as we have seen, were sold at public auction, especially in the early eighteenth century. Others were returned to their owners in Curaçao, as happened to a woman named Mariana and her young daughter in 1748.[96] Curaçaoan slave owners, like their chattel, often took their cases to Venezuelan courts.

Sometimes fugitives gave each other critical support. For example, several freemen from Curaçao, including the head of the local free black militia, testified in the cases of three fugitives who petitioned for their freedom in the early 1740s.[97] However, there was no guarantee of solidarity or common cause with other people of color. At midcentury a free black ship captain from Curaçao named Gaspar Antonio Quirigazo made a handsome living regularly traveling to Coro to hunt down fugitives on commission from island authorities. On at least one occasion (the case of Mariana and her daughter) he testified on behalf of their owners in a Venezuelan court.[98] Residents of Curiepe were embroiled in an extended land dispute that pitted locally born blacks against those from Curaçao.[99] Sometimes there was even a kind of revolving door. In 1743 Nicolás Pérez de Campo, a midlevel Spanish colonial administrator, complained that two runaways whom he had purchased at public auction had returned to the island, and that his attempts to obtain redress from Dutch authorities were completely unsuccessful.[100]

Slaves also fled to the Spanish realm from Dutch and French colonies on the Wild Coast. Some fugitives from Essequibo escaped to Trinidad, where, in the second half of the century, they found official sanctuary.[101] Others trekked through the swamps and jungles to Venezuela. In the early 1770s the governor of Essequibo and Demerara informed officials of the Dutch West India Company that local plantations faced sure ruin if marronage to Venezuela were not stemmed. Officers of the militias in both colonies noted that their ranks were being similarly depleted as enslaved militiamen escaped. Colonial officials in Venezuela, as well as those in the Netherlands, repeatedly petitioned the Spanish for a treaty of restitution.[102]

Changing Colonial Configurations and the End of an Era

Wherever fugitives crossed political boundaries, their owners might be expected to seek compensation for the loss of their property, return of the runaways, or both. Authorities wrestled with the problems of compensation and restitution throughout the eighteenth century. Here again, the interests and perspective of local administrators could be markedly different from those of imperial authorities in distant Europe. Sometimes local authorities made arrangements on an ad hoc basis. At other times the European powers signed treaties. Some of these more formal agreements applied to places where the Spanish had offered sanctuary. Others did not. One of the earliest accords for the reciprocal restitution of runaways was signed between the Spanish and French on Hispaniola soon after the 1697 Treaty of Rijswijk, which formally recognized French Saint Domingue.[103] Geography may have been a factor in this and other cases. The seemingly impenetrable jungles of northeastern South America were especially alluring to escaping slaves and thus spurred early cooperation among competing powers. Dutch and French colonial authorities on the Wild Coast signed a treaty of reciprocal restitution in 1713.[104] The French and Portuguese signed treaties promising to return each other's slaves in the Amazon region in 1732 and 1753.[105] On sparsely populated Trinidad, site of the original royal decrees, authorities faced "a greatly increased number of slaves, some criminals, who have come from French, Dutch and English colonies to seek refuge," and bucked the trend toward manumission by proposing to reenslave them in the mid-1780s.[106]

Authorities grappled with the issues of compensation and restitution in Spanish Florida for several decades, even as they contemplated the fate of runaways who arrived from British colonies. In 1727, legal counsel to the Crown recommended that the slaves be granted freedom but that they also assume responsibility for compensating their English owners.[107] Four years later the Council of the Indies recommended that the British owners not be compensated, which was the policy that was adopted in the corresponding *reales cédulas* of 1733.[108] In 1750, just months before the Crown issued its most encompassing sanctuary decree, the governor of British South Carolina sent a representative to St. Augustine to demand that his counterpart return fugitive slaves or face "disagreeable consequences." The governor of Florida responded by fortifying the defenses at Mose.[109] In 1750 the Crown noted that its previous royal decrees had prohibited restitution "because the English and the Dutch did not practice equal correspondence with fugitives who fled from my domain to their colonies."[110] The pace of demands for restitution appears to have picked up in the second half of the eighteenth century, partly due to the changing geopolitical climate. Increasingly, the Spanish Crown now saw foreign fugitives as a threat to its interests, rather than as an opportunity to boost colonial loyalty and provide manpower to underpopulated areas. The Spanish signed treaties of restitution with both the British (for slaves who had escaped to Puerto Rico) and the Danish in 1767, and with the French (relating to Saint Domingue) in 1776.[111] All three of these treaties covered areas where slaves previously had found sanctuary.

The Crown ordered Venezuelans to compensate Curaçaoan slaveholders for their runaways as early as 1704 and again in 1718, although it is not clear how rigorously these dictates were followed.[112] Throughout the first half of the eighteenth century the owners regularly made their cases for restitution, either in person or by proxy, in Venezuelan courts. These efforts, which often were successful, were made variously by individuals, by groups of slave owners, and occasionally by official representatives of the WIC.[113] Such attempts declined following the promulgation of the 1750 *real cédula*.[114] Throughout the second half of the century, as fugitives continued to arrive from the island and elsewhere, local officials apparently felt that the Crown was being unresponsive to their growing concerns. In 1771 the commander of the Caracas battalion warned of "the suspicion and fear which is being caused by the continued flight of black slaves from Curaçao."[115] In 1784 high-level Venezuelan authorities requested that the Crown sign "a convention with foreign powers for the mutual restitution of fugitive slaves" in order to avoid foreign-born slaves being allowed to stay "under the cloak of religion."[116] They pointed out that certain slaves might be handpicked and introduced intentionally by Spain's enemies for purposes of espionage.[117]

When such a pact was not forthcoming, locals took matters into their own hands. In 1790 the governor of Caracas issued a royal order that declared a "halt [to] freedom to fugitive slaves from foreign powers" and authorized the return of seven Curaçaoan runaways, in direct violation of royal policy. The order noted that foreign-born slaves were "prejudicial to these provinces" and ordered that "for now compliance with the royal decrees is suspended."[118] Nevertheless, the governor recognized the logistical and political impossibility of meeting the demands of Curaçaoan authorities to return all the fugitives who had arrived over the past forty years. "There are serious drawbacks" to such a demand, the governor noted, "as with such a long possession of liberty it will be extremely difficult to return to slavery the extensive free black population . . . and very dangerous to attempt it."[119] Even slaves who came via more established channels were now suspect. When a schooner arrived in Puerto Cabello from Curaçao in September 1790 with a shipment of thirty-one slaves to sell, local authorities opposed the disembarkation of those who had been born in Curaçao. "It has been observed that creole slaves or those who have been educated in foreign colonies are detrimental to these provinces," a local official wrote a few months later.[120]

On 23 June 1791, almost a year after Venezuelan authorities had ceased complying with the *reales cédulas*, Spain and the Netherlands signed an agreement for the reciprocal return of fugitive slaves and deserters.[121] The nine-point treaty specified that slaves would be returned from Puerto Rico to St. Eustatius, from Coro to Curaçao, and from Venezuelan holdings in Orinoco to the Dutch colonies on the Wild Coast. It had a one-year statute of limitations, required owners to cover the transportation costs involved in reclaiming their chattel, stipulated that the runaways would not be punished and that they be allowed to exercise their religion freely upon their return to the Dutch domain, and specified that any fugitives who had committed crimes must fully serve their sentences in Spanish territory before being returned. Two years before, Spain had opened up the slave trade to Venezuela (as well as to Cuba, Santo Domingo, and Puerto Rico), thus dealing an economic blow to those who did a brisk business in the contraband trade in chattel.[122]

Abolishing the legal framework that encouraged marronage did not completely halt it. If slaves had fled from the Dutch island to the Spanish mainland well before the Crown had sought to entice them, they continued to do so after the incentives were revoked. One Curaçaoan slaveholder reported that one hundred of her chattel escaped to Venezuela between 1786 and 1792.[123] At least three groups of Afro-Curaçaoans arrived in Venezuela in 1795; authorities returned some but not others, reflecting an ongoing ambivalence in policy.[124] Marronage also continued from Dutch and French colonies on the Wild Coast into eastern Venezuela. Some fugitives continued to get satisfaction from the legal system in spite of the 1791 Treaty of Restitution. One of the longest cases on record is that of Teresa Ayuba, who arrived in eastern Venezuela at age nine as part of a large, multiethnic group that had fled from Essequibo. Ayuba's legal path to freedom seemingly was as long and arduous as her jungle trek. She was sold along with thirty-three others in 1767, shortly after arriving, and again in 1780. After the French temporarily seized Essequibo from the Dutch in 1781, the French ambassador officially requested return of twenty-four of the fugitives, including Ayuba, even though their emigration had predated the takeover by well over a decade. The governor recommended that all be returned except those who were married to locals or who performed useful occupations. But in 1787 the Spanish Crown rejected this request and instead granted freedom to all blacks, mulattos, and Indians who had arrived in Venezuela from Essequibo, citing the *real cédula* that freed all fugitives who arrived in Trinidad from Tobago and Essequibo. There followed several years of repeated petitions on the part of both Ayuba and her daughter. In 1794 Ayuba claimed that her initial sale had violated royal policy. Her owner countered that, since her arrival had predated the corresponding royal decree, the latter did not apply and that, in any event, the Treaty for the Reciprocal Restitution of Deserters and Fugitives was now in effect. Authorities in Venezuelan Guayana apparently disagreed. They finally granted freedom to Teresa Ayuba and her children in March 1799, over thirty years after she had arrived. The fate of her original travel-mates is unclear.[125]

Marronage from Curaçao to Venezuela continued into the nineteenth century.[126] New geopolitical realities produced new incentives. The brief creation of the federation of Gran Colombia in 1821, followed by the independence of Venezuela in 1823 and the subsequent eventual abolition of slavery, renewed the attraction of the mainland for Curaçaoan slaves, who remained under Dutch rule and would have to wait until 1863 for their own emancipation. The uneven pace of emancipation in the different imperial and rising national spheres, beginning with the Age of Revolutions and continuing well into the nineteenth century, spurred new waves of intercolonial marronage around the circum-Caribbean, ones that responded to particular political and economic currents.[127]

Conclusions

This chapter has explored several dimensions of legal pluralism that played out in the slave societies of the eighteenth-century Caribbean related to inter-imperial marronage. First, the evidence points to jurisdictional complexity within the Spanish empire. The Crown's struggle to tighten its tenuous hold over some of its most peripheral areas spurred the promulgation of a series of royal decrees that granted freedom to some of the area's most marginalized people. The intersection of the interests of fugitive slaves with those of the Spanish Crown guided changes to the Spanish legal order.[128] Venezuela's constant shifting between the Audiencia of Santo Domingo and the Viceroyalty of Nueva Granada provided another level of jurisdictional complexity, and gave exceptionally wide latitude for a variety of colonial actors, including authorities, to interpret—or ignore—royal proclamations as they saw fit.[129]

A second level of legal pluralism is evident in the complex relationship between the Dutch island of Curaçao and the nearby Spanish American mainland. While politically Curaçao and Venezuela belonged to two separate imperial spheres, the transimperial jurisdiction of the Roman Catholic Church, and the centrality of intercolonial smuggling as the region's economic bedrock, created a vibrant inter-imperial area of interaction, one that facilitated the development of an inter-imperial legal zone. Here again, Venezuela's shifting position in the colonial hierarchy both facilitated and complicated the relationship. Thus, issues of internal and inter-imperial legal pluralism were intertwined. It is notable, for example, that Curaçaoan slaveholders often appealed to colonial Venezuelan courts for the return of their chattel—the very courts that were freeing fugitives from the Dutch island.[130]

The distinction between jurisdictional and normative plurality was no doubt often unclear to the various actors involved. The runaway slaves, like others who crossed imperial boundaries, learned to navigate multiple, often contradictory, legal regimes and normative orders.[131] Simply by crossing from the Dutch to the Spanish realm, most (if not all) of the fugitives would have been aware that they were "subject to more than one body of law."[132] Sometimes simply changing jurisdiction could result in altered legal status for a slave, what Rebecca Scott has termed a "rupture in legality," without appeal to the formal judicial system.[133] However, in many cases, the runaways sought recourse in colonial courts to obtain legal freedom, land, etc. It is difficult to know how the fugitives themselves interpreted the opportunities and various normative orders available to them in their new homeland, and how their understanding of these various orders guided their choices as to whether or not to pursue formal court cases.

Legal pluralism played out in complex ways in the slave societies of the Americas. As the evidence here has shown, the question was not always one of a simple dichotomy between a powerful, repressive state versus subaltern normative orders created by marginalized people seeking to carve out small, subversive spaces of relative freedom. As Rebecca Scott has noted, rather than a "unitary project of state control," slavery's intersection with the law was sometimes complicated and multifaceted.[134] The evidence presented here provides an intriguing glimpse into an even more complex legal order, one in which mobile slaves who were able and willing to cross imperial boundaries actively contributed to the formation of plural legal orders both within and across empires. Recourse to the law was only one of several strategies they employed as they adroitly managed complex jurisdictional issues.

One must be careful not to overstate the case here, however. The overwhelming majority of slaves in the eighteenth-century Caribbean were tightly bound to plantations where the established legal order supported conditions of unmitigated repression and horror, with very few opportunities for even the simplest freedoms. Questions of imperial sovereignty and jurisdictional complexity were simply irrelevant to most Caribbean slaves, whose only recourse may well have been to develop subversive, informal, alternative responses to highly repressive official legal codes. Nevertheless, a minority of slaves throughout the circum-Caribbean found themselves in circumstances where means, motives, and opportunity came together to create what historians have categorized variously as a continuum, a dialectic, or a "vexed and permeable boundary" between slavery and freedom.[135] Fugitive slaves who crossed imperial boundaries and took advantage of the Spanish royal decrees sometimes also took advantage of the similarly permeable political demarcations between empires, even as they became caught up in the complicated power dynamics that such vagaries produced.[136]

NOTES

1. Portions of this chapter were presented at the Triangle Legal History Seminar (National Humanities Center, Research Triangle Park, NC, February 2010) and at the Symposium on Comparative Early Modern Legal History, "New Perspectives on Legal Pluralism" (Newberry Library Center for Renaissance Studies, Chicago, April 2010). Most of the research was conducted during a leave that was funded by an ACLS/SSRC/NEH International and Area Studies Fellowship. Some material is adapted and expanded from the first section of Rupert, "Marronage, Manumission, and Maritime Trade in the Early Modern Caribbean," *Slavery and Abolition* 30, no. 3 (September 2009): 361-82. I am grateful for the excellent critique and insights I received from seminar participants and others and for the specific comments on this version by Lauren Benton, Richard Ross, Peter Wood, David Geggus, and Peter Villella. I regret that I have not yet been able to incorporate all of the suggestions. This is the seed of a new research project, based on an initial survey of a limited selection of the relevant archival material.
2. "Sobre la libertad de esclavos" (1704?), in Carlos Gonzalez Batista, comp., *Documentos para la historia de las antillas neerlandesas* (Coro, Venezuela: Centro de Investigaciones Historicas Pedro Manuel Arcaya, 1987), Causas Civiles #8, 120-21. The quotation is from 120. The case is also described in Lucas Guillermo Castillo Lara, *Apuntes para la historia colonial de Barlovento* (Caracas: Academia Nacional de la Historia, 1981), 345-47; Ramón Aizpurua, "En busca de la libertad: Los esclavos fugados de Curazao a Coro en el siglo XVIII," in *Influencias africanas en las culturas tradicionales de los paises andinos* (Bogotá, Colombia: Dupligráfica, 2002), 88-89; and Robert J. Ferry, *The Colonial Elite of Early Caracas: Formation and Crisis, 1567-1767* (Berkeley: University of California Press, 1989), 111-12.
3. Aizpurua, "En busca de la libertad," 80.
4. Recent analysis is beginning to reframe this, however. See Rebecca J. Scott, "Slavery and the Law in Atlantic Perspective: Jurisdiction, Jurisprudence, and Justice," *Law and Historical Review* 29, no. 4 (November 2011): 915. Sue Peabody and Keila Grinberg have noted how the creation of areas of so-called free soil contributed to processes of state building throughout the early modern world. See Sue Peabody and Keila Grinberg, "Free Soil: The Generation and Circulation of an Atlantic Legal Principle," *Slavery and Abolition* 32, no. 3 (September 2011): 333. Walter Johnson makes a similar argument for jurisdiction at the level of individual states in the nineteenth-century United States. See Walter Johnson, "Resetting the Legal History of Slavery: Divination, Torture, Poisoning, Murder, Revolution, Emancipation, and Re-enslavement," *Law and History Review* 29, no. 4 (November 2011): 1095.

5. Both *reales cédulas* are reproduced in Archivo de la Academia Nacional de la Historia (AANH) Archivo del Registro del Distrito Federal, Cajas Negras (ARDF CN) T-1742-CG-PRSUZ Exp. 9 (20 August 1740), 8-10. The May one is also reproduced in Ermila Troconis de Veracoechea, comp., *Apuntes para el estudio de los esclavos negros en Venezuela* (Caracas: Biblioteca de la Academia Nacional de la Historia), #48, 222-23. The wording of the two is almost identical except that the second one references the Capuchin Order. It is not clear if they were intended as two separate pronouncements or if, more likely, the second is simply a reissue of the first. Apparently the Crown issued another such *real cédula* for Trinidad almost one hundred years later, which was applicable to fugitives from Tobago and Essequibo. See Aizpurua, "En busca de la libertad," 93-94, and Cármen Torres Pantín, comp., *Indice sobre esclavos y esclavitud: sección civiles-esclavos* (Caracas: Biblioteca de la Academia Nacional de la Historia, 1997), 53. Aizpurua lists the date of this third decree as 20 February 1773 while Torres puts it ten years earlier, on 2 February 1763. I have yet to find a copy.
6. Baptism was often a prerequisite for manumission in the seventeenth and eighteenth centuries. See Peabody and Grinberg, "Free Soil: The Generation and Circulation of an Atlantic Legal Principle," 332.
7. In addition to the three royal decrees for Trinidad (see footnote 5), there were three for Spanish Florida (7 November 1693, 4 October and 29 October 1733), at least one each for Central America and Hispaniola (19 December 1739 and 21 October 1764, respectively), and a more general one for all of the Americas (24 September 1750). See "R. C. para que en las provincias de la Nueva España se guarde y compla lo resuelto en punto de que se tengan por libres los negros esclavos que se huyesen a ellas con el fin de abrazar nuestra santa fe católica" (24 September 1750), in Richard Konetzke, ed., *Colección de documentos para la historia de la formación social de Hispanoamérica, 1493-1810* (Madrid: Consejo Superior de Investigaciones Científicas, 1953), 3:1 #152, 248; John J. TePaske, "The Fugitive Slave: Intercolonial Rivalry and Spanish Slave Policy, 1687-1764," in Samuel Proctor, ed., *Eighteenth-Century Florida and Its Borderlands* (Gainesville: University of Florida Press, 1975), 6; Jane Landers, "Gracia Real de Santa Teresa de Mose: A Free Black Town in Spanish Colonial Florida," in Colin Palmer, ed., *The Worlds of Unfree Labor: From Indentured Servitude to Slavery* (Aldershot, UK: Ashgate, 1998), 17; Oakah L. Jones Jr., *Guatemala in the Spanish Colonial Period* (Norman: University of Oklahoma Press, 1994), 112; Torres, comp., *Indice*, 49. The text of the 1750 royal decree also mentions two others, dated 11 March and 11 November 1740, but it does not provide specifics and I have yet to find a more complete reference. There may well have been others, in addition to a variety of royal provisions, royal orders, and other proclamations on the topic that were issued by different imperial and colonial authorities.
8. Jane Landers, "Maroon Women in Colonial Spanish America: Case Studies in the Circum-Caribbean from the Sixteenth through the Eighteenth Centuries," in David Barry Gaspar and Darlene Clark Hine, eds., *Beyond Bondage: Free Women of Color in the Americas* (Urbana: University of Illinois Press, 2004), 13–14; Peter H. Wood, *Black Majority: Negroes in Colonial South Carolina from 1670 through the Stono Rebellion* (New York: Norton, 1996 [1974]), 306; N. A. T. Hall, "Maritime Maroons: *Grand Marronage* from the Danish West Indies," *William and Mary Quarterly*, 3rd series, 42 (October 1985): 483–84; Robert J. Ferry, *The Colonial Elite of Early Caracas: Formation and Crisis, 1567-1767* (Berkeley: University of California Press, 1989), 111–12; Oakah L. Jones Jr., *Guatemala in*

the Spanish Colonial Period (Norman: University of Oklahoma Press, 1994), 112; Torres, comp., *Indice*, 84, 85, 92, 126; O. Nigel Bolland, "Timber Extraction and the Shaping of Enslaved People's Culture in Belize," in Verene A. Shepherd, ed., *Slavery without Sugar: Diversity in Caribbean Economy and Society since the 17th Century* (Gainesville: University Press of Florida, 2002), 56.

9. These decrees, and their usefulness in attracting immigrants to settle on the frontiers of empire, had their roots in medieval Spain. See Peabody and Grinberg, "Free Soil: The Generation and Circulation of an Atlantic Legal Principle," 334, 336. Spanish codification of specific ways slaves could obtain freedom dated from the Siete Partidas of the thirteenth century. See Aurelia Martín Casares and Margarita García Barranco, "Legislation on Free Soil in Nineteenth-Century Spain: The Case of the Slave Rufino and Its Consequences," *Slavery and Abolition* 32, no. 3 (September 2011): 462.
10. For analysis of the concept of free soil and corresponding case studies across time and place see "Free Soil," ed. Sue Peabody and Keila Grinberg, special issue, *Slavery and Abolition* 32, no. 3 (September 2011).
11. Alvin O. Thompson, *Flight to Freedom: African Runaways and Maroons in the Americas* (Jamaica: University of the West Indies Press, 2006), 273-74; Guillermo Morón, *Los orígenes históricos de Venezuela*. Vol. 1, *Introducción al siglo XVI* (Madrid: Consejo Superior de Investigaciones Científicas, Instituto Gonzalo Fernandez de Oviedo, 1954), 42.
12. Thompson, *Flight to Freedom*, 272; Joshua M. Torres and Reniel Rodríguez Ramos, "The Caribbean: A Continent Divided by Water," in Basil A. Reid, ed., *Archaeology and Geoinformatics: Case Studies from the Caribbean* (Tuscaloosa: University of Alabama Press), 13-29.
13. Hilary Beckles, "From Land to Sea: Runaway Barbados Slaves and Servants, 1630-1700," in Gad Heuman, ed., *Out of the House of Bondage: Runaways, Resistance, and Marronage in Africa and the New World* (London: Frank Cass, 1986), 79-94; N. A. T. Hall, "Maritime Maroons: *Grand Marronage* from the Danish West Indies," *William and Mary Quarterly*, 3rd series, 42 (October 1985): 476-97; Michael J. Jarvis, "Maritime Masters and Seafaring Slaves in Bermuda, 1680-1783," *William and Mary Quarterly* 59, no. 3 (July 2002): 585-622; Julius C. Scott, "The Common Wind: Currents of Afro-American Communication in the Era of the Haitian Revolution" (Ph.D. dissertation, Duke University, 1986), *passim*.
14. Thompson, *Flight to Freedom*, 272; Philip D. Morgan, "Introduction," in "Maritime Slavery," special issue of *Slavery and Abolition* 31, no. 3 (September 2010): 316; Michael J. Jarvis, *In the Eye of all Trade: Bermuda, Bermudians, and the Maritime Atlantic World, 1680-1783* (Chapel Hill: University of North Carolina Press), especially 147-51 and *passim*; Pedro L. V. Welch, *Slave Society in the City: Bridgetown, Barbados, 1680-1834* (Kingston: Ian Randel, 2004), especially chapter 8. Cities offered similar protection for terrestrial runaways. See John Hope Franklin and Loren Schweninger, *Runaway Slaves: Rebels on the Plantation* (New York: Oxford University Press, 1999), 125.
15. "Consejo de Indias a S. M." (12 April 1731), in Irene A. Wright, comp., "Dispatches of Spanish Officials Bearing on the Free Negro Settlement of Gracia Real de Santa Teresa de Mose, Florida," *Journal of Negro History* 9, no. 2 (1924): 168-70.
16. "R. C. para que en las provincias de la Nueva España se guarde y compla lo resuelto en punto de que se tengan por libres los negros esclavos que se huyesen a ellas con el fin de abrazar nuestra Santa Fe Católica" (24 September 1750), in Konetzke, ed., *Colección de documentos* 3:1 #152, 248-49.

17. "R. C. al Fiscal de la Audiencia de Santo Domingo sobre los esclavos fugitives de franceses" (25 November 1679), in Konetzke, ed., *Colección de documentos*, 2:2 #468, 688.
18. "R. C. al Presidente de Santo Domingo" (3 September 1680), in Konetzke, ed., *Colección de documentos* 2:2, #483, 708-9. This communiqué does not reference the *reales cédulas* related to Trinidad, although they clearly were germane.
19. Thompson, *Flight to Freedom*, 274.
20. "Consejo de Indias a S. M." (12 April 1731), in Wright, comp., "Dispatches of Spanish Officials," 168-69; TePaske, "The Fugitive Slave," 5.
21. TePaske, "The Fugitive Slave," 5.
22. Thompson, *Flight to Freedom*, 275.
23. "R. C. al Gobernador de Santo Domingo" (21 October 1764), in Konetzke, ed., *Colección de documentos* 2:2, #194, 322-23.
24. "Los oficials reales de la Florida a S. M." (8 March 1689), in Wright, comp., "Dispatches," 151.
25. Antonio de Benavides to the Crown (2 November 1725), in Wright, comp., "Dispatches,"164. The extensive reports by the governor and others are reproduced in Wright, comp., "Dispatches," 150-64. These communiqués are filled with religious justification both for the marronage and for allowing the fugitives to remain in Florida.
26. TePaske, "The Fugitive Slave," 4-5.
27. Four small groups of fugitives who arrived in the 1680s and '90s apparently were allowed to stay, but it is not clear whether they obtained their freedom (Landers, "Gracia Real de Santa Teresa de Mose," 14). Three particularly unfortunate would-be runaways were caught by the British in 1697 and tortured (TePaske, "The Fugitive Slave," 4). Thereafter, apparently there were no reports of runaway slaves arriving in Florida from British North America for over a quarter of a century. It is unclear whether this is due to gaps in the archival records or to local, regional, and geopolitical factors during the War of the Spanish Succession and its aftermath. Landers says the group that arrived in 1724 numbered ten; the documents reproduced by Wright mention just seven (Landers, "Gracia Real de Santa Teresa de Mose," 15; Wright, comp., "Dispatches," 145, 164).
28. Antonio de Benavides to the Crown, 2 November 1725, in Wright, comp., "Dispatches,"164-65; Landers, "Gracia Real de Santa Teresa de Mose," 15. TePaske says the fugitives arrived in 1725, but this may be a reference to the first official communiqué about them, in November 1725 (TePaske, "The Fugitive Slave," 4; Wright, comp., "Dispatches," 145, 164).
29. John TePaske has noted that the 1693 royal decree "was the first step in defining a fugitive slave policy" for Spanish Florida (TePaske, "The Fugitive Slave," 3).
30. "Consejo de Indias a S. M." (12 April 1731), in Wright, comp., "Dispatches," 166-73.
31. "Consejo de Indias a S. M." (12 April 1731), in Wright, comp., "Dispatches," 168, 169.
32. "Consejo de Indias a S. M." (12 April 1731), in Wright, comp., "Dispatches," 170.
33. "Consejo de Indias a S. M." (12 April 1731), in Wright, comp., "Dispatches," 171.
34. TePaske, "The Fugitive Slave," 6; Landers, "Gracia Real de Santa Teresa de Mose," 17.
35. Governor Montiano to the Crown (31 May 1738) in Wright, comp., "Dispatches," 173; Landers, "Gracia Real de Santa Teresa de Mose," 17.
36. Governor Montiano to the Crown (16 February 1739) in Wright, comp., "Dispatches," 176. The town had a precarious existence, however. It was evacuated in 1740 for the duration

of the War of Jenkins's Ear, resettled in 1748, and finally disbanded in 1763 or 1764 when the British took Florida (TePaske, "The Fugitive Slave," 8-10). It is not clear to what extent Mose actually served as a magnet for fugitive slaves, the concerns of British American slaveholders notwithstanding. By the time of its final evacuation the settlement counted just seventy-nine inhabitants, who apparently represented the entire free black population of Spanish Florida, as compared to the territory's 350 slaves (TePaske, "The Fugitive Slave," 11).

37. Landers, "Gracia Real de Santa Teresa de Mose," 18.
38. Landers, "Gracia Real de Santa Teresa de Mose," 18.
39. "Instructie voor Jacob Pietersz Tolck, Direkteur van Curaçao" (1638), in J. A. Schiltkamp and J. T. Smidt, eds., *West Indisch Plakaatboek: Publicaties en andere Wetten alsmede de oudste Resoluties Betrekking hebbende op Curaçao, Aruba, Bonaire* (Amsterdam: S. Emmering, 1978), 1: 6; Governor Fuenmayor (20 April 1638), cited in Aizpurua, "En busca de la libertad," 75.
40. Resolution of island directors of Curaçao (26 May 1644), in Charles T. Gehring and J. A. Schiltkamp, eds., *New Netherland Documents.* Vol. 17, *Curaçao Papers, 1640-1665* (Interlaken, NY: Heart of the Lakes, 1987), #8c, 39.
41. L. Rodenburch to Amsterdam Directors (2 April 1654), in Gehring and Schiltkamp, eds., *New Netherland Documents,* #14, 59.
42. Letter from Governor of Curaçao to Directors of the Dutch West India Company (11 June 1657), in Gehring and Schiltkamp, eds., *New Netherland Documents,* #27, 98.
43. Archivo de Falcón (Coro, Venezuela) Causas Civiles #914 (9 September 1688). For more on this case see Linda M. Rupert, "Waters of Faith, Currents of Freedom: Gender, Religion, and Ethnicity in Inter-imperial Trade between Curaçao and Tierra Firme," in Nora Jaffary, ed., *Race, Religion, and Gender in the Colonization of the Americas* (Aldershot, UK: Ashgate, 2007), 151-64.
44. Peter Stuyvesant et al. Resolution (26 May 1644), in Gehring and Schiltkamp, eds., *New Netherland Documents,* #8c, 39.
45. For further development of this point see Linda M. Rupert, *Creolization and Contraband: Curaçao in the Early Modern Atlantic World* (Athens: University of Georgia Press, 2012), chapter 5; and Linda M. Rupert, "Inter-colonial Networks and Revolutionary Ferment in Eighteenth-Century Curaçao and Tierra Firme," in Wim Klooster and Gert Oostindie, eds., *Curaçao in the Age of Revolutions, 1795-1800* (Leiden, the Netherlands: KITLV Press, 2011), 75-96.
46. For the pre-Columbian era see Jay B. Haviser, "Amerindian Cultural Geography on Curaçao" (Ph.D. diss., Rijksuniversiteit, Amsterdam, the Netherlands, 1987), 11, 51–54; 73–79, 140–49, and the introduction to Neil L. Whitehead, ed., *Wolves from the Sea: Readings in the Anthropology of the Native Caribbean* (Leiden, the Netherlands: KITLV Press, 1995). For the Spanish era (1499–1634) see the following in Irene Wright, comp., *Nederlandsche Zeevaarders op de Eilanden in de Caribische Zee en aan de Kust van Colombia en Venezuela Gedurende de Jaren 1621-1648(9): Documenten hoofdzakekijk uit het Archivo General de Indias te Sevilla.* Vol., 1, *1621-1641* (Utrecht, the Netherlands: Kemink en Zoon, 1935): Francisco Nuñez Melian (11 February 1635 and 15 July 1635), 200; Domingo Antonio Francisco (12–13 July 1635), 211; Juan Mateos (19 October 1635), 215–16; Memorandum (1641), 248.
47. For the concept of colonial centers, see Amy Turner Bushnell and Jack P. Greene, "Peripheries, Centers, and the Construction of Early Modern American Empires," in Christine

Daniels and Michael V. Kennedy, eds., *Negotiated Empires: Centers and Peripheries in the Americas, 1500-1820* (New York: Routledge, 2002), 3–6.

48. Wim Klooster, *Illicit Riches: Dutch Trade in the Caribbean, 1648-1795* (Leiden, the Netherlands: KITLV Press, 1998), 68.
49. John Jay TePaske, "Integral to Empire: The Vital Peripheries of Colonial Spanish America," in Daniels and Kennedy, eds., *Negotiated Empires*, 29, 33.
50. For analysis of contraband's importance for Venezuela and Curaçao in the eighteenth century, and the symbiosis between the two economies, see Rupert, *Creolization and Contraband*; Ramón Aizpurua, *Curaçao y la costa de Caracas: Introducción al estudio del contrabando en tiempos de la Compañía Guipuzcoana, 1730-1788* (Caracas, Venezuela: Biblioteca de la Academia Nacional de la Historia, 1993); Celestino Andrés Arauz Monfante, *El contrabando Holandés en el Caribe durante la primera mitad del siglo XVIII*, vols. 1 and 2 (Caracas: Biblioteca de la Academia Nacional de la Historia, 1984); Jeremy David Cohen, "Informal Commercial Networks, Social Control, and Political Power in the Province of Venezuela, 1700-1757" (Ph.D. diss., University of Florida, 2003); Klooster, *Illicit Riches*, especially chapters 3, 5, and 7; and Cornelis C. Goslinga, *Dutch in the Caribbean and in the Guianas, 1680-1791* (Assen, The Netherlands: van Gorcum, 1985), especially chapters 3, 6, 7, and 14.
51. This also was the case for the neighboring Dutch islands of Aruba and Bonaire, which were sparsely inhabited during the time period covered here.
52. This recalls Tamanaha's analysis of the complex interface between state and religious law, although he does not consider cases that cross political jurisdictions. See Brian Z. Tamanaha, "A Non-Essentialist Version of Legal Pluralism," *Journal of Law and Society* 27, no. 2 (June 2000): 318.
53. Carlos Felice Cardot, *Curaçao hispánico: Antagonismo flamenco-español* (Caracas: Ediciones de la Presidencia de la República, 1982), 404-6, 412; Goslinga, *The Dutch in the Caribbean*, 247.
54. For further elaboration on this point see Rupert, "Inter-colonial Networks and Revolutionary Ferment."
55. Some historians argue that territorial conquest was always subordinate to commerce in the Dutch overseas enterprise. Others contend that, at least in the early to mid-seventeenth century, territorial expansion was as important to the Dutch as it was to other European powers. For the former, see Victor Enthoven, "Early Dutch Expansion in the Atlantic Region," in Johannes Postma and Victor Enthoven, eds., *Riches from Atlantic Commerce: Dutch Transatlantic Trade and Shipping, 1585-1817* (Leiden: Brill, 2003),17-47, and Patricia Seed, *Ceremonies of Possession in Europe's Conquest of the New World, 1492-1640* (Cambridge: Cambridge University Press, 1995), 154-60. For the latter, see Benjamin Schmidt, "The Dutch Atlantic: From Provincialism to Globalism," in Jack P. Greene and Philip D. Morgan, eds., *Atlantic History: A Critical Appraisal* (Oxford: Oxford University Press, 2009), 171-75. The relationship between territorial claims and commercial networks in the Dutch realm merits further study. As early as 1609, decades before the Dutch reached their apogee, Hugo Grotius argued that territorial possession was fully compatible with a mercantile project (Hugo Grotius, *De mare liberum*, cited in Claudia Schnurmann, "'Wherever Profit Leads Us, to Every Sea and Shore . . . ': The VOC, the WIC, and Dutch Methods of Globalization in the Seventeenth Century," *Renaissance Studies* 17, no. 3 (2003): 480. As Lauren Benton has noted,

imperial sovereignty in the early modern era often was exercised in ways other than via the strict claiming of territory. See Lauren Benton, *A Search for Sovereignty, Law, and Geography in European Empires, 1400-1900* (Cambridge: Cambridge University Press, 2010), 3-5.

56. Venezuela was under the jurisdiction of the Audiencia of Santo Domingo until 1717, that of the Viceroyalty of Nueva Granada in the period 1717-1726 (although communications were so poor that news of the administrative change did not arrive in Caracas until 1719), Santo Domingo again from 1726 to 1739, Nueva Granada between 1739 and 1742, and, finally, Santo Domingo in the period 1742-1777. Thereafter it obtained its own separate jurisdiction within the Spanish realm, roughly corresponding to the contours of the eventual independent nation-state.
57. Klooster, *Illicit Riches*, 175.
58. Aizpurua, *Curazao y la Costa de Caracas*, 293.
59. Nationaal Archief, The Hague, the Netherlands (NAN) Oud Archief Curaçao (OAC) 806 #622–624 (22 June 1737); NAN OAC 820: 11 (6 January 1749).
60. Calculated from Rik van Welie, "Slave Trading and Slavery in the Dutch Colonial Empire: A Global Comparison," *New West Indian Guide* 82, nos. 1 and 2 (2008): table 3, 56.
61. The first three are reproduced in David Marley, comp., *Reales asientos y licencias para la introducción de esclavos negros a la América Española (1667-1789)* (Colección documenta novae hispaniae volúmen B-9. Edición facsimilar Windsor, Ontario and Mexico: Rolston-Bain, 1985), documents III and V, no pagination. The 1705 decree is in Ermila Troconis de Veracoechea, comp., *Apuntes para el estudio de los esclavos negros en Venezuela* (Caracas: Biblioteca de la Academia Nacional de la Historia, 1969), *Documentos* #57, 240-43.
62. *Real cédula* (30 January 1690), reproduced in "Banda sobre negros 'de mala entrada'" (24 March 1692), in Marley, comp., *Reales asientos y licencias*, document V, no pagination.
63. The case is summarized in Castillo, *Apuntes para la historia colonial de Barlovento*, 343.
64. The problem of foreign fugitives in Venezuela also became intertwined with the issue of internal marronage. In 1702 the Crown issued a royal decree that expressed concern about the many escaped slaves who wandered around the Venezuelan countryside and ordered that they be rounded up into towns (Castillo, *Apuntes para la historia colonial de Barlovento*, 345). For more on the topic of internal marronage see Castillo, *Apuntes para la historia colonial de Barlovento*, 337-48.
65. Ferry, *The Colonial Elite of Early Caracas*, 111.
66. "Sobre la libertad de esclavos" (1704?), in Batista, comp., *Documentos*, Causas Civiles #8, 120-21; Ferry, *The Colonial Elite of Early Caracas*, 111. The quotations are from the former.
67. Castillo, *Apuntes para la historia colonial de Barlovento*, 350.
68. Castillo, *Apuntes para la historia colonial de Barlovento*, 351, 369.
69. According to Ramón Aizpurua a total of twenty-three people arrived in two canoes in 1703 (Aizpurua, "En busca de la libertad," 76). Fugitives arrived individually as well as in groups. In early 1703 a man named Juan Antonio landed in a canoe; like others he was sold at public auction. See "Cuentas de la Real Hacienda" (2 January 1703-30 January 1704), in Gonzalez, comp., *Documentos*, Causas Civiles #7, 120. It is not clear whether he is included in Aizpurua's numbers. Not everyone who arrived in a canoe had made the entire trip in one. In some cases people traveled in larger trading vessels whose launches they commandeered upon arriving at the mainland coast.
70. The various cases appear in Gonzalez, comp., *Documentos*, Instrumentos Públicos: Colonia, 35-38.

71. Ferry, *The Colonial Elite of Early Caracas*, 112. According to Ferry, the total number of fugitives was forty, most of whom were auctioned into slavery. Those who were not traveled to Caracas, accompanied by several of the previously freed Curaçaoans.
72. Castillo, *Apuntes para la historia colonial de Barlovento*, 347. Apparently there was also a relevant communiqué from the Audiencia of Santo Domingo on 11 October 1706, which is mentioned in "Solicitud de un traslado de real provision" (26 February 1726 or 1727), in Gonzalez, comp., *Documentos*, Causas Civiles #13, 122-23.
73. "Solicitud de un traslado de real provision" (26 February 1726 or 1727), in Gonzalez, comp., *Documentos*, Causas Civiles #13, 122-23. He cited three royal provisions, dated 7 [June] 1704, 11 October 1706, and 5 January 1711.
74. The drawn-out decisions as to where exactly to found the town, and ensuing disputes with local white landowners, as well as Curiepe's full history, are chronicled in minuscule detail in Castillo, *Apuntes para la historia colonial de Barlovento*, chapters 12-22, and, more succinctly, in Ferry, *The Colonial Elite of Early Caracas*, 108-20. Ferry focuses on how the jurisdictional confusion resulting from the repeated transfer of Venezuela between the Audiencia of Santo Domingo and the Viceroyalty of Nueva Granada played out in the complicated power dynamics between the newly arrived free blacks, the area's established white landowners, and various local and regional authorities.
75. Castillo, *Apuntes para la historia colonial de Barlovento*, 375.
76. "Sobre la libertad de esclavos" (1704?), in Batista, comp., *Documentos*, Causas Civiles #8, 121.
77. See Ferry, *The Colonial Elite of Early Caracas*, 120-29, for the size of local cacao holdings.
78. Castillo, *Apuntes para la historia colonial de Barlovento*, 359.
79. "Ana María Motete, morena libre, contra oficiales de Real Hacienda," Archivo General de la Nación, Caracas, Venezuela (AGN) Archivo del Registro del Distrito Federal, Tierras (ARDF-T) 1767-M-1. The case is also discussed in Rupert, *Creolization and Contraband*, 163-64, and in Castillo, *Apuntes para la historia colonial de Barlovento*, 325-26, 378-79, 577. He incorrectly transcribes her last name as Mohele.
80. The Netherlands provided ample opportunities for slaves to obtain their freedom, even while restricting the entry of slaves from its colonial possessions. See Dienke Hondius, "Access to the Netherlands of Enslaved and Free Black Africans: Exploring Legal and Social Historical Practices in the Sixteenth–Nineteenth Centuries," *Slavery and Abolition* 32, no. 3 (September 2010): 377-95. However, the logistics of crossing the Atlantic were prohibitive compared to the relative opportunities for mobility within the Caribbean.
81. NAN Nieuwe West Indische Compagnie (hereafter, NWIC) 1166:124, "Lijste der Slaven" (7 July 1775). Ramón Aizpurua puts the count at 605, citing a different archival document, and analyzes the list extensively (Aizpurua, "En busca de la libertad," 78-81).
82. Aizpurua, "En busca de la libertad," 80.
83. AANH 1753-JP 1, cited in Torres, comp., *Indice*, 92.
84. AANH 1743-BSWS 3, cited in Torres, comp., *Indice*, 85.
85. "Instancia promovida por Juan Lorenzo Rodríguez" (15 September 1746), in Gonzalez, comp., *Documentos*, Causas Civiles #21, 125-26.
86. AANH 1740 G#283 Arch. 1. It is not clear from the documents whether they fled in 1738 or 1739. Among those who testified on their behalf was the head of the free black militia, himself from Curaçao.

87. "Gabriel de Zuluaga sobre tres negros q binieron de Curazao" (29 August 1740), AANH ARDF-CN T-1742-CGPRSUZ, Exp. 9. The case is also described in Torres, comp., *Indice*, 50-52, and in Marianella Ponce, *El Ordenamiento Jurídico y el Ejercicio del Derecho de Libertad de los Esclavos en la Provincia de Venezuela, 1730-1768* (Caracas: Biblioteca de la Academia Nacional de la Historia, 1994), 73-76.
88. AANH ARDF CN T-1742-CGPRSUZ Exp. 9 (20 August 1740), 8-10.
89. "Sobre la libertad de esclavos" (1704?), in Gonzalez, comp., *Documentos,* Causas Civiles #8, 121. Marronage within Venezuela dated from the earliest days of Spanish occupancy and slavery. By the early 1700s contemporary observers were commenting on the large numbers of fugitive slaves who roamed the countryside (Pedro Jose de Olavarriaga, *Instruction General y Particular del Estado Presente de la Provincia de Venezuela en los Años de 1720 y 1721.* Preliminary study by Mario Briceno Perozo. [Caracas,Venezuela: Biblioteca de la Academia Nacional de la Historia 1965], 215).
90. "Sobre la libertad de esclavos" (1704?) in Gonzalez, comp., *Documentos,* Causas Civiles #8, 121; Castillo, *Apuntes para la historia colonial de Barlovento*, 350.
91. Rafael Diego Mérida (1 February 1797), in *Documentos de la Insurrección de José Leonardo Chirinos,* vol. 1 (Caracas, Venezuela: Editorial Metrópolis, 1994), 207; Carlos Gonzalez Batista, *Antillas y Tierra Firme. Historia de la Influencia de Curazao en la Arquitectura Antigua de Venezuela* (Caracas: Refinería Isla (Curazao) S.A., 1990), 50-52; Castillo, *Apuntes para la historia colonial de Barlovento*, 605.
92. Castillo, *Apuntes*, 610. Gonzalez, *Antillas y Tierra Firme,* 96.
93. Don Manuel de Carreta report (2 June 1795) in *Documentos de la Insurrección de José Leonardo Chirinos* 1: 44-46.
94. Archivo de Falcón (Coro, Venezuela) Causas Civiles #914 (9 September 1688).
95. "Sobre esclavos fugitivos (3-4 August 1751) in Gonzalez, comp., *Documentos*, Causas Civiles #27, 131.
96. "Sobre la propiedad de una esclava curazoleña" (October 1748), in Gonzalez, comp., *Documentos*, Causas Civiles #23, 126.
97. AANH 1740 G#283 Arch. 1. Local blacks also had helped some of the fourteen fugitives who arrived in 1690 elude capture (Castillo, *Apuntes para la historia colonial de Barlovento*, 343).
98. NAN OAC 820:17-30, Captain Gaspar Antonio de Quirigazo (11 January 1749); and the following in Gonzalez, comp., *Documentos*: Gaspar Antonio de Quirijazo (29 November 1748), Instrumentos Públicos #1, 80-81; "Sobre la propiedad de una esclava curazoleña" (October 1748), Causas Civiles #23, 126; "Sobre negros fugitivos de Curazao" (22 April 1751-1 February 1752), Causas Civiles #26, 130. The spelling of his last name varies in the different documents
99. Castillo, *Apuntes para la historia colonial de Barlovento*, 376-77, and chapter 18.
100. "Sobre negros fugitivos de Curazao" (22 April 1751-1 February 1752), in Gonzalez, comp., *Documentos*, Causas Civiles, #26, 129.
101. Aizpurua, "En busca de la libertad," 9; Torres, comp., *Indice*, 53.
102. Thompson, *Flight to Freedom*, 276.
103. Thompson, *Flight to Freedom*, 274. It is not clear to what extent authorities in Santo Domingo attempted to enforce the agreement, as marronage continued throughout the next century.
104. Thompson, *Flight to Freedom*, 273.

105. Thompson, *Flight to Freedom*, 273.
106. "Se propone convención con las potencias extranjeras para la mutual restitución de esclavos fugitivos" (29 August 1784), cited in Aizpurua, "En busca de la libertad," 93.
107. TePaske, "The Fugitive Slave," 5.
108. "Consejo de Indias a S. M." (12 April 1731), in Wright, comp., "Dispatches," 171-72; TePaske, "The Fugitive Slave," 6; Landers, "Gracia Real de Santa Teresa de Mose," 17.
109. TePaske, "The Fugitive Slave," 10.
110. "R. C. para que en las provincias de la Nueva España se guarde y compla lo resuelto en punto de que se tengan por libres los negros esclavos que se huyesen a ellas con el fin de abrazar nuestra santa fe católica" (24 September 1750), in Konetzke, ed., *Colección de documentos* 3:1 #152, 248.
111. Thompson, *Flight to Freedom*, 277-78; Torres, comp., *Indice*, 50. According to Thompson, the treaties rescinding sanctuary resulted in a decline in marronage to the corresponding areas.
112. From Gonzalez, comp., *Documentos*, Causas Civiles: "Sobre la libertad de esclavos" (1704?), #8, 120-21; Captain Matías Christiansz (8 November 1718), unnumbered footnote, 129-32.
113. From Gonzalez, comp., *Documentos*, Causas Civiles: "D. Juan Casalonga" (7 January 1734), #17, 123-24; "Sobre la propieded de una esclava curazoleña" (1-2 October 1748), #23, 126; "Sobre negros fugitivos de Curazao" (22 April 1751-1 February 1752), #26, 127-30; Aizpurua, "En busca de la libertad," 90-93.
114. According to Aizpurua they ceased completely after the decree was issued (Aizpurua, "En busca de la libertad," 92). However, there are at least two cases on record of successful restitutions from the early 1750s. Although one case apparently involved slaves who had fled prior to the 1750 decree ("Sobre negros fugitivos de Curazao" [22 April 1751-1 February 1752], in Gonzalez, comp., *Documentos*, Causas Civiles #26, 127-30), the other involved fugitives who had arrived in 1751 ("Sobre esclavos fugitivos" [3-4 August 1751], in Gonzalez, comp., *Documentos*, Causas Civiles #27, 130-31).
115. Quoted in Gonzales, *Antillas y Tierra Firme*, 52.
116. "Se propone convención con las potencias extranjeras para la mutual restitución de esclavos fugitivos" (29 August 1784), cited in Aizpurua, "En busca de la libertad," 93.
117. "Se propone convención con las potencias extranjeras..." (29 August 1784), cited in Aizpurua, "En busca de la libertad," 93.
118. "Orden Real comunicada por el Intendente de Caracas (Juan de Guillelmi) a los Jueces y Subdelegados de su Jurisdicción" (19 July 1790), cited in Aizpurua, "En busca de la libertad," 94.
119. "Orden Real" (19 July 1790), cited in Aizpurua, "En busca de la libertad," 95.
120. Cited in Miguel Acosta Saignes, *La trata de esclavos en Venezuela* (Caracas: Centro de Estudios Históricos, Revista de Historia, 1961), 39.
121. "Convención entre el Rey nuestro Señor y los Estados generals de las Provincias Unidas, para la recíproca restitución de desertores y fugitivos entre las colonias de América" (19 August 1791). The treaty is reproduced in its entirety in Aizpurua, "En busca de la libertad," 100-102.
122. "Real Cédula de su Magestad Concediendo Libertad para el Comercio de Negros con las Islas de Cuba, Santo Domingo, Puerto Rico, y Provincia de Caracas" (28 February 1789),

reproduced in Marley, comp., *Reales asientos y licencias,* Document X, no pagination. The contraband slave trade, however, continued alongside legal commerce.

123. Aizpurua, "En busca de la libertad," 84-88.
124. "El comandante militar de Coro" (22 September 1795), in *Documentos de la insurrección de José Leonardo Chirinos* 1: 133; Aizpurua, "En busca de la libertad," 95-97.
125. Information about this case comes from AANH ARDF-CN 1787-A1, and Torres, comp., *Indice*, 52–55, 126. The group, which numbered at least thirty-four, included five Indians and at least one mulatto, skilled slaves such as carpenters and shipwrights, and agricultural laborers.
126. For example, "Contra los esclavos fugitivos" (24 June–14 November 1828) in Gonzalez, comp., *Documentos*, Causas Criminales #18(86), 172.
127. Thompson, *Flight to Freedom,* 278. The Haitian Revolution, in particular, created multiple opportunities for increased mobility to intersect with chances for freedom. This included slaves who fled to the island in search of freedom after the revolution, and also refugees from the island. See Ada Ferrer, "Haiti, Free Soil, and Antislavery in the Revolutionary Atlantic," *American Historical Review* 117 (2012): 40-66; Martha S. Jones, "Time, Space, and Jurisdiction in Atlantic World Slavery: The Volunbrun Household in Gradual Emancipation in New York," *Law and History Review* 29, no. 4 (November 2011): 1031-60; Rebecca J. Scott, "Paper Thin: Freedom and Re-enslavement in the Diaspora of the Haitian Revolution," *Law and History Review* 29, no. 4 (November 2011): 1061-87. In all these cases, issues of jurisdiction and sovereignty intersected with and were informed by legal codes of slavery. As these studies clearly demonstrate, however, not all cases of mobility resulted in greater freedom.
128. This symbiosis did not go unnoticed or unchallenged by a broad range of colonial groups, whose own interests intersected and sometimes clashed with those of the Crown and the fugitives. Future research will explore the ways in which these various colonial groups (including political, legal, and religious authorities; middling sectors such as merchants and planters; and local slaves, free people of color, and internal runaways) interacted with the foreign fugitives as the latter created new lives and sometimes sought to legitimate themselves through Spanish colonial courts. Intermediaries played a similarly vital role, and had a similarly complex relationship with fugitives seeking freedom, in a very different time and place: nineteenth-century Philadelphia. See Richard S. Newman, "'Lucky to be Born in Pennsylvania': Free Soil, Fugitive Slaves, and the Making of Pennsylvania's Anti-Slavery Borderland," *Slavery and Abolition* 32, no. 3 (September 2011): 418-19, 421-25.
129. Here, Merry's examination of the tensions between state and local regulations, and the interaction between local situations and larger systems, is relevant. See Sally Engle Merry, "Legal Pluralism," *Law and Society Review* 22, no. 5 (1988): 885, 891.
130. This recalls Tamanaha's notion of a "plurality of legal pluralisms." Brian Z. Tamanaha, "A Non-Essentialist Version of Legal Pluralism," *Journal of Law and Society* 27, no. 2 (June 2000): 297.
131. See, for example, Jones, "Time, Space, and Jurisdiction in Atlantic World Slavery"; Scott, "Paper Thin"; Jane G. Landers, *Atlantic Creoles in the Age of Revolutions* (Cambridge, MA: Harvard University Press, 2010).
132. This, in Woodman's view, is the central implication of legal pluralism viewed from the point of view of the individual. Woodman, "Legal Pluralism and the Search for Justice," *Journal of African Law* 40, no. 2 (1996): 157.

133. Scott, "Paper Thin," 1080.
134. Scott, "Slavery and the Law in Atlantic Perspective: Jurisdiction, Jurisprudence, and Justice," 919.
135. Linda M. Rupert, "Marronage, Manumission, and Maritime Trade in the Early Modern Caribbean," *Slavery and Abolition* 30, no. 3 (September 2009): 361, 374; Johnson, "Resetting the Legal History of Slavery," 1093.
136. TePaske, "The Fugitive Slave," 11.

9

"A Pretty Gov[ernment]!"

The "Confederation of United Tribes" and Britain's Quest for Imperial Order in the New Zealand Islands during the 1830s

P. G. McHUGH

During the 1830s a wild assortment of British subjects was resorting to the New Zealand islands with an array of motives, not all of them savory or evangelical. This was an unruly cast and one that was getting unrulier by the day, fomenting unrest among Maori and liable to explode into violence. Increasingly imperial authorities realized that the Crown would have to establish formally some kind of local presence (*imperium* or formal governance) in the islands so as to bring ruliness to its subjects and in their dealings with the indigenous Maori tribes. As this necessity pulled into focus during the 1830s, two types of jurisdiction were successively entertained: the first involved a form of pluralism transposed (though never explicitly identified as such) from the East Indies and the Ohio Basin of British authorities. It involved British authorities working with and through native government(s). By the 1830s those late-eighteenth-century models were becoming somewhat stale, their African reinvention as indirect rule still some decades away. However, they were still far from discredited or superseded by a juridical standard of civilization and more absolutist formulations of sovereignty such as later shaped (and to some extent was then infiltrating) British imperial practice. Nonetheless, for British authorities the viability of this option, a vicarious jurisdiction levered through native sovereignty, depended upon the stability and orderliness (or at least their perception of it) of native government and the political ascendance of Maori. By the late 1830s these were no longer safe suppositions, especially with the specter of large-scale English settlement spreading to new settlements south of what had mostly been a European concentration in the northern isthmus. The second option—British sovereignty—then reared quickly into view and soon prevailed. In 1840 the Crown entered into a treaty with the Maori chiefs, who ceded their sovereignty over the islands to Britain (the Treaty of Waitangi, named after the seaside promontory where it was first signed). This essay is about the first stage, as British authorities explored jurisdictional options short of full sovereignty and premised on the continuance of the Maori.

From the outset, imperial officials depicted the nature of any formal intervention mostly as a matter of acquiring and asserting some form of jurisdiction over their subjects (with Maori only figuring later in the day). Except mostly in the disavowal, the language of sovereignty barely entered the vocabulary of this official deliberation. Even when it started to figure in the official mind in the very late 1830s, forced by the mounting pace of events, it was mostly linked still to the more fundamental question of the foothold for a British jurisdiction over its own troublesome subjects in New Zealand. Official policy, with the cupidity that always marked British imperialism, began by seeking the lowest level of jurisdictional presence but eventually capitulated to the fullest. Nevertheless, annexation of the entire country was not an outcome the Colonial Office regarded as inevitable or even saw itself as faced with through most of that decade. And when it reared as an option, it was necessitated less by considerations attached to an active management of Maori than by anxieties (possibly no more than faint) over the designs of the French and, most especially, the precipitate action of the New Zealand Company spreading and intensifying British settlement to the southern parts. Further, when the acquisition of sovereignty became an actively considered tool in the box of jurisdictional possibilities, it was conceived initially as extending to parts, rather than the whole, as necessitating Maori consent, and, primarily, as providing the legal wherewithal for the Crown to protect Maori from and to govern over its interloping subjects. What is notable about official deliberation during the 1830s is the primacy of a British concern with jurisdiction, particularly over its own subjects, and its recognition of the (potential if not real) viability of the Maori.

This construing of imperial presence as a matter of jurisdiction is consistent with the British practice in that era and as it had developed till then. It is known that British imperial practice and political thought did not move fully into an absolute, territorialized notion of sovereignty until later in the nineteenth century. Prior to that, the legal formats of its imperialism were a variegated pattern of jurisdictionalism, trails of *imperium* reflecting the improvisational and essentially ad hoc nature of empire in the century after the renowned military victories of the late 1750s. Famously, the empire was acquired in the fit of an absent mind, and as this happened, as Britain found itself in new and extending theaters of activity with an array of indigenous polities, the legalism surrounding that was essentially cobbled pragmatically from the material already at hand. Certainly that legalism became more coherent and its deployment more overtly governed by overarching principle during the nineteenth century, the second half especially. That tendency was surely oiled by the establishment of the Colonial Office (in1801 as a department of the War Office and in 1854 in its own right) with a permanent under-secretary (1825) and the growing recourse during the nineteenth century to professional legal advice (in the Foreign as well as Colonial Office). Statutes also came to set out general legal platforms that integrated imperial practice after the mid–late Victorian era and beyond, but these were not in force in the 1830s and were not consolidated until the last quarter of the century. The unifying effects of professionalization and principle began to appear more consistently in the positivizing and consolidating legalism of empire, but that was mostly a consequence of the more managerial mindset of a later era of politician and bureaucrat and the formation of the imperial administrative state, rather than of the more improvisational 1830s when that approach was no more (perhaps) than an emergent tendency. The legalism of empire in the period of the Treaty of Waitangi (1840) was fluid, situational, as ad hoc as ever, and apt to be conceived in jurisdictional terms that looked at the amenability of certain classes of persons to British jurisdiction rather than a blanket and absolute territorial reach. This approach was necessarily pluralistic in that it recognized the possibility—indeed, acknowledged the reality—of other jurisdictions such as Maori. By the 1840s the British understood that territorial sovereignty carried such stark connotations, and, when pressed, its officials were perfectly capable of expressing the nature of Crown authority in that blunt and thoroughgoing manner. At that time, though, questions of jurisdiction were not as clear-cut as the late-nineteenth-century model would depict them.

Still, in the second quarter of the nineteenth century, it was not usual to describe Crown *imperium* primarily in terms of sovereignty in that thoroughgoing absolute sense, even if something like that was its consequence. Officials reached into a repertoire of jurisdiction. Questions persisted through the second quarter of the nineteenth century in Australasia and Upper Canada that showed that transition into the absolutist model of settler-state sovereignty was still occurring. Imperial practice incorporated pluralism, particularly of the non-Christian variety, without any problematizing or Austinian anxiety about its integrity or character as "law" emanating from a stable sovereign commander. Within realm and empire, jurisdictional complexity did not excite concern. It had long been the norm in the East Indies, even if by the 1830s mosaic jurisdictionalism was being superseded by more centralist and unifying forces. So when the British encountered its intensively tribalized forms in New Zealand, there was willingness to work with it, if it could be made to work (and Christianized at the same time). In that period an important sign of the lingering remnants of jurisdictionalism in the legal map of empire concerned the uncertainty over the jurisdiction of colonial courts over tribe members for serious crimes *inter se* (murder especially). This was not an uncertainty and slipperiness that would have arisen had the absolutist Diceyan model of Crown sovereignty of a later (more markedly state-centric) era been the impregnable orthodoxy of the earlier one. Certainly, as the pattern set in the East Indies during the early nineteenth century showed and as the history of New Zealand was also to illustrate, full territorial sovereignty became the option when lesser, more minimalist (and less costly) forms of *imperium* had been exhausted or overwhelmed by creeping British acquisitiveness. Necessarily, legal format was cut to suit imperial interests but that imperial legalism was vastly more subtle and modulated jurisdictionally than the grinding leviathan of crushing Crown sovereignty. That pulverizing constitutionalism was the hallmark of colonial sovereignty (as wielded by Anglo-settler governments) rather than an imperial design.

A. Early Attempts at Establishing British Jurisdiction

The earliest attempts to establish British authority in the New Zealand islands were made by Governor Lachlan Macquarie of New South Wales. Relying upon the terms of his commission giving him jurisdiction over "adjacent islands,"[1] he appointed Kent as a justice of the peace in New Zealand (1810), but the appointment never became effective. In December 1813 Macquarie proclaimed Maori to be under British protection but, as with Cook's declarations of sovereignty, this unilateral action was unauthorized by the Crown and received no subsequent approval. His proclamation invoked the *jus gentium* to protect Maori and was aimed directly and personally at lawless Europeans, British in particular (convict escapees from New South Wales).[2] Macquarie followed this with the appointment (1814) of Thomas Kendall, a Church Missionary Society missionary in the Bay of Islands in the northern isthmus of the North Island (then one of the most visited parts), as magistrate. An order was also addressed to British seamen in the New Zealand islands:

> His Excellency being equally solicitous to protect the natives of New Zealand and the Bay of Islands in all their just rights and privileges as those of every other dependency of the territory of New South Wales, hereby orders and directs that no master or seamen of any ship or vessel belonging to any British port, or to any of the colonies of Great Britain, resorting to the said islands of New Zealand, shall in future remove or carry therefrom any of the natives without first obtaining the permission of the chief or chiefs of the districts within which the natives so to be embarked may happen to reside, which permission is to be certified in writing under the hand of Mr. Thomas Kendall, the Resident Magistrate of the Bay of Islands, or of the Magistrate for the time being in the said districts.[3]

The order went on to prohibit the landing of any British seaman in the islands without, again, the permission of the local chief(s) and certificate of the Resident Magistrate. The order warned that disobedience would "subject the offenders to be proceeded against with the utmost vigour of the law upon their return hither." The chiefs "Dewaterra, Sunger and Kora Kora" were "invested with power and authority" for the purposes of ensuring compliance with the order. Crucially, the order did not establish any formal authority over British subjects in the islands, much less Maori, but simply advised the former of their amenability to the "utmost rigour of the law" on their return across the Tasman. To that extent the designation of Kendall as "Magistrate" was misleading, and doubtless intended to intimidate. There was certainly no legal basis upon which British seamen's compliance with the order could have been enforced in New South Wales and so it must be treated as mere and ineffectual bluff.[4] Nonetheless, the order contained one of the earliest signs of what was to become a consistent feature of British practice in New Zealand in the pre-sovereignty era. The order recognized the power and authority of the chiefs and through them purported to establish some British authority over its own seafaring subjects. By the 1820s that recognition of chiefly authority was quickly becoming the norm. British officials insisted that any British trading posts (or factories) must be established with Maori permission.[5]

In 1819 Macquarie appointed Butler as a justice of the peace in New Zealand.[6] In so doing, he again described New Zealand as a "dependency" of New South Wales, a description that was unfounded but, again, bluff: two years previously imperial legislation, the Murders Abroad Act 1817,[7] had expressly disavowed any sovereignty over New Zealand.

Macquarie's successor, Brisbane, wrote to Bathurst, the colonial secretary, in February 1825 asking whether his commission gave him jurisdiction over the islands of the South Pacific and the extent of the term "the Islands adjacent."[8] Although Brisbane's recall rendered reply unnecessary, as Tapp observes,[9] by redefining the governor of New South Wales' jurisdiction within a latitude bisecting the North Island, the Instructions and Commission to Governor Darling[10] strongly indicated a negative response to Brisbane's inquiry. If that were not clear enough, imperial legislation of 1823[11] and 1828[12] (besides that of 1817) was enacted on the clear basis of a lack of British sovereign authority in New Zealand.

B. "Jurisdiction by Legislation"

The problem of lawlessness among the British seamen, traders, and whalers in New Zealand became more pressing during the 1830s. Samuel Marsden reminded Governor Darling that there was "no legal authority, Civil, Military, or Naval"—in other words, no jurisdiction in any of those forms—"to restrain the conduct of the Masters and Crews of those ships which put into the Harbors of New Zealand." He worried that Maori would retaliate with violence "if no remedy is provided to do them justice."[13] By then a series of imperial acts had been passed establishing what might be termed "jurisdiction by legislation" over New Zealand. The Murders Abroad Act 1817 made British subjects liable to trial on British soil for offenses committed in "Otaheite, New Zealand, the Honduras and other places now within His Majesty's dominions." This jurisdiction received further provision through imperial legislation of 1823 and 1828 enabling courts in New South Wales to try British subjects for serious offenses committed in New Zealand. These acts were expressly founded upon a disavowal of any sovereignty over New Zealand and deliberately avoided erection of an *imperium* in the islands.

The crucial shortcoming in "jurisdiction by legislation" lay in the disavowal of any local *imperium*. It simply made British subjects liable to trial for serious crimes upon their return to British soil. The practical difficulty and hence impotence of this form of jurisdiction was revealed in the "*Elizabeth* affair" (1831) although by then the shortcomings had been noted many times before.[14]

During early 1831 Captain Stewart of the *Elizabeth* sailed Te Rauparaha, a Maori chief, and his war party to Akaroa to enable the slaughter of virtually all the Ngai Tahu inhabitants and the capture of the chief, Tamariharanui, and his family (who were subsequently killed). Te Rauparaha's fare was a cargo of flax. Governor Darling condemned English involvement as "an Act of premeditated atrocity."[15] He immediately set in train the machinery to prosecute the British perpetrators under the Imperial Act 9 Geo 4 cap

83 giving New South Wales' courts jurisdiction under the Murders Abroad Act 1817. His attempts to invoke this act against Stewart and his crew met difficulty at every turn. The Crown solicitor of New South Wales worried about whether the depositions disclosed "a sufficient body of facts to warrant a commitment by the Magistrates."[16] In addition, there was doubt whether Stewart and crew had even committed an offense recognized by the criminal law of England. The two tribes had been in a state of "legitimate warfare, according to the usages of their country,"[17] and so could not have been considered to have murdered the Ngai Tahu victims. Given that, Stewart and crew could hardly have been charged as accessories to murder. Moreover, by the time bench warrants were obtained, only Stewart could be detained, the others "keeping out of the way."[18] No prosecutions eventuated.

This experience graphically underlined the argument then being made, especially by the missionaries, for some form of local British authority, one to be exercised within the New Zealand islands.[19] The call for the exercise by the Crown of a local judicial power faced two problems. On the one hand, the Crown would not erect unilaterally a local *imperium* for it had recognized the Maori tribes as "the owners and sovereigns of the soil."[20] This refusal to use the royal prerogative to erect a local judicial power over British subjects without previous grant from the local sovereign, as by "capitulation," was consistent with established British practice in Ottoman and Mughal Asia. The possibility of an informally acquired jurisdiction by informal grant, sufferance, or usage was not recognized in British practice until the innovation licensed by the Foreign Jurisdiction Act 1843. In addition and even further from the range of options then at hand was the use of imperial legislation statutorily to endow the Crown with the facility to erect local jurisdiction over its own subjects in uncivilized territory. This step was not made legally possible until 1875, and, as with the 1843 measure, when it was statutorily incorporated into the Crown's jurisdictional repertoire, it was regarded as an innovation. Indeed, an attempt in 1832 to pass an act giving New South Wales power to legislate for serious crimes committed by British subjects in New Zealand failed because of Westminster's refusal to legislate for foreign territory wherein the Crown through conduct of its foreign relations had not previously come to some arrangement with the local sovereign.[21] This perception was acting as a real brake upon official options, and it was an example of the integration of *jus gentium* and constitutional practice into their legal way of thinking.

There was, then, a perceived lack of any prerogative or statutory constituent power available to imperial officials despite the obvious and increasingly pressing need during the 1830s for the establishment and exercise of some local British authority. That need was accentuated by the worry that France was about to annex the country. The fear was unfounded, it transpired, but it was an understandable anxiety of a generation still in the aftermath of long and brutal warfare with France. So worried were missionaries that Yate dispatched a petition of thirteen chiefs for Governor Darling to forward to William IV requesting British protection from "the tribe of Marion" as well as those "troublesome" subjects who were "vicious to us."[22]

In April 1831 Darling resolved[23] and eventually obtained permission[24] to send a "British Resident" to represent and protect British interests in New Zealand. The perceived lack of any constituent power in the Crown meant the Resident could not be warranted as a magistrate with formal power over British subjects. Consequently Bourke, who had waited in vain for the Bill of 1832 to pass the Imperial Parliament, was forced to instruct the appointee, James Busby,[25] "You are aware that you cannot be clothed with any legal power, or jurisdiction by virtue of which you might be enabled to arrest British subjects offending against British or Colonial Law in New Zealand." It had been intended to supply that defect by means of local legislation under authority of an imperial statute but, Bourke regretted, that had not ensued: "You can, therefore, rely but little on the force of Law, and must lay the foundation of your measures upon the influence which you shall obtain over the Native Chiefs. Something, however, may be effected under the Law as it stands at present." Bourke advised Busby that he might invoke the Act 9 Geo IV cap 83; however, his description of the procedure under an act that had proven so wanting in the case of the *Elizabeth* only highlighted its inadequacy:

> If, therefore, you should at any times have the means of sending to this Colony any one or more persons capable of lodging an information before the proper authority here of an offence committed in New Zealand, you will if you think the case of sufficient magnitude and importance send a detailed report of the transaction to the Colonial Secretary by such persons who will be required to depose the facts sufficient to support an information upon which a Bench Warrant may be obtained from the Supreme Court for the apprehension of the offender, and transmitted to you for execution. You will perceive at once that this process which is at best but a prolix and inconvenient operation . . . will be totally useless unless you should have some well founded expectation of securing the Offender upon or after the arrival of the Warrant. . . .[26]

Admitting the impotence of the format of "jurisdiction by legislation" across a sea hundreds of miles from the nearest British court, Bourke was forced, therefore, into advising Busby to work through the Maori chiefs.[27]

It must be noted at this stage that resort to a "British Resident" was hardly novel but drew upon long-established practice in Mughal and Maratha India. There, Residents were regularly appointed to represent British interests in court and exert a local control over British subjects, although (with the exception of soldiers under their military command) this was usually done through the agency of the host sovereign. Residents exercised an authority of suasion and influence derived less from Crown authorization than from delegation and integration into the legal system of the host court. Indeed, the most effective Residents in the Company Raj before the Mutiny (1857) were those who were able to deploy indigenous custom and legalism in a courtly setting of high diplomacy and ritualism (as well as intrigue).[28] Their track record became vastly less effective where (as increasingly during the second quarter of the nineteenth century) an evangelical sense of Christian and/or anglicizing mission intruded. The use of Residents was, then, well-known practice at the time of Busby's appointment. The governing suppositions were disavowal of British sovereignty—that being in India partly, if not mostly, a company strategy to deflect Crown oversight—and, for the same reason, a building up of the ostensible integrity of the indigenous polity (for machinating by the Resident). The East Indies provided models, but there the effectiveness of each Resident was essentially a reflection of his personal manipulative capacities: and so it proved also, and less illustriously, for Busby.[29]

Bourke's instructions placed Busby in a delicate position. There was no question of the application of Maori law to the "troublesome" and "vicious" British subjects within New Zealand, but, equally, it was clear that no British subject could exercise any judicial or legal authority over another without warrant from the Crown. This, for example, had been the ground for doubt over the legality of the jurisdiction that one George Maclean had been exercising in the same period over British subjects along the Gold Coast, an informality eventually condoned by the Foreign Jurisdiction Act 1843.[30] Busby, then, had to keep a delicate balance between the recognition and judicious guiding of chiefly authority, this being permissible, and the assertion of an irregular unlawful jurisdiction over British subjects. Recognizing the fine line a Resident without formal royal warrant would have to tread and the inevitability of its transgression, Goderich advised Bourke that given the absence of "any established system of Jurisprudence" among the tribes, the Resident might take reasonable action against lawless British subjects. He thought such "measures of coercion and restraint . . . may be vindicated on the ground of necessity, even if they cannot be strictly as legal." Accordingly he recommended the Resident be indemnified against "the risk of any litigation on such ground."[31]

It is doubtful whether the Resident's position, which at least from a legal point of view was precarious, might have been handled more effectively by a person of less officiousness and pettiness than Busby displayed.[32] Certainly his contemporary, Maclean of the Gold Coast, a man of greater ability and canniness as well as less excitable temperament, was unable and unwilling to control the Gold Coast by simple influence and reliance upon the indigenous authorities. He had the chutzpah to take matters into his own hands without reference to the chiefs' permission. Indeed, he proceeded in willful defiance of it.

Nonetheless, the professed inability of the Crown to give Busby's office as Resident the formal authority of magistrate, governed as it was by punctilious regard for the sovereignty of Maori, set the scene for the transformation of what was essentially a negative and passive recognition into more positive forms. Until the early 1830s the recognition of Maori sovereignty had been negative in that it was used as a restraint upon British involvement in the islands, an excuse as it were for inaction. However, by then the need for some local and official presence had become too acute. The appointment of a Resident, however informal his office, inevitably meant that the recognition of Maori sovereignty would become more positive and active. At that stage and given the position taken by imperial officials in London, the authority of the chiefs was the only means at hand through which some order could possibly have been brought to the New Zealand frontier.

C. The British Resident and "He Whakaputanga" or the Declaration of Independence (1835)

Having been delayed some months in Sydney as Bourke waited in vain for imperial legislation authorizing the grant of formal power to a British official in the islands, Busby reached the Bay of Islands in mid-1833 convinced "how desirable it is that the chiefs of New Zealand, in any transaction which might be considered of an international character, [be dealt with] *in their collective capacity only*."[33] Busby had brought a new element into the picture, talking of the chiefs collectively and of a "Confederation"[34] as the basis for an established government of the Maori tribes. This concern—it became a virtual obsession—with the collective rather than tribalized sovereignty was to characterize his office as British Resident.

Again, Busby was not acting in the dark. By that time the British were used to dealing with confederations of indigenous polities, such as the Powhatan of the north Atlantic coast, the loyal Iroqouis in the Ohio Valley interior, the Creek and Cherokee along the southern Atlantic seaboard, and the robust Maratha Confederation of the Deccan Plateau in India. In the midwestern plains the early republic was also dealing with the Comanche, Wichita, and Lakota (Sioux) confederacies. These confederations had enjoyed highly ritualized relations with the Anglo-European arriviste, as powerful allies and potentially devastating enemies whose support was to be solicited and the authority of whose leaders was fully recognized. Certainly the fame of one influential superintendent, the legendary Sir William Johnson, would have been known to Busby, whose efforts to cultivate his own *mana* by the theatrical harnessing of Anglo pageantry (such as 21-gun salutes, flag-flying, and associated flamboyance) and the performative elements of Maori culture (such as *hui* and their distinctive highly ritualized declamatory oratory) echoed the famous Irish superintendent: there are words and phrases as well as his rather theatrical efforts to erect a confederate Maori state buzzing around Busby's conduct of office that suggest, though faintly (and, in his case, rather unimpressively), this emulation. Given that charisma had often filled the void where royal warrant did not run, recourse to this was not surprising. It was just that unlike some of the glittering examples of British emissary sprinkled across what had become a culturally diverse empire in British North America, Africa, and the East Indies, Busby was not such a figure.

One of Busby's first steps upon arriving in New Zealand as Resident was to give some tangible expression to this "Confederation" that he planned to convocate. After securing approval from New South Wales,[35] he prevailed upon the chiefs in the vicinity of the Bay of Islands to adopt a national flag "for the Tribes of that Country in their Collective Capacity."[36] This measure was approved by the Colonial Office and Lords of the Admiralty,[37] who instructed the commander-in-chief on the East India station to recognize the register of vessels flying under the flag as "valid instruments [to be] . . . respected as such in the intercourse such vessels hold with British Possessions."[38]

Soon after, however, the weakness of the Resident's position was revealed in the debacle surrounding the whaling barque *Harriet* (1834). The ship was wrecked off the Taranaki coast of the western North Island, those on board reaching shore where Maori attacked them. The survivors were taken prisoner and incorporated into the tribe, except for a handful who were released on the understanding that they would return with a cask of gunpowder as ransom for the rest. Eventually at Bourke's orders, amid great slaughter, HMS *Alligator* came to the bloody rescue. No effort had been made to consult Busby or the missionaries, or even to consider the Maori side of the matter (who in accordance with custom had been expecting negotiation for release of the captives). In reporting the rescue to the Colonial Office,

Bourke stressed the weakness of the Resident's position and the need either for a ship of war to be stationed permanently in New Zealand waters or for Busby to be equipped with real legal authority. The mere air of it, moral suasion alone, was insufficient. Bourke had reiterated this point in his despatches to London during the mid-1830s,[39] although the long-awaited imperial legislation authorizing him to erect judicial authority in the New Zealand islands never eventuated.

In October 1835 Busby received a letter from a person styling himself the Baron de Thierry. This letter informed "His Britannic Majesty's Consular Agent at the Bay of Island" that he was planning to establish a "Sovereign Government" upon his arrival in New Zealand.[40] De Thierry's "Address to the New Zealand settlers" described his plan to lift the Maori tribes through European settlement, trade, and religious education under his auspices, to make them an "Independent Sovereignty" (as opposed to a colony of Great Britain).[41] Busby took immediate fright at these designs. He circulated an address to British subjects in the New Zealand islands—then mainly concentrated in the northern isthmus—noting that "His Majesty, after having acknowledged the Sovereignty of the Chiefs of New Zealand in their collective capacity, by the recognition of their flag" would not "permit his Humble and Confiding Allies to be Deprived of their Independence upon such Pretensions." Busby announced his intention to convene the chiefs of the region to tell them of "this proposed Attempt upon their Independence, and to advise them of what is Due to Themselves and to their Country."[42]

The northern chiefs assembled, and on 28 October 1835 there issued a "Declaration of Independence" or "He Whakaputanga." The first articles of this declaration stated,

> 1. We the hereditary Chiefs and Heads of the Tribes of the Northern Parts of New Zealand, being assembled at Waitangi in the Bay of Islands on the 28th day of October 1835, declare the Independence of our Country, which is hereby constituted and declared to be an Independent State, under the designation of The United Tribes of New Zealand.
> 2. All Sovereign power and authority within the Territories of the United Tribes of New Zealand is hereby declared to reside, entirely and exclusively in the Hereditary Chiefs and Heads of Tribes in their Collective Capacity: Who also declare that they will not permit any legislative Authority separate from themselves in their Collective Capacity to exist, nor any functions of Government to be exercised within the Said Territories unless by persons appointed by them and acting under the Authority of Laws regularly enacted by them in Congress Assembled.[43]

That last phrase, "in Congress Assembled," was, of course, directly lifted from the American example (not the first time such echoes occurred in the New Zealand setting of this period). The third article continued,

> 3. The Hereditary Chiefs and Heads of Tribes agree to meet in Congress at Waitangi in Autumn of each year, for the purpose of passing laws for the disposition of Justice, the preservation of peace and good order and the regulation of Trade; And they candidly invite the Southern Tribes to lay aside their private animosities, and to consult the Safety and Welfare of our Common Country by joining the Confederation of the United Tribes.

The United Tribes asked King William to "continue to be the parent of their infant State" and to "become its Protector from all attempts upon its independence." Other tribes were invited to sign the declaration, and by 1839 the number of signatories had reached fifty-two, most from the north of the North Island.

This declaration received wholehearted approval from the governor of New South Wales[44] and the Colonial Office, save in one respect to which I come soon. The Colonial Office replied with the assurance that the king would protect the Maori people, provided this protection was consistent with a due regard to "the just rights of others and to the interests of His Majesty's subjects."[45] The recognition of Maori sovereignty in the declaration was accepted straightforwardly: it was a logical, if somewhat dramatic, corollary and extension from what had gone before.

The second article was criticized, however, as an attempt by Busby to manipulate the recognition of the chiefs in their collective capacity to his own ends. In July 1834 one McDonnell had secured his appointment as additional British Resident at Hokianga, not far from Busby's seat in the Bay of Islands. The appointment had rankled Busby. Late in September 1835, shortly before "He Whakaputanga," McDonnell had persuaded the chiefs of the Hokianga neighborhood to pass a law against the importation into their district of ardent spirits. Bourke approved this law and notified it in the New South Wales *Sydney Gazette*.[46] Busby, watchful of his *mana*, took exception to the law on the grounds that the sole legislative authority in the northern region was the United Tribes, that is, the confederacy of tribes that he saw himself as orchestrating. It was no accident that he had sought the declaration so quickly after learning of McDonnell's "law." Busby justified subscription to a confederated as opposed to tribalized view of Maori sovereignty on the grounds that it might become a lawful authority with legislative and judicial capacities over all inhabitants of the island.

He knew enough of the competitive character of tribal politics to realize that recognizing tribalized sovereignty would invite disunity and incoherent if not contradictory legalism. It would be "little better than authorized outrage, in which . . . it would be derogatory to a civilized nation to participate." The only sound native legislature, he argued, was a collective, confederated one over which the Resident could exert a strong guiding influence.[47] Although the authorities in New South Wales and Britain were not persuaded by Busby's insistence upon confederated sovereignty only, the more general recognition of Maori sovereignty contained in the declaration was endorsed.

Within a short while events revealed the impossibility of an early convening of Busby's cherished Congress of the United Tribes. It soon was clear that the rivalrous tribes could not convene peaceably. By early 1836, it was conceded that the use of the congress to establish more European-like authority over the islands was unlikely to succeed.[48] On 18 January Busby advised Bourke that the question of formal British intervention could "no longer be deferred . . . that interference should be prompt, decided, and effectual." Nonetheless, the Resident still clung to the idea of the congress despite its impracticability and continued to raise it in suggesting formats and options for Britain in New Zealand.[49]

The start-stop experience with the United Tribes during late 1835 through early 1836 highlighted both the general recognition of tribalized sovereignty by imperial authorities in Sydney and London and the practical difficulties with that. Nonetheless, these authorities were fully committed to that recognition, as their affirmation of "He Whakaputanga" showed. Events by this stage—which is to say, the tempo of British presence in New Zealand—were moving such that some formal presence was becoming inevitable. It was clear that a local commissioned authority was necessary rather than the impotence of "jurisdiction by legislation" or the moral suasion of a thin-skinned ineffectual Resident. The growing acceptance that some formal presence was necessary kept to the themes already noted: a perception of response cast in the language of jurisdiction put mostly in personalized terms directed towards British subjects, and the recognition that New Zealand was, somehow, an independent country under tribalized Maori sovereignty. What constrained British action according to the understanding of the *jus gentium* also affected its constitutional capacity—the international and municipal spheres were not distinct zones but part of the same integrated one.

By the second half of the 1830s and putting aside the ongoing missionary effort, British interests were moving swiftly from itinerant coastal trade toward more permanent settlement. Land purchasing from the tribes had begun and was on the increase, bringing with it disputes between and among the settlers and tribes.[50] The failure of the United Tribes was, in retrospect, the last gasp of the attempt to establish order in New Zealand exclusively through the agency of Maori sovereignty. By 1837, despite the Colonial Office's inaction, it was becoming clear that some formal lawful authority in New Zealand would have to be commissioned through the Crown rather than under the mantle of Maori sovereignty. Inevitably, the way in which the format of this intervention became contemplated was governed by what had gone before: the British were committed to recognition of Maori sovereignty but needed to establish jurisdictional presence over its own wayfaring, wayward, and way-staying subjects.

D. December 1837: The Critical Juncture

Throughout 1837 the British government received a growing number of deputations, letters, petitions, and the like on the New Zealand question. In general, these approaches emanated either from the evangelical quarter or from those associated with the colonial reform movement, which sought the regulated colonization of the country. By the end of that year it was becoming clear that formal British action was necessary and the defensive invocation of Maori sovereignty insufficient. The willingness to attempt to work through forms of confederate Maori jurisdiction was disappearing very quickly.

The Colonial Office did not begin to move positively toward the establishment of formal British authority in New Zealand until 1838. The possibility of strengthening the "jurisdiction by legislation" approach came and went. A draft Punishment Act for New Zealand was prepared in August 1836,[51] at the same time as the eventual Cape of Good Hope Punishment Act 1836,[52] but was still-born.[53]

In June and November 1837 the New Zealand Association, with Edward Gibbon Wakefield at the helm, had sent Glenelg the abstract of an act enabling the Crown to charter the "Founders of Settlement" in New Zealand. The use of charters of incorporation and proprietary grant was one of the oldest techniques of British imperial activity, and by the mid-nineteenth century this device was making something of a comeback. It had gone into an eclipse from the mid-eighteenth century when the Crown Colony became the more favored mode with its more centralized—some say autocratic—constitutional form. Clause 5 of the association's draft act presupposed that the Crown held sovereignty over the land in New Zealand already acquired by purchase from the chiefs. Collapsing the acquisition of *dominium* with an *imperium*, it authorized the company to obtain further land by treaty with the chiefs.[54]

Glenelg's response in December 1837 signaled an upping of the pace of official deliberation. He recognized and refused to condone the fudging of *imperium* and *dominuium*. Drawing from principles of Scottish stadialism and with echoes of Vattel's insistence that the "dwarf state" was to be regarded as being equally as sovereign as the larger, he insisted that the Crown could not and would not exercise any constituent power for New Zealand to erect some local jurisdiction without Maori consent:

> 1. It is difficult or impossible to find in the History of British Colonization an Example of a Colony having ever been founded in derogation of such Rights, whether of Sovereignty or Property, as are those of the Chiefs and People of New Zealand. They are not Savages living by the Chase, but Tribes who have apportioned the country between them, having fixed Abodes, with an acknowledged Property in the Soil, that Great Britain has no legal or moral right to establish a Colony in New Zealand, without the free consent of the Natives, deliberately given, without Compulsion, and without Fraud. To impart to any Individuals an Authority to establish such a Colony, without first ascertaining the consent of the New Zealanders, or without taking the most effectual security that the Contract which is to be made with them shall be freely and fairly made, would, as it should seem, be to make an unrighteous use of our superior Power.[55]

Glenelg saw that the association's proposal was moving things from an inquiry into establishing forms of local jurisdiction over and among British subjects to the more committed option of a colony. If anything, that accentuated rather than diminished the need for such a form of *imperium* to be obtained with Maori consent "deliberately given." Among imperial officials there was no question of any jurisdictional rights, much less the fullest form of colony, being asserted by "usage" or "sufferance" (modes the Foreign Jurisdiction Act 1843 was soon to license) or on the strength of British land purchases allegedly made already. The association had used the Crown's seventeenth-century proprietary grants to Penn (their status almost iconic in the mid-nineteenth century) as a precedent, but these were regarded officially as impossible to issue unless preceded by Maori consent.

Glenelg was aware that recently the Select Committee on Aborigines (1837) had "expressly dissuaded the Colonization of New Zealand." He noted too that there were many American citizens in the islands, and he observed the likelihood of their rejecting British sovereignty as it would mean their liability to taxation for the support of a British colony.[56] The Crown's assertion of jurisdiction over them was problematic, he realized.[57] And he was aware also of the touchiness of British settlers on the question of taxation. In fact, the association was proposing a governing arrangement not unlike that of the East India Company. Although not referring explicitly to that model, Glenelg seems to have grasped the similarity. Inferentially, revenue reaping through Mughal structures might work in India, but with British settlers a form of corporate governance based in London making such tax-farming demands would not work. (The moral of the American Revolution reverberated here, too, though also tacitly.) The usual imperial practice was that powers of legislation and taxation

> must . . . be left to the local legislature, except in reference to a very few anomalous Cases. The possibility of governing by a Legislature composed of Nominees of a Body of private Persons residing in England [as proposed by the Association] seems very questionable. Experience shows in these Times English Colonists will scarcely brook such an Authority, though derived directly from the sovereign power.

Glenelg was also worried that the proposal, in requiring legislation, impugned the prerogative of the Crown. He observed that colonial governments had been erected through the prerogative “from the infancy of Colonization, in the reign of Elizabeth, to the present Day, without a single Interruption, until the recent Case of South Australia”:

> All the Precedents in which a delegated Sovereignty has been given to the Founders of Colonies are Precedents of Charters; not Acts of Parliament. Her Majesty may lawfully transfer the Exercise of Parts of Her Prerogative; but it would be a very startling Innovation if this should be done by an Act of Parliament.[58]

Glenelg's memorandum was tabled the next year before the Lords Committee on New Zealand.

At that stage he had not seen a report written by Captain Hobson of HMS *Rattlesnake* in August 1837 after a spell in New Zealand seas. Yet by the end of 1837, as this report was en route, two alternatives were forming clearly in the deliberations inside the Colonial Office. The first option was to erect the tribes into the semblance of a government that the British could recognize as competent to govern all inhabitants of the island—the Busby line—or, secondly, to establish a local jurisdiction through erection of a colonial government. The imperial authorities were already tending toward the latter option. Hobson's report chimed with that outlook and it commended him to London.

Hobson's report confirmed the Colonial Office's growing albeit reluctant disposition toward some form of colonial government. He had seen that the obvious problem with "jurisdiction by legislation" was the distance from the New South Wales courts. He proposed that the Crown establish "factories" in small pockets of New Zealand (at Cloudy Bay, the Bay of Islands, and Hokianga). These would "afford a safe retreat to our Fellow Countrymen who will become powerful by concentration."[59] They would be established with Maori consent and as dependencies of New South Wales. All British settlers' purchases of land would be registered in the factory. The "Heads of Factories should be Magistrates, and the Chief Factor should, in addition, be accredited to the United Chiefs of New Zealand as a Political Agent and Consul."[60] Jurisdictional treaties could then be concluded giving the factory courts authority over British subjects beyond the confines of the towns.[61] The establishment of such factories and jurisdictional treaties would not be confined to "the mere legal protection they are calculated to afford." It was to be hoped that they would "be the means of introducing amongst the Natives a System of Civil Government . . . which may hereafter be adopted and enlarged. . . ."[62] The factory model that Hobson advocated was taken directly from the East Indies, the station where his ship HMS *Rattlesnake* was based.

Around this time—in mid-December 1837—the Colonial Office had received the "outline of a plan of Government" conceived by James Busby in his capacity as British Resident and dated 16 June 1837. Busby's plan amplified and modified his earlier position on the collective character of Maori sovereignty. Whereas previously, especially in the context of his dispute with McDonnell, he had insisted that Maori sovereignty resided only in the chiefs collectively, he now conceded that it vested in them in both their tribal and their collective capacities, but that with the recognition of the confederation's flag all diplomatic relations were to be with latter only:

> The Articles of Confederation having centralized the powers of Sovereignty exercised both *de jure* and *de facto* by the Several Chiefs; and having established and declared the basis of a Constitution of Government founded upon the Union of those powers—I cannot, I think, greatly err in assuming that the Congress of Chiefs, the Depositary of the powers of the State, as declared by its constitution, is competent to become a party to a treaty with a Foreign Power, and to avail itself of

> Foreign assistance in reducing the Country under its authority to order, and this principle being once admitted, all difficulty appears to me to vanish.[63]

The "foreign power" he meant was, of course, Great Britain. By such treaty, the Congress would be protected from foreign interference in exactly the same way as the Ionian Islands and princely states in the East Indies.[64]

Busby went on to propose that the Congress should enact laws for all the population, observing, contradictorily, that "in truth the present race of Chiefs could not be entrusted with any discretion whatever, in the adoption or rejection of any measure" that the Resident might present to them. "In theory and ostensibly," he said, "the Government would be that of the Confederated Chiefs, but in reality it must necessarily be that of the representative of the protecting power." This meant the Congress "would, in fact be a School, in which the Chiefs would be instructed." The Colonial Office marginalia was scathing: "a pretty Gov[ernment]!!"[65] Nonetheless, he proceeded somewhat diffidently though (as typically) at browbeating length, the chiefs might enact laws for the white as well as the Maori inhabitants of New Zealand, where the content and form was supervised and controlled by Her Majesty's Government: "Whatever laws His Majesty's Government should consider suitable for the protection and Control of the King's subjects, would be proposed to and, as of course, become acts of the Legislature of NZ—Whatever laws of judicature H.M. might deem necessary would be established under the same sanction."[66]

A Colonial Office line was drawn heavily alongside the above paragraph with James Stephen's marginalia: "This is the real point." Busby then discussed the courts of civil and criminal jurisdiction that might be erected for the white population to be established by congressional legislation, approved by the Crown, and with an executive body comprised of three settlers and three missionaries advising the Resident.

Should that option prove infeasible, Busby suggested that the Crown simply grant a charter to the settlers already established in New Zealand, a version of the New Zealand Association's proposal that also supposed the Crown had sovereignty over the areas in white settlement acquired by purchase from Maori. This land purchasing was a phenomenon of growing concern, as the Colonial Office underlining of references to it in his report demonstrated. However, the official position by then was clear: no formal act of Crown sovereignty would occur without previous Maori consent. There would be no supposition that the acquisition of land by settlers entailed the simultaneous acquisition of British sovereignty.

Busby's report arrived in London in December 1837, a crucial juncture. It confirmed, unwittingly, the futility of pursuing a policy that sought to preserve and confederatively to consolidate exclusive Maori sovereignty. On 29 December Glenelg wrote to Lord Durham, referring to their pre-Christmas interview offering a charter. The Select Committee on Aborigines had only recently advised against British colonization and treaty making as contrary to the interests of tribal peoples. This committee had strong evangelical presence and its report, directed mostly toward southern Africa, tended to support the missionaries, who resisted colonization as likely to degrade and disrupt Christianization. The fervent belief of the missionary societies—and the Select Committee—was that it was advisable to begin with Christianity in order to lead to civilization, rather than the other way around.[67] For most of the mid-1830s the missionary societies thought this hands-off, or at most light-touch, approach to British presence would prevail. This was oiled no doubt by their feeling—not always soundly—that they held considerable sway in the Colonial Office of James Stephen's stewardship. And it was buoyed also by their recent success in securing abolition of slavery (1834). The tactic of the evangelical pressure groups throughout the mid-1830s had been to persuade British authorities to leave the New Zealand islands to their work in spreading His Word, but with some local judicial authority over misbehaving interloping seamen (vested in the local missionaries). By late 1837 that was no longer a viable possibility.

The Select Committee on Aborigines recommendations, though fresh, appeared to Glenelg "inadequate to meet the existing Evil, and the Repression of Practices of the most injurious Tendency to the Natives of New Zealand." These could now "be accomplished only by the Establishment of some settled Form of Government within that Territory, and in the Neighbourhood of the places resorted to by British Settlers." The Crown wished to avoid the "Calamities by which the Aborigines of the American and African Continents have been afflicted." Some colonial establishment was, therefore, necessary, the choice being between "a Colonization, desultory without Law, and fatal to the Natives, and a Colonization organized and salutary."[68]

Late in December 1837, the missionary societies got wind of what struck them as a u-turn by the Colonial Office on the question of intervention in New Zealand and protested vocally. In any event, the New Zealand Association declined the offer, which required formation on a joint-stock basis. It was withdrawn soon after.[69]

By the end of 1837, then, pushed by the pace of events—increasing settlement in New Zealand and unregulated if not chaotic land purchasing from Maori, the city-based maneuvering of the colonial reform movement, and pressure from evangelical societies to protect aboriginal peoples—the Colonial Office accepted that formal British authority would have to be established. This would be accomplished through Crown sovereignty, but that was conceived in terms of being limited to parts of the islands and as necessitating Maori consent. The conceptualizing remained primarily jurisdictional in orientation: it was just that events now were necessitating contemplation of fuller rather than minimal forms.

E. Seeking Imperial Order

Lauren Benton has looked at the jurisprudence of abolition in the British Empire of the post-Napoleonic period. Carefully unpacking vice-admiralty litigation, she demonstrates persuasively that efforts to implement and enforce abolition through the law merged with a project of consolidating the legal orders of empires. She shows how discussion of the treatment of liberated captives developed in the context of conflicts over slave owners' legal prerogatives and the imperial government's authority to restructure those prerogatives. "The dominant constitutional issue," she argues, "was one of order and not of rights."[70]

The characterization of imperial practice and law as fixated with order rather than conceptualized through a language of rights certainly transposes to the New Zealand setting of the mid-1830s, where the recognition of Maori jurisdiction was not in principle problematic for British authorities (however sceptical) until, in practice, it proved infeasible.[71] Imperial policy, its formal guise not least, was based upon a willingness to recognize confederate and mediated Maori jurisdiction until 1838 when the specter of full-scale settlement beyond the northern isthmus as well as fuller appreciation of the incessant turbulence of intertribal rivalry dislodged that predicate. To describe that willingness to work through Maori jurisdiction as an unqualified recognition of Maori sovereignty risks infusing that term ("sovereignty") with a rights-bearing meaning it was subsequently argued to hold, rather than its more jurisdictional connotation in this era. Sovereignty was not the substantive interest—the thing in itself held by Maori—that the British sought to protect but the consciously selected starting predicate from which the appropriate forms of guardianship and facilitation of imperial enterprise ("imperial order") might flow. The recognition of "Maori sovereignty" that was occurring through the 1830s was less concerned with endowing Maori with substantive rights in their dealings with British authorities (and settlers) than with guiding the pursuit of imperial order. For all its dressing in the modish language of humanitarianism and evangelism, ultimately the recognition of that sovereignty—as with British recognition elsewhere of the sovereignty of non-Christian polities—supplied the frame for action rather than acted as a substantive brake upon the imperial project.

The British approach toward lawlessness in the New Zealand islands during the mid-1830s demonstrates how recognition of the sovereign status of non-Christian polities was not starting primarily from a rights-oriented outlook so much as an order-based one. Further, British recognition of Maori sovereignty did not depend upon some criterion of civilization so much as a more pragmatic test of effectiveness that London realized the tribes individually and collectively could not meet, especially in the mounting pressure of the late 1830s. The official commitment to that sovereignty thus became the basis for its replacement by cession through the Treaty of Waitangi. Through this progression, from working through tribal sovereignty (the story told here) to arranging its cession (the next installment), the primary consideration was imperial order and the balancing of interests that this quest entailed. Maori sovereignty was a means to that end. For imperial officials it was never an end of itself.

NOTES

1. E. J. Tapp, *Early New Zealand: A Dependency of New South Wales, 1788-1841* (Melbourne: Melbourne University Press, 1958), 4, 66; Peter Adams, *Fatal Necessity: British Intervention in New Zealand, 1830-1847* (Auckland: Auckland University Press, 1977), 52. Later argued (unsuccessfully) as proof of British sovereignty over New Zealand: Petition of London Merchants, 22 May 1840, *Report of the Select Committee on New Zealand* (1840) [hereafter *RSCNZ* (1840)], *British Parliamentary Papers* [hereafter *BPP*] *1840*, vol. 1 [582], App. 1.
2. Robert McNab, ed., *Historical Records of New Zealand* (Wellington: Government Publisher, 1908), I at 317.
3. Government and General Order, 9 November 1814, id., 328-29.
4. James Hight and Harry Bamford, *The Constitutional Law and History of New Zealand* (Christchurch: Whitecombe and Tombs, 1914), 42; Adams, *Fatal Necessity*, 52. British seamen did not take the appointment seriously: Nicholas, evidence, *Lords Committee on New Zealand* (1838), *BPP 1837-38* [68], 11.
5. Macquarie to Bathurst, 24 June 1815, *RSCNZ* (1840), App. 2; Bathurst to Macquarie, 9 April 1816, id.
6. Hight and Bamford, *Constitutional History of New Zealand*, 42-43.
7. 57 Geo. 3, cap 83.
8. Brisbane to Bathurst, 8 February 1825, *Historical Records of Australia* [hereafter *HRA*], 1st series, 26 volumes (Canberra: Commonwealth Library, 1914), xi, 296.
9. Tapp, *Early New Zealand*, 72.
10. In *HRA*, xii, 496-97.
11. 4 Geo. 4, cap 96.
12. 9 Geo. 4, cap 83.

13. Reverend Samuel Marsden to Governor Darling, 2 August 1830, Colonial Office [hereafter CO] 209/1: 15 at 17.
14. For instance, Reverend Marsden to Darling, 2 August 1830, CO 209/1: 15-18; Darling to Murray, 12 August 1830, CO 201/175: 29; Barrow to Hay, 24 March 1832, CO 201/228; 27-31 (including abstract of Colonial Office correspondence on the topic); and, generally, Adams, *Fatal Necessity*, 59-60, 66.
15. Darling to Goderich, 13 April 1831, CO 209/1: 28-34 (with enclosures at 36-50).
16. Moore to Colonial Secretary (NSW), 7 February 1831, encl. in Darling to Goderich, 13 April 1831, CO 209/1: 51.
17. So described in Goderich to Bourke, 31 January 1832, CO 209/1: 66 at 68.
18. Moore to Colonial Secretary (NSW), 12 April 1831, encl. in Darling to Goderich, 13 April 1831, CO 209/1: 53.
19. A similar problem arose in 1836 regarding the prosecution of Reverend William Yate for sodomy: Busby to Colonial Secretary (NSW), 11 November 1836, CO 209/2: 279, and on this matter see Judith Binney, "Whatever Happened to Poor Mr Yate? An Exercise in Voyeurism," *New Zealand Journal of History* 9, no. 2 (1975): 111-12. To avoid the need for a warrant Busby later sought to obtain one from the native chiefs (as "a bar to any action for false imprisonment" by litigious British miscreants), 1 July 1837, CO 209/2: 30-37. Hobson treated his transportation of the British culprits as being lawfully based upon the chiefs' formal permission: Hobson Report, copy enclosed in Bourke to Glenelg, 9 September 1837, CO 209/2: 30-37, encl. A. In evidence, Flatt advised the *Lords Committee* (1838), evidence, at 32, of two murders among the European population having gone unpunished because "Mr Busby had not the power."
20. Stephen, recorded opinion, 25 May 1830, CO 201/215: 696-97.
21. Bill of 7 June 1832, text in CO 209/1: 102: British Parliamentary Debates: Great Britain. Parliament. *Hansard's Parliamentary Debates,* 3rd series, 365 vols, (London: T.C. Hansard 1829-1891), 43: 505-6; Glenelg to Bourke, 28 October 1835, CO 209/1: 163-68; Stephen to Russell, 16 November 1839, CO 209/5: 51.
22. Petition of Thirteen Chiefs to William IV signed in the presence of the Committee of Merchants, encl. in Yate to Colonial Secretary (NSW), 16 November 1831, CO 201/221: 384-48 and CO 209/1: 96-98. The French were so described after the visit of Marion du Fresne, which brought disastrous consequences for both sides: Tapp, *Early New Zealand*, 80, n. 63. Goderich to Maori Chiefs, 14 June 1832, CO 209/1: 104-5.
23. Darling to Goderich, 13 April 1831, CO 209/1: 28-34.
24. Goderich to Bourke, 31 January 1832, CO 209/1: 66.
25. Bourke to Busby, instructions, 13 April 1833, CO 209/1: 107-17 at 111. Busby had written a pamphlet recommending the appointment of an agent with Magisterial authority over British subjects after treaties with the chiefs had been concluded: *A Brief Memoir relative to the Islands of New Zealand* (June 1831) in CO 209/1: 183, 197-98.
26. Id. at 112.
27. Admiralty powers were limited to naval commanders and therefore those limited powers could not be given to Busby.
28. As portrayed in William Dalrymple's popular history *White Mughals: Love and Betrayal in 18th-Century India* (London: HarperCollins, 2002).
29. Though he did share with many East India Company "nabobs" the disposition to make personal gain while in office. During the 1840s he was one of the most vociferous of the

"old settlers" demanding that the Crown validate direct land purchases from the tribes predating British annexation, activity in which he had been a not inactive participant.

30. Graham Metcalfe, *MacLean of the Gold Coast: The Life and Times of George MacLean, 1801-1847* (Oxford: Oxford University Press, 1962), 170-71 and 177; W. Ross Johnston, *Sovereignty and Protection: A Study of British Jurisdictional Imperialism in the Late Nineteenth Century* (Durham, NC: Duke University Press, 1973), 58-59. As to the legality of MacLean's assumption of jurisdiction without tribal grant see Stanley to Hill, 16 December 1843, CO 96/5; MacLean argued (unsuccessfully) that Britain held the sovereignty *de facto* of the region: MacLean to Stanley, 2 February 1844, ibid.
31. Goderich to Bourke, 31 January 1832, CO 209/1: 66.
32. Adams, *Fatal Necessity* at 64-71, gives an assessment of Busby's character.
33. Busby to Bourke, 13 May 1833, CO 209/2: 210 at 211.
34. Id. at 212.
35. Bourke to Stanley, 29 April 1934, CO 209/1: 121, 123 (extracts from the Minutes of Proceedings of the NSW Executive Council, 7 September 1833).
36. Busby to Hay, 3 April 1834, CO 209/1: 121-24, 213-36 (enclosures).
37. Abderdeen to Bourke, 21 December 1834, CO 209/1: 129.
38. Barrow (Admiralty) to Hay (Colonial Office), 24 November 1834, enclosure 2 in Bourke to Stanley, 29 April 1834, CO 209/1: 121, 123.
39. Bourke to Stanley, 23 September 1834, CO 209/1: 132; Bourke to Rice, 1 February, CO 2091: 139.
40. De Thierry to Busby, 14 September 1835, CO 209/2: 85 (copy).
41. De Thierry, "Address to the New Zealand Settlers," CO 209/2: 87.
42. Busby, "The British Resident as New Zealand to His Britannic Majesty's Subjects who are residing or trading in New Zealand" (10 October 1835), copy in CO 209/2: 94.
43. Declaration of the United Tribes, 28 October 1835, CO 209/2: 102-3 (duplicate copy).
44. Colonial Secretary (NSW) to Busby, 12 February 1936, CO 209/2: 16.
45. Glenelg to Bourke, 26 May 1836, CO 209/1: 268 at 269. Tabled 1 May 1838 before the *Lords Committee* (1838), App. 2 at 159.
46. Bourke to Glenelg, 19 March 1836, CO 209/2: 10.
47. Busby to Bourke, 30 November 1835, CO 209/2: 111. Several despatches were exchanged on the matter of the Hokianga ardent spirit law, the matter soon degenerating into a personal battle between Busby and McDonnell, its vehemence and long-winded character doubtless compromising the credibility of the former. See especially Busby to Bourke, 27 July 1836, CO 209/2: 256-78.
48. Busby to Bourke, 18 January 1836, CO 209/2: 140; Busby to Bourke, 26 January 1836, CO 209/2: 152; Church Missionary Society clergy to Busby, 13 May 1836, CO 209/2: 240; Busby to Bourke, 18 May 1836, CO 209/2: 232; Petition of British missionaries, 20 April 1837, CO 209/2: 231; Hobson to Bourke, 8 August 1837, CO 209/2: 30.
49. Busby to Bourke, 20 February 1836, CO 209/2: 160; Busby to Bourke, 12 March 1836, CO 209/2: 178; Busby, "Memorandum for the Missionaries of the Church Missionary Society," 18 May 1836, CO 209/2: 238; Busby to Bourke, 15 June 1836, CO 209/2: 248; Busby to Bourke, 22 March 1837, CO 209/2: 311, and, especially, Busby to Colonial Secretary (NSW), 9 November 1838, CO 209/4: 6. Ian Wards, *The Shadow of the Land* (Wellington, NZ: Historical Publications Branch, Department of Internal Affairs, 1968), 14-22, argues that after *He Whakaputanga* the Crown recognized only the confederated sovereignty of the United Tribes. In fact (as the Hokianga law incident illustrated), the Colonial Office recognized Maori sovereignty as fundamentally *tribal* in character.

50. For instance, Busby to Governor NSW, 26 January 1836, CO 209/2: 152; 20 February 1836, CO 209/2: 160; 30 January 1837, CO 209/2: 301-7; 28 March 1837, CO 209/2: 313-16; 16 June 1837, CO 209/2: 333-54 at 335, stating formal intervention was necessary, otherwise he could not "see the least prospect of any permanent peace."
51. Draft Punishment Act for New Zealand, encl. in Glenelg to Bourke, 23 August 1836, CO 201/248: 311 at 318-19.
52. 6 & 7 Will 4 cap 57. This act was based upon the recognition of the "Kafir Nation": Merivale, Memorandum for Cabinet: April 1851, CO 879/1: xx.
53. Glenelg to Bourke, 26 August 1836, CO 209/2: 20. See Adams, *Fatal Necessity*, 70.
54. Outline of a Bill for New Zealand drafted by the New Zealand Association, 14 June 1837, CO 209/2: 388.
55. Glenelg, Memorandum, 15 December 1837, CO 209/2: 409.
56. "In illustration of this may be mentioned the strenuous Objections, which the United States have made to the Payment of Duties of Customs at Honduras, founded on the imperfect Title under which Great Britain holds that settlement." Id. The layout of the draft of this Memorandum 209/2: 411-21 suggests this came as an afterthought before printing.
57. Indeed, some of the issues relating to American citizens prior to British sovereignty reached the Anglo-American Claims Tribunal: *Successors of William Webster (United States) v. Great Britain* (Determination of 12 December 1925), *American Journal of International Law* 20, no. 2 (1926): 391-97.
58. By the late 1830s legislation was being sought on a case-by-case basis to modify the Crown's constituent power, in particular prospective colonies (especially those being designated officially as acquired by settlement). However, this legislation was no more than facilitative. It did not replace the prerogative of the Crown with a parliamentary constitution, so much as extend the scope of the former. This legislation was necessitated by the interpretation being given *Campbell v. Hall* (1774) that colonists of British settlers in uninhabited or uncivilized territory were entitled at common law to a representative assembly (see discussion below). This meant that legislation was needed to enlarge the Crown's constituent power in the erection of a Crown colony with other than a representative assembly (taken to mean, a chamber with at least half its members elected). See McHugh, "The Common Law Status of Colonies and Aboriginal 'Rights': How Lawyers and Historians Treat the Past," *Saskatchewan Law Review* 61, no. 2 (1998): 393–429. Glenelg regarded the South Australia format ("that Colony of feuds and schisms") as having the "great failing" of splitting the legislative power between London and Adelaide.
59. Hobson's Report, 8 August 1837, enclosure in Bourke to Glenelg, 9 September 1937, CO 209/2: 37.
60. Id. at 36.
61. Id. at 30.
62. Busby reacted to this rather pettily, arguing that the civil government Hobson hankered after was already in place as the (i.e., his) United Tribes: Busby to New South Wales, 30 November 1838. CO 209/4: 43-5.
63. Busby to Bourke, 16 June 1837, CO 209/2: 333 at 340.
64. Id. at 339 stating that his proposal "is founded upon the principle of a protecting state administering in chief the affairs of another state in trust for the Inhabitants, as sanctioned by the Treaty of Paris in the instance of Great Britain and the Ionian Islands, and as applied, I believe, in various instances, on the borders of our Indian possessions."

65. Id. at 341.
66. Id. at 343.
67. See for example the extracts published in Dandeson Coates (Secretary to the Church Missionary Society), John Beecham (Weslyan Missionary Society), and William Ellis (London Missionary Society), *Christianity, the Means of Civilization: Shown in the Evidence Given before a Committee of the House of Commons, Selections from the Evidence of Witnesses* (London: Seeley and Burnside, 1837).
68. Glenelg to Durham, 29 December 1837, CO 209/2: 423-32, quotations at 424-25.
69. Glenelg to Durham, 5 February 1838, CO 209/4: 295. Adams, *Fatal Necessity*, 112-14.
70. Lauren Benton, "'Slave trading is not a piratical offense': Abolition, Prize Law, and the Imperial Constitution," paper presented at the 2010 Symposium on Comparative Early Modern Legal History: "New Perspectives on Legal Pluralism," 23 April 2010, at the Newberry Library, Chicago; Lauren Benton and Lisa Ford, "Magistrates in Empire: Convicts, Slaves, and the Remaking of the Plural Legal Order in the British Empire," in this volume.
71. Also, along similar lines, Lisa Ford, *Settler Sovereignty: Jurisdiction and Indigenous People in America and Australia, 1788-1836* (Cambridge, MA: Harvard University Press, 2010).

PART IV

Concluding Perspectives

10

Laws' Histories

Pluralisms, Pluralities, Diversity

PAUL D. HALLIDAY

Edward Byam condemned the "breach of the laws of the empire" he saw all around Mauritius in late 1822.[1] As British commissary general of the police in the island, he struggled to work within a "radically bad and vicious" system. Its radical badness arose from the fact that French laws that sustained the slave trade persisted alongside British laws that prohibited it. The solution was to constrain the plurality of laws by a "full and entire execution" of the "laws of the empire in regard to the slave trade." The rule of law would end a chaos of laws.

After Britain's conquest of Mauritius in 1810, maintaining French law had been seen as one of the means by which French colonists might be peacefully co-opted into a foreign empire. Slavery remained legal; the trade in slaves did not. But laying British law atop parts of French law created spaces in which the trade survived. Prohibitions against the slave trade were undermined by the assertion of the norms of slave traders and owners whose choices subverted that law. Grand juries found reasons not to indict even the most blatant illegal traders; judges found reasons not to convict them. A British statute permitting importation of slaves to Mauritius from the Seychelles simply widened the space in which the trade might persist with the appearance of legality.[2] Meanwhile, maroonage increased rapidly in the 1820s. Slaves fled their masters. Work stoppages and other forms of protest sent a similar message: that norms opposed to slavery competed with laws that sustained it.[3]

Imperial places like Mauritius lived with many kinds of law. In the interstices among them lurked all kinds of normative possibilities. Slaves and slavers alike exploited those possibilities to act according to expectations that were often at odds with law in one or more forms. For some, laws' pluralities represented opportunities; to others, they permitted the unforgivable. Byam branded slave-trading opportunists as a "cabal . . . of revolutionary, low, and ignorant persons" who "waged war against British principles."[4] By enlisting help from his colonial office superiors in Westminster, he sought imposition of a single law—a reduction of plurality—and thereby an end to the unforgivable.

We call this countervailing multiplicity of laws "legal pluralism": a device scholars use to impose interpretive order on otherwise chaotic worlds of both present and past. We also use the term because we like the variety, the diversity that it calls to mind. Perhaps owing to our unspoken liberal premises, we believe this represents possibilities for choosing, and thus for individual and collective self-realization, through law. We may call it pluralism, but in the living of laws in the past, they were simply pluralities. Mauritian slave traders must have celebrated laws' pluralities. Edward Byam condemned them. Laws' pluralities showed their capacity both to liberate and to oppress. Historical explanation makes this clear. But before we can work on pluralities, we must first deal with pluralisms.

Legal Pluralisms

"Legal pluralism" has a past. By touring that past, we can appreciate the sorts of work the term does now and understand whether it's the term we want to keep using for the work before us. In the essays gathered above, legal pluralism has returned to its postcolonial point of origin, serving as a way to consider the consequences of imperial and colonial legal orders and their interaction with the lives those legal orders encountered around the globe. But it now serves very different analytic purposes. In the hands of historians, pluralism has become pluralities.

In the 1950s, '60s, and '70s, legal pluralism provided the medium through which legal planners considered the circumstances of new nations, especially in Africa. In their hands, "legal pluralism" indicated "a situation in which we have not just one law equal for all, but where we find a plurality of legal orders, each applying to a particular group."[5] Such pluralism occurred for two reasons: because of the cultural plurality of what were called "tribal societies," and because "tribal" plurality was overlaid by European law.[6] Indigenous multiplicity was compounded in places—Mauritius, for example—where successive and sometimes composite European legal forms once held sway.

Pluralism provided postcolonial planners with a diagnostic label, a way to identify a problem in need of solution. The problem was that different sorts of people had different sorts of law. This offended dominant positivist and rule-of-law sensibilities, which required that all within a given area be subject to the same legal demands and procedures. Colonial and customary legal orders' multiplicity militated against legal uniformity and thus the rule of law.[7] It also militated against national unity. Legal reform would contribute to "modernization": "to the evolution of national legal systems and their role in nation-building." Curing pluralism provided a "great opportunity . . . to do a major job of social engineering."[8]

Nation building through legal reform: doing this required a strong state; it would also help to make such a state. Just as they hired civil engineers to design massive infrastructure projects that would build postcolonial nation-states, new states in the 1960s needed to hire socio-legal engineers to design constitutions that would co-opt or lop off awkward pluralities in the name of nation building. National unity would arise from and contribute to the legal uniformity presumed to be the hallmark of a proper state.

Modernization, uniformity, rationalization: the effort would extend to postcolonial Africa and Asia an evolutionary process European societies had presumably passed through long before. History, it seemed, had lessons to teach. After all, Europe had found itself in much the same pluralist predicament in the millennium following the collapse of Rome. It was then that Europe's evolution began, culminating in what in retrospect seemed the inevitable point of arrival: hegemonic states, recognized by arrangements made in the Treaty of Westphalia in 1648 and capable of enacting and enforcing uniform legal expectations across internally unified territories.[9] Adoption and adaptation of European legal ideas and practices, "appropriate to those needs of Western civilization of which Africa is now to become a part," would allow new nations to become "adult members of an international society."[10] The success of these new states would depend on the degree to which the legal engineers could reduce legal pluralism by reproducing a presumed European model.

At first blush, legal sociologist John Griffiths's definition of legal pluralism looked like the one used by the postcolonial legal engineers. Legal pluralism appears whenever "in a social field more than one source of 'law,' more than one 'legal order,' is observable."[11] But where the engineers celebrated the state in the interest of a unity to be won by containing pluralism, Griffiths celebrated pluralism and challenged the engineers' central premise: that the state has and should have sole authority to generate what counts as law. Griffiths skewered the "myth" of "legal centralism." It was nothing more than an "ideology" perpetuated by "false comparisons" with so-called "primitive society." The problem was not pluralism, but a myopia that insisted that the legal engineers' centralist expectations—that "unification is inevitable, necessary, normal, modern, and good"—should guide understanding about what really happened in colonial societies and thus about what must happen in postcolonial ones.[12]

For Griffiths, legal pluralism was "an attribute of a social field and not of a 'law' or of a 'legal system'" conceived as an autonomous realm of ideas and institutions presided over by professionals. Every social field is filled with "normative material," all constitutive of law, whether or not it manifests itself in the work of state actors and institutions. Given the rich world of norm making and imposing that we all inhabit—made and imposed by courts and by daily interactions governed by everything from the rules of local softball leagues to the expectation that a 35-mile-per-hour speed limit really means forty-five—there is always "more than one source of 'law,' more than one 'legal order,'" in any social field.[13]

Griffiths set the terms of subsequent debate over legal pluralism. He had helpfully moved discussion past the simple statism of the legal engineers. But his own scare quotes around "law" and "legal order," and his slippage between "law" and "norms," pointed to a problem. If law is any activity involving "the self-regulation of a 'semi-autonomous social field,'" then just what is law? More to the point, what *isn't* law? Griffiths's suggestion that law might be anything "more or less 'legal'" did little to answer this central question.[14]

Griffiths's law-norm elision dulled legal pluralism's analytic edge. Sally Engle Merry agreed that legal pluralism happened wherever "two or more legal systems coexist in the same social field." And like Griffiths, Merry critiqued the privileged position of the state relative to what might count as law. But she significantly modified Griffiths's all-norms-included account of legal pluralism. "State law" had to be understood as a site of action distinct from "other normative orders."[15] The means by which to distinguish law from norm was the very thing Griffiths sought to diminish: the state. In a string of articles, Brian Tamanaha extended this line of thinking in order to understand law as a particular kind of norm-making activity. "[S]tate law norms and non-state 'law' norms are two starkly contrasting phenomena, not at all alike. Stated more strongly, they are ontologically distinct."[16] Countering the myth of state centralization required neither dismissing nor diminishing the state by pretending that its actions existed on an undifferentiated spectrum with other sites for making and enforcing norms. It required the reverse: that we understand the differences between state law and nonstate norms. Then we might explain the interaction between them.[17]

Arguably the richest examination of laws' multiplicity and its interaction with other norms had been made a few years earlier from outside the pluralism debate. Robert Cover identified what he called a "jurisgenerative principle" that proliferates across the many communities found in any society. This principle operates beyond as well as within state institutions. But distinguishing the state from other sites of norm making matters. Only by doing that might we make sense of the work done by the state, and especially by courts. The social pervasiveness of jurisgenesis—the endless capacity to create norms that compete with those of the state—created the need for the state and its courts. "It is the multiplicity of laws, the fecundity of the jurisgenerative principle, that creates the problem to which the court and the state are the solution." Judges do not create law; they bury it. "Theirs is the jurispathic office. Confronting the luxuriant growth of a hundred legal traditions, they assert that *this one* is law and destroy or try to destroy the rest."[18] In Cover's account, there is less a rule of law than a rule of courts. That rule, performed through words, is violent.[19]

For Cover, state centralism was no myth; it was the hardest of realities. But just as Cover seemed ready to condemn state law for its centralism, and thus as destructive of the *nomoi* generated by living communities, he redeemed the judicial function, in admittedly American separation-of-power terms. Courts are the "least dangerous branch." The judge's violence operates not only on nonstate norms claiming to be law. It also restricts other organs of the state that might inhibit the enjoyment of norms to which self-selecting communities might peacefully submit themselves. Thus the judicial office is arrayed against "the violence and coercion of the other organs of the state." "In a truly violent, authoritarian situation, nothing is more revolutionary than the insistence of a judge that he exercises such a 'jurisdiction.'"[20] The jurispathic office protects even as it destroys. In plural legal environments, the state's law might emancipate as well as oppress.

Cover did not use the language of legal pluralism, but in many ways, he was its most subtle student. While Griffiths placed the law of the state on a continuum with what he contended were other legal forms, Cover distinguished the state's law from the norms of distinct communities (for instance, Mennonites or Mormons).[21] He thereby demonstrated how we *need* the state: both as we inhabit our own social worlds and as we attempt to explain the living work of law—present, past, and perhaps future—in relation to the other kinds of norms that compete with it. How then shall we understand the operation of law and of other norms in the social worlds people inhabit?

Griffiths offered an account of legal pluralism that encompassed all normative assertions to challenge the all-encompassing claims of the nation-state. This left law so broadly defined as to be of little use. Merry answered by moving beyond definition: by asserting that "[d]efining the essence of law or custom is less valuable than situating these concepts in particular sets of relations between particular legal orders in particular historical contexts."[22] Brian Tamanaha went one methodological step further. "[N]o attempt to formulate a single scientific or cross-cultural definition of law can succeed."[23]

Tamanaha suggested that Griffiths's version of "legal pluralism," by running law and norm together, might be more helpfully called "normative pluralism."[24] To avoid confusion, law had to be understood as a distinct kind of normative ordering. Griffiths's essentializing version of legal pluralism, by which all normative ordering might be called "legal," defied understanding the world as people live in it: a world in which people use words like "law" to refer to ideas and practices distinct from those they associate with their other normative commitments. Thus what should count as law may only be "determined by the people in the social arena through their own common usages, not in advance by the social scientist or theorist."[25] Another way to put this is to say that what counts as law is context dependent and defies the modeling impulse. Of course, history had already taught us this.

Or more precisely, E. P. Thompson had. Long before Griffiths wrote about the work performed by multiple legal and extralegal norms, Thompson struggled, then failed, to find the social "level" where law might be isolated from other kinds of social interaction. "[L]aw did not keep politely to a 'level' but was at *every* bloody level."[26] Like Griffiths, Thompson viewed law and the norms that struggle with it as socially pervasive. Unlike Griffiths—but like Merry, Cover, and Tamanaha—Thompson distinguished law making in and through the state from other processes by which norms arise and operate. The state and its law marked a site of contest where normative claims competed for recognition. For instance, in the eighteenth century, innovative claims about the freedom of producers and sellers of grain to export or set prices clashed with customary claims about just price. Statutes, the pronouncement of judges, and the actions of local magistrates played the jurispathic role as one normative order supplanted another by winning the endorsement of state legality.[27]

Thompson developed three points about laws' pluralities as he explored the contrapuntal relationship of law and custom. First, there was a larger temporal pattern in the experience of legal pluralism that did not sit neatly within the traditional progressive models associated with the Westphalian state and the ability or desirability of reproducing such states in postcolonial settings. By exploring the example of English law's endorsement of market innovation, Thompson gave an account of legal pluralism at the moment of its containment. In the eighteenth and nineteenth centuries, a world of mixed and overlapping customary interests in soil fell before innovative property claims. The containment of plurality by state law marked a liberation for novel market interests at the same time it marked the destruction of customary interests in just prices and mixed land use. Second, this pattern was extended across Britain's empire at the same time it extended across England. The same state that aided the enclosure of England's commons abetted the extension of novel forms of property to the Scottish Highlands, North America, and India. Plurality and its restriction in the empire's core provided a template for the same pattern across the empire's farther reaches.[28]

Finally—perhaps surprisingly—there was another side to this. The same state law that restricted pluralism provided the conceptual, rhetorical, and procedural tools to constrain, reverse, or at least ameliorate the effects of this pattern. Here, law as a site of norm making different from others became crucial to the analysis. As Thompson put it, "the forms and rhetoric of law acquire a distinct identity which may, on occasion, inhibit power and afford some protection to the powerless." Or, as Thompson noted when considering state law's imperial possibilities, if law is and was a mask of power, "it was a mask which Gandhi and Nehru were to borrow, at the head of a million masked supporters."[29] In Britain and across its empire, the rule of law was at once an instrument of containment and an instrument by which the state might be contained.

As Thompson's work implied, "legal pluralism," as a term identifying a debate about how to model a supposedly transhistorical human experience, has been undermined from the beginning by the specificities of historical explanation. These specificities highlight the role of the state and of temporal and spatial patterns that defy the making of models. The less we focus on how to theorize law—on how to model plural*ism*—the more we do history: the more we see pluralities.

Laws' Pluralities

The essays in this volume account for pluralities rather than pluralism. They heed the oldest yet perhaps still boldest of claims. In the words of R. G. Collingwood, the things historians address "are not abstract but concrete, not universal but individual, not indifferent to space and time but having a where and a when of their own."[30] These essays tell stories filled with individuals; they attend to geographic and temporal precision; they recover languages of legal argument that are unreadable to the modern eye unless aided by contextualizing instruments of linguistic analysis.

Throughout, the state's the thing. As we've seen, one problem with the initial socio-legal formulation of legal pluralism was its boundless idea of law—that which is "more or less legal."[31] But there was a bigger problem: legal pluralism's bounded idea of the state. For all legal pluralism's sharp critique of state centrism, that critique was made possible only by accepting the hoariest conception of the state: the so-called Westphalian model of internally coherent, territorially defined states, each an equal in an international order of states. The legal pluralism critique yearned to undo this condition—to create a post-Westphalian world—by eliding the state's norms with nonstate ones. This, it was hoped, would open the spaces in which those other normative orders might flourish. But creating a post-Westphalian world requires that there has first been a Westphalian one.[32] And it is here that the kind of historically particular essays in this collection suggest how narrow is the conception of the state that has informed the pluralism debate. For the early modern state was not simply a site of pluralities. It was made by them.

For all the prominence of Jean Bodin and Thomas Hobbes, their discourses of unitary sovereignty arose for a reason: to counter insistent discourses of divided sovereignty and plural legality in the world they inhabited. To show this, Richard Ross and Philip Stern take an approach reminiscent of Quentin Skinner (himself influenced by Collingwood): "any act of communication will always constitute the taking up of some determinate position in relation to some pre-existing conversation or argument."[33] Bodin and Hobbes entered a preexisting conversation. For centuries, everyone had been talking about pluralist forms of sovereignty.

We have had a hard time hearing those other voices because the canonical theorists of sovereignty largely drowned them out as later generations accepted the Westphalian model of the state, whose existence the likes of Bodin and Hobbes seemed to explain. Ross and Stern remind us that the best way we can hear those other voices is by listening for the scriptural texts on which they relied. Once we retell the stories of the tribes of Israel and reread Romans 13, we discover how God's Word, as the ultimate justification of authority, resolved as readily in pluralist ideals as in the kind of sovereign unity we imagine every time we read Bodin or look at the frontispiece of *Leviathan*.[34] But as Ross and Stern point out, Leviathan and plurality did not present an either/or proposition.[35] They constituted one another. Early modern states, in their cores and on their peripheries, became strong not by squelching plurality and thereby approximating the unity apparently required by our Hobbesian and Westphalian expectations. They became strong *because* of plurality.[36]

We might go one step further. The exercise of sovereignty was extended by dividing it. This is the lesson we learn from the archetypal form of imperial extension: the chartered company, whether Dutch, French, or British. The traditional theory of corporations required the "concession" of the state for their creation. This concession was typically signaled in a charter, by which the king gave life to a "body in fiction of law."[37] Sovereigns formally created and supervised corporations. But Philip Stern and Helen Dewar remind us how different the lives of those collective fictional beings were in the living. Each corporation took on a life of its own, independent and sometimes defiant of its creator. Like kings, the Dutch and English East India Companies made treaties with Asian sovereigns. They created courts, regulated property, collected taxes, and hired armies. From St. Helena to Bengkulu, they built fortresses as well as factories. More than mere traders, they made and managed the commonweal, and in so doing, offered a competing locus of loyalty, an alternate form of subjecthood, for both the indigenes and the Europeans living in the places they ruled.[38]

Pluralities of law and loyalty operating through corporations point to a basic problem in the Westphalian idea of sovereignty. The modern legal-political imagination is sustained by an illusion of neat boundaries containing internally coherent entities, each dealing with the others as theoretical equals in an international "order." This illusion is as much a product of our geographical imaginations as of our political imaginations. Our minds color in the whole of each space called a nation-state with a single crayon. We don't use pastels, overlap tints, or paint outside the lines.

But consider the map of early modern France as Helen Dewar asks us to see it.[39] The modern imagination simply sees a French kingdom. Early modern subjects of that kingdom saw a patchwork of tiny, often overlapping spaces. Our metaphors now fail us. However much we blur the lines and overlap the patches, two dimensions won't do. Perhaps we should think in terms of three-dimensional multimedia installations used as props in an improvisational dance. Thinking about jurisdictional politics in these terms, we begin to see that the spaces covered by the performance were less important than the people who performed and the things they made each time the performance occurred.

Actual people—subjects and sovereigns—defined the early modern imperial state in its core and on its peripheries. In the British Isles, we might reasonably observe that the laws of Berwick and the Channel Isles differed from the laws of England. In France, we can use territorial tags—Brittany,

Normandy—to identify different legal assumptions and practices. But in each case, legal variations arose from the personal relationships at work at the moments when those places became associated with particular sovereigns. Plurality arising from variations in the personal relationships within Britain and France then reached across the Atlantic, shaping laws' pluralities on the ocean's far side. Place—distance, topography, territorial bounds of different degrees of clarity—conditioned how relationships of sovereignty and subjecthood played out in empires.[40] And territorial aspects of jurisdiction became more pronounced in the later eighteenth and nineteenth centuries.[41] But throughout, human beings and the relationships among them defined the state in all its plurality.

The state arose from and depended upon the relationship called subjecthood. The modern mind sees sovereignty manifesting itself through a uniform, depersonalized collective being called the state, possessed of will and mind but no body. The early modern mind saw sovereignty in a living, bleeding person, possessed of will, mind, *and* body. Subjecthood was a personal connection between two souls and minds, each contained in a living body. Spatial situation might indicate aspects of the relationship, but it did not constitute it. Allegiance—the heart of subjecthood—was a matter of faith and truth. As Sir Edward Coke put it, these "are qualities of the mind and soul of man, and cannot be circumscribed within the predicament of *ubi*."[42]

This relationship of sovereign and subject explains how laws' pluralities grew from and sustained states that bore few of the qualities the modern mind expects of a state. But many were the king's subjects. Each person or group of persons—owing to territory, social status, or other markers of difference—stood in a slightly different relationship of mutual obligation with the king. Indians in Mexico looked to the king in Spain for justice, just like his Castilian subjects, though each received his justice by different jurisdictional means.[43] British overseas trading companies, like their French counterparts, received life from the monarch's grant of corporate privileges. But those privileges varied from one instance to the next. In the Ottoman empire, Jews, Christians, and Muslims stood in distinct positions relative to the sultan. And though it may seem paradoxical at first glance, as Karen Barkey suggests, the management of diversity by offering each community its own instruments of justice bound different peoples together into a single subjecthood.

When looking at subjecthood, the modern liberal democratic eye focuses on obedience. To the early modern eye, subjecthood appeared as a condition of possibility, one arising from the protection—provided by laws—given in return for obedience. This explains how subjecthood was not simply invoked by people who might have seemed self-evidently to be subjects. It was chosen. Linda Rupert recounts how Dutch slaves crossed dangerous waters and porous borders in order to become the Spanish king's subjects. That sovereign's pronouncements, in the form of multiple decrees, created the spaces where their choosing might be possible: where subjecthood might be the condition by which they might leave the subjugation of slavery. Subjecthood was an invitation accepted. Winning Spanish subjects from Dutch slaves in this way legitimated the claims of the sovereign's state.[44] Subjection to the sovereign as the means to liberation was a strategy of long standing: it was the same move Mexican Indians had long made to assert their own claims to freedom from the oppressions of others.[45]

The operation of subjecthood also reminds us how plural legal spaces could be as productive of tyrannies—typically imposed by lesser tyrants we call by the name of masters, landlords, or local magistrates—as they were of liberation. These tyrannies might only be curtailed by the sovereign's actions in response to the subject's pleas.[46] Given the proliferation of such tyrannies where left unchecked by sovereign power, we encounter another problem raised by the socio-legal account of legal pluralism: what Boaventura de Sousa Santos has called its "romantic or pseudo-radical anti-state stance." By this stance, laws (or norms) made outside the state are presumed to liberate while those made in the state are presumed to stifle. But these poles might easily be flipped: all we need to do is recall the memory of lynch mobs and U.S. law's ultimate response to them. E. P. Thompson's paean to the rule of law at the end of *Whigs and Hunters* points to the same possibility.[47] Santos has put the corollary to this more bluntly: there is "nothing inherently good, progressive, or emancipatory about 'legal pluralism' . . . there is no intrinsic reason why state law should be less despotic or, for that matter, less democratic than non-state law."[48] Claims of liberty and other moral goods often needed the sovereign's might for protection in a plural legal world.

We sometimes have a hard time appreciating this. After all, consider the possibilities for adjudication of differences Christians and Jews enjoyed under Ottoman law—even more possibilities than Muslims.[49] Or consider the capacity of Dutch slaves to win freedom by deciding to be Spanish subjects. One reason we tend to celebrate plurality is that it involves choosing, and we take choosing to be a means of moral and social self-realization. It is, we presume, "emancipatory." But perhaps we deceive ourselves. After all, within and among the places we call courts, choosing is usually the prerogative of people called plaintiffs or prosecutors. There is always someone on the receiving end of their choices. Plural environments multiply possibilities for people to choose; those choices close down the choices of others.

Choosing and being the object of choosing also help us understand work done among the personnel of the tribunals and other sites of official action in legally plural imperial settings. Edward Byam did not like the choices Mauritian slave traders had found in the spaces left open by laws' pluralities. So he appealed to higher authorities in an effort to narrow the range of choosing that sustained their illegal trade. The solution to local tyrannies was the imposition of the sovereign's will to protect the empire's subjects.[50] Byam's complaints exemplify one way this worked: by enlisting the help of a greater authority in an imperial hierarchy. Doing so narrowed the range of others' choices: in this case, of slave traders.

Byam's complaints also suggest how the reduction of plurality and the resulting homogenization of imperial practices occurred in a particular moment: in the late eighteenth and nineteenth centuries. Reducing plurality became a matter of policy, one often driven by concerns about economic productivity. That concern replaced the relationship of subject and sovereign as the glue that held together polyglot empires. As Brian Owensby notes, Spanish imperial debates of the eighteenth century set a novel market economy against a traditional moral economy.[51] Law's pluralities diminished as economic efficiency supplanted justice as the chief purpose of the imperial state.

Owensby offers an elegiac account of the moral commitments that bound empire together at the moment those commitments began to shrivel, an account not unlike the one Thompson offered of the enclosure of England's commons. But the containment of plurality might emancipate as well as constrain.[52] We can only guess that people like Ann Rumsby felt safer in their choices as the choices of magistrates in New South Wales were restricted as a result of imperial policy.[53] In the 1810s, '20s, and '30s, dominions across Britain's empire were recast in similar ways in response to comprehensive reviews of judicial institutions made by special commissioners. Over the course of a generation, the legal pluralities that had been the hallmark of early modern states and empires had been significantly reduced.[54]

Reducing laws' pluralities improved the lot of many imperial subjects. Sending new judges with new powers to watch over the petty tyrants who served as magistrates in places like the Leeward Islands or New South Wales was one way this happened. Such judges, in the words of Robert Cover, might "use their interpretive acts to oppose . . . the violence and coercion of the other organs of the state."[55] Chief Justice Francis Forbes of New South Wales was just the sort of professional judge who worked to stamp out corrupt regimes sustained on empire's outer reaches by laws' pluralities.[56] The rights claims of people like Ann Rumsby probably received a better hearing as a result. But imperial planners were at least as concerned with order as with rights as they did the work of homogenization. P. G. McHugh puts it nicely: "by the 1830s, mosaic jurisdictionalism was being superseded by more centralist and unifying forces." New Zealand's sovereignty was recognized so that it might be taken away by the Treaty of Waitangi in 1840. All across the British and other empires, "pulverizing constitutionalism" crushed laws' pluralities.[57] The imperial state had finally become the modern state. But that state, however much it dominates our imagination, was evanescent.

Diversity

By thinking historically about law in and among empires, we have moved from pluralism—as a way an observer might see things from without—to pluralities: to seeing the world as experienced by those who inhabited it. The state that generated and sustained imperial laws' pluralities bore little resemblance to an ostensibly Westphalian or Hobbesian ideal. And no sooner had such a state finally come into being in the nineteenth century than it was forced into retreat. As this has happened, laws' pluralities have asserted themselves in new forms. In the last generation or two, state sovereignty has been punctured from without by demands about the rights due to individuals and by the actions of transnational beings of many kinds: by treaty organizations, international tribunals, nongovernmental organizations, multinational corporations, and so on.

Since the final breakup of Europe's empires, the tendency to apply legal pluralism "indiscriminately to almost any kind of complexity" has reduced any analytic force the term may once have possessed.[58] And despite the warnings of Santos and others, the belief persists in many quarters that pluralism is an inherent good. This is especially evident in the recent tendency to describe pluralism as "diversity." Like each brightly colored insect in a tropical rainforest, we assume that every legal usage, however strange it looks or however difficult it may be for us to identify its place in the legal habitat, serves some good and requires preservation. We are encouraged to pursue "sustainable diversity," to replace the rule of law with the rule of laws.[59] Histories of laws' pluralities may suggest otherwise.

An ancient tension lies within the call to sustain diversity, to live by the rule of laws rather than the rule of law. It is a tension as old as liberal ideals, a tension between the desirability of choosing and the danger posed by others' capacity to choose. As Santos notes, the debate over legal pluralism "challenges liberal political theory."[60] Yes. But the reverse is also true. Thompson's recognition of the rule of law as "a cultural achievement of universal significance" suggests how liberal political theory challenges pluralism.[61] Happily, it is not the role of histories or their authors to adjudicate the moral claims of laws' pluralities. All they may do is observe them. And perhaps wonder if Edward Byam might not have been right to desire the end of diversity.

NOTES

1. Byam's account of the island, from December 1822, is in the National Archives, London, CO172/38, quotations at 2, 6, and 9.
2. On fluctuations in the illegal slave trade in the 1810s and '20s and the economic and political dynamics behind them, see Richard B. Allen, "Licentious and Unbridled Proceedings: The Illegal Slave Trade to Mauritius and the Seychelles during the Early Nineteenth Century," *Journal of African History* 42 (2001): 91-116, especially 105-6.
3. Richard B. Allen, *Slaves, Freedmen, and Indentured Laborers in Colonial Mauritius* (Cambridge: Cambridge University Press, 1999), 49-53.
4. National Archives, London, CO172/38, 2 and 6.
5. Max Rheinstein, "Law and Social Changes in Africa," *Washington University Law Quarterly* (1962): 444.
6. As Lloyd Fallers put it, legal pluralism was simply "the legal aspect of the general cultural fragmentation which is so characteristic of the new African states." "Customary Law in the New African States," *Law and Contemporary Problems* 27 (1962): 605.
7. For an account of the classic rule of law position put by A. V. Dicey, though overlaid by a modern commitment to human rights, see Tom Bingham, *The Rule of Law* (London: Allen Lane, 2010), 3-5.
8. Denis V. Cowen, "African Legal Studies: A Survey of the Field and the Role of the United States," *Law and Contemporary Problems* 27 (1962): 546-47.
9. This view of Europe's past was infused with the kind of stadial thinking that was made famous by leading Scottish Enlightenment figures and that formed the foundation of modern historical sociology. For a critique of this evolutionary thinking in debates about legal "development" toward a presumably positivist end condition, see Lawrence M. Friedman, "On Legal Development," *Rutgers Law Review* 24 (1969): 16-25.
10. Rheinstein, "Law and Social Change in Africa," 443, with quotation at 448-49. Cowen, "African Legal Studies," 558, with quotation at 546. M. B. Hooker provided a subtler synthetic look at those varieties of pluralism that had resulted "from the transfer of whole legal systems across cultural boundaries." But his account, too, required a vigorous state to contain the centrifugal dangers of legal pluralism through the use of conflict-of-laws rules. As he put it, "The competence of the national law is absolute over the whole of the nation-state. . . . Although there may be a variety of legal systems operative within the nation-state, only one will be dominant, and it will be that which constitutes the organs of the nation-state." *Legal Pluralism: An Introduction to Colonial and Neo-Colonial Laws* (Oxford: Oxford University Press, 1975), 1, 454.
11. John Griffiths, "What Is Legal Pluralism?" *Journal of Legal Pluralism and Unofficial Law* 24 (1986): 38.
12. Griffiths, "Legal Pluralism?" 4, 8.
13. Griffiths thus applied to law Sally Falk Moore's notion of a "semi-autonomous social field." Griffiths, "Legal Pluralism?" 34, 38.

14. Griffiths, "Legal Pluralism?" 38.
15. Sally Engle Merry, "Legal Pluralism," *Law and Society Review* 22 (1988): 870 and 879.
16. Brian Z. Tamanaha, "The Folly of the 'Social Scientific' Concept of Legal Pluralism," *Journal of Law and Society* 20 (1993): 209. Idem, "Understanding Legal Pluralism: Past to Present, Local to Global," *Sydney Law Review* 30 (2008): 410.
17. On the desirability but difficulty of "individuation" of laws, norms, and other kinds of ordering, see William Twining, "Normative and Legal Pluralism: A Global Perspective," *Duke Journal of Comparative and International Law* 20 (2010): 482-85.
18. Robert Cover, "Nomos and Narrative," *Harvard Law Review* 97 (1983-84): 40, 53.
19. Cover elaborated this point in "Violence and the Word," *Yale Law Journal* 95 (1985-86): 1601-29.
20. Cover, "Nomos and Narrative," 57-59.
21. Cover was particularly interested in the claims of separatist religious communities: "New law is constantly created through the sectarian separation of communities." Cover, "Nomos and Narrative," 15.
22. Merry, "Legal Pluralism," 889.
23. Tamanaha, "Folly," 192.
24. Twining has likewise suggested that it would be helpful to treat legal pluralism "as a species of normative pluralism." "Normative and Legal Pluralism," 515.
25. Tamanaha, "A Non-Essentialist Version of Legal Pluralism," *Journal of Law and Society* 27 (2000): 314. Idem, "Folly," 199.
26. E. P. Thompson, *The Poverty of Theory and Other Essays* (New York: Monthly Review Press, 1978), 96.
27. The classic statement of this appeared in Thompson's "The Moral Economy of the English Crowd in the Eighteenth Century," *Past and Present* 50 (1971): 76-136. "[L]aw, as definition or as rules . . . was a place not of consensus, but of conflict . . . and the law, like other institutions . . . has its own characteristics, its own independent history and logic of evolution." E. P. Thompson, *Whigs and Hunters: The Origin of the Black Act* (New York: Pantheon, 1975), 261-62.
28. E. P. Thompson, "Custom, Law, and Common Right," in *Customs in Common: Studies in Traditional Popular Culture* (New York: New Press, 1993), 163-75.
29. Thompson, *Whigs and Hunters*, 266. For an important discussion of Thompson's mapping of developments within English law and society onto colonial history, see Lauren Benton, *Law and Colonial Cultures: Legal Regimes in World History, 1400-1900* (Cambridge: Cambridge University Press, 2002), chapter 7.
30. Collingwood concluded with a flourish: "History, therefore, cannot be made to square with theories according to which the object of knowledge is abstract and changeless." *The Idea of History* (reprinted, Oxford: Oxford University Press, 1993 [1946]), 234. It's worth noting that what remains one of the most influential considerations of the nature of legal history operates at what we might say is the intersection of E. P. Thompson's awareness of law's social situations and Collingwood's strict historicism. Robert Gordon has made these debts clear by implication throughout much of his work, and more explicitly in "Critical Legal Histories," *Stanford Law Review* 36 (1984): 99, 123.
31. One response to which was to follow Brian Tamanaha in saying that what Griffiths, Santos, and others were really talking about was not legal pluralism, but "normative pluralism" or "rule systems." Tamanaha, "Folly," 199; and idem, "Non-Essentialist Version,"

302. Griffiths seems now to accept this suggestion, though for rather different reasons. Griffiths, "The Idea of Sociology of Law and Its Relation to Law and to Sociology," in Michael Freeman, ed., *Law and Sociology* (Oxford: Oxford University Press, 2006), 62-64.

32. "To suggest that the 'Westphalian system' is collapsing is to give that system an importance that it had never had in the past, except if one myopically concentrates on the historical experience of European states." Edward Keene, *Beyond the Anarchical Society: Grotius, Colonialism, and Order in World Politics* (Cambridge: Cambridge University Press, 2002), 148-49.
33. Quentin Skinner, *Regarding Method*. Vol. 1, *Visions of Politics* (Cambridge: Cambridge University Press, 2002), 115.
34. Ross and Stern, especially 116–125.
35. Ross and Stern, especially 110 and 132.
36. This point was nicely developed in the English domestic case, especially as concerns litigation, by Steve Hindle, *The State and Social Change in Early Modern England, c. 1550-1640* (London: Macmillan, 2000). See also Michael Braddick, *State Formation in Early Modern England, c. 1550-1700* (Cambridge: Cambridge University Press, 2000), especially 101-76.
37. William Shepheard [Sheppard], *Of Corporations, Fraternities, and Guilds* (London, 1659), 1. On concession theory, see C. T. Carr, *The General Principles of the Law of Corporations* (Cambridge: Cambridge University Press, 1905), chapter 13.
38. Stern, especially 28–37.
39. Dewar, especially 49–53.
40. For a more full consideration of the impact of topographical variety, see Lauren Benton, *A Search for Sovereignty: Law and Geography in European Empires, 1400-1900* (Cambridge: Cambridge University Press, 2010).
41. On territorial jurisdictions as "relatively new and intuitively surprising technological developments," see Richard Ford, "Law's Territory (A History of Jurisdiction)," *Michigan Law Review* 97 (1999): 843. Also Shaunnagh Dorsett, "Mapping Territories," in Shaun McVeigh, ed., *Jurisprudence of Jurisdiction* (New York: Routledge, 2007), 138-54.
42. *The English Reports* (London, 1907-09), v. 77, 385 (7 Co. Rep. 7b).
43. Owensby, especially 145–149. On Indian justice more generally, see Brian P. Owensby, *Empire of Law and Indian Justice in Colonial Mexico* (Stanford, CA: Stanford University Press, 2008).
44. Rupert, especially 201–206.
45. Owensby, *Empire of Law*, especially chapter 2.
46. On subjecthood and the containment of lesser magistrates by judges in response to the claims of subjecthood, see Paul D. Halliday, *Habeas Corpus: From England to Empire* (Cambridge, MA: Harvard University Press, 2010), especially chapters 3, 6, and 8.
47. Thompson's account of the idea of the rule of law became an object of criticism in certain quarters, especially as it might be applied to colonial settings. For a salvaging of Thompson from the criticisms of Ranajit Guha, see Benton, *Law and Colonial Cultures*, 254-60.
48. Boaventura de Sousa Santos, *Toward a New Legal Common Sense: Law, Globalization, and Emancipation*, 2nd ed. (London: Butterworths, 2002), 89, 98.
49. Barkey, especially 94–95.
50. Lauren Benton, "Historical Perspectives on Legal Pluralism," in Brian Tamanaha, Caroline Sage, and Michael Woolcock, eds., *Legal Pluralism and Development: Scholars and Practitioners in Dialogue* (Cambridge: Cambridge University Press, 2012), 27.
51. Owensby, especially 145.

52. As Lauren Benton has noted generally in thinking about how this history may relate to current problems in world legal order, "in global reform movements, assistance to people in positions of social weakness has been advanced effectively through reforms designed to scale back the legal prerogatives attached to some jurisdictions." Thus offering legal protection to them involves less an assertion of right than a containment of the institutional means by which wrong may be perpetuated. Benton, "Historical Perspectives," 31.
53. Benton and Ford, 181–187.
54. D. M. Young, *The Colonial Office in the Early Nineteenth Century* (London: Longmans, 1961), chapters 2 and 3. For the centrality of one person to this process, see Paul Knaplund, *James Stephen and the British Colonial System, 1813-1847* (Madison: University of Wisconsin Press, 1953), chapter 9.
55. Cover, "Nomos and Narrative," 57-58.
56. Benton and Ford, 183–185. Halliday, *Habeas Corpus*, 294-96.
57. McHugh, 236.
58. Twining, "Normative and Legal Pluralism," 516. Twining is skeptical about a *global* legal pluralism, since what we may take to be global amounts to nothing more than the geographical transposition of our own assumptions and values: ibid., 509-14. For another view, see Ralf Michaels, "Global Legal Pluralism," *Annual Review of Law and Social Science* 5 (2009): 2432-62.
59. H. Patrick Glenn, "Sustainable Diversity in Law," in Tamanaha et al., eds., *Legal Pluralism and Development*, 95-111.
60. Santos, *Toward a New Legal Common Sense*, 93.
61. Thompson, *Whigs and Hunters*, 265.

11

Rules of Law, Politics of Empire

JANE BURBANK AND FREDERICK COOPER

The Normality of Legal Pluralism

All legal systems attempt to work by providing rules for social interaction and asserting the validity of these rules for individuals subject to them. Occasionally, rule makers and their advisors make extensive claims for applications of their laws: that they apply or should be applied to all who share a faith, to all in a single polity, in the extreme to all the peoples of the earth. But the ordinary state of law depends upon a selective and multiform approach to rules—to the range of their applicability, to their appropriate sources, and to the entitlement to implement them. Empires of the sixteenth to nineteenth centuries, as the authors of this volume show, followed conventional practice: they extended legal rule in multiple and unlike ways to subjects and would-be subjects as they strove to expand or maintain their power near and far. The normality of legal pluralism in many forms—different rules for different groups, devolved authority to interpret and enforce them, sustenance of multiple and sometimes conflicting jurisdictions—explains in part why rulers, legal theorists, politically minded explorers, theologians, and other writers at that time do not seem to have needed a concept for it, or considered it worthy of debate. Legal pluralism was not an abstraction; it was a habit. More theoretically, it was a *habitus.*[1] For this reason, one should be careful not to read too much into the "ism" of legal pluralism.

The unremarkable habit of being legally pluralistic was connected to the more conspicuous problems of defending and extending imperial power. Empires set themselves the tasks of bringing different peoples and places under their control and of exploiting these resources effectively and securely. They did not all do this in the same way, but there were strategies that all avoided. The option of one law for all, applied consistently and thoroughly to all subjects and to their relations with each other and the state, was sure to fail. Successful imperial law had to be variegated and adaptable to multiple and changing circumstances, while affirming the sovereign's ultimate authority.

How to carry off the trick of being sufficiently attentive to a myriad of local contexts and simultaneously ensuring their subordination to a single, recognizable superior power? There was no master recipe for how to rule an empire, even for Europeans, including the Ottomans, who shared a distant Roman ancestor that had left an influential legal legacy. Roman law, through its multiple transformations, provided a common language for imperial lawmakers; more profoundly, Roman practices of legal rule, in particular the emphasis on legal commentary, advocacy, and interpretation, enabled creative, open-ended considerations and refinements of imperial legalism. If legal pluralism was a requirement for imperial survival, Rome's legitimation of debate over law gave Europeans spacious room for imagining, institutionalizing, and reforming their ways of legal rule.

In no way was it obligatory for imperial law to be uniform, fixed, or neatly bounded in permanent ways. Over the centuries of European empires' gradual extension of their claims around the world, jurisdictional issues were treated differentially depending on context—both material and ideological. In secured regions, empires might put in place apparently long-term and distinction-marking structures—the "republica de indios" and "republica de espanoles" in Spanish America, for example.[2] In areas where power was contested among empires or with unruly others, the question of jurisdiction was best left open-ended. Overlapping jurisdictions put room for play into imperial legalism, sometimes setting the high stakes of acquiring new resources, sometimes offering a breathing space while rulers tried to figure out a means to get their way. The multiple and conflicting proposals involving British jurisdiction in New Zealand in the early nineteenth century described in P. G. McHugh's chapter can be read not as ineffectual dithering but as enabling London to adjust its legal mechanisms as new challenges to maintaining order and productive capacity on the islands arose.

The emphasis of the authors in this volume is on the jurisdictional complexity produced by expanding, contending, and defending empires.

Together the chapters suggest attributes and implications of empires' legal strategies. First, pluralistic legal structures were the norm (although of course not identical in their makeup) inside empires, both in spaces considered homeland (provinces in France, confessional assemblies in the Ottoman empire, corporations in England and the Netherlands) as well as in more distant regions into which empires expanded.

Second, legal pluralism offered a medium for interactions among empires. A multiplicity of imperial legal regimes intersected unevenly over the globe; this network of jumbled jurisdictions enabled legal settlements, albeit tentative, of disputed property (prize courts being an obvious case in point) but also possibilities for both competition and negotiation among empires. Spain, having lost Curaçao to the Dutch in 1634, eventually tried to make good on its losses through royal laws that offered legal manumission to slaves who escaped to Spanish Venezuela with the stated purpose of making themselves Catholics. The assertion of Spanish jurisdiction in this instance was intended to weaken a rival empire. But after a century of competition and litigation over runaways, Spanish rulers mobilized the law in a different cause—the interests of slave owners in their domains—by signing restitution treaties with their rival empires (Britain, France, and the Netherlands) in the region.[3] The language of law, declarative but subject to revision, enabled these contradictory and pragmatic initiatives on the part of Spanish rulers.

A third characteristic of the normal complexity of jurisdictional settings, within and among empires, was their mobilization by multiple actors, in their own conflicting interests. Empires' institutionalization of law in multiple jurisdictions offered opportunities not only to the rule makers but also to rule users. At issue here is not simply forum shopping—the possibility for litigants to choose among courts—but the more general condition of enabling suits, claims, and discipline to be decided upon in legal fora legitimated by a superior authority but connected to local practices in various ways. As Helen Dewar writes, "law was an instrument that both extended the monarch's sovereignty and provided subjects with a framework within which to affirm and defend their own privileges and challenge other claims."[4] Coexistence of multiple sources of law (customary, religious, of a prior polity, devolved authorities, the emperor, etc.) combined with a multiplicity of instances for obtaining legal decisions meant that justice was not just a moving target but a many-centered one in any empire.

Connected to the situation of jurisdictional melanges—what we might call normal imperial legal pluralism—was the crucial role of the authorities who tried to hold sway in the middle range of adjudication. In legal matters, as in military and economic ones, the most critical challenge for empires was securing the effective and loyal service from intermediaries.[5] The intermediary problem in legal matters could take on different guises: a tribal representative, a clerical defender of a faith and its requirements, a colonial official, a local notable, a magistrate, etc. The multiple locations of legal expression—courts of many kinds, advisory councils, religious institutions, imperial commissions, regional administrations—meant that intermediaries could enact imperial law at different intersections in the web of legal rule.

Empires took different approaches to the task of empowering intermediaries: a personalized method in the French empire where the royal commissioner was the preferred, but not the only, agent of legal expansion; reliance on the chartered corporation for the British; leadership of religious authorities in the Ottoman empire. But everywhere and in every variant, the power of intermediaries was a two-edged sword: vested officials had a great deal to say about whether any law or legal judgment would be enforced and in whose interests. One result was the proliferation of layers and types of controls, as overlords tried to constrain their own creations with other sources of authority: commissioners to overrule corporations, appeals instances to review lower-level judgments, royal decrees to trump provincial councils, and the like. Because intermediaries were both essential and challenging to legal rule in any extensive polity, efforts to govern an empire were directly related to the expansion of legal pluralism.

Of course, intermediation in empires did not function through law alone. Vertical relations of authority could be established and maintained by other means: people could be persuaded to partake in imperial expansion through access to loot, slaves, and women, as well as to positions of authority and to rule-bound activities. Legal norms and institutions might restrain the improvisations of clientelism; at the same time, extralegal clients could facilitate the incorporation of diverse peoples into an imperial structure. Here is another reason to be careful about the "ism" in "legal pluralism," as well as about the "legal" and its relation to imperial controls.

Normal imperial legal pluralism was thus not self-containing. The institutionalization of legal authority in one form entailed sharing out powers that would sooner or later need correction—and more institutions, or at least supervisors. Jurisdictional multiplicity had ideological implications as well: the pluralism of sites where legal decisions could be argued and reviewed created possibilities for reimagination of how the empire's justice might work. Administrators could be aware—or not—of tactics used in other areas of an empire or in other empires. The fluidity of imperial legalism offered room for maneuver to leaders at many levels and to canny subjects. The overlapping of jurisdictions had a constructive function in this sense: at multiple intersections between subjects and authorities, practices and ideals of governance were articulated and at least potentially put into the wider play of imperial law making.

Who Makes the Rules of Law and Why and How?

The tendency of jurisdictional complexity to instigate interventions by imperial authorities leads us to questions of sovereignty: who made the laws of empire; how and why did particular solutions to the general problem of imperial rule emerge?

One suggestion that arises from these chapters is that law making was shared out in imperial polities; law was enacted, if not created, in the multiple jurisdictions that empires legitimized, at least for a time. Two qualifications need to be made. First, even in situations of local empowerment, obstructionism, and self-serving interpretation—all common phenomena—an underlying assumption for most people involved was that the emperor (the king, the queen, the sultan, etc.) was the head of state and responsible for its provision of legal governance. No one argued that ultimate sovereignty was located in one of the parts of the realm; in the terms of the time, no one defended the condition of *imperium in imperio*. Even those who theorize sovereignty as originating in the empire's component parts—in civic assemblies, for example—must argue (if they are concerned to keep the polity together) that these several parts are somehow associated in a greater union, which may have complex ways of parceling and locating legislative competence. Some notion of verticality imbued even the controversies over imperial law and its potential.

Second, empires were not alike in their ways of distributing or theorizing sovereign power. Philip Stern argues in this volume that sovereignty in the British Empire was lodged in corporations, linked to the state in multiple and contested ways. Much law making went on inside the many corporate bodies, where members exercised powers conferred upon them by their own institutions, including judicial operations, political duties, and rule making that intersected with these same functions as carried on by other corporations and by institutions more directly controlled by the state.[6] This location of sovereignty in associations of persons, whose corporations are connected to but not superseded by the state, constituted a natural recourse for the British Empire as it extended itself overseas by chartering corporations or recognizing older sovereignties as components of a wider imperial system. At the same time, this multiplex associational model of sovereignty meant that the struggle over who makes the rules took place on an uneven and obstacle-laden terrain.

But this corporatist reflex was only one way of conceiving of imperial sovereignty. Other variants treated in this volume include the more vertical conception of law in the French case, where sovereignty was delegated "down" by the king, who was in theory informed by multiple sources of law.[7] Spanish imperial rulers had to deal with the claims of Catholic jurists, who held the king to the requirements of Christian community (interpreted variously), where sovereignty devolved from God was vested in a social collective.[8] These conceptions of legitimate authority affected the particular strategies of jurisdictional configuration in French and Spanish empires.

Even this small selection from among the many theorized locations of sovereignty and the strong distinctions among them—civic associations, royal stewardship, godly community—suggests that empires worked with very different assumptions about the sources and limits of their capacity to govern. Each empire acted with ideological tools it had developed in the past, as well as under the impact of recent experience, negative or positive, in extending and maintaining power. The Ottoman empire combined a refined, state-sheltered Islamic jurisprudence with the long-term reality of a multiconfessional populace to configure a multiplex legal system that recognized confessionally derived law.[9] Reference points for British policy makers in the early nineteenth century included India, where the strategy of a British "Residency" hosted by a local sovereign seemed be working, as well as North America, where their colonial policy had blown up disastrously.[10]

Distinctive conceptions of sovereignty and particular political experience (lessons learned the hard way) set empires off on different tracks toward the configuration of law in their domains.[11] But as some of these chapters suggest, both initiatives and results depended a great deal on extralegal considerations, in particular on the challenges presented by other empires, by rapacious intermediaries (especially colonial settlers), and by supposedly subjected or subjectable people who wanted things their own way. In all these circumstances, imperial law gave way or took a different course to meet the exigencies of power—military, economic, or both. In the British case, according to P. G. McHugh's account, formally theorized consideration for Maori sovereignty had little to do with considerations of the presumed rights of another people and everything to do with imperial control.[12]

In addition to the overwhelmingly determinate considerations of power and money, posed by other empires and by colonials also greedy for both, empires had to contend with less transparent initiatives explicitly directed at obtaining justice for imperial populations. The efforts of abolitionists to control and then abolish the slave trade were both a product of empires that had established the traffic in humans between Africa and the Americas in the first place and a thorn in their side. As Lauren Benton and Lisa Ford show, British efforts to regulate slavery—an essential first step from the abolitionists' point of view—were frustrated by planters in the Caribbean. The result was a series of institutional experiments, borrowed from Spanish precedents, transformed and implanted in the highly contested West Indies, and ultimately productive, as in New South Wales, of a new imperial intermediary—the colonial magistrate empowered to regulate and control unfree labor in the empire.[13]

Thus, while it is certain that law was a tool of empire, questions about who actually wielded this tool and for which goals and with which results open up a wide field of inquiry and conceptualization. It is critical to emphasize that law was not the only means that empires had at their disposal and even more vital to note that there was no single "rule of law." Empires deployed law in multiple ways, shaped by contingency and cultural predispositions. But whatever institutions or authorities an empire legitimated or tried to empower, these became a field of political play for imperial rulers, intermediaries, and subjects. Convicts, slaves, merchants, pirates, landlords, officials came or were taken to courts, whose judgments were in turn open to discipline and surveillance by Protectors, Residents, commissions of inquiry, religious authorities, and other imperial agents. These endeavors brought intellectuals and politicians into the action—the action of imagining and transforming the flexible legalism of imperial rule.

Dynamics of Imperial Transformation

Working against conventional assumptions, the authors of this volume manage to jettison the idea that there is something the matter with contradictory legal phenomena within one political regime. We should be able to acknowledge that the ideal of universal law—that laws are to be exactly the same for every subject—is itself a creation and one that "contradicts" the inequalities everywhere present in social life at all times. But once legal pluralism is understood as a usual practice, what impact did this way of rule have on political developments over time? The editors of the volume put an accent on conflict among legal authorities as a motor of transformations in sovereignty. Their claim is not linked to a narrative of progress or other normative teleology, but instead to two "patterns" of historical change. The first claim is that the expansion of empires produced "clusters of conflict" around legal issues in ever wider areas and over more populations; the second is that jurisdictional complexity "within and across empires" is linked to "the move toward a more hierarchically structured legal order."[14]

The first pattern seems at first glance indisputable, but also important. Imperial rule asserted through law did indeed draw new people, with their prior legal arrangements, into juridical settings that, if they were to last, had to be defined in multiple and unlike ways. Similarly, the carrying out of imperial rule meant that officials, settlers, prisoners, sailors, commanders, etc., were able to settle or open disputes in new jurisdictional settings. That conflicts arose from myriad claims to different types of justice and to different legitimating authorities in these expanded zones of asserted imperial control is not surprising; the grounds for action and the possible actors go well beyond tensions between "colonizers and colonized." Investigation of jurisdictional complexity opens up to view a far richer cast of characters engaged in legal and other conflicts than did the early phase of colonial studies with its dichotomies between rulers and ruled.

But is the accent on conflict helpful in understanding the consequences of legal pluralism for empires? Much depends on how wide the compass of institutional inclusion is imagined to extend as well as on the ways that law was understood by its participants in particular imperial situations. As Karen Barkey shows, in the Ottoman empire a systemic commitment to differentiated legal fora did not entail conflict. Instead, an acceptance by communal leaders of the powers of other groups' elites and of the overall sovereign meant that the Ottoman kind of jurisdictional carve-up contributed to peace and stability, not to speak of the effectiveness of proximate justice for subjects.[15] This kind of strongly institutionalized and only modestly overlapping juridictional practice internal to a state is what Richard Ross and Philip Stern call "weak" legal pluralism.[16] But seen from other perspectives and focusing on what legal structures offer to multiple users in complex systems, we might call the Ottomans' legal pluralism "strong"—strong in the sense that it both preserved state power and localized notions of rights.

In Barkey's account, the disruptive factor in the late Ottoman period was not the multiplicity of legal venues with their different confessional bases, but the intrusion of other empires' jurisdictional claims into Ottoman space. These ventures, linked to the ambitions of the Ottomans' competitor empires—"Western" but also Russian, all drawing ahead in the competition for economic gain and military might—invaded the Ottomans' imperial justice regime. It made matters worse that some outsiders' claims to take over the care of Ottoman subjects relied on the same moral foundations that the empire itself projected. The Russians insisted on the protection of Orthodox subjects, for example, playing the same game of imperial oversight as Istanbul, but with different cards. When the focus on juridical institutions is widened to include multiple empires, it is probably quite safe to bet that overlapping jurisdictions and jurisdictional assertions do present greater potential for conflict than for enhancing social harmony.

Nonetheless, within the empire, jurisdictional complexity could have positive, state-reinforcing consequences. As Barkey suggests, the acculturation of imperial elites played a critical role in making legal pluralism work. When Ottoman elites were mutually attentive to each others' legal rights and interactive with other community leaders, the strategy of distinctive legal regimes preserved and enhanced peaceful conduct and subjects' well-being. The Ottoman empire, a long-lasting one, derived much of its ability to be so big for so long precisely from its composite kind of legalism. Only in the nineteenth century was Ottoman security afflicted by competitions with other, now stronger empires over jurisdictional issues; these conflicting claims to legal authority pulled the state apart, rather than forming it.

The second pattern Benton and Ross propose relates to the prickly issue of change in the structures and viability of states. Was there a "global legal transformation" going on during the centuries under consideration here, or, relating to the editors' stronger claim, was there a transformation in a particular direction, toward a "more hierarchically structured legal order"? Certainly, the international legal specialists who were taking up their professional arms at the time would have seen things this way and were engaged in the project of making a superior coordinating authority among states.[17] But while evidence from chapters in this volume suggests the disruptive potential of jurisdictional overlaps and contests, it is not clear that these disruptions led toward more hierarchical legal order. Several chapters describe instead a condition of ongoing revisionism by individual empires of their own legal systems, accompanied by interventions, engagements, and contestations with other empires as well as with their often unruly subjects, including their intermediaries. In short, an ongoing multidimensional story of adjustments and initiatives and change, but not in a single direction.

Lurking in the background of discussions of emerging hierarchy, it seems, is the old notion that somehow a more "modern," more centralized sovereignty emerged sometime after the "early modern" centuries. One step toward dethroning the idea of an "early modern" to "modern" trajectory is recognizing the tautology of the chronological categories themselves. Periods themselves determine nothing.[18] This volume has trouble setting a conventional end to the "early modern" of its title, and for good reason. The narratives of some chapters run well into the nineteenth century, at least in part because the work of imperial law and sovereignty was ongoing. Even chapters in this volume that seem to support a thesis of transition to a "modern" state are appropriately vague about this purported political restructuration and its timing.

As for state theory, Ross and Stern's discussion brings forward the pluralist conceptions that were articulated in discussions of imperial sovereignty from the sixteenth century on. Is there a tenable story about sovereignty that could designate unambiguously distinctive chapters in the legal history of European empires as they expanded and competed in what turned out to be their period of global hegemony? Or in Stern and Ross's words, are centralism and pluralism two "interlinked discursive poles" that provoke a "perennial tussle" among theorists of sovereignty? Empires were still going full guns in the so-called modern period, but they were not going toward a definitive endpoint. Whether they were significantly less pluralistic in their manners of rule is a question for another volume to consider.

Whither Legal Pluralism and Empires?

This volume, with its focus on European empires and their legal regimes, opens up questions about law and sovereignty in other contexts—in other times and other spaces. As the remarks above suggest, the problems and possibilities engendered by pluralistic legal systems did not recede in the nineteenth century. European and other empires continued to deploy multiple kinds of legal frameworks to their subjects, and to struggle with the consequences of doing so.

Let us mention briefly what might seem like the worst possible case for the continuities of legal pluralism in the nineteenth and twentieth centuries—France. The idea of a republic of citizens posits equality before the law. Napoleon's imperial variant on civil equivalence—the Code Civil of 1804—made explicit a mono-legal notion applied to an expanding polity. Except that Napoleon knew quite well that he should not apply the Code Civil everywhere, and in parts of his "outer empire" where he needed the support of local or regional nobilities he was careful to give them a wide space to rule in their own ways. Napoleon was in another sense a restorationist; in 1802 he revoked the revolution's decision (the product of pragmatism as much as principle) to emancipate slaves on French territories (1793 and 1794) and returned to the notion that in colonies different rules applied.[19]

The renewal of French empire after Napoleon seems at first glance to be based on a legal dualism (rather than monism or pluralism) that made a neat distinction between citizens to whom one form of law applied and subjects who came under a second and inferior form of "justice." Yet the revived imperial configuration was more complicated than that. With the conquest of the Ottoman province of Algeria in 1830 (when France was under monarchical rule), France promised in effect to follow Ottoman practices—to recognize Muslim and Jewish people's rights to maintain their own jurisdictions. This colonial pluralism turned sour for subjects in the context of France's crooked path to republicanism: different meant inferior, deprivation of the rights of the citizen, the power of local administrators to inflict arbitrary punishments up to a certain level (a practice known as the *indigénat*, since it applied only to indigenous peoples), and at times compulsory labor, even after the abolition of slavery in French colonies in 1848. Discrimination was frequently justified on the basis of the different personal status regimes that non-Christian people came under with regard to civil life: the Sharia for Muslims, Mosaic law for Jews, "customary law" for many others.

But many French politicians and administrators were ill at ease with distinctions of this sort, particularly during the Second (1848-52) and Third (1871-40) Republics. The French government never could bring itself to give the *indigénat* a permanent juridical standing—it remained a temporary measure, renewed every time it expired until, in the case of French Africa, 1946. In the 1880s and again during World War I, some influential legislators tried, unsuccessfully, to enact "*citoyenneté dans le statut*"—extending the rights of citizenship to all French subjects even if they came under their own personal status regime.[20] There was an exception to the exception: in the four enclave-colonies in Senegal (the "Quatre Communes"), the original inhabitants had the rights of citizens even though their personal affairs were administered by Islamic courts; from 1848 these Africans could vote in local and national elections. In 1916, the French legislature made explicit the citizenship status of the people of the Quatre Communes.[21]

Most remarkably, in 1946, when French leaders were pressed to make good on the contribution of their colonies to two world wars and finally came to understand that the co-optation of indigenous elites was essential if the empire were to be preserved, the Senegalese model was extended to the overseas territories generally. In the constitution of the Fourth Republic, subjects acquired the "quality" of the French citizen without having to give up their personal status. Citizenship gave former subjects civil rights, the right to move anywhere in the empire, including European France, and—although it took a decade to implement fully—the right to vote and be represented in the legislature. Exactly what citizenship would mean was, not surprisingly, a complex and contested issue between 1946 and the end of French rule in sub-Saharan Africa in 1960 and Algeria in 1962.[22]

The question in the present context is why this complex reconfiguration of fundamental laws—multiple civil law regimes administered in distinct jurisdictions—was available to a supposedly modern state in 1946. How could distinct status regimes be recognized in a polity that claimed to be egalitarian? The underlying logic comes clear, however, if one abandons the narrative of the nineteenth and twentieth centuries as a transition from empire to nation-state and avoids the assumption that "modern" states are supposed to move toward uniformity. Empires govern different people differently, and they adjust, or try to adjust, the way they do so in the context of threats to their existence and opportunities to enhance their power. Actually pulling off a system that combined multiple institutions and norms for civil law with the egalitarianism of republican politics—and the new presumptions of social and economic as well as political citizenship—was another story. But writing a constitution that attempted to do so was not just imaginable in 1946. It was done.

Other empires had foundered earlier in the twentieth century on the rock of too much equal treatment. The Habsburg monarchy over centuries had managed its multiple populations with extensive attention to powerful hierarchies and their requirements; in the eighteenth and nineteenth centuries, rulers enlarged educational access and cultural amenities in outlying regions. Straight through revolutionary and other challenges, Hungarian nobles held onto their privileges and managed to achieve a distinctive solution to their aspirations. In 1867, the empire was transformed into the "dual monarchy," surely a testimony to the possibilities of a pluralistic political imagination: one emperor, who was also the king of Hungary; joint ministries for some matters, not for others; separate parliaments and civil services in the two components of the empire. No march toward a single hierarchy here. Unfortunately, for the empire anyway, its tolerance of difference could be taken in conflicting directions by nationalists who insisted on the primacy of their language and culture. And the equalizing politics of universal (male only, but still) citizenship opened up conflicts over whose values and language should predominate in matters of state. Democracy in the context of equal rights, rather than the strategy of differentiated jurisdictions, was the disruptive factor for Austria-Hungary.

Other empires went other ways. After 1917, revolutionaries in Russia made a choice for a kind of differentiated jurisdiction that was to have long-term consequences for political reformations around the globe. The winning Bolshevik faction did not reject the imperial composition of the state they inherited; instead they reinterpreted it. The form taken by the world's first communist polity was not a unified, hierarchically ordered national state, but a federation of soviet republics, formed on the principle of devolving selected aspects of authority to ethnically representative elites. Nothing could be more fluid, opaque, assertive, and overlapping than the murky jurisdictional parallels and intersections among party, state, nationality, and territory in the new Soviet empire.

This empire thrived, for decades anyway, on complex, unevenly distributed, retractable powers, but ones that recognized ethnic and, reluctantly, religious difference. The Bolsheviks attempted a unique solution to the intermediary problem: responsible positions in the state were to be filled at the discretion of the communist party leadership, which was supposed to be controlled from above. However, obstreperous, self-seeking, even good-willed intermediaries challenged Soviet power, once the discipline of sheer terror wore off. The multijurisdictional constitution of the USSR was invoked and deployed against the command of the Soviet party's top leaders when dissident communists, led by Boris Yeltsin, made the Supreme Soviet of the Russian (vs. the Soviet) Republic, whose powers were earlier thought to be minimal, into a meaningful political actor. The polity's second revolutionary transformation within one century affirmed the tenacity of the imperial, multijurisdictional model—the Russian Federation has eighty-three component parts, of unequal status—as well as new challenges inherent in the empowerment of supposedly loyal subordinates.

As these twentieth- and twenty-first-century perspectives suggest, the capacity for innovations in sovereignty was not exhausted as European empires lost their grip on the world's resources. The "West" in its much-predicted decline still encompasses states of a variety of compositions—take Switzerland, the United States, Spain, and Germany, for example, each with its own way of devolving aspects of sovereignty and designing jurisdictions. In matters of marriage, inheritance, legitimized weaponry, and medical assistance, jurisdiction makes a great deal of difference in the United States under its rules of law.

But this is only to touch on one part of the world. A next step in the exploration of legal pluralism and complex sovereignty would take us outside the Euro-American empires to explore these issues in Eurasia, the Middle East, and Africa. From ancient times to the present, polities in these areas, too, have dealt with the dilemmas of empire and law. A basic question arises from the evidence and arguments of this book: Did the linkages among imperial expansion, governance, and law in these other contexts provoke transformations in sovereignty and political imagination? A starting assumption is that in Asia as well, plurality of jurisdiction, inside and between empires, today as in the past, offers multiple agents opportunities to defend interests or put forward ideals in ways that may, or may not, upset the presumed status quo.

NOTES

1. Bourdieu's category works well to describe the unrecognized self-reproducing and adjusting field of imperial political theory. For the classic statement, see Pierre Bourdieu, *Outline of a Theory of Practice*, trans. Richard Nice (Cambridge: Cambridge University Press, 1977), 72-95.
2. See Brian Owensby, "Between Justice and Economics: 'Indians' and Reformism in Eighteenth-Century Spanish Imperial Thought," in this volume.
3. See Linda Rupert, "'Seeking the Water of Baptism': Fugitive Slaves and Imperial Jurisdiction in the Early Modern Caribbean," in this volume.
4. Helen Dewar, "Litigating Empire: The Role of French Courts in Establishing Colonial Sovereignties," in this volume.
5. On intermediaries and empire, see Jane Burbank and Frederick Cooper, *Empires in World History: Power and the Politics of Difference* (Princeton, NJ: Princeton University Press, 2010), 13-14.
6. See "'Bundles of Hyphens': Corporations as Legal Communities in the Early Modern British Empire," in this volume.
7. See Dewar, "Litigating Empire," in this volume: "All justice emanated from the king throughout France in theory, but there were multiple sources of law: provincial custom and local usage, Roman law (especially equity), and royal statutes, in descending order of influence."
8. See Owensby, "Between Justice and Economics," in this volume.
9. See Karen Barkey, "Aspects of Legal Pluralism in the Ottoman Empire," in this volume.
10. See P. G. McHugh, "'A Pretty Gov[ernment]!': The 'Confederation of United Tribes' and Britain's Quest for Imperial Order in the New Zealand Islands during the 1830s," in this volume.
11. For a discussion of the distinctiveness of imperial strategies, see Burbank and Cooper, *Empires in World History*, 11-13.
12. See McHugh, "'A Pretty Gov[ernment]!'" in this volume.
13. See Lauren Benton and Lisa Ford, "Magistrates in Empire: Convicts, Slaves, and the Remaking of the Plural Legal Order in the British Empire," in this volume.
14. See Lauren Benton and Richard Ross, "Empires and Legal Pluralism: Jurisdiction, Sovereignty, and Political Imagination in the Early Modern World," in this volume.
15. See Barkey, "Aspects of Legal Pluralism in the Ottoman Empire," in this volume. On the impact of proximate courts at different times in the Ottoman empire, see Leslie Peirce, *Morality Tales: Law and Gender in the Ottoman Court of Aintab* (Berkeley: University of California Press, 2003) and Iris Agmon, *Family and Court: Legal Culture and Modernity in Late Ottoman Palestine* (Syracuse, NY: Syracuse University Press, 2006).
16. See Richard J. Ross and Philip Stern, "Reconstructing Early Modern Notions of Legal Pluralism," in this volume.
17. See Martti Koskenniemi, *The Gentle Civilizer of Nations: The Rise and Fall of International Law, 1870-1960* (Cambridge: Cambridge University Press, 2001).
18. For a critique of the analytical usefulness of the concept of "modern," see Frederick Cooper, *Colonialism in Question: Theory, Knowledge, History* (Berkeley: University of California Press, 2005), chapter 5.
19. Frederick Cooper, "Provincializing France," in Ann Stoler, Peter Perdue, and Carole McGlanaghan, eds., *Imperial Formations*, 341-78 (Santa Fe, NM: School for Advanced Research Press, 2007).

20. Alix Héricord-Gorre, "Eléments pour une histoire de l'administration des colonisés de l'Empire français. Le 'régime de l'indigénat' et son fonctionnement depuis sa matrice algérienne (1881-c. 1920)," Thèse du doctorat, European University Institute, 2008; Emmanuelle Saada, *Empire's Children: Race, Filiation, and Citizenship in the French Colonies*, trans. Arthur Goldhammer (Chicago: University of Chicago Press, 2012); Isabelle Merle, «Retour sur le regime de l'indigénat: genèse et contradictions des principes repressifs dans l'empire français,» *French Politics, Culture, and Society* 20 (2002): 77–97.
21. Mamadou Diouf, «The French Colonial Policy of Assimilation and the Civility of the Originaires of the Four Communes (Senegal): A Nineteenth-Century Globalization Project,» *Development and Change* 29 (1998): 671–96.
22. Frederick Cooper, "From Imperial Inclusion to Republican Exclusion? France's Ambiguous Post-War Trajectory," in Charles Tshimanga, Charles Didier Gondolas, and Peter J. Bloom, eds., *Frenchness and the African Diaspora: Identity and Uprising in Contemporary France* (Bloomington: Indiana University Press, 2009), 91–119.

ABOUT THE CONTRIBUTORS

Karen Barkey, Professor of Sociology and History at Columbia University, has worked on state-society relations in her main empirical site, the Ottoman Empire, in comparison with the French, Habsburg, and Russian empires. She also pays attention to the Roman and Byzantine worlds as important predecessors of the Ottomans. Her latest work, *Empire of Difference* (2008), was awarded the 2009 Barrington Moore Award from the Comparative Historical Sociology section of the American Sociology Association and the 2009 J. David Greenstone Book Prize from the Politics and History section of the Political Science Association.

Lauren Benton is Professor of History and Affiliated Professor of Law at New York University. Her research focuses on the comparative legal history of empires, and her books include *A Search for Sovereignty: Law and Geography in European Empires, 1400-1900* (2010) and *Law and Colonial Cultures: Legal Regimes in World History, 1400-1900* (2002). Benton received her Ph.D. in History and Anthropology from Johns Hopkins University, and her A.B. from Harvard University. She is currently Dean of the Graduate School at NYU.

Jane Burbank is Collegiate Professor and Professor of History and Russian and Slavic Studies at New York University. She is the author of *Intelligentsia and Revolution: Russian Views of Bolshevism, 1917-1922* (1986), *Russian Peasants Go to Court: Legal Culture in the Countryside, 1905-1917* (2004), and, with Frederick Cooper, *Empires in World History: Power and the Politics of Difference* (2010).

Frederick Cooper is Professor of History at New York University. A specialist on the history of colonization and decolonization in Africa, he is the author most recently of *Colonialism in Question: Theory, Knowledge, History* (2005) and coauthor with Jane Burbank of *Empires in World History: Power and the Politics of Difference* (2010). He is completing a study of citizenship in French Africa, 1945-1960.

Helen Dewar is an SSHRC Postdoctoral Fellow at McGill University in Montreal, Quebec. She recently completed her dissertation, entitled "'*Y establir nostre auctorité*': Assertions of Imperial Sovereignty through Proprietorships and Chartered Companies in New France, 1598-1663," at the University of Toronto. She has published articles in the *Canadian Historical Review*, the *Journal of the Canadian Historical Association*, and the *Revue d'histoire de l'Amerique francaise*.

Lisa Ford is Senior Lecturer in the School of Humanities at the University of New South Wales. Her work centers on ideas and practices of legal order in the post-1763 Anglophone world. Her prize-winning book, *Settler Sovereignty* (2010), explains how and why North American and Australasian settler polities defined their sovereignty against indigenous customary law after 1800.

Paul D. Halliday is Julian Bishko Professor of History and Professor of Law at the University of Virginia. He is the author of *Habeas Corpus: From England to Empire* (2010), among other works.

P. G. McHugh is a Fellow of Sidney Sussex College and Professor of Law and Legal History at the University of Cambridge. His books include *Aboriginal Societies and the Common Law: A History of Sovereignty, Status, and Self-Determination* (2004) and *Aboriginal Title: The Modern Jurisprudence of Tribal Land Rights* (2011). His present project is looking at the impact of the tumultuous 1860s on Anglo-imperial constitutional thought and practice.

Brian P. Owensby is Professor and Former Chair of the Corcoran Department of History at the University of Virginia. He is the author of *Intimate Ironies: Making Middle-Class Lives in Brazil* (1999) and *Empire of Law and Indian Justice in Colonial Mexico* (2008).

Richard J. Ross is Professor of Law and History at the University of Illinois–Urbana/Champaign and Director of the Symposium on Comparative Early Modern Legal History. Representative publications on law and comparative colonialism include "Puritan Godly Discipline in Comparative Perspective: Legal Pluralism and the Sources of 'Intensity,'" *American Historical Review* 113 (2008); and "Legal Communications and Imperial Governance: British North America and Spanish America Compared," in *Cambridge History of Law in America*, volume 1, *Early America (1580-1815)*, ed. Christopher L. Tomlins and Michael Grossberg (2008). With Steven Wilf, he is currently working on a book, entitled *The Beginnings of American Law: A Comparative History* (forthcoming).

Linda M. Rupert is Assistant Professor (early modern Atlantic and Caribbean) in the Department of History at the University of North Carolina–Greensboro. She is the author of *Creolization and Contraband: Curacao in the Early Modern Atlantic World* (2012). She also has published articles in *Slavery and Abolition*, *Itinerario*, and *Jewish Culture and History*.

Philip J. Stern, Assistant Professor of History at Duke University, is a historian of the early modern British Empire. He is the author, most recently, of *The Company-State: Corporate Sovereignty and the Early Modern Foundations of the British Empire in India* (2011).

INDEX

Made in the USA
Monee, IL
04 January 2020

19840922R00189